CITIZENSHIP D WARS

The early years of democracy in France were those of a society divided by civil war, class war and violent conflict. *Citizenship and Wars* explores the concept of citizenship in a time of social and political upheaval, and considers what the conflict meant for citizen-soldiers, women, children and the elderly. This highly original argument based on primary research brings new life to debates about the making of French identity in the nineteenth century.

Putting the latest theoretical thinking into empirical use, the author assesses how the function of the state and its citizens changed during the Paris Commune and the Franco-Prussian War. The study considers fresh issues such as:

- how the people coped with the collapse of their government
- what the upheaval meant for the provinces of France
- how religious identities affected the issue of citizenship
- the differences between colonial Algeria and metropolitan France

This seminal study will appeal to students of history at undergraduate and post-graduate level. It is also an invaluable insight into the political and sociological aspects of the period.

Bertrand Taithe is Senior Lecturer in Cultural History at the University of
Manch

CITIZENSHIP AND WARS

France in turmoil 1870–1871

Bertrand Taithe

London and New York

First published 2001
by Routledge
11 New Fetter Lane, London EC4P 4EE

Simultaneously published in the USA and Canada
by Routledge
29 West 35th Street, New York, NY 10001

Routledge is an imprint of the Taylor & Francis Group

© 2001 Bertrand Taithe

Typeset in Baskerville by Taylor & Francis Books Ltd
Printed and bound in Great Britain by Biddles Ltd, Guildford and King's Lynn

British Library Cataloguing in Publication Data
A catalogue record for this book is available from the British Library

Library of Congress Cataloging in Publication Data
Taithe, Bertrand.
Citizenship and wars: France in turmoil, 1870–1/Bertrand Taithe.
Includes bibliographical references and index.
1. Citizenship–France–History–19th century. 2. Franco-Prussian War, 1870–1871.
3. Paris (France)–History–Commune, 1871. I. Title.

JN2919 .T34   2001
943.08'21–dc21   00-051719

ISBN 0–415–23927–3 (hbk)
ISBN 0–415–23928–1 (pbk)

I dedicate this book to Vicky, to my children Louis and, Emily, and to the memory of my father, forever in these pages

CONTENTS

ILLUSTRATIONS

Tables

Figures

ACKNOWLEDGEMENTS

This book concludes a long-term project, laboured over for many years, which has tested the patience of even my most devoted friends and family. Over the years many people have read elements of this research. Roger Cooter, Mark Jenner, Tim Thornton, Colin Jones and Ruth Harris have all, at some stage, been generous with their time and their advice. David Taylor has gone one step further by reading the entire manuscript, and I am grateful for his advice and generous help.

I have other, often more literal debts: first of all to the Wellcome Trust, for funding the research fellowship which fostered this project from 1992 to 1994. Second, chronologically at least, to the British Academy, which awarded me study leave at a time when breathing space and research time were most needed. My previous department at the University of Huddersfield and my current department at the University of Manchester have been friendly and generous with travel funds and research time; I hope this will repay some of my debts. Marie-Armelle and Georges Bayard have long understood that research on a shoestring meant frequent gate-crashing and long visits in their Paris home. As a consequence, they had to invest in a larger flat. I would also like to thank Mr Paul Montelimard for his welcome in Aix-en-Provence. My brother and sister have also helped this project go further.

Over the years I have spent much time in the following archives and libraries and I have always found the archivists and librarians patient, helpful and friendly: Archives nationales, Archives du département de la Seine et de la Ville de Paris, Bibliothèque historique de la ville de Paris, Bibliothèque administrative de la ville de Paris, Archives de la préfecture de Police de Paris, Archives Épiscopales de l'Archevêché de Paris, Archives du Grand Orient de France, Archives du service de santé des armées de Terre, Archives des Armées de Terre de Vincennes, Archives de l'Assistance Publique de Paris, Archives Départementales de l'Hérault, de la Creuse, de la Corrèze, de la Haute Vienne, du Rhône, the Bibliothèque Nationale, the British Library, the University of Huddersfield Library, the Brotherton Library at Leeds University, and the John Rylands Library of Manchester University.

ABBREVIATIONS

AAP	Archives de l'assistance publique de Paris
ADC	Archives départementales de la Corrèze
ADCr	Archives départementales de la Creuze
ADH	Archives départementales de l'Hérault
ADHV	Archives départementales de la Haute-Vienne
ADR	Archives départementales du Rhône
AEP	Archives épiscopales de la ville de Paris
AGOF	Archives du Grand Orient de France
AIT	Association Internationale des Travailleurs
AML	Archives municipales de la ville de Lyon
AMM	Archives municipales de la ville de Montpellier
AN	Archives nationales
AOM	Archives nationales d'Outre Mer (Aix-en-Provence)
APdP	Archives de la préfecture de Police de Paris
ASSAT	Archives du service de santé des armées de Terre
AVdP	Archives du département de la Seine et de la Ville de Paris
BAIM	*Bulletin de l'Académie Impériale de médecine*
BAVP	Bibliothèque administrative de la ville de Paris
BHVP	Bibliothèque historique de la ville de Paris
GMP	*La Gazette médicale de Paris*
JORC	*Journal Officiel de la République, édition de la Commune*
Red Cross	Société de secours aux blessés des armées de terre et de mer, & Société de secours dite de la Presse (unless otherwise stated, the two organisations are merged under one collective label)
SAT	Service historique de l'Armée de Terre de Vincennes

1

INTRODUCTION

Citizenship, wars and revolutions

Citizenship

The concept of citizenship, particularly French citizenship, has been overshadowed by one overwhelming but misconceived metaphor: that citizenship is akin to education.[1] To put it another way, the political investment of the Third Republic, continuing into the modern age, in the *teaching* of citizenship through schools or through the *Ligue de l'enseignement* or any such pressure group, has paid historiographical dividends.[2] This assimilation of citizenship to education, developed in all central texts on citizenship in nineteenth-century Europe and America, makes a number of comforting, if flawed, assumptions.

The first one is that citizenship is liberating knowledge which can be learned. By implication, citizenship can be taught. Teachers of citizenship therefore belong to the ranks of those who have come to master this knowledge, usually from their formal, liberal education at school – the *gymnasium*, the *lycée* – or through a convoluted political career in opposition to oppressive political practices.[3] Central to this are the intellectuals, the politicians who manage to claim to be simultaneously the voice of the silent masses and the leaders at the vanguard of the citizenship revolution. Instrumental in the propagation of this scholarly truth are the school system, the voluntary associations and the republican or liberal political formations that they dominated and still control.[4] Citizenship thus becomes a practice of exclusion of past immaturity and dependence.[5] In a sense, it is therefore the achievement of strong individuals who obtain and maintain their freedom through their will and the practice of legally or ethically defined rights. It becomes the domain of a liberal vanguard which, in the course of time, shaped our modern society. Looking at its salient features, citizenship is no more than the old concept of civilisation revisited. It fits roughly with Comtian utilitarianism[6] and could even be reconciled with a middle-of-the-road reading of Marx's views on emancipation.

The second assumption, which follows from the first, is that citizenship is a stage in the history of mankind reached after long and convoluted travels in the darkness of subjection. Since citizenship can be taught, until citizens achieve political maturity, the whole nineteenth century can be depicted as the pubescent age of citizenship. Entire periods of mixed political identities, such as the French Second Empire, serve as necessary stages on the road to emancipatory democracy.

1

This emphasis on education became, in the years following 1871, a fervent '*démopédie*', to use Rosanvallon's phrase,[7] a mixture of democracy and pedagogy which attempted to create electors worthy of their own political system.[8] As in puberty crises, revolutions appear as untimely manifestations of future identity, petulant outbursts of suppressed passion or as necessary rites of passage.

Another related metaphor, which has a less lofty tone, is that of apprenticeship. The apprentice learns a trade at the side of the master, which can either be defined in individualistic terms – Garibaldi, Mazzini – or in a more abstract way, as in the romantic notion of the silent but inspiring 'People' in the work of Michelet.[9] In 1870 Jules Vallès, a debased, petit-bourgeois intellectual sunken in poverty and grim bohemia,[10] described his apprenticeship as a series of encounters with the people, while stressing his hard-earned education.[11] He thus maintained the leadership of the intellectual who alone could make text out of unspoken popular aspirations. One of the key tensions in Vallès' work is precisely the knowledge that his scholarly learning should not give him the power others recognised in him. He therefore regularly denounces the sterile and aged scholarship of education. 'It will take a gun to destroy the cardboard schools as well as the stones of the Tuileries [palace].'[12] His entire literary effort, with its deliberate use of vernacular and broken-down sentences, aims to express this frustration with being a reluctant author, witness and leader of an unfinished revolution.[13]

Many other radicals did not harbour such self-doubt and were only fleetingly aware that they were merely spectators and not leaders.[14] The Commune of Paris on 4 May 1871 set examinations for its aspiring officers, with questions on recent history, including the analysis of the defeat of 1848, the role of the National Guard, and the meaning of social questions.[15] The jury pontificated on the value of these intellects while the revolution they lived in approached its end. Some of the radical literature on citizenship may attribute different values to the concept, but on the whole it respects the positivist assumptions which shaped the historiography of citizenship. Anarchists such as Bakunin might disagree with Marx or, later, Lenin on the necessity of a leadership of vanguard teachers, but instead put the emphasis on self-learning processes, following invisible guidelines set up by historical conditions of a more abstract kind.

Emphasising education comes naturally to historians who tend to be practitioners of education and who feel, rightly or foolishly, that they deliver a public service in producing the citizens of today and the subjects and leaders of tomorrow. This is a fundamental 'mission statement' and it seems almost cruel to question it,[16] yet it is obvious that the whole narration of citizenship constructed since Rousseau has stuck with dated educational thinking and with positivist teleology. The type of education implicit in this view of citizenship is not developed from the western practice of pedagogy over the last two hundred years: instead, it harks back to the rhetorical tropes of *Émile* and modern inventions of the educated self.[17]

If we accept that this particular construct of citizenship is false or merely not terribly useful, we can consider different forms of narratives of the self, collective and individual. We can then reconcile what we know of our own practice of citizenship with the more abstract rights and duties delineated in our written or implicit constitutions. Starting with the view that citizenship is not necessarily what shaped individual identities, or that this shaping is not the result of gentle character-forming, bending and bonding over the formative years, we might accept that citizenship might 'erupt' as a central part of one's being. We might consider that practices and micro-practices, as pointed out by Michel de Certeau,[18] are more important than electoral propaganda and political speeches. A more existential approach accepts that events also shape identity, and allows for sudden re-inventions, self-assertion and rediscovery. This approach also implies that the narrative of citizenship, individually and collectively, is not linear and progressive, but staccato and replete with discontinuities. In other words, one could re-introduce the experimental register of citizenship. Yet this does not mean that all experiments in citizenship are necessarily treasured, understood and accumulated as knowledge that can be passed on. In fact, these experiments are not necessarily acceptable memories or practices cherished by the temporary citizens. The writings of Veuillot, a fiercely Ultramontane Catholic opposed to any revolutionary heritage, contain some strange uses of the term 'citizenship' and an unprecedented willingness to entertain more inclusive political futures for France.[19] Many of the respectable republicans and moderate bourgeois who had suddenly discovered in them the stuff of a Danton or even a Robespierre reverted to more sober identities after 1870–1. France, currently led by the 1968 generation, can only wonder at the chasm between current neo-liberal political leaders, politicians and bank managers and their hairy Maoist former selves. They may have cherished the 1968 experience, but it had a much-mellowed impact on their later development. Their vision of active citizenship and of militancy is now a faded historical construct. There is no betrayal; it is their understanding of citizenship that has changed.

Citizenship, being part of a collective and individual narrative of the self, is necessarily integrated and made logical, just like other elements of any autobiographical account.[20] The same is true of many people in the France of 1870.

Citizenship thus exists on two related planes, one constitutional and defined by the recorded laws of the nation, and the other the practice of the rights and duties associated with the title of citizen which make citizenship more than a paper identity. This particular dimension is found in the work of T.H. Marshall, whose concept of welfare citizenship divides the substance of citizenship into three parts, civil, political and social.[21] While this concept is particularly apt in societies which have reshaped their ideal of a social contract to provide a safety net for the poorest, it also exists in nineteenth-century societies, albeit as aspiration or through more convoluted channels of exchanges and philanthropy.

In cultural and ideological terms the duties and rights compete, so that historians, philosophers, sociologists, historians of law and anthropologists tend to talk at cross-purposes on the subject of citizenship.[22] This book is not intended to rescue any orthodoxy or master narrative from any historical false consciousness. However, the central theme of this book is citizenship not only as it was theorised in a centralist state, but as it was practised in the city, the village, the hamlet.[23] Citizenship is not simply a conceptual right: it is or it is not in the detail of its practice.[24] Recent sociological work on citizenship and nationality, often inspired by Elias,[25] shows in some depth that the citizen is defined by his interrelation with other citizens within the remits of a state – in French, *concitoyen*. The work on the ordinariness of citizenship (and by implication the ordinariness of the state) points to the central importance of the experience of citizenship and its ritual and codified practices, as well as the more spontaneous recognition of implicit rights and duties of other citizens.[26] The experience of citizenship during the Franco-Prussian war and the Commune period was certainly more intense than anything lived hitherto or since, but its individual and collective impact needs some reassessment. In 1870 we do not start from a *tabula rasa*: the Second Empire had a complex and rich definition of citizenship, with a definition of how citizens and state interacted which varied in time.[27] Citizenship also varied in space: the rights of a small city-dweller were infinitely more developed than those of an inhabitant of Lyons or Paris, even though the latter received more attention and paternalistic handouts than the former.[28] Providing the state exists ordinarily, so does citizenship. But what happens when the government collapses, when the territory is invaded and when the nature of the state itself is in question, as it was in 1870–1?

How the French renegotiated their citizenship in relation to a state in chaos is the thematic backbone of the whole book and will recur throughout each chapter. The central argument of this book is that citizenship proved itself to be flexible and was represented as a set of practices and exchanges.[29] The National Guard, whose role has become central to most recent explorations of the period, was the crucial institution of the 4 September republic regime and the Communard movement, precisely because it codified exchanges based on handouts, gifts and sacrifice. At the heart of this exchange was the concept of honour, both national and individual.[30] The rituals of death, funerals and processions, which inscribed the national guardsmen within the civic tradition, had a tremendous importance.[31]

The aim of this book is not, therefore, to narrate the history of the war and Commune in strictly sequential order: the war and then the Commune, Paris and then the provinces. This will not do, precisely because this narrative is flawed, however appealing its simplicity. Only a thematic approach will allow us to reflect simultaneously on different places and people, on social, gender and political issues. In Appendix 1, a chronology will help the reader to follow some of the great dates and episodes. The fact that this story has previously been told from the Parisian viewpoint is not only a reflection on the centralisation of scholarship: the politics of Paris, its sufferings during the siege and its strategic importance dominated all nationwide discussions of how the war should be fought and, to some extent, how France should be redefined after the empire.

Paris attracted much attention; in its tragic phase of the Commune, many of the people who had been active revolutionaries in the provinces went to Paris, where the Commune of Paris resembled an alternative state.

Many of the other political experiments that had taken place earlier in the provinces did not present the same bombastic decorum or claim sovereignty. When policies are looked at, however, it must be recognised that revolutionary aspirations were expressed and acted upon in many great urban centres of France, to an extent unknown in Paris and with consequences that went deeper into the meshing of the subsequent political fabric.

This wide-angled approach is not meant to minimise the importance of 1870 and 1871 in French history. On the contrary, it posits this period as a watershed in the political and social thinking which contributed to the making of modern France.

Historiography

Historiographical developments since 1870 are intimately intertwined with the making of a canonical chronology, and this section will recall the great 'dates' of 1870–1, introducing vital elements of the historical narrative and the debates to which they gave rise.

The first debate concerns the origins of the Franco-Prussian war. This issue is crucial because by determining Napoleon III's guilt it fundamentally undermined Bonapartist ideology and forced the French to think their society afresh.

Since July 1870, when the war started, historians have been attempting to explain what appeared a very confused crisis. The French government of the Third Republic after 1871 heaped the blame on the Second Empire regime and its adventurer leader, Napoleon III. On the material available, its bona fide historians apportioned the responsibility for the conflict equally between Bismarck's Machiavellian plans and Napoleon III's incompetence.[32] At a popular level, the entire blame fell upon Napoleon III for agreeing to a war planned by his foreign and reactionary wife. Lurking behind the empress were the authoritarian ex-ministers Persigny and Rouher.[33] A more scholarly approach stressed the deterioration of Napoleonic diplomacy, which since 1849 had attempted to restore France's *grandeur* and international prestige while acquiring land and wealth.[34] The many wars of the imperial regime had made a joke of the phrase 'empire is peace', declared in Bordeaux in the first year of the dictatorship. There had been the wars in the Crimea, in Italy to help unite Italy and then to preserve the Papal State,[35] in Lebanon (1860), in China (1862–3), in the Far East ostensibly to protect Catholic missionaries, and in Algeria to increase French colonial interests. More damagingly, the expedition in Mexico, initially launched to recover debts,[36] eventually established a straw empire for Maximillian of Habsburg (1863–6), and had in the long run exhausted the French army and undermined the credibility of the French diplomacy.[37]

This trigger-happy diplomacy, mixing gun-boats, financial speculation and grand designs, had dispelled the chance of any alliance the French had attempted to establish. Napoleon III's calls for a new European order, a new congress of the nations, remained unanswered.[38] By 1865 the Second Empire also began to run out of steam: the Mexican adventure proved costly and point-less, the defence of the Papal State had alienated the Piedmontese government, and the European order appeared more threatened than protected by the French. In 1864 France and Britain had been unwilling to respect their 1720 convention to defend Denmark against the Austrian and Prussian armies coming to the rescue of Schleswig-Holstein German subjects of the Danish crown. This local and rapid war of the Duchies saw the rapid demise of Denmark and the creation of an exclusive German sphere divided between Austria, the old power, and Prussia, the rising force of Germany.

The crisis which followed in 1866 between Prussia and Austria witnessed a similarly passive attitude from the French, who attempted to negotiate territorial gains with Prussia in exchange for their neutrality. The battle of Sadowa ended these secret negotiations, and left French diplomats stranded while Prussia achieved almost complete supremacy over the German-speaking world.[39] The events of 1866 were perceived as a major defeat for the French European order, which had always played on the balance of power in Germany to prevent polit-ical unification and the reconstruction of a solid German empire.[40] Albert Sorel and Benedetti, writing immediately after the war of 1870, saw in Sadowa the first step towards a major Franco-German conflict.[41] Culturally, Sadowa cast Prussia in a new light. The French press and public figures such as Edgar Quinet denounced the romantic myths of the Germans as a peace-loving people of dreamy poets and confused philosophers. This imagery, which had prevailed in France since the writings of Madame de Staël, gradually disappeared, to be replaced with a militarised Prussian stereotype.[42] In other words, the French began to perceive the German unification as a cultural and political danger. The striking German victories had also been a great surprise. Baron Stoffel, writing just before the war from the French embassy in Berlin, had accumulated reports on the efficiency drive which had turned an outmoded army into a new model army based on conscription and territorial reserves (*Landwehr*). His very alarmist reports were ignored, and this later served as an indictment of the regime when they were published in 1871.[43] The tone of these reports undermined their cred-ibility, and the French reacted to Sadowa by mimicking German reforms in the *Loi* promoted by Marshal Niel in 1868.[44]

This law was never fully implemented or given the financial muscle it required. It does matter, however, for the later developments of 1870, as this half-baked reform created the military and political tool at the disposal of the 4 September republic. Originally, Niel wanted to complement the long military service nucleus of the French army with a reserve of territorial soldiers called the *garde mobile*, composed of ex-soldiers and young men who had been fortu-nate enough to avoid conscription in the first place. French conscription since 1818 had been based literally on a lottery: the picking of a wrong number could mean a seven-year spell in uniform or the expense of paying for a substitute. The latter practice meant that the middle class and the wealthier farmers could save for this eventuality and avoid military service. The Niel reform thus confronted a long tradition of non-participation in the defence of the nation. Furthermore, France had not been threatened since 1815, and many remembered the appalling human cost of the revolutionary and imperial wars of 1792–1815. Historians are now familiar with estimates approaching the losses of the First World War, but contemporaries usually thought that conscription had cost them a million men. Statisticians and demographers were already concerned at the low French birth rate, which made France a slow-growing anomaly in Europe by 1870.[45] Niel's reform, postulating a long and a short military service, thus faced some very serious local opposition to the costs incurred and the political danger implied. The Second Empire had originated in the military coup of 1851, and the army remained a pillar of the regime, while rural votes gave it huge majorities in frequent elections and thus the appearance of democratic legitimacy.

The third central debate was on the nature of the caesarean polity towards the end of the Second Empire. By 1868 the Second Empire was in a phase of remarkable political and social reforms leading to the short-lived liberal empire. Napoleon III gradually granted debate rights to the chamber of deputies and strike and temporary association rights to workers; he made his ministers individually accountable and began to move towards his Orleanist and republican opponents in shifting the regime more to the middle ground of French politics. This evolution startled the more intransigent Bonapartists and the more reactionary supporters of the muscular first incarnation of the regime. It was the fruit of Napoleon III's own personal 'social reveries' and of his advancing physical decline.[46] By 1868 the empire had to evolve sufficiently to make the transition to Napoleon IV possible, and thus it needed to find real constitutional stability. The constitutional role of the ruler had to diminish to enable this transition to take place.

Because of this evolution the government found itself no longer able to push through any major piece of legislation. The Niel reform was cut to size and opposed by many Bonapartist rural deputies unwilling to lose their support and by most urban opposition deputies fearing a new militarisation of the regime. The cost of modernising the army and the price of a million new standard needle rifles had already horrified the deputies; the idea of civilians in arms terrified the reactionaries and exasperated many professional soldiers. After Niel's untimely death, the French reforms were starved of cash and political will. The price of a new artillery could not be supported by normal budgets, and the French who saw the new steel Krupp guns at their own Universal Exhibition of 1867 could neither afford to purchase them nor imitate their breech-loading design.

All these questions on social and military reforms later fed the debate on the causes of the French defeat of 1870. In July 1870 the Spanish crisis brought the

French government to war against Prussia. Spain, in an intense political crisis, lacked a head of state, and the dictator Prim sought to appoint Leopold von Hohenzollern to the throne.[47] The French emperor, although closely related to Leopold, could not accept this candidature for the fear that it might recreate the sixteenth-century encirclement of France. Although this historical thinking was largely obsolete by 1870, the implication that a branch of the house of Bourbon would lose its throne in Spain shortly after the fall of the Sicilian Bourbon monarchy could have revived internal royalist opposition to the empire. To cut a convoluted story short, Leopold withdrew at French insistence, and the French attempted to obtain Prussian assurances that the house of Hohenzollern would not entertain any further design on Spain. In many ways this was a terribly old-fashioned crisis, reflecting the dynastic diplomacy that ruled Europe even in the last few decades of the nineteenth century. The French liberal Émile Ollivier, who was recently rallied to the emperor and whose government represented the new face of the regime, was already facing much opposition from the chamber at the time of the crisis. Ollivier needed to assert himself nationally and internationally.[48] This may seem surprising, as the reforms had obtained a massive electoral approval in the plebiscite of May 1870 and the empire looked stronger than ever. In the chamber of deputies, however, the government was weak and could rely on neither left nor right. The political dynamics behind the crisis were thus very diverse: the liberal government wanted war to assert itself, the reactionary Bonapartists wanted glory to re-establish a conservative regime, and the republicans feared it might consolidate the regime. A few, like Adolphe Thiers, warned against the war.

On the Prussian side, Bismarck probably exaggerated his Machiavellian role, but his Ems telegram, with its insulting description of the last encounter between the French ambassador Benedetti and King Wilhelm, made the war inevitable. Prussian military high command was also eager to face the French before they could reform their armies.

Stéphane Audoin-Rouzeau has shown that for the ordinary Frenchman and woman the war came as a great surprise after a short crisis.[49] In a sense, the complexity of the political crisis remained a challenge for historians. Much was made for a while of street opinion in favour of war. Newspapers in Paris might have given that impression at first glance, but there was little enthusiasm in many quarters of the nation's public opinion and scenes of enthusiasm were limited to Paris. Throughout the country the idea of a war slowly sank in as the *gardes mobiles*, barely trained, if at all, were called to arms and the army gathered at the border. Another body of men, *Gardes Nationaux*, originally recruited among bourgeois sections of the population, formed a reserve of armed men who later played a considerable role when the units began to recruit more widely.[50]

The fourth great historiographical debate – great in terms of volume of writing, perhaps, rather than interest – concerns the causes of the defeat of the imperial army in July and August 1870. On paper the French army seemed comparable with its German counterparts; in reality, however, recent studies have demonstrated that French confusion between the concentration and mobilisation phases of the war had disastrous consequences, preventing any rapid attack. It meant that French soldiers were first sent to one site to be equipped and then went for their regiment, sometimes in the greatest confusion.[51] The scale and nature of war was markedly different from anything the French had fought since 1854.

The Franco-Prussian war was a conflict of masses of infantry, in which the heavy cavalry lost its battlefield relevance while reconnaissance missions became more crucial. The French gathered by the Rhine, invaded Saarbrücken, retreated and were defeated in a series of murderous battles where officers showed conclusively that they had not fully comprehended the consequences of the new fire-power. Needle rifles, lethal up to a mile away, new guns firing further and more rapidly than before, and French *mitrailleuses* (a bullet gun) could kill and maim more effectively than before and favoured defensive positions. The first victims of changes in the nature of warfare were the cavalry squadrons. Many historians of the war, notably Michael Howard in Britain, have stressed the violence of the first month of the war. Casualties were extremely high on both sides. Split in two, the French armies moved to Sedan and to Metz, where they were captured and besieged respectively. Sedan and Napoleon III, so cruelly depicted in Zola's *La Débâcle*, surrendered on 2 September.

When the news reached the rest of France, the regime collapsed and the republic was proclaimed on 4 September simultaneously in Lyons and Paris.[52] Debates arose here again as to the nature of the regime proclaimed in Paris. Trochu, the head of the government, was a token Catholic, vaguely Orleanist officer; he owed his sudden promotion to a pessimistic book of 1867 on the French army, which had achieved sudden prophetic status, and to his recent promotion as governor of Paris.[53] All the other members of the government were deputies of Paris and popular names, such as the radical journalist Rochefort. The 4 September revolution in Paris proclaimed the republic, and could be considered to be the founding act of the Third Republic, even though it opened a period of constitutional uncertainty which only ended five years later.[54] This government of national defence attempted to be as inclusive as possible to compensate for the fact that it was undoubtedly the representation of a minority in the country as a whole.

There is something deeply puzzling in the sudden melting away of the Bonapartist support. Even within the army, protests against any imperial restoration were issued from Germany in 1871 by officers of the captive French army.[55] After twelve months the threat of an imperial restoration had all but vanished. Was Bonapartism an aberration in French politics?

Many historians have silenced their doubts about this in stressing the lack of cohesion of the Bonapartist majority,[56] while the recent historiography contradicts this by stressing the enduring peculiarities of its politics. The Bonapartist myth of a country rejecting parties to favour national unity certainly had enduring qualities which have led some, like René Rémond, to consider Gaullism a direct avatar of this tradition.[57]

9

In 1870, however, the myth of Napoleon I suffered an immense blow in the hands of his militarily incompetent nephew. The only military myth that remained in the face of an invasion was the revolutionary ideal of Valmy and the great victories of the French Revolution. To revive 1792 became the propaganda goal of all republicans and Bonapartists, while the more cautious monarchist factions supporting the competing Bourbon dynasties had to join in for a while to avoid being branded as defeatist. 'We will support the government of 4 September because in the current circumstances we have to unite for the public salvation,' stated a Legitimist provincial sheet.[58]

The French Revolution had acquired almost mythical status through the works of a number of historians, from Thiers to Michelet, who had developed the notion of a nation in arms as a great founding moment of French citizenship.[59] The popular incarnation of patriotic feelings was the popular poetry of Béranger, which had contributed powerfully to xenophobic definitions of the foreigners against whom the nation in arms existed.[60] In 1870, this myth of the nation in arms was given new vigour through the contested work of a young and charismatic politician, Léon Gambetta. Sadly, re-enactment and parody are closely related, and the heroic prism through which the Revolution was magnified proved to have fatal consequences as it highlighted enthusiasm over preparation, improvisation over training. The anxieties voiced in Laon in early September, when the local people refused to defend their city in spite of the prefect's bombastic calls to patriotism, could also be found in many a sleepy provincial town. When a Prussian army approached, heroics seemed of little relevance in the face of overwhelming danger.[61]

The government in Paris soon became nothing much more than the government *of* Paris. The siege of Paris, which started around 16–19 September 1870 only to end on 28 January 1871, isolated the capital city from the provinces and left Gambetta republican dictator of most of France. Gambetta's efforts from Tours, where he settled after 8 October, have been belittled by the conservative historiography[62] and defended by a now largely defunct Third Republic hagiography, yet were considerable.[63] A total of 635,838 men were recruited and equipped to serve in the many armies of the republic as *Gardes Nationaux mobilisés*, while 250,000 were still in training camps at the time of the armistice.[64]

Figure 1.1 clearly illustrates the scale of the debacle and the rapid advance of the enemy in France. Were this map put against another map illustrating the wealth of the nation, it would become even more obvious that much of the modern, productive and wealthier part of France had fallen under the German onslaught.

In the face of immense difficulties, Gambetta managed to keep the country together behind the war effort in spite of secessionist aspirations. The historiography thus focused on Paris on two accounts. The capital city had a revolutionary tradition which was most active during and after the siege and on which Marxist and neo-Marxist analytical theories could be anchored, and Paris became the obsession of the French and Germans who knew that its fall would

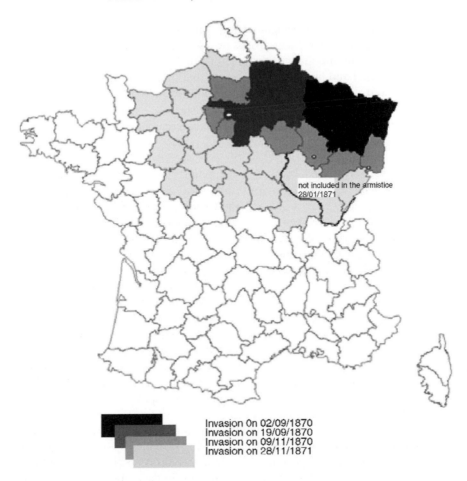

not included in the armistice
28/01/1871

Invasion On 02/09/1870
Invasion on 19/09/1870
Invasion on 09/11/1870
Invasion on 28/11/1871

Figure 1.1   The invasion of France 1870–1

lead to peace. Much of what happened in Paris during the siege then became part of a separate historiographical tradition, which will be discussed later. What took place in the country was critically analysed at different periods.

A post-war parliamentary inquiry into the acts of the government of national defence attempted to judge its action through a series of very leading question naires aimed at discrediting the 4 September republic. The questionnaire was so partisan and so leading that even conservative ministers chose to 'withdraw a number of questions to which I could not provide answers that could be made public' and the prefects only answered 'the questions which could not involve the responsibility of the administration'.[65] The Catholic and royalist media criticised the mayhem of major cities where local municipalities were allowed to legislate and enforce radical reforms and anti-clerical politics. France in 1870 suffered from a real power vacuum which decentralist forces, discussed in Sudhir

11

Hazareesingh's recent work, sought to fill.[66] Much of this rich eruption of local politics has been neglected by historians or has been complacently described as sister movements of the great Commune of Paris.[67] As the following chapters will show, the vital and lively forms of debate that took place almost everywhere in France owed nothing to the specifically Parisian political developments and followed a different political, cultural and social agenda.

In the provinces the war took many non-governmental forms. The most mythical, perhaps, in the sense that we do not have a clear notion of the numbers involved or of their efficiency, were the *francs-tireurs*, private armies which had been recruited by their self-appointed officers and had received authorisation. These irregular troops specialised in ambushes and guerrilla warfare. They usually wore a uniform and were not really civilians in arms, yet the occupying forces developed a deep anxiety about civilians and reacted with great brutality in reprisal. These irregulars allowed for different and often competing forms of nationalistic feelings, and enabled anti-clerical and Catholic elements of the political landscape to fight the common enemy under their respective flags.[68] Another novelty of the war was the intervention of an international brigade led by Guiseppe Garibaldi. International private armies had existed in the past, in Greece for instance, but this particular army came to the rescue not of France but of the republic, and played an important political role in the Rhône valley, which it defended. Historiographically, the role of this force is much more contested, although it did capture the only enemy flag won by a French army.[69] This book argues that this volunteering played an important role in reshaping the idea of modern war and the relationship between French people and their state.

Further controversy is linked to the behaviour of the French officers during the republican phase of the war. In Metz, Marshal Bazaine, a powerful representative of a new officer caste owing everything to Napoleon III, surrendered at the end of October without so much as a real fight. In Paris, the left criticised the generals who seemed unwilling to use the 400,000 men at their disposal to their full potential.[70] That hastily equipped civilians were not good soldiers seemed to be the case in the earlier skirmishes, but in the later battles they showed a willingness to fight which was not matched by their superiors. In all places incompetent, routine-prone and defeatist minds limited the effectiveness of the war effort. Few names survived this war (for military reasons), save, perhaps, that of Chanzy.[71]

Within Paris the siege proved to be an untenable position for the government. Hunger led the political agenda, and the government was hostage to the population that had acclaimed it in September. The news of military defeats could only trickle into the capital, which had to survive on an impoverished diet of third-hand news and rumours. While street publications flourished in considerable numbers, they had little of importance to say. In this climate of deep anxiety, the tension was increased by the news that the government had attempted to negotiate peace in vain and had postponed elections, both municipal and national, to a later date. The news of the surrender of Metz led to a failed insurrection in Paris on 31 October, when radical forces led by Blanqui attempted to seize the town hall, a traditional centre of revolutionary sovereignty. This first insurrection ended in farce as government forces literally crowded into the building. Another insurrection attempt on 22 January ended in a bloodbath. These two insurrections have received far more attention than the ones that took place in Lyons in September or December because their protagonists were prominent later during the Commune of Paris.

The Commune of Paris, which dominates the historiography of the period, has many deep roots in French history. As a political movement, the term 'commune' had many different meanings, ranging from municipalism to communism, and the term was strongly reminiscent of the 1793 Commune which enabled the most radical revolutionaries to control the capital city during the Terror. All these meanings were juxtaposed in the political language of 1870, and the contradictions of the term were rarely openly addressed. The Commune of Paris as a political movement started in August 1870 with the raid on the fire station of La Villette; it was called for in Paris for many weeks during the siege and became a political alternative only after the sudden armistice of January 1871. At the end of January 1871, the food reserves of Paris ran short and the besieged government, without informing Gambetta or enquiring into the provincial situation, decided to sign an armistice for the whole of France. The signed armistice thus excluded the east of France (marked on the map in Figure 1.1) where an army led by Bourbaki attempted to cut German supply lines.

This omission created much confusion and contributed to the destruction of the last operational French forces. To establish a vote between peace and continuation of the war, elections to a national assembly were called for 8 February. After a seven-day campaign, fought almost exclusively on a peace-versus-war platform, the elections returned a solidly conservative and even monarchist majority, which chose the veteran politician Adolphe Thiers as chief of the executive.[72] The list system used for the elections meant that the political leaning of one list or the other was not always clear.[73] The conservative list of the *Salut Public* in Lyons, ostensibly in favour of peace, was thus led by Trochu, Jules Favre, Le Royer (*procureur général*), Bérenger (judge), Morel (previous mayor of Villefranche-sur-Saône) and a number of conservative figures, while the pro-war list of the National Guard contained precisely the same names with the addition of Garibaldi, Chanzy, Hénon (mayor of Lyons), Dolphus (mayor of Mulhouse) and Gambetta.[74] In other words, the substance of a list was often in the minor names which, following the multiple nomination system, were the ones most likely to take the seats. Eventually the conservative Thiers could thus be elected in twenty-six departments, while the 'republican dictator' Gambetta only made it in nine departments (Figure 1.2) and was thus the third most popular politician.

This system gave a degree of presidential legitimacy to the most frequently elected character. The newspapers thus calculated that 1,664,612 Frenchmen had elected Thiers while only 464,605 voters had chosen the nearest republican

THIERS.

GAMBETTA.

Figure 1.2   Thiers and Gambetta, two popular portraits

rival.[75] As they could accept only one seat, the others were made vacant and later enabled less well-known figures to enter the political fray. This confusing system allowed for a number of established names to be elected by virtue of their local notoriety. Ancient names had a field day, and February 1871 represents the last electoral victory of the *notables*. One of the paradoxes of the list vote was that it was meant to elect representatives who were not directly accountable to constituents but only to the nation as a whole. It was meant as an assembly of representatives of the nation, and not of regional or local interests.

Some republicans, like Gambetta, remained attached to this principle throughout their careers because they objected to local control.

The elections seem to prove that the French did not embrace the warmongering republic and, indeed, left the door open for a restoration of the constitutional monarchy. Meeting first in Bordeaux, the assembly refused to return to Paris, and Parisians felt to a greater extent than before the divide between urban minority and rural majority. A series of blunders by the new government, which contained only a handful of known republicans, created the political situation of the Commune insurrection. The end of a moratorium on rent and trade debts suddenly threatened many with bankruptcy. The humiliation of a German parade in Paris and the harsh terms of the peace settlement, condemning the French to five thousand million francs reparation, a long occupation of the north of France and the loss of Alsace and German-speaking Lorraine, added to the Parisian furore.[76] In Bordeaux, the assembly produced a succession of provocative moves such as refusing a seat to Garibaldi (elected four times), laughing at Victor Hugo, and attacking Gambetta in his absence.[77] The 18 March 1871 insurrection was the response to the last provocation, when the army attempted to remove the guns paid for by Paris from the camps of the *Gardes Nationaux*. While the rest of this book will consider the Commune at length, it is worth stressing the general lines taken by the recent historiography which are relevant here.

Traditionally the Commune has been perceived as the culmination of an insurrection campaign led by vanguard groups such as the Blanquists. This theory roughly fitted within the Marxist–Leninist orthodoxy. Also important to this historiography was the role of a handful of members of the Workers' International, far fewer in proportion than in the making of the Lyons Commune in September 1870. A second generation of historical writing, concentrated in terms of publication dates around 1968–71, stressed the anarchistic traditions of the Parisian people and made the Commune a halfway house between old-style revolutionary impulses and new class-consciousness and anti-state politics. Those who attempted to find some left-wing common ground about the Commune questioned its value as a Kuhnian 'paradigm for revolution'.[78] Since the 1980s, a revival of interest in the forms taken by the Commune has stressed its importance as a republican moment, as Philip Nord would describe it – a moment during which the conciliatory forces attempting to bridge the differences between radicals and conservatives were denied their legitimate role.[79] Others, more traditional in a sense, stressed the continuity of political associationism in Paris since the beginning of the 1860s. Dalotel *et al.* emphasised this long story of republican and Utopian socialist underground work.[80] While they may have exaggerated the very Thompsonian undertones of their story of the making of the French working class and its secret nature, they rightly emphasised the vitality of associations before and after the insurrection. Martin Johnson devoted his entire study to the associationist component of the Commune and to the club culture[81] that stirred and developed the revolutionary theories of the Paris Commune.[82] This renewal of emphasis on associations oddly revives the conspiracy historiography of the socialist school or of the reactionary historians who saw in the Commune a Masonic and Internationalist plot.[83]

Historical sociologists such as Harvey[84] or Gould[85] paid more attention to the neighbourhood dimension of the revolutionary movement, and argued that the relative Communard silence on class issues reflected the fact that the Parisians rebelled against the new urban order of Prefect Haussmann.[86] They reacted against the extreme pressures on housing and working-class neighbourhoods inflicted by the prefect's slum-clearing and boulevard-opening schemes.[87] When they rebelled, they fought within the framework of established local sociability which was rarely exclusively work-centred.[88] The National Guard, which established the Commune and remained its principal source of legitimacy, cut through class and professional forms of associations to recompose itself along local lines.

These studies present a rich reassessment of some of the forms of political communalism; it seems less certain that they can be defended as the only sources of the Commune. For the other movements in France which will be studied in this book, the scholarship is old and roughly follows Lissagaray's study. Louis Greenberg's *Sisters of Liberty* is certainly the work that paid most attention to the depth of other Communard movements but, like Jeanne Gaillard's *Commune de province, Commune de Paris*, it centres its narrative too narrowly on the propagation of the Parisian experience. This myopia is obvious when one considers the fact that major figures such as Cluseret or Lissagaray had begun their revolutionary career in the provinces. There was cross-fertilisation and an exchange of people and ideas between Paris and the provinces.

The nature of the Commune of Paris's programme is the final great controversy of the historiography to interest us. Some elements of it, such as the greater transgression of gender boundaries, have been rescued from oblivion as pointing towards a modernity of sorts. The women of the Commune, who later had to walk to Versailles under a shower of stones and spittle, were deemed emblematic of its freedom and dangers.[89] Yet in many ways the Paris Commune fell well short of a socialist agenda. It explicitly referred to notions of right to work and did not innovate in terms of income tax; it promoted healthy economic management rather than redistribution. It used old scapegoats instead of denouncing class inequality. Lyonese leaders went much further: the programme of the Commune of Lyons, as enacted between September 1870 and May 1871, showed a much deeper concern with socialist issues than the Parisians had the time or inclination to display.[90] The final element of this story concerns the civil war, so masterfully studied by Robert Tombs in *The War Against Paris*. The final massacres of May 1871, which killed up to 25,000 Parisians and signalled the beginnings of an era of systematic political violence, led to a polarisation in French politics, later accentuated by the Dreyfus affair, which took over a hundred years to fade.

One of the great 'lessons' of this year of conflicts is undoubtedly the brutalisation of warfare and of French politics. Even though the story has been told many times, there are still many gaps to be filled and many ways, perhaps, of subverting war narratives and revolutionary myths.

Citizenship and wars, 1870–1

This book comprises nine chapters, this introduction included, which develop the themes sketched out above. Because the intention is to deal with more than Paris, the book focuses on specific areas of France which are not often more 'representative' of anything but themselves but which can still be regarded as interesting exemplars or highly suggestive instances of what took place in France.

Another approach, using prefectoral reports such as that of Audoin-Rouzeau, might have been used, but the generalities established from administrative reports are not necessarily representative of anything more than the survival of administrative practices.[91] The departments that have interested me belong to very different social and political arenas. Paris and the Seine were long at the heart of my research, and much of the material for this book originates from the capital city. Lyons, for reasons that will be explained later, became central to much of my narrative. The Hérault gave an interesting instance of a political region which no longer supported the empire but remained in many ways a traditional agricultural department. The three other departments, Creuse, Corrèze, and Haute-Vienne, which form the modern region of Limousin, represent three traditionally supportive regions of the empire where agriculture, migratory workforces and small-scale industry meant that some of the social conflicts were intensely developed while some of the social bonding of the *ancien régime* survived. Moreover, the works of John Merriman and Alain Corbin have made the historiography all the richer.[92]

Appendix 1 gives a chronology of the Franco-Prussian war, while Chapter 2 tackles the recent debates on 'total war' which tend to have been applied principally to the American Civil War and the First World War. As a concept, 'total war' is flawed because the application of war to the totality of a nation is impossible; as an ideal, of a Kantian type, total war has enabled strategists and historians to reflect on the creation of what Daniel Pick labelled a 'war machine'.[93] This war machine has obvious implications in the way modern citizenship has been conceived as a fully and voluntarily integrated cog in a military structure. Total war thus represents the expression of full modernity. Before total war, it is argued, societies at war can be deeply involved in a conflict and yet not be fully mobilised towards the war effort, so that its industrial, commercial and exchange structures are not, in the longer run, affected by the conflict. The year 1870 presents a complex case. France was invaded and many areas of normal life were severely disturbed, much industry was redirected to provide for the war effort and much tax pressure was applied to the French to enable them to import foreign weapons or machinery. In literary terms the war effort was intense, and the proliferation of newspapers and books during the conflict reflects not only an internal propaganda war but also the deep involvement of many literary figures. This involvement was perhaps proportionately greater than in the First World War. Many traditional historians have been reluctant to accept the label, quoting as counterfactual the lack of popular support for the revolutionary wars or the military reluctance to employ the masses of men in arms at their disposal. That the French army was reluctant is not in doubt; that many rural areas saw with dismay the crop of 1871 compromised and the exchange of goods thwarted is also not in question. Yet the war went further than many realised even then.

The war of 1870 saw the rise of a humanitarian consciousness throughout Europe[94] which enabled French women and children to take part in the conflict. The trains of wounded and sick soldiers crossing France brought home

17

the realities of modern war. Even the support for 'war to the last' was not really questioned until defeat after defeat had eroded the French reserves. In theoretical terms, 'war to the last', stating absolute gains as a priority objective, demonstrated a neo-Clausewitzian rejection of negotiated settlements.[95] The modernity of this war was recognised in the immediate post-war period, especially as it highlighted political violence arising from the proletarianisation of France, and had deep cultural and social implications which substantially shaped the making of modern France.

Chapters 3 and 4 follow from this first assessment to consider the ways in which citizenship was structured to face the challenge of the invading armies. The myth of the revolutionary wars of 1792 stirred some deep passions and debates. The whole call-to-arms campaign of Gambetta restated the exchange between citizen and state, and this propaganda campaign backfired in the sense that the revolutionary debates became integral to a contest of the state. François Furet used some of this material to justify his views that the Revolution ended in this period of maturation.[96] The great debates – such as decentralisation – of the late empire were obviously at the heart of this collective rethinking of citizenship. *La sociale*, the general term that encompasses the whole social aspirations of the new working-class and old artisan communities, also had particular echoes in 1870. The war effort supported by Paris or Lyons, for instance, was largely justified by the social gains established through a new compact between patriotic citizens and the nation in danger.[97] Law and order measures and repressive policies could only be cast in this light. Ultimately, there was a breakdown of this new compact largely because it remained tacit and unexplained.

The new compact did not find its best expression at the state level. It was on the municipal scale that these issues arose, and the devotion to the 'commune' in its simplest meaning cannot be justified solely as an instinctive reaction against centralisation. What took place in Lyons, Montpellier, or any city one cares to look at, was a fuller debate on citizenship in relation to local democracy. The politics of care developed by municipalities for the poor or the families of the soldiers, and the development of often secularist education policies, demonstrated the maturation of local politics. Moreover, the decentralist label, applied to all provincial movements by Louis Greenberg, could be challenged on many instances of heavily centralist discourse originating from emancipated communes.

Chapter 5 develops this appraisal but on a smaller scale, by looking at individual identities and how religion could or could not be integrated into discourse on citizenship. Since the Revolution, French definitions of citizenship tended in theory to dissociate citizenship and religious identities from one another. In practice, however, the French had behaved consistently in contradiction with their ideals. The North African territories of Algeria were thus ruled through religious definitions of citizenship and subjection. The Jews, Muslims and 'non-natives' were treated differently by the military and civilian authorities which enjoyed condominium over the territories. The 1870 Crémieux decree gave full, officially non-religious citizenship to the North African Jewry while it confirmed the subjection of the Arabs and submitted the 'Muslim' community to the 'non-native' civilian authorities. The end result was that the militantly racist and proselytising French people of North Africa saw their citizenship reinforced and gained sovereignty over second-class Muslim citizens/subjects. This conundrum, which was not resolved until the Algerian uprising of 1956, led directly to a major insurrection in Algeria in 1870–1. The Jews of France had, through Adolphe Crémieux's decree, gained fuller control over their brethren of North Africa, whom they regarded with some colonialist dismay, but as a religious community they also took part in the revival of the republic. Philip Nord has shown how this minority and the Protestant minority embraced republicanism. Freemasons, themselves in the midst of a deep doctrinal controversy on theism, also allied themselves vigorously to the revolutionary impulse of 1870.

The real religious question in the republic of 1870 was thus the Catholic question. Chapter 5 looks at the ways in which the Church moved to negotiate with the republic, and how it retreated over the Commune uprising to its traditional monarchist allies and a generation-long opposition to the republic.

Chapters 6 and 7 examine the tensions that led to such breakdowns of communication and to the brutalisation of French politics. By looking at the enemy within, Chapter 6 considers how gender and age were discussed in relation to citizenship. The situation in radical cities gave rise to many debates on the military or paramilitary role of women in the war effort.[98] Women of the Commune have thus received much critical attention, from Lissagaray to Gay Gullickson.[99] Children of the Commune or of the siege of Paris did not become as central in French thinking on gender, but the way they were treated reflects on the social contextualisation of childhood in France. Ageism was also contested, and legions of volunteers, civilian brigades uniting children and old men or women, were ways in which significant numbers of individuals reasserted their social value and their active citizenship during the war and Commune. On the other hand, the conflicts which led to the exclusions of a number of individuals or enemies within also deserve some attention as to their social mechanics. Traitors and spies were universally denounced throughout the war and Commune. When a rural baker was sentenced to death for spying on behalf of distant enemies, when a German immigrant father of two French soldiers had to flee his neighbourhood, or when a Communard crowd murdered one of their own on the grounds of treason, a whole process of exclusion and inclusion was taking place which defined citizenship.[100] This process led to the murder of 'innocent' people, precisely because their identity and their citizenship seemed in contradiction with each other. The number of priests arrested for spying also reflects this tension between their marginal, professional, confessional or other identity and French citizenship.

Chapter 7 investigates a number of incidents of internecine violence that led to the greater brutalisation of French politics. The three instances looked at here are also good examples of a patchy but tragic evolution leading to the breakdown of civility and the end of a civil order. The murder of Hautefaye, studied in detail by Alain Corbin in the light of the *longue durée*, in its more contemporary context led to a reflection on civilisation, rurality and barbarity.[101] In this instance, a Bonapartist mob slaughtered a young royalist like a pig and roasted the corpse on a spit. In spite of its atrocity, this murder fitted within a whole tradition of rural violence. The murder by his own men of Commandant Arnaud, officer of the *Garde Nationale*, also fitted with urban violence, except that it targeted a well-liked working man, Freemason and radical. Arnaud's death and the rites that followed his burial, as well as the trial of his murderers, led directly to the reciprocal and calculated violence of the Commune of Paris. While most insurrections of 1870–1 had ended in a negoti-ated settlement, as in Narbonne or even in Paris on 31 October 1870, the insurrection of 18 March 1871 used violence and was repressed in a calculated way, making murder the ultimate argument on both sides and creating a polit-ical chasm that the Third Republic never managed to bridge.

The following two chapters attempt to pull together the experience of the war and Commune and to assess their impact on the making of modern France. Chapter 8 reflects on the Eugen Weber hypothesis and on the fragility and strength of French national identity.[102] By looking at the French state more broadly – that is, looking beyond the state-paid administration – one can attempt to analyse some of the elements of a desire for centralisation. Throughout the war the republic had to use and attempt to modify an administration that was not shaped by its ideals; after the war it negotiated with this civil service, while it also found some of its stronger support in elected magistrates, professions and other organised groups. The conclusion deals with the political and social constraints on the development of a post-war regime.

Odile Rudelle and Claude Nicolet have seriously begun an in-depth revision of the Third Republic, but their work alone has not changed the prevailing negative opinion.[103] Yet the Third Republic was the longest lasting form of government enjoyed by the French since 1789. How the political regime that divided the French least became the strongest, while constantly in crisis, remains a difficult issue to address. The war and Commune experience provided the matrix of post-war developments and froze some of the possible political devel-opments of France. The religious question, which first focused on the Catholics and then on the Jews, the hunt for the enemy within which found much expres-sion in medicine and culture, the conflicting aspirations to a mystical or materialistic national regeneration, and the dream of a unifying saviour, all became embedded issues of the new regime. On the other hand, practical concerns, including the social issues or even innovations of the war such as the capital gains tax and income tax promoted in Lyons, were not brought to the fore of French politics for many years. In conclusion, this book will consider how the experience, practice and memory of citizenship at war contributed to the making of that most odd regime called the Third Republic.

2

TOTAL WAR, CIVIL WAR AND 'MODERNITY'

> I have always feared that the principle of nationalities would turn
> the struggle between peoples into racial extermination and would
> remove from the rules of *droit des gens* the temperament, the civil
> behaviour accepted in the small political and dynastic wars of the
> past.[1]

The Franco-Prussian war has always been considered in relation to the
American Civil War.[2] This comparison was not new in any way, since the
American Civil War provided a model of military developments frequently
invoked during the Franco-Prussian war and the war against the Commune.[3]
The American Civil War analogy was used in both Communard and Versaillais
discourses. In the Communard discourse, it was to justify a belief in the effectiveness of a 'people in arms'.[4] This was reinforced by the fact that Cluseret, one of
the most prominent revolutionaries in Lyons in September 1870 and in Paris in
March 1871, was himself a veteran general of the US war. In the Versailles
usage, the Communards were compared with confederates,[5] the term *federates*
being actually used by the Communards themselves to refer to their decentralist
political project while the *Ligue du Midi*, led by Esquiros, had declared earlier that
'there is ground to create a provisional confederation'.[6] If we go beyond the
rhetoric and generalities which this 'American' model represented[7] the picture is
more blurred, at least for the period preceding the war itself. In fact, the lessons
of the American Civil War were only learnt the hard way, and it seems that the
large literature produced between 1865 and 1870 in French had but little impact
on the ways the French rulers thought about their army or modern warfare. The
French army had few self-critical agencies or 'think tanks' to go by, and certainly
did not possess the reflective tools provided by the Prussian high command
around Von Moltke. The American war had been ground-breaking in many
tragic ways. The great slaughter of Gettysburg and the use of novel ways of
killing had been matched in theoretical terms by the appearance of new
concepts, such as war crimes, which led to the trial and execution of Captain
Henry Wintz, commandant of Andersonville confederate prisoner camp.[8]
Paradoxically, most of the key developments in warfare and attitudes to war

did not travel well or lost much of their substance in translation. This chapter will thus look at the Franco-Prussian war in the light of this comparative approach, and consider three contested analytical tools to broaden our under-standing of this crucial period. The first contested concept is borrowed from the work of Clausewitz and relates to 'total war', a term until recently applied to world wars only.[9] The second concept is that of a social war or ideological war between bourgeois and proletarians. This debate still runs deep in the historiog-raphy, and contributed substantially to all understanding of the period. The third and last relates to modernity and seeks to establish why the Franco-Prussian war and Commune have recently been re-evaluated as forerunning moments of modernity.

Total war

Daniel Pick, in his recent *War Machine*, attributed great importance to the Franco-Prussian war in the making of modernity in feeding industrial war machinery.[10] The fact that the war was mostly fought in a manner reminiscent of earlier conflicts rather than later ones did not undermine his teleological argu-ment that this war was a first step towards a more integrated society, running like a nightmarish machine without leadership or other purpose than destruction. In a recent collection devoted to this subject, historians failed to find a common historical register to discuss the issue of total warfare.[11] Part of this problem comes from the work of Clausewitz himself, who, writing in the 1820s, could not have anticipated the destructive industrial warfare of attrition of the Western Front in 1914–18, but could reflect on the mass wars of the revolutionary period. The notion of total war is thus less associated with the means of war – industry need not be part of the equation if the parties involved are devoid of industrial strength – and more with war objectives. Total wars of the revolu-tionary period seem to imply a war to the last, intent on destroying the enemy's military might, its political system or even its culture. Uncompromising war aims would thus term war as the opposite of diplomacy, carried through other means. If we analyse the Franco-Prussian war, it soon becomes obvious that some of its features make it relatively close to a Clausewitzian *type* of war. Since we are still talking about theoretical models and a conceptual typology, it is obvious that the relationship between theory and practice may be quite problematic.

In 1870, the war effort on the part of the French gradually stepped up and became almost universal. The first mobilisation effort had recruited all soldiers, including reserves and others. In August the mobilisation was applied to all single men under the age of 40. Gambetta then extended universal conscription to all men (including married men) under the age of 40, while all men up to the age of 65 joined a military force of one kind or another.[12] Some workers, such as those working in the manufacture of weapons or in vital supply areas such as the bakeries of Paris, were exempt from actual military service.[13] When Gambetta reiterated his calls to mass mobilisation, he stated clearly the new social obligations that the war imposed on the state in exchange for the abolition of all family exemptions and special cases: 'The republic will provide for the needs of the families recognised as necessitating help ... The republic will adopt the children of the citizens who succumb for the defence of the fatherland.'[14] Those who joined the ranks of inflated army reserves of one sort or another often joined in the war effort in another capacity, and various night watch, fire and even vigilante organisations were set up by volunteers who could not enlist in the ranks of the army.

In besieged Paris, civilian victims were equated to soldiers in terms of pension or disability allowances. In other cities involved in the earlier phases of the war, civilians were not treated the same way, even though the families and orphans of guardsmen[15] mobilised in October 1870 had rights to certain poor relief.[16]

The war became a total war because of the republican regime. Irregulars could obtain *francs-tireurs* guerrilla certificates easily, so soldiers regarded as unfit to serve the state would still be able to fight for themselves, equipped at their Commune's expense. Total warfare supposed a strict management of manpower towards the war effort, and indeed it seems that Gambetta and his acolyte Freycinet, while ignorant of Clausewitz, were drawn to similar conclusions on the importance of mass armies in the age of nation-making wars.[17] This was not in itself surprising, since they all used the French Revolution and its armies as the basis for their analysis.

While the republican war effort was important, many rightly complained that the troops already gathered in units had few weapons, officers or instructors and that their equipment was often very inadequate. The government itself was aware of this, and a number of memoranda made that point as firmly as possible.[18] These critics probably missed the point: this mass mobilisation, which reached every village of rural France, was meant to involve the whole population in a struggle, which was increasingly represented as a struggle to the death. The slightly ridiculous parades of the military strength of small village militias mattered.[19] Archive boxes are full of their requests for more weapons and for more military training.[20] In Lyons, the municipality established an ammunition factory which served the dual purpose of employing unemployed female workers and of equipping local conscripts.[21]

If we take the pragmatic view that money is a better indicator of political support than memoranda, administrative reports and demonstrations of enthusiasm, we have mixed results. On the one hand, public war subscriptions were often relatively unsuccessful in the rural areas; on the other, the vast public expenses ordered by the weak government were carried through, and departmental elites put their weight behind expensive projects such as the creation of new departmental artillery batteries. Of the 382 new artillery batteries ordered by decree on 3 November 1870, 98 were complete in February 1871, 254 were nearly complete and only 30 had not been contracted out.[22] That many of these guns were not up to the best military standards does not matter here, as it would have been easy for local mayors, *conseils généraux* at departmental level or administrators to slow down or even block any spending. In reality, this war effort over a period of less than three months is remarkable. As for the public's relative lack of enthusiasm for war subscriptions, this may be partially explained in terms of credit rating. The government of 4 September simply did not have the established track record required to guarantee these loans. Furthermore, many of the municipalities or local authorities issuing the bonds were even more fragile, and citizens could only view with some suspicion a debt issued by, for instance, Lyonese revolutionaries, which could easily be repudiated by following administrations.

Chronologically there was perhaps less enthusiasm for the war after the defeats of November or December 1870. Yet we should not be unduly obsessed with figures. Enthusiasm in times of war is often a result of careful public opinion management, and historians have long seen through the great myth of war unity during either the First World War or the Second World War.[23] The Franco-Prussian war lasted little more than six months, and while Gambetta's propaganda machine went disastrously astray it does not undermine the fundamental issue of a total war argument.[24]

The process of mass militarisation was well under way when the Paris government signed the peace. It may not have been very productive in the very short term, but the 1870 revolutionaries were prompt to demonstrate that the early phases of the revolutionary wars of 1792–3 were not immediately successful. One difference with later mass militarisation, or indeed even with its predecessors, was that this 'massification' did not originate from the army, which had only a loose grasp on its management. It was largely a result of mass participation in an improvised civilian war effort. The leaders of this mass militarisation rejected the military values associated with working within traditional army discipline. The elected officers of the new army had to negotiate, and stated coyly that 'the captain hopes that he will never have to use such means of repression and relies on the *esprit de corps* and the conciliatory and fraternal spirit which have always been here since the formation of the Compagnie'.[25] While calling all men to arms, revolutionary leaders like Flourens denounced the traditional military systems.[26] The traditional categories or spheres of 'civilian' and 'military' are only valid when one excludes the other: they disappear when one sphere embraces the values of the other.

Historians have been scathing about the French lack of enthusiasm and about the growing unease cultivated by conservative newspapers, which seemed to have changed their minds over Gambetta in mid-November. They have contrasted the number of volunteers of August with those of January as an indication of the decline of the French war effort. In August, 36,000 men left their homes to enter the ranks of active military life, while in January only 5,700 still wished to risk their lives.[27] However striking these figures may be, they are misleading in the sense that there was far less scope to volunteer in January than there was in August. Most men had by then been registered and enrolled in National Guard or *garde mobile* units, and many of the reserve units were now destined for active service. In Haute-Vienne, for instance, a department of about 319,000 inhabitants, 400 men belonged to the normal call of conscripts of 1870; 3,000 men were part of the *mobile*, 5,432 men were mobilised after the decree of 29 September 1870, and 1,650 had volunteered to serve for the duration of the war. Another 170 served in the *francs-tireurs* units of Les Amis de Paris and Les Francs-tireurs de la Haute-Vienne. Of this mass of 10,652 men, only 3,570 served in the Loire armies; they suffered the loss of 354 men, nearly 10 per cent of the total, and 47 per cent of these died of an illness.[28] The total cost to the department, including a new field artillery battery and the relief work involved in mass mobilisation, was over ten million francs. Evidence suggests, however, that apart from a few incidents where the rural conscripts challenged the republican order, shouting 'Long live the emperor!' or even '*Vive la Prusse!*',[29] most soldiers did not flee and most joined their National Guard or *mobile* units without trouble.

Dissatisfaction arose from the lack of training or equipment provided to the various units. This under-provision meant that the military camps created by Gambetta to harden his soldiers and isolate them from the constant restlessness of urban politics were only partially successful and had yet to bear fruit when the armistice was signed.

Appendix 2 details the number of guardsmen mobilised during the second phase of the war after the decrees of 22 October and 5 November 1870, together with the number of registered *corps-francs*. With Figure 2.1, it also indicates the percentage this mobilisation represents of the department's population. In terms of *corps-francs*, A. Martinier established that this form of anarchistic mobilisation created 91 battalions of infantry and 450 squads (*compagnies formant corps*), 28 *escadrons* of cavalry and 18 *pelotons* and 31 batteries of artillery. The bulk of this mass of *francs-tireurs* was in Garibaldi's army[30] and was composed of small units, some of them short-lived, originating from all the departments listed below and with 166 of them from extra-departmental organisations.[31] Volunteers from Spain, Belgium, the United States, South America, the Middle East, Greece, Ireland (O'Kelly's Regiment), Egypt and Italy formed units where the foreign element was not always the majority. Whatever their origins, irregulars all seemed to borrow their uniforms and posturing from melodramatic theatres.

The detailed table on which this map is based represents the second wave of the war effort, after the army and the *gardes mobiles* had already gone, and is thus only representative of the efforts of the National Guard to create operational units. To establish a comparative framework with the First World War would be difficult. Becker established that, in real terms, 168 men per thousand inhabitants went to war over the four years of the conflict, and that the French suffered losses of 34 per cent.

In Haute-Vienne, using the data mentioned earlier, the 1870 figure for war conscripts would stand at 33 per thousand if we include all the men involved in the war effort. In other words, even though this calculation is limited by the demographic evidence and the gender balance, the mobilisation effort of the

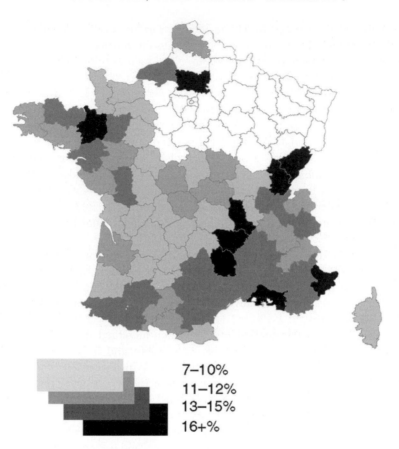

7–10%
11–12%
13–15%
16+%

Figure 2.1 The French war effort by department[32]

republican war of 1870 compares well with the later conflict in spite of a much
more desperate and disorganised situation. The percentages have to be read,
moreover, with the caveats imposed by the peculiarities of the locality. For
instance, the Creuse department, led by Martin Nadaud, was one of intense
male migration, and many men were then already in Paris or Lyons. This
explains why that particular department also suffered such disproportionate
losses during the bloody week of May 1871.[33] On the other hand, the excep-
tionally high percentages for the department of Oise are the result of
confusion between sedentary guardsmen and mobilised ones. In the Rhône
department the numbers are also flawed, in the sense that Lyons considered
itself a city at risk and maintained within its limits many of the guardsmen
equipped and trained since September 1870. The variations are not all clearly
explained by local diversity. It is important to consider where the war took
place to understand better why departments such as the Jura, which were near
the front line, afforded twice as many soldiers as the Tarn-et-Garonne, which

was a long way from any battlefields. The geographical proximity to the war influenced participation.

In Paris and major republican hotbeds like Lyons or Marseilles, the enthusiasm for war went on unabated and was only undermined by enforced idleness and the suspiciously cautious attitude of professional soldiers. Heroes of war such as Sergeant Hoff in Paris maintained the morale of the besieged Parisians. Hoff, almost a character from a melodrama, was a soldier who bore a particular grudge against the invaders and who specialised in guerrilla warfare and night-time sniping.[34] In the first few weeks of the siege, Hoff, carrying back various trophies, was fêted as a hero. A little later he disappeared and was promptly denounced as a spy who had staged his exploits with Prussian help. In fact, the bombastic Hoff had been wounded, and he never recovered from this reversal of fortune.

The war thus mobilised more men than could be used, and the war efforts implied a better adjusted management of manpower. The French government only realised the extent of its role as it was called to intervene in different sectors of economic and social life. Mobilisation had created real hardship for many families, and specially created departmental committees were set up to provide for the families of soldiers at war.[35] These families were granted goods and occasional funds, while in Paris the state and municipalities had to manage the new poverty created by war. The conflict affected all walks of life, and the economic crisis in the besieged cities and in the country at large had a real impact on the conduct of the war. Economically, many industries were set up to convert an outmoded weapon design into something approaching a modern rifle or to produce ammunition. Many industrialists and profiteers tried to take a share of a chaotic market in which state and municipalities competed.[36]

Francs-tireurs did not necessarily deserve the bad press they received after the end of the war. They suffered relatively heavy losses, and even though their action was not orthodox it forced the invaders to maintain a considerable force in the field to protect their supply lines. A variety of men were found in these units: for instance, the small unit of the *francs-tireurs de la Haute-Vienne* contained men aged 21 to 51, with the majority in their thirties. They occupied a diversity of activities: 14 were porcelain workers from Limoges, 10 were shopkeepers, 17 were Limousin builders (itinerant builders), 7 were farmers and labourers, 4 lived off their private income, 16 were either artisans or working in a trade, and 3 were clerks.[37] This motley group contracted an engagement with one officer, who then joined his private army to the forces of the Loire army. This particular group went through three battles of some importance and walked several hundred miles, with only four deserters on what was a harrowing adventure.

Even if we ignore the strictly military aspect of war, the conflict changed a number of perceptions and involved a greater number of people than before. The French Red Cross – in fact, two competing societies, the *Société de Secours* and the *Comité de la Presse* – was established to serve a diversity of purposes.[38] New institutions, created around notions of compassion, care for the heroic wounded and a whole martyrology, also served to promote individuals and their causes to a national level. French Protestants,[39] Freemasons,[40] Jews, Catholics, aristocrats and notables grasped the humanitarian ideals[41] as a helpful buoy in troubled waters.[42]

If we consider this a good indicator of war involvement, the evidence from the provinces and Paris is overwhelming. The smallest communes such as Toy-Viam, hardly more than a hamlet on the poverty-stricken high plateau of Corrèze, offered four beds for the war wounded.[43] The communes organised collections which were successful in terms of the limited income these municipalities would have access to in normal times. Many civilians also opened makeshift hospitals, named 'ambulances', in their own homes after it became widely known that the Geneva Convention protected the belongings of such charitable institutions. Here again, the army watched as the war effort increased its remits to include forms of civilian participation, which were not subject to its control, even nominally, until 31 December 1870.[44] The number of beds involved and the resources devoted to the humanitarian agencies turned whole cities into giant hospitals. Parisian ambulances represented 25,182 beds, not including a number of ambulances closed down by the authorities.[45]

In Le Mans, a smaller city of the centre west of France eventually reached by the German armies after the defeat of the Loire armies, seventy ambulances were added to the eighty-two others of the department. Le Mans thus offered 635 beds and the department 1,405, receiving 2,601 and 5,410 patients respectively for a grand total of 141,364 days, or an average of about seventeen days per patient, before the battle. In the heat of the conflict, the number of beds multiplied to 3,697 beds for 19,348 wounded and sick soldiers. The German invaders were exasperated by this mass hospitalisation: under the terms of the Geneva Convention, they were prevented from billeting their soldiers in makeshift hospitals. In Le Mans, they violated the Convention and occupied fifty-six ambulances, sacking thirteen.[46]

More than simply redistributing resources towards forms of the war effort, the humanitarian logic emphasising the rules of war and codes of behaviour of modern warfare meant that the enemy could be cast in the role of villain in a much-simplified representation of the conflict. A number of atrocities reflected the ideological loading of the conflict whereby the enemy became demonised and embodied the whole burden of war violence and atrocities. This process took place on both sides, but the French especially had cause to complain of German exaction and severe retribution for guerrilla warfare. The doctor serving humanity became the embodiment of the universal values of citizenship at war. While soldiers in arms were the citizens answering the nation's call, doctors and nurses could represent a less directly militarised and gender-neutral form of citizenship.[47] When nurses and doctors were shot or raped, the values of universalism were themselves undermined by the invader, who cast himself as the enemy of mankind.[48] War representations abound of the relatively few infringements of the Geneva Convention; see Figure 2.2.

This crude woodcarving, published in 1871, reflects the growing use of medical neutrality to feed nationalistic bipolar representations. The doctor shot

CHIRURGIEN FRANÇAIS TUÉ PAR UN PRUSSIEN
PENDANT QU'IL SOIGNE UN BLESSÉ.

Figure 2.2   French surgeon murdered by a Prussian while tending the wounded[49]

in the back by the Prussian trooper is the representation of humanity as the victim of barbarity, and the caption leaves no room for the imagination. This picture, while realistic in style, does not refer to any specific instance of the war but simply to a wider range of atrocities in Le Mans, at the Saône-et-Loire ambulance or in Sedan.[50]

The statistics of casualties were not very reliable but estimated French losses at 470,521, of whom 131,100 died or went missing, a figure comparable with the

French losses of the first semester of the First World War. This meant that a significant percentage of the French population brought home the scars of modern warfare. Gambetta's use of hospital trains to distribute victims across France reflected past military practice in Italy.[51] In 1870, however, many wounded soldiers ended up travelling hundreds of miles before finding a bed, while large reserves of beds went unused in the cities they crossed.[52] This migration of the dying brought home images of the war, however, and the conflict became a reality for many French people.[53] The railway network of ambulances as created by Gambetta had ramifications throughout the whole of France.[54] When trains crossed the country and stopped at the local station, there would be spontaneous demonstrations of nationalistic fervour and care, which greatly helped provincial French people to comprehend the violence of the conflict. Like most crude governmental propaganda, this could backfire and chill the enthusiasm of the volunteers.

The spectacle of maimed bodies and dying young men did not entice volunteers to flock in large numbers. In terms of public health, there is no doubt that this policy helped spread the smallpox epidemic which raged among the unvaccinated soldiers.[55]

Considering the many negative consequences of the war, the message of the necessity of carrying on the war rather than surrendering on humiliating terms was notoriously difficult to pass on. The situation in Paris was made worse by the atrocious weather of December 1870. In the vacuum of imagery, artists took it upon themselves to step in and fulfil their patriotic duties. The works of Puvy de Chavannes and other major painters are familiar, but one of the most inspired and odd uses of arts during the siege of Paris was the creation of a 'Museum of Snow' near Fort 85 of the 7th Company of the 19th Battalion. The 'statues' produced created a real sensation and became a very popular tourist attraction for besieged Parisians. The one statue which achieved national notoriety and which was reported in almost every newspaper and account of the war was the statue of *Resistance* by Falguière (Figure 2.3). Beside it, a monstrous bust of the Republic paled into insignificance.

> The delicate artist has not given to *Resistance* the solid, almost manly forms or the large muscles inspired by Michelangelo that the topic seemed to require. He understood that it was a moral resistance rather than a physical one and instead of embodying her with the features of a female Hercules ready to fight, he gave her the grace of a woman of Paris today ... her delightful feet pushing, the toes attached to the stone seemed to become part of the soil.[56]

Falguière never converted this design into a marble statue, and the snow soon returned to the soil. By the time of the armistice a sudden thaw had removed this fragile symbol. Symbols did not go amiss in 1870, but the speed of events tarnished even the brightest reputation. Like this snow statue, the propaganda of war could not escape defeat.

Figure 2.3   La Résistance, a snow statue by Falguière

Social war

Another element of the 1870–1 period which bears comparison with 1914–18, and particularly 1917, is the manner in which the great national show of unity dissolved and revealed greater tensions and social hatreds. There were a great number of insurrections in 1870. Two took place in August against the empire, one in Paris and the other in Lyons. The major revolution of 4 September started in Lyons and Paris almost simultaneously, and established a national republican government in the latter and a radical municipal democracy in the former. In Paris, as in Lyons, the imperial regime had kept a direct rule, and there were no intermediate echelons to mollify the revolutionaries as in Saint-Étienne or Marseilles, where newly elected town councils had the local democratic mandate to fill a power vacuum.[57] The regime of 4 September was broadly based and attempted to unite the moderate conservatives and republicans in a national defence government, which left behind many of the more radical aspirations of the left. The way the war had been fought and lost led many factions of the left to distrust the moderate republicans. Aborted insurrections in Paris and the provinces gradually undermined the government's grasp on its radical republican constituency. Not all insurrections were Parisian, and indeed the Communard movement that seized power in Paris in March 1871 had many provincial brethren throughout France and Algeria.

31

The war was only a month old when the first insurrection attacked a barracks in Paris in an attempt to capture weapons. The old revolutionary Blanqui and his clique, who were at the heart of this first failed insurrection, had been active since the 1830s. They were the hard core of revolutionaries who believed in the revolution for revolution's sake. In many ways, this elitist vanguard referred back to the extreme left of the French revolution but did not have a full programme for the aftermath of the revolution. Blanqui did not believe that there would be a period free of the revolution or that he and his men would live to see it.[58] This ideology of action, almost of permanent revolution, had an obvious influence on the development of the great revolutionary traditions of the late nineteenth century and early twentieth century. The most obvious link was with the Russian anarchist and theorist Bakunin, who inspired – if not led – a failed insurrection in Lyons on 28 September 1870.[59] Lenin later reflected on the success of the Bolshevik insurrection in relation to the Paris Commune.

The Lyons affairs of 1870 are less well known.[60] On 4 September, while a crowd invaded the *chambre des députés*, the republicans of Lyons had already proclaimed the abolition of the empire and established their own revolutionary commune under the red flag. Following the well-established and long-serving republican Hénon, motley opposition groups constituted a municipality which included Freemasons, members of the workers' international and conservative republicans. Under their leadership the Lyons administration threw away the shackles of despotism and organised itself as a city-state, using its soldiers to organise the defence of the Rhône valley. The union between republicans was then stronger than their ideological divisions on the nature of the society that would follow. Splits soon appeared, however, between republican and socialist leaderships. Yet when Cluseret, Bakunin and Albert Richard attempted to lead the ultra-revolutionary groups of the working-class areas of Lyons to the town hall, it was officially to negotiate a pay increase for defence labour and military service. They had found a few hundred volunteers to whom it did not seem particularly novel to petition their municipality aggressively.[61] In general, parade-demonstration had many equivocal meanings, but in this instance it was not revolutionary in intent, and while Cluseret and Bakunin did seize the town hall they found their troops despondent and unwilling to topple the new municipality for a handful of rhetorical phrases and platitudes.[62] Eventually, the 30,000 or so men who had gathered turned against the new revolutionaries. From the town hall, where the revolutionaries indecisively signed arrest orders, they could hear the prefect being acclaimed by the National Guardsmen gathered outside. Finally, Cluseret, the leader of the Lyonese movement, went to negotiate the surrender with the prefect.

Not a shot was fired in this tragi-comic incident, which was typical of the ideologically motivated incidents of the beginning of the war. What made it worthy of notice was the presence of Bakunin and the anarchistic message addressed to France. In fact, most contemporaries ignored this radical inspiration and blamed better-known leaders of the Association Internationale des Travailleurs (AIT).[63]

The 31 October crisis in Paris, much more important in some ways, was a reaction against the fall of Metz, and caused Blanqui, Flourens and their friends to lead the Belleville northern guardsmen of Paris to attack the town hall. Here again, they managed to seize the government. While the revolutionaries discussed their own governmental alternative, the army coming through the underground passage literally crowded them out, to the point where it became impossible to move in the town hall. The crisis was resolved without a shot. The government, severely shaken, had to organise a referendum to find a new political legitimacy in Paris. It also signalled the end of the municipal dreams of the old Étienne Arago, who had wanted to 'make of the town hall a sort of house made of glass'.[64] The ideals of political transparency and anonymous collective leadership had been badly shaken and discredited. The budding republic of 1870 could not resume the narrative of 1848. Through these crises, the political adversaries of the left found in each other a more dangerous enemy than the royalists or even the Prussian invaders. While it is important not to overstate the cohesiveness of republican opposition to the Second Empire, channels of communications still existed between centre-left and extreme-left people, and so did much friendship and mutual respect. The failed insurrections of 1870 tested this republican fabric and gradually tore it apart.

In all these instances, the elements of class warfare were not dominant. The revolutionary culture of the insurrectionists and governing forces was the same, and they shared social origins. The differences were on the margins of ideology, and often rested on a handful of tactical choices or policies. It is, however, significant that after so many years of dictatorship the only technique of dissidence with which revolutionary forces were familiar was the use of guardsmen and armed demonstration, occasionally barricades. The revolutionary idiom inherited from the French Revolution was singularly impoverished in 1870 and limited to shows of power. This technique was common to both sides. In this power game, violence remained limited to a display. This was a dangerous courting game which could easily turn violent but which was perhaps not meant to do so, and it is significant that most of these parades ended in peaceful talks and negotiation. Those who witnessed it right to the end were cynically comparing notes with the historical accounts available: 'The Commune settled in yesterday ... There are also some Garibaldians, a real masked ball. A simulacrum of the feast of the Federation of the First Republic '[65]

It was when sections of the population unfamiliar with these displays of working-class force, first manifested during the great strikes of the 1868–70 period, seized power from within the republican establishment that these regular crises turned sour. When members of the military started to exercise greater influence on the government in Paris, the attitude towards civilian unrest gradually became more violent verbally until, on 22 January, the negotiation did not even start and led to a fusillade on the Place de l'Hôtel de Ville in Paris.

33

The role of military ideology in the hardening of political discussion should not be underestimated, yet the active role of military figures should not be over-stated. The government's leader was a verbose general, Trochu, who did not impart to his government many of the rigid qualities associated with military regimes.[66] Indeed, the civilian members of the government, such as Jules Ferry, were often seen as more directly involved in a toughening of the government's politics.[67] The head of the National Guard, Clément Thomas, was a veteran authoritarian republican who had taken part in the repression of the June days in 1848, and he also led in the militarisation of the government. This drift to a more authoritarian regime can be dated from the 31 October insurrection. As mentioned earlier, this had been a very serious attempt at seizing power, and had been narrowly defeated by a mixture of cajoling and superior force. The dialogue that took place led to a negotiated solution, the terms of which were that the insurrection itself was not to be treated as a crime. Central to the negoti-ations were the left-wing republicans who later gathered under the label 'radical'. Edmond Adam, then prefect of police, and various mayors of arrondissements, like Georges Clemenceau, served as go-betweens.[68] When the government went back on its word and actually attempted to arrest the leaders of the 31 October insurrection, these intermediaries were either pushed into the arms of more radical groups or lost much of their own political credibility.

Edmond Adam resigned, to be replaced by a more conservative prefect;[69] radical republicans set themselves in cautious opposition. This tension was later followed with the denouncing of radical troops as cowardly. In many symbolic ways, the government attempted to humiliate the radicals as ineffective, warmongering hotheads. All these measures – the betrayal of the word given on 31 October, the public humiliations and the insults – led to a gradual breaking down of the central links of citizenship between rulers and ruled. The honour of the left had been insulted and the honourability of a treacherous government seemed more than dubious. In a situation where the government's only legitimacy was that of popular acclaim, when they owed the power they had to the street, which had given them the right to rule, it seems incredible that the government was so careless and wasteful of its popularity and good reputation. Throughout the war, republican solidarity broke down and republi-cans lost a common idiom.[70] In sociological terms, it took place mostly where the military dominated the state apparatus. Lyons came to this level of violence only after the murder of Arnaud, while many provincial insurrections, such as the one in Narbonne studied in detail by Marc César, were negotiated and diffused precisely because the army played a very small part in the negotiations.[71]

A similar pattern applied to tribunals. Where the military established war tribunals punishment grew in severity, while the civilian courts which judged the Narbonne affair freed most participants precisely because the insurrection was still recognised as part of the common political idiom and did not necessarily call for repression.[72] In some ways, then, the conflict was not a social war to start with but ended up being so. It could be read as an attack on the state or even a taking over of the state by associative organisations.

One of the most pregnant interpretative models was that offered by Marx in 1871. Karl Marx's comments on 1870–1 set the commune movements within his vast teleological construct and construed the Commune as an attack on the bourgeois state. Lenin picked up the analysis of Marx, arguing that the Russian revolution should mirror the Commune in creating an alternative form of the state.[73] The debate between Kautsky, Lenin and Trotsky in 1918 entirely revolved on the interpretation of the Commune of Paris as the first instance of a dictatorship of the proletariat, and, in scholastic terms, on what elements of the Commune's practices Marx had approved. The defence of terrorism articulated by Trotsky reverberated in all revolutionary movements of the twentieth century, including those of Mao and Castro. Communists and anarchists never doubted the relevance of the Commune of Paris, even though their reading of the movement differs in major ways. For the more conservative historians and writers, the Commune has increasingly been dismissed as a nostalgic movement grounded in a masquerade of the French Revolution. It is only through the wider angle of the Franco-Prussian war and the Commune seen as a continuum that the recent literature has emphasised its modernity.

Modernity

Modernity is a contested cultural concept which may well be empty of demonstrable meaning but which refers to notions of progress and positivism and to the economic and social developments of the Industrial Revolution. In relation to warfare, modernity is intimately tied to the development of an industrial state, something which did not exist fully in either France or Germany by 1870.[74] The meshing of industrial and military concerns may be the weak link in any demonstration of total war using First World War paradigms for the Franco-Prussian war.[75]

By 1870, the French had only partially integrated the industrial within the military. One of the most developed forms of modern capitalism, namely the railway sector, had been put under the authority of a commission of the Niel military reform of 1868 but had not really been integrated within the war effort. Other industries such as the national armouries of Tulle or Saint-Étienne produced weapons at a higher rate, while various industries improvised new techniques to convert old equipment or issue new weapons, notably new models of the *mitrailleuse*. These bullet guns (not really machine-guns) had an exaggerated reputation as the ultimate weapon of destruction because most fired 50g bullets, which could remove limbs at some distance, and because, like the eponymous machine-guns, they signalled a more undifferentiated killing process and greater efficiency.[76] As weapons, they were not the most efficient, but they were symbolic of new warfare. Other innovations and symbols of modernity were the armoured trains or the electrical spotlights converted from their Universal Exhibition purpose into instruments of war. The small pleasure boats, *bateaux mouches*, of the exhibition were also used as ambulances. The French used hot air balloons – ballooning had been a popular sport among the adventurous before the war – for communication and escape from besieged Paris. They also used microfilms to carry a maximum of information, attached to the feet of pigeons.

There is a modernism of sorts attached to the war of 1870 during which a scientific committee was established to study the claims of myriad inventors and amateur scientists. The French academicians studied means of resisting the siege and various weapons, but even though the intentions were obvious there were few of any value identified over the period.[77] If modernity is to be assessed in relation to the rapid acceptance of slightly marginal but cutting-edge technology or the smooth integration of the complementary elements of a societal war machine, the French failed to be modern in 1870.

In other terms, and considering modernity as a literary and metaphorical set of representations, there is a case to be made. The war had a very important impact on literary and artistic representation. French painters, varying from symbolism to the gritty realism of Detaille's popular panoramas, tried to place the war at the heart of their work. Even Manet drew the war against the Commune. In literature, apart from a mass of literary expressions of remembrance, sense of defeat or personal accounts, generations of thinkers and philosophers reflected on the war experience as a central experience of modernity. The work of Claude Digeon on the 'German crisis of French thought' reflected on the generations of 1830, 1840 or 1850, and sought to assess the impact of the conflict on each new literary wave. This way of thinking has a strong logic: the war took a central part in people's lives and they later reflected on its novelty as an experience and on its deeper consequences. Émile Zola, Alphonse Daudet and Guy de Maupassant all returned to the theme of the war in their later writings and structured it as a central part of their work.[78] Some of Arthur Rimbaud's poetry, which literally changed the poetic idioms of French literature, can only be read with a chronology and glossary of the war in hand.

In less literary terms, the war and representations of the war shook the notion of self and many concepts of identity. The self of the wounded and disfigured soldiers was never the same again; regional identities were also shaken, and many reports of 1871 show that older people were contested by younger citizens who had served. The experience of defeat in 1870 and the Commune also questioned gender identities. It is very interesting to follow the fate of 'lost cause' soldiers, who felt exhilaration in the struggle only to be cut down to size in the post-war period.[79] Rossel, a Protestant soldier with some theoretical knowledge, thus ended up with the Commune, carrying on a struggle which had turned into civil war, while republicans ended up on both sides of the barricade defending very similar values.[80]

The defeated masculinity of professional soldiers was only asserted through a victory against barbarians of the lower orders. The language of class, which had so little footing in French political discourse, gained a kind of prominence through the civil war and under the pen of many rabid reactionaries.[81] Working-men's identities were thus reinforced and demonised simultaneously, while women's identity and gender politics were undermined by the war. The work of Gay Gullickson and Schulkind shows French women of the war, after a positive phase of assertion of their role in ambulances or as auxiliaries, losing ground in the moral order restoration which followed the defeat of the Commune.[82] Many historians of French feminism have argued that the Commune's defeat inflicted a severe setback on the struggle for gender equality. This implies a certain linearity in gender history, but it is demonstrable that the role of women during the war was perceived to be negative and that femininity and decadence were then closely associated in political and artistic representations.[83] Last but not least, sentimentalised representations saturated narratives of the war and set the whole conflict in a wider scheme of things and within the struggle between good and evil. Humanitarianism, which saved perhaps few lives, was the key new ideological construct at work during this conflict.

The Franco-Prussian war and the Commune were truly international events in which foreign powers played an active part, eventually pouring most help where it was most needed, on the French side. Out of this humiliating position as the recipient of alms the French obtained a moral victory of sorts by reversing their responsibility in the conflict to that of victim.[84] In putting so much emphasis on the sentimental representation of civilians suffering at the hands of their German tormentors, the French turned the war into a conflict of values and civilisation. The modernity of 1870 is to be most clearly found in the spectacle of war reported in the popular press and immediately translated in images and pictorial anecdotes, and in the manner in which it became historicised. Unlike the Napoleonic or revolutionary epic narratives, the war did not become shrouded in myth, and the number of stories that were produced after the war did not engender a comforting collective story. The divisions of the Commune and of the war were the most salient aspect of the period and remained the bitterest memory of the *année terrible*. The period 1870–1 also signalled a radical break with a whole political and cultural period of French history. At a European level, the Commune of Paris had a substantial impact which made most governments in Europe sensitive to a new form of revolutionary threat symbolised by the Association Internationale des Travailleurs. Similarly pan-European, the new humanitarian agenda and the greater coverage by news media shaped the perception of this local war as a forerunner of wars to come. Many foreign observers had no doubts about the inevitability of a future European conflagration. The Frankfurt peace treaty did not bode well for future peace.[85]

Humanitarianism, which integrated the civilian within the military, had already started to challenge the existence of a peace order opposed to war.[86] Thus the modernity of this year of turmoil may well lie in its epistemological position as a break with both past and future, in the knowledge that these wars would shape future wars, and in the certainty that history would not be written the same way thereafter.

3

THE CRISIS OF CITIZENSHIP
AND *LA SOCIALE*

La sociale, la Marianne – two enemies![1]

The crisis of 1870 comes at a crucial time in the making of world class politics and the rise of socialism as a mass movement and coherent political idiom. In Europe, the revolution of 4 September 1870 made France a republic for the third time in seventy-eight years and threatened the old European order. The Commune, which challenged the new republic in many thwarted or successful insurrections, had direct links with the First International, particularly in the provinces; it used a class-politics idiom and often referred to general socialist principles. The fact that Lenin's mummified body in Moscow lay under a Paris Commune red flag has been seen as the logical consequence of a clear affiliation between twentieth-century revolutionary Marxism and the nineteenth-century romantic cult of the insurrection. The crisis of 1870 was thus a crisis of European politics, and was perceived as such by foreign observers, states and organisations. In effect, it was a crisis of French citizenship.

To take some of the intellectual tools developed about Britain by Patrick Joyce, Gareth Stedman-Jones and James Vernon,[2] this crisis was largely about the language of class, constitution, politics and people in French politics. The way the French reorganised their political world in the great vacuum of the collapsed empire revived old political forms and gave new credence to minor and marginal political dialects. They had to imagine the constitutional framework in which their state operated in effect (*état de fait*) and they could not refer to a text-based organisation of society (*état de droit*). The way people thought and felt about politics changed. In other words, the debate on language, which will be used here to a certain extent, does not refer to pure concepts and conscious forms of politics but rather to the way people construe their universe. Under the particular duress of a war situation, they also had to think over their individual role in defending or changing the nature of the state as they came to comprehend and express its fundamental essence. All of this was effected in 1870 but did not come as a complete surprise.

The Second Empire had not been a dead moment in French politics. Bonapartism, which claimed to embody popular sovereignty over the existence of parties,[3] may well have belittled parliamentary forms of democracy or the right to debate, but it had made frequent calls to the people and the people's right to approve their leader's policies.[4] Over the twenty-two years of the presidency and then empire, Napoleon's political game had worked on forces of both the left and the right. Even though some, like Jules Ferry,[5] believed that the republic of 1848 could be resuscitated, all political forces, be they the party of 'law and order' or revolutionaries, had evolved and changed dramatically.[6] Regular use of universal male suffrage rooted the practice of elections in the fabric of French life.[7] Over eighteen times during the reign, the French went to the polls and chose either a yes or no answer – usually to a convoluted referendum – or voted for a local council or a candidate to an increasingly powerful chamber of deputies. All the local and national chambers, from the municipal council to parliament, enjoyed increased rights.

Electoral practice in the 1860s had seen the end of openly rigged elections and the decline of the official candidatures.[8] The paradox of a Bonapartism without a Bonapartist party structure[9] was that as it opened up to the parliamentarianism favoured by republicans and Orleanists,[10] it also allowed competing forms of politics to thrive. Opposition parties could build on their own well-established networks while Bonapartists were lacking the apparatus and roots to counter-attack on those grounds. Bonapartism was a cult of success, with a strong meritocratic dimension borne out of the revolution, which asserted technical ability over popularity and, in practice, used a growing civil service as a technocratic backbone of French politics. The civil service was the display cabinet of imperial politics and was thus intensely political, and so attacked. A mismanaged civil service and scandalous abuses of power were easier targets than the emperor.

Under the Bonapartist umbrella many survivors of the previous regimes, Catholic Legitimist monarchists and parliamentarian Orleanists joined in with the empire, switching allegiance to maintain law and order. They widened the middle- and upper-class power base of the regime but remained somewhat aloof. Many rural mayors described themselves as men of order, without much of a preference as to who guaranteed that order. The rural vote and the masses were the great Bonapartist strongholds, while urban workers tended to be more sensitive to republican traditions.[11] There were many exceptions: migrants voted differently from their neighbours and religious issues could colour the vote in either direction. In other words, much had changed since 1848, even though some of the 1848 electoral results had deep cultural roots which continue to influence electoral patterns in France.

What the regime had tried to do was steer to the centre and centre left. With the widening of political rights in the 1860s and the granting of meeting rights, the authorisation of workers' strikes and the granting of debating rights in parliament, the political spectrum had broadened, putting the imperial majority further to the conservative, often openly aristocratic, right than the emperor had wanted. Imperial reforms of 1869–70 were thus an attempt to reconcile the

Bonapartist myth with its ideal constituency: the people. Using ex-republican politicians like Émile Ollivier was an attempt to enrol the moderate republicans under the Bonapartist flag. The parliamentary reforms which made the ministers individually accountable diminished the emperor's power but increased his constitutional distance from politics, in many ways reviving his direct bond with the people as a whole by making him more truly the emperor of the French. It is highly probable that this strategy, or a variant of it, would have resulted in making anti-constitutional opposition marginal in the long run and would have enabled a smooth transition to Napoleon IV. What this meant in 1870–1 was that democracy was already part of political practice and the French were fully citizens, even though many had not been represented by the deputies of their choice or seen their views debated in parliament.

In other words, when the government of General Palikao crumbled in the wake of the Sedan defeat, the revolution of 4 September had to find a legitimacy superior to that of the previous regime. There is a paradox in the fact that the deputies of Paris, who thus recognised the representativeness of their own election under the empire, proclaimed the new republic. The year 1870 resembled neither 1789 nor 1848.

This chapter explores the rhetoric of citizenship and the key institutions through which it was defined. In the first section it considers the National Guard, which became the central tool of militarisation and democratisation of society, while the second section looks at the deployment in space of regional visions of citizenship. The third section adds the social dimension, reified and politicised linguistically as *la sociale*, to this revision of the concept of citizenship, and examines how republicans attempted to use this concept to establish the primacy of their ideals of citizenship.

The National Guard, 1792 and *La Marseillaise*

The moral superiority of 1870 republicans could not be achieved by simply accounting for the votes they had collected before the war. Republicans were a minority, and in some departments their support had been waning under the liberal empire. They could not look back to the 1849–51 period when the republic was led by conservatives who restricted electoral rights, but they could look back to February–June 1848 and to the First Republic. The First Republic especially had an important mythical role in the military imagination of the French people. Major historians of the anti-Bonapartist opposition, Jules Michelet, Adolphe Thiers and Henri Martin, had celebrated Valmy, the volunteers of 1792–3. Their writings on the Revolution had been major publishing successes running to dozens of editions, popular texts and illustrations. In the words of Michelet in the introduction to the history of the Revolution published in 1862,

> nothing was comparable to the *élan* of the federations. The absolute, the infinite sacrifice, in all its greatness, the gift of the self which does not

hold anything back, appeared in this sublime uproar of 1792. Holy war for the peace of the world, for the freedom of the world.[12]

This later translated in the enthusiastic claim, 'We only have to shout, as at the battle of Valmy, the cry of "*Vive la nation!*" This cry so enflames [the people] that it generates heroes.'[13]

The Second Empire had largely benefited from this propagandistic remembrance of French military glory, but it was defiant of revolutionary myths. The *Marseillaise*, for instance, was banned, while 14 July gave rise to annual student demonstrations and well-policed celebratory banquets.[14] The war changed this, and the regime allowed the *Marseillaise* to be sung once again as a portent of military might. The collapse of the French army in August witnessed the devaluation of the imperial legend, only to see it replaced by the cult of the revolutionary mass-war. In Paris the republicans staged the war effort like a re-enactment of 1792. In Lyons they went further, using the guns to sound the alarm, staging enlistment and beating the drums for days on end. This ended up being counterproductive:

> The committee believed it could raise [support] and enthuse by using memories of 93, grand words, *la Patrie en danger*! And the alarm gun … it worked well for a few days but little by little it became small and ridiculous, it became fake enthusiasm … One was forgetting, by trying to imitate this great era, that the people of 93 was a new, virgin and lively people; that it had not been influenced by twenty years of unnerving corruption; that it had new things to defend, rights and land; and that over the previous four years the Revolution had been boiling, which had prepared and forged the men and set the nation to be up to the task.[15]

Despite the cynicism this historical posturing necessarily generated and despite the lack of renewal in the vocabulary or genuine originality in the revolutionary discourse, the people in arms was a deeply rooted theory which proved relevant to the aspirations of the French people in 1870 and 1871. The people in arms theory was twofold. First, the revolutionary wars had shown that large masses motivated by enthusiasm could defeat smaller mercenary armies, a model which did not fit with the conscripted Prussian army; second, the people in arms was the best expression of the duties and rights of citizenship. As such, it played a more important political role than even its military purpose. The people in arms was the nation in arms, and ought to establish the republic in the soul of its defenders. In practice, in 1870, as Michael Howard and Holmes have shown, the problem was not to conscript large forces or even to equip them with roughly adequate weapons, but to find the NCOs or officers able and willing to train and use a popular army.[16]

The deputies of Paris refused to go as far as the Lyons republicans and tried to cajole the military establishment into serving them. Gambetta chose his generals from among the Bonapartist clique, with people such as Bourbaki, older aristocrats like d'Aurelles de Palladine and the precious few republicans like Chanzy who were willing to believe in such an army. One of the political objectives of a mass army was not simply to oppose large forces in a battle of the bulks against the Prussian military machine, but also to bring home the virtues of 1792. The republican message of the Revolution was widely perceived to have been a result of revolutionary wars themselves. Arms could make the citizens. Foreigners serving with the French thus became citizens *de facto*. The best examples were Garibaldi, elected in several departments to the national assembly, or the multitude of international volunteers who had joined the irregular troops.[17]

This link between citizenship and military service in time of war explains largely why the republicans thought it useful to revert to the election of officers in the two reserves of the new army. They knew the National Guard to be a much more important institution in civic terms than in military ones, and they hoped that universal suffrage might allow new elites to be formed through a self-reflexive, educational process.[18] Guardsmen and *mobiles* chose their officers in regular elections which soon acquired a truly democratic dimension.[19] In some instances the elections were stating the obvious, because there was no choice of candidate and nominated officers stood unopposed. Even though these elections did not correspond to the theory of a balanced and fair election, they still recast the bond between hierarchical superiors and inferiors within terms of mutual dependency.[20] In the words of Henri Durangel, writing his report in the first days of the peace, 'One might ask oneself if the direct nomination right granted to the government, considering the circumstances and the speed required, would have given perceptively better results [than the ones obtained through elections].'[21] This viewpoint was hotly debated, and most military-minded individuals thought that elections undermined the principles of authority without which army discipline could not exist.[22]

Indeed, some of the choices were based on local reputation and contacts rather than military expertise:

> I went to find my equipment [wrote the Gambettist Sutter-Laumann, then a member of the National Guard, 7th Cie 32 Battalion of Paris] at my captain's. He was a retired NCO who had served in the Crimea and in Italy, he had been elected unanimously not only because of his military reputation and of his known courage, but also because of his influence in the neighbourhood where he was a publican [*marchand de vin–limonadier*].[23]

The guards nevertheless sometimes took a very grand view of their role,[24] and this went much further than the legislators had anticipated:

Need I tell you that you appoint your leaders of any kind, that these officers, from the humblest corporal, appoint by delegation the commander-in-chief whose powers do not extend beyond a year? Are you not eternally the source of all powers?[25]

In this Lyonese definition, the National Guard's role was further enhanced.

We talk of the National Guard not as an armed body submissive to its chiefs, which would go against all our principles, but as a constituted body providing from now on the basis of a good organisation and offering all the guarantees needed for the free deliberations [of the people] and for rational choices.[26]

The guardsmen were civilians in arms, defending the nation if they were *mobiles* likely to go to the front line, or their homes if they were sedentary *Gardes Nationaux*. Much was made of the new bonds of comradeship and of the ways in which each neighbourhood rallied together, organising communities of defence to contribute equally to the common struggle.[27] This idealised representation touched a raw nerve, in the sense that it appealed to the democrats and to those who had already served in similar bodies which were formerly bonded by class. The National Guardsmen were not segregated by class but by neighbourhood, and the spatial distribution of most cities of France was such that classes did mingle in the guard units. Also fundamental was the notion that rights and duties of citizenship 'were embedded', in Hazareesingh's words, 'in experiences and expectations about local and collective life'.[28] The central experience of the identity of the citizen was one of belonging and excluding.[29] The National Guard played an important part in reinforcing this idea. Acquiring the right to serve in the guard was a great revolutionary move of 1870. That this right entailed voting rights and practices reinforced the municipal message. In the words of the old 1848 republican Martin Nadaud to guardsmen of his prefecture of Creuse:

Yes, Citizens, you are the real support of the governments which respect the rights of the people; in a word, you are the Commune in arms, the basis of social order ... Citizens, National Guardsmen, the Republic will soon equip you. From this day onwards keep these weapons, these tools of your freedom, hold them as sacred as your honour, break them rather than surrendering them; use them to defend your rights and to regain your supremacy over Europe![30]

This was rhetoric pandering to real aspirations for a revitalised local democracy empowering the local guardsmen, and the speech also included some tropes borrowed from Napoleon and the revolutionary period. While Nadaud belonged to the more exalted revolutionary group in a relatively 'politically advanced' rural but also migrant-proletarian department, his speech was not exceptional in its tone and content.[31] The vision of the National Guard as the instrument of the Commune and of the Commune as the basis of social organisation and national resistance was fundamental in the way republicans defined the national defence movement. In this context, the demonstrations in Paris in the autumn, when the men shouted 'Long live the Commune!' should not be read with the Commune of Paris insurrection in mind, although the Commune insurrection built on the ambiguities of the term 'commune'. The diaries of a number of writers, from the extreme right of Louis Veuillot and the surviving Goncourt brother to the writings of moderate left-wing figures, show an almost universal belief that the Commune was the unit enabling both a national war and a deep political renewal.[32]

Some royalists even declared that 'The Commune is today the serious basis of any organisation able to guarantee order and security'.[33] At a less theoretical level the closeness experienced by men serving together may be overstated, but National Guard service was a daily practice of the values of the republic. There is much anecdotal and statistical evidence that the National Guard contributed to shaping the values they were meant to defend.[34] Most of the peculiarities of democracy in 1870, its stubborn insistence on mandate and its insistence on

LA GARDE NATIONALE AUX REMPARTS. — LE FEU DE BIVOUAC.

Figure 3.1   National Guardsmen near the walls of Paris

armed demonstrations, can be traced back to the National Guard and their fear that a national vote might be against revolutionary interests.[35]

In the engraving in Figure 3.1, which was published in 1870, the men in the blue overalls (*blouses*) mixed with the men in frock coats and tall hats. Gathered together around the fire, they shared in the fundamental comradeship of their recently renewed citizenship.[36] This experience could unsettle the moderates or unnerve familial and social links. Family members who did not share in this enthusiasm could only report with some anxiety on their relatives' 'political exaltation, which cannot be expressed'.[37]

The National Guard could indeed serve as a surrogate family and reinforce or create sociability networks at the level of the neighbourhood, as noted by Gould.[38] The units organised their *conseils de familles*, which allocated help to needy families.[39] The key word used about *conseils de familles*, and one which would later form a central part of the social discourse of the Third Republic, was 'solidarity'.[40] Unlike an anonymous charity,

> solidarity between the members of a social family ... between the members of a common city or rather a great nation must establish a sort of association to distribute as fairly as possible the burden created by a great common misfortune for which no one should be made responsible. An ideal of justice and reparation.[41]

In the light of an impending defeat, the *conseils de familles*, a most patriarchal institution, had, the journalists insisted, to play a part in extending the reach and purpose of mutual societies.[42] The *conseils de familles* were elected and co-opted, mixing hierarchy and elected representatives. They were composed of the elected officers of the Compagnie: two sergeants, two corporals and two elected guardsmen. There were thus a dozen *conseils de familles* for one arrondissement of Paris, depending on the size of the population. In some areas they were renamed *conseils de familles de quartier*, to better express their civilian status and their roots in the neighbourhood. In the terms used by the mayors of Paris, their aim was to 'prevent this numerous class of citizens [workers] from falling into the dangers of idleness'.[43] In fact, this institution went much further than adding a few menial tasks to the workload of the sedentary guardsmen: it singularly empowered them and enabled them to become the masters of their own destiny, often for the first time.

Conseils de familles had charge of the budget of the squad and collected the monthly subscription to the mutual help fund of the National Guard. In many instances they had democratic credentials deemed to be superior to the hierarchy, and could make or break an officer. For instance, the captain of the 12th Battalion of the 1st Legion of Paris, Blondin, had to resign after the *conseil de familles* organised a petition of 128 guardsmen against his authoritarian manners.[44] Beyond the bread-and-butter aspects, the *conseil de familles* also checked the squad's morale and arbitrated on conflicts that might have arisen.

To conservative observers, its activities freed the people for revolutionary activities.[45] Furthermore, it was in charge of defining who was or was not a pauper in
the neighbourhood,[46] thus replacing the imperial institution of the Assistance
Publique.[47] The Assistance Publique in Paris had been abolished by Jules Ferry,
and its responsibilities had been split three ways between a *conseil des hospices* in
charge of the hospitals, the arrondissement mayor, managing the budget of
home-relief and soup kitchens,[48] and the National Guard. The guardsmen alone
had the means of distributing this help on the ground.[49] In other cities where the
National Guard were slower to organise themselves, as in Montpellier[50] or
Lyons, improvised revolutionary committees such as the *Comité révolutionnaire de la
Guillotière*, dominated by Dr Crestin, took over the duty of feeding the poor. The
paupers came to them as they had gone to the *bureaux de bienfaisance* before, cap in
hand and negotiating their political passivity in exchange for material support.[51]

Uneasy with this power, revolutionary committees often found it more useful
to pass on the responsibility and the precise management of the welfare
measures to the guardsmen, who could use them more effectively to support the
war effort. The committee would pass on this duty to the local battalion of the
National Guard, who only lost this responsibility on 10 July 1871.[52] Looking at
the scanty records surviving from their extensive activities (few complete sets of
minutes exist) one finds that the *conseil de familles* of the VIII arrondissement of
Paris, for instance, established a clear criterion for the distribution of help. They
rejected idle young men and single mothers 'ill behaving', and established short
but lively profiles of the people coming to them. The help the *conseil* gave was
often in small sums of cash, and gave most consideration to matters of health
and behaviour. The profile established specified the age and marital status, the
rent and the state of the furniture, and the physical profile of the claimants, and
attempted to define whether they were helped by other charities or other means.
A National Guard could only establish this profile after an intrusive visit.[53] In
some instances, the guardsmen resented this inspection chore and refused to
collect additional information.[54] When peace returned, the municipal authorities
attempted to recreate their own welfare institutions in an attempt to summon up
support in preparation for the dissolution of most National Guard units.[55] In
Paris, the situation was somewhat mixed, as the local authorities of the
arrondissements kept their control over food supplies in association with the
guardsmen.[56]

A similar process of devolution of social responsibility, and therefore power,
took place in most of France. Early on in the republican war, the provincial help
structures shifted from the department and the canton to the locality.[57]
Throughout France, municipalities attempted to map poverty, the people in need
and the sites of political emergencies, using National Guard reports and visits.[58]
The government was attuned to these needs, and this devolution of administrative
decision-making was both a pragmatic answer to a crisis and an ideological choice.

Within Paris, the central government, having relinquished most of its power
and authority, was criticised for not managing the unmanageable. To react to

well-founded complaints, it attempted to keep the moral high ground by marking its liberality through timely gifts such as *étrennes* for New Year.[59] The recently explored central role of gift-giving in France was shaping the public sphere.[60] The government attempted to make good its democratic deficit through the usual demonstration of benevolence. The balance of power between governed and governors had never tipped so precariously in the direction of the governed. The guardsmen petitioned and wished to preserve their double role as protectors of the nation and the republic. In the words of Jules Ferry:

> We were a government resting on moral support, we had nothing else at our disposal: what did we have to maintain order against the anarchist party, who were but a small part of the people? The National Guard and nothing but the National Guard. So, what the National Guard allowed, the people could do, and our fate was always in the hands of the National Guard.[61]

This fine meshing of politics and armies was most accentuated in urban centres of some importance. In the local elections that took place in Lyons and Paris in September and November respectively, the National Guard acted like a republican electoral committee.[62] While republicans had been well organised and often successful in winning over the large cities of France, their record in the countryside had been disastrous. There they were seen as *partageux*, communists ready to steal and redistribute the land. This urban implantation was perceived as a reflection of the political maturity of the French. 'Rural' or 'rustic' were words of opprobrium; the French republicans made direct links between *civis*, *citoyen*, and *civilisation*. This attitude was very deeply ingrained, and probably backfired in the sense that even the most passionate appeals to the common sense of the *paysans* were at best patronising, if not downright insulting.[63] J. Midor of the National Guard of the 3rd Cie, 7th Battalion of Lyons, thus addressed his 'advice to the rural people at the eve of the elections of 8 February'. This electoral pamphlet contained a large number of promises on the reduction of the army to one-sixth of what it had been under the empire. He also promised firemen and free medical help in the villages, denounced the cost of a priest's salary, and concluded: 'The revolution of 1789 delivering you from villeinage and feudal duties has given you all the rights of citizenship.'[64] Talked down to and ignored in the mainstream political discourse, many *paysans*, like 35 per cent of those of Thizy, did not bother voting.[65] Neglected by the republican institutions, often loosely bound to local guardsmen's units, isolated rural voters were neither involved nor invited to partake in the comradeship of citizens in arms. In fairness, the split between rural and urban was moderated in many regions where the urban world had made inroads into the rural fabric.[66]

The democratic practices of the urban militias were to be found, much attenuated, in the provinces. Small villages in the low-density Limousin landscape had their guardsmen, but they had few weapons and their hunting rifles did not give them a military aspect. When these deeply rural men went to the more densely populated urban areas, they were looked at with some puzzlement. The French citizens of the west of France, Vendée or Brittany, apparently closer to the Chouans of the royalist insurrection of the 1790s, did not mingle much with the Parisian population.[67] The various regions represented in Paris, for instance, kept their regional identity or even reinforced it. This exotic perception of what Frenchmen really were reflected the Parisian centrality in the tools of French cultural self-representation.[68] In fact, the contact of the capital city had some impact on the soldiers themselves, and they eventually proved unreliable when it came to civil war.

The republican black legend of the countryside, where citizenship remained crushed under the feudal structure, should not be exaggerated. The opportunity to punish the arrogance of Paris was shunned by most. When Thiers tried to recruit his army to fight the Commune, reports from many areas showed complete hostility to civil war. Rural citizens of the provinces had not lived the war with the same intensity, and their values and interests were often more at risk than those of urban dwellers, but they nevertheless recognised in the National Guard institutions a familiar and unthreatening picture. Provincialism could be expressed through these local structures, and provincialism was a political force to be reckoned with in 1870.

Federalism and war, *ligues*, the *Ligue du Midi* and separatism

The paradox of the republican movement was, of course, that most if not all members of the new government had come from the provinces to Paris. Yet when they branded themselves as deputies of Paris they signalled their espousal of the values of centralised republicanism. As Hazareesingh and Nord have shown, the debates on centralisation had been crucial in late Second Empire politics.[69] The committee reporting on decentralisation never had time to present its views in 1870, but the views of many members of the 4 September government were in line with the *programme de Nancy* of 1865, supporting greater local democracy and decentralisation.[70] France since the Revolution had become a centralised country, where the prefects had overwhelming powers in their departments, nominating the mayors of most cities and villages and even choosing the complete administration of Paris, Lyons and, to a lesser extent, Marseilles. Members of most political persuasions, for different reasons, demanded administrative decentralisation. The royalists were the most active in this respect, founding various journals such as *La Décentralisation* or *Le Réveil de la Province*, which exploited anti-Parisian feeling to revive monarchists' beliefs in the values of the land and the meanings of organic communities structured around their legitimate elites and religion.[71]

The republicans were divided, as they had been during the Revolution, between Girondin and Jacobin. Gambetta was more Jacobin than most of his colleagues, who, being moderate republicans, preferred the Girondin's democratic ideals to Robespierre's centralism and excess. In 1871 the moderates of the *Ligue d'union républicaine des droits de Paris* stated in their project of municipal law the differences between their decentralist views and those of Thiers and conservative Jacobins.

> The head of the executive remembers the conflicts he has witnessed during his long political career between prefects and mayors of major cities. For a centralist and authoritarian mind conflicts are disorderly. Instead of diminishing the causes of conflicts by limiting the attributions of the protagonists, one is getting rid of one side of the conflict instead of resolving it; and as the prefects are a sacred consular institution for the government, the mayors are suppressed by making them puppets of the central power and thus the subordinates of the prefect. For us the solution must be radically different. The institution of the prefects, created by the constitution of An VIII, is condemned; it must either disappear or be substantially modified. That the central power should have, in territorial divisions, some delegates in charge of making sure that the general laws are not violated and the national interest undermined could not be better; but that these delegates under the excuse of *administrative tutelage* should be the directors of departmental or communal affairs, that is unacceptable.[72]

In fact, this conflict over the way the state should be managed ran deep even within the Paris Commune, where the partisans of a dictatorial sovereignty of the people opposed the federalist communalists who wished to defend the contractual nature of communal democracies federating into a nation state.[73] These seventy-year-old debates were revived in 1870 and found a particular echo in places like Lyons and the south of France, which had had to suffer from centralisation since 1789.

In Lyons and the Lyonese region and in Beaujolais, home-grown local heroes like Madame Roland from Villefranche-sur-Saône had been moderate Girondins. Lyons republicans constantly recalled the violence of the Jacobins. Some of this defiance of centralisation was articulated less in the distant past than in the more recent experience of imperial policies. The notion of federalism, especially around the local democratic forum of the Commune, was an integral part of the French socialist tradition. Socialist writings of 1870 at the communal level revived the Utopian socialism of Cabet and Fourier. A federation of the communes of France resembling a web of *phalanstères* and communities was the fundamental Utopia of most provincial socialists in September 1870.

A Lyonese theoretician saw in the revival of the communal ideology a combination of old-fashioned political reformism and new collectivist socialism developed through the work of the AIT. In his opinion, the particular history of

Lyons, at loggerheads with most Parisian-based regimes since 1793 or even earlier, meant that

> this idea of the suppression of the state in the social relations was too much in the Lyonese instinct not to be welcomed. But many were opposed to the slow economic renovation thus undertaken [through mutualism] and were obstinate, perhaps rightly, in their belief that a revolution might change brusquely the order of things.[74]

This notion that small is beautiful was linked to the idea that the commune was the legitimate site for democratic debates, and that only at that scale could the imperative mandate so many desired be monitored.[75] This called for representatives of the locality instead of representatives of the nation, and this change in the mode of representation postulated a democracy of constituencies working together rather than a central representative body speaking for the common good. In other words, locally accountable representatives went against the grain of French centralist traditions.

The organisations created in 1870, like the *Ligue du Midi*, were thus attempts not at breaking openly from the nation state but at changing its remit.[76] It is very interesting that, of all political terms, the word *ligue* should be the one chosen by republicans. *Ligue* referred obviously to the anti-Corn Law leagues of Britain[77] but the term *ligue* in French had more rebellious connotations. It referred almost directly to the Catholic organisation of the wars of religion, which had opposed the monarchy while attempting to defend the country. In this sense, the term was appropriate to the 1870 situation. *Ligues* tend to be confederate rather than centralist. Major *ligues* in 1870 were the *Ligue de l'Est*,[78] the *Ligue du Midi* and the *Ligue du Sud-Ouest*. Of the three there is little doubt that the *Ligue du Midi*, led by Esquiros, the deputy of Marseilles later made prefect by Gambetta, was by far the most important.[79] It was also the one that managed to establish itself before the arrival of Gambetta in Tours. In the words of Bauquier, who was then *sous-préfet* in Pontarlier, reporting to Besançon, home of the *Ligue de l'Est* led by Ordinaire, deputy-prefect:

> The delegation in Tours had been, in principle, favourable to such important *ligues*, which presented the benefits of taking over some of the responsibility of the defence and of having a civilian administrator leading them, which could impress the Bonapartist generals. A secret message advised the prefects to counterbalance the powers of generals by using energetic men who could 'make a civilian spirit penetrate the military'. But when Gambetta arrived from Paris and took over the ministry of war he only saw in these *ligues* attempts at federalism that he needed to thwart at all costs.[80]

The *Ligue du Midi* has been looked at and described by Greenberg in the light of the later Paris Commune, and it is the most common paradox that the later movement is so often seen by historians as inspiring movements preceding it. This is truly an instance of a centralisation of thoughts and historical imagination. Far from being a homogenous institution, the *ligue* was a debating arena which allowed many nuances to emerge. The Marquis de Volfans thus managed to address the *ligue* to contest its legitimacy:

> you want to create a government which could paralyse the one of Tours, you want to raise one against the other, in other words, you will disorganise ... [protests] The government of Tours is the only one that we must recognise [no! no! shouting].[81]

Even though this type of internal contest rapidly became more rare, it was never a closed shop. More importantly, it always positioned itself towards the government of Tours, the triumvirate led by Gambetta, rather than towards the government of Paris, which was largely irrelevant to the country at large. What the *ligue* stood for was a dual struggle against the despotism of the invasion and of the monarchical state. In its many declarations the social content was neglected for rhetoric, calls to arms and vociferous declarations of universal mobilisation. In its federative organisation of departments, however, the *ligue* demonstrated its reluctance to submit to any central authority. In the words of Esquiros, the *commissaire extraordinaire des Bouches du Rhône*: 'There is ground to form a kind of provisional confederation which will allow us to act together. The Midi will perhaps save the north ... It is a regional and Provençal defence that we wish to establish.'[82]

This group of active decisive revolutionaries who claimed that 'the true military forces now are the popular forces' wished to unite the energies of the departments of Bouche du Rhône, Rhône, Isère, Vaucluse, Drôme, Hérault, Gard, Var, Ardèche, Hautes Alpes and Alpes Maritime, a federation which would have created a solid block of departments on both sides of the mighty river. The *Ligue du Midi* was completed, and to a certain extent rivalled by Lyonese ambitions to create a *ligue de Lyon* to unite the war effort of fourteen neighbouring departments.[83] The *ligues* appeared to be carving France into zones of influence. It is important to notice, however, that even in their declaration of 25 October the organisers and Esquiros stated in bold that they were speaking in the name of the 'Republic, **one and indivisible**'.[84] In Toulouse, the committee of public salvation at the heart of a less important *ligue du Sud-Ouest* announced a six-point programme in preparation for the election of the constituent assembly:

1 The candidates undertake to support and defend the republic, one and indivisible, and to risk their lives for this;
2 *to outlaw all pretenders to the throne;*

3   to lead, *as delegates*, the armies of national defence following the glorious example of our forefathers of 92;
4   to deal with and solve social questions in the best interests of the working class;
5   to separate Church and state;
6   to be accountable for their mandate to the electors.[85]

The issues raised variously tackled local social conflicts, deep-seated religious conflicts and the nature of the regime, but they rarely challenged the existence of the nation state. Separatism was not really a political option of real weight.[86] In all these ebullient manifestations of regionalism, the constitution of France emerged as a central theme. The constitution wanted by provincial republicans had the trappings of a radical lay state and a mechanism to keep representatives close to their electors.

The absence of a national politics and constitution inspired a lively revival of political culture at the departmental level. Lyons perhaps went furthest in its assertion of local and national character. When the councillors of Lyons invited Gambetta to establish his capital in the second city of France, they were seriously considering a change of capital city or even calling for a centralisation of the war effort on Lyons. There was a real and meaningful contest of the nation state, which we will consider in more depth in Chapters 4 and 8.

Provincial politics fragmented the debate on citizenship, and the variations between local newspapers of a similar persuasion show that being republican or reactionary in Lyons or Tulle was not the same. Even though all newspapers borrowed from each other and practised the cut-and-paste technique to fill their columns, which were starved of war news by self- and state censorship, the editorial line changed and reflected localised political cultures.

Since the political void of the empire was so great, moderate republicans had to fill it. This was a right recognised even by some decidedly reactionary newspapers, advocating a return to a God-chosen king. Some royalist newspapers briefly supported Gambetta in October and November 1870.[87] 'Mr Gambetta has signed a message that lacks neither energy nor strength. Mr Gambetta seems to have arrived [in Tours] to seize the power which dwindled in the hands of the old men of Tours, Crémieux and Bizoin.'[88]

As a figurehead, Gambetta provided the conservatives with the image they craved: a strong man 'able to resist the Parisian riot if it wanted to overturn him. The province, which wants, above all, the salvation of France, would energetically support him.'[89]

The concept of citizenship exposed by the right-wing press and other right-wing sources was fundamentally reduced to its lowest common denominator of patriotism, ready to sacrifice political preferences temporarily to promote the ideal of the nation. In practical terms there were not many demonstrations of this ideal, if we exclude the marginal and very limited additions of *zouaves pontificaux* and ultra-Catholic soldiers to the common cause.[90]

Republican titles promoted citizenship through an active propaganda campaign, and through the guardsmen the republicans created their own constituency of democratic practice. The chief absentee, although it had controlled most press titles until then, was the Bonapartist party. Bonapartists had been stunned by defeat and cloaked their political allegiances under their patriotism. Patriotism thus became the one common language of all political sides, even though all knew that it was a transient form of unity. Even though decentralisation remained a central constitutional dream, decentralist efforts were thus drowned in the mass of patriotic feeling which did not allow for a more vigorous debate. Meanwhile, only one form of political contest threatened to subvert this great show of unity: *la sociale*.

La sociale and the poor

La sociale is a problematic term which even native French speakers find difficult to define as a noun. 'Social' is more often an adjective, but it is as a noun that it acquired real political significance in 1870–1, becoming a political rallying cry. What it meant is complicated. It sums up all aspirations to a social state, a democratic and redistributing form of government integrating what was called 'the social question'. Under the term 'social question' all sorts of political agendas could be filed, from Napoleon III's 'extinction of pauperism' to hygienic slum clearance or trade unionism.[91] *La sociale* also encompassed a complete renegotiation of all social relationships and all hierarchies and especially the establishment of a society of equals before the judiciary and economic laws.

The many socialist groups had kept the *sociale* ideal alive in most cities of France. Since the late 1860s trade corporations had been allowed to exist in order to fight for specific causes, and not as full organisations. Under these rules strikes had multiplied in 1870 in the great industrial centres like Le Creusot or Lyons.[92] The First Internationale (AIT) was particularly active in attempting to federate the various trade unions and create permanent structures with a fully developed political agenda.[93] This attempt had been severely hindered in the spring of 1870 when a crackdown on the political activities of secret societies had led to a series of arrests and trials.[94] On 4 September the amnesty of all political crimes enabled members of the AIT to take more active political roles. The importance of this socialist international has been much exaggerated for the Paris Commune.[95] Even the more serious analysts like Oscar Testut, used by the police as source of vital information, blamed the uprising of 18 March 1871 on the AIT.[96]

This said, the AIT did play a role, but perhaps more so in the provinces where, in Lyons, Marseilles and many provincial centres, the members of the AIT claimed political rights in the new administrations on the grounds that they represented organised labour. The names most active on the Lyons scene, for instance, were later discredited because they attempted to revolt against the republicans of the city or later joined the ranks of the proletarian Bonapartists.

The members of the AIT who attempted to impose their views on Lyons on 28 September lost the battle that day through simple unarmed negotiating and an obvious realisation that they had not mobilised public support behind their coup. These people later reunited in a 'Central Committee for the Salvation of France'[97] which self-dissolved on 9 October and whose final declaration illustrated the contradictions of any radical politics at the time of the invasion:

> We have done everything in our power to have the great revolutionary measures adopted, which alone, according to us, can save our poor motherland from ruin and shame. We wanted to use the last month to arouse the masses everywhere and to organise the revolutionary unleashing of all the live forces of France against Prussia. We wanted the united citizens, with no exceptions except for the traitors to the national cause, to create more solid and democratic institutions than the hierarchy and administrative centralisation, the old judicial system and the old military organisation which are the seeds of despotism and the guarantors of the current social inequalities.
>
> We wanted there to be in France only one great army of brothers, holding hands to achieve victory. Our proposals were rejected.
>
> But we want to avoid troubles and divisions at all costs and we do not want to be considered ambitious or agitators. Therefore, we leave the people to judge the situation and we proclaim the dissolution of the Central Committee for the Salvation of France.[98]

While the aims were wide-ranging and somewhat similar to those proclaimed on 31 October 1870 by the partisans of Blanqui and Flourens, the means remained ill-defined and revolved around the notion that revolutionary energies lay dormant and waited only to be unleashed.[99] This idealism, which we find also in the belief in the strength of the nation in arms, reflected the romantic vulgate of the French Revolution historiography. Fundamentally, the issues at stake were wide-ranging and diverse – the abolition of the judicial, military and administrative states – but the means to achieve this universal dissolution of the French body politic remained unclear. One of the key debates among *la sociale* supporters was the primacy of political issues over social ones: political reforms were needed to increase workers' rights. This meant that strikes were subordinated to revolutionary aims.

This undermined the efforts of associations such as the AIT, which attempted to use social issues for political purposes. The primacy of what the Marxists named 'the superstructure' meant that these movements lacked relevance to many workers unwilling to engage in costly disputes over theoretical issues. More representative, perhaps, were the many co-operatives which, while politically under-theorised, were most active in practical terms and expected to obtain rights in order to change the political system. Co-operatives had been accepted by the empire and, if not flourishing, were at least a force to be reckoned with.

Even though mutual societies and co-operation did not provide a remedy for poverty or even a workable way of dealing with social issues on a grand scale, they worked locally.[100] Experiments in co-operation were limited throughout France, and even during the Commune of Paris new co-operatives were relatively few.[101] State agencies remained central to any imagined or real answer to the crisis of *la sociale*.

In answer to the issues raised by the debate on poverty, guardsmen led the only real political experimentation. The *conseils de familles* played a far more important role in the tangible associationist culture than most clubs and hot-air debating rooms ever did.[102] This is a role historians have on the whole completely neglected.[103] They are not alone: the emphasis on the repression of the Commune was also similarly permeated with notions of secret organisations when most organisations were functioning in the open.[104] In the departments, committees were created which reflected a different social representation and often pushed a different political agenda, yet they all had in common a shared responsibility in alleviating the hardship of a substantial population.[105] In Montereau-Faut-Yonne, a humble town in the Yonne department, a *société de secours aux blessés et aux familles nécessiteuses des soldats sous les drapeaux* was created as early as 22 July and attempted to alleviate the sufferings of 102 families.[106] The number of poor people in France was in itself a debate, in the sense that poverty is a relative concept often established either by using a set of moral values or by applying sophisticated and abstract statistical tools. While for Paris or other major urban centres statistics did exist that could enable a general perception of poverty, the same was not true in the provinces. Poverty as defined by the Assistance Publique in Paris or Lyons differentiated between *indigents* and *nécessiteux*.[107] The criterion to qualify for relief was that residence had to be established for a sufficient period of time to allow an inquiry into the morality of the recipient.

The war changed this. Mass conscription suddenly impoverished families reliant on the income of a younger male member of the family. Like the family of Martin Nadaud, many depended on a young worker in town for the cash supply of small subsistence farming. The charitable organisations created in the departments attempted to cover for the families of war prisoners and the sick.[108] The war also slowed down most exchanges of goods and capital, and paralysed the national market. All this led to some anxiety over the food supply of the country in 1871, many believing that bread might be running out soon.[109]

In Paris the state had serious problems relating to feeding and looked back in history, reviving some rules dating from before 1511.[110] The Germans had halted the food supply, and the logic of rationing went against bourgeois values whilst requisitions were anathema to the rich. The partisans of *la sociale* called for both requisitions and rationing. The first Parisian 'red poster' in September 1870 called for immediate rationing. In fact, the political equilibrium of Paris meant that the government came to impose rationing measures only slowly.[111]

As the picture in Figure 3.2, engraved in 1870, indicates, the *cantine municipale* under the control of armed guardsmen became the site of a renewal of the spectacle of poverty. The whole picture indicates that the power relations have changed: the guardsmen and the clerk stand in the light watching in a detached way as the paupers walk by with the food the new structures have provided.[112] In Lyons, rationing never had to take place, but symbolic requisitions of ecclesiastical wealth answered the calls of the ultra-left. Revolutionary jurisprudence and precedents legalised requisitions.[113] In terms of alleviating poverty, most provincial committees relied on money handouts which, while often small, demonstrated the state's willingness to intervene and reciprocate in times of war. In Paris, each arrondissement behaved like a small city with its own political agenda. In the words of Arago, then mayor of Paris, 'It was in the arrondissement town halls that the city's life existed, and when it appeared elsewhere it went to these centres of republican action to be employed.'[114] The XX arrondissement, led by the Jacobin Delescluze, multiplied the number of soup kitchens and recorded ten times more paupers than before the war.[115]

In many respects the municipality came to know its constituents and acquired this level of detailed knowledge through democratic practices. Municipalities had equipped and largely financed the soldiers and volunteers; they maintained some links with their soldiers even when they had left the vicinity, and they learnt to know their families much better.[116] Giving food or money served a purpose. These handouts were not large in general, and soup kitchens could

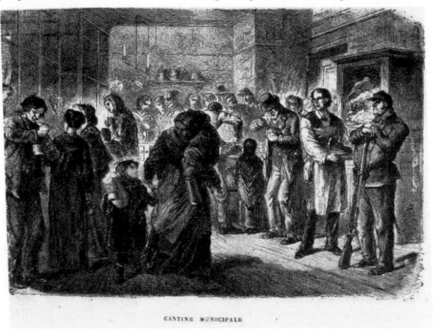

CANTINE MUNICIPALE

Figure 3.2 Municipal soup kitchen during the siege of Paris

only partly compensate for the loss of wages due to war-induced unemployment. The state used the National Guard to distribute wages of 1.50 francs to each guard and 70 centimes to their spouses. This handout was a small income for a Parisian, when the average salary fluctuated between 3 and 5 francs a day between 1870 and 1875. In Lyons, the municipality created national workshops to modernise the defence system of the city and help revive the 'right to work' agenda of 1848. The creation of ammunition factories, of shoes or military clothing workshops, also went in the same direction of state intervention.

Towards a national social compact?

Some economic historians have denounced this state interventionism as the beginnings of the over-active French state meddling with liberal practices and biasing the economy in an unhealthy way. This seems quite exaggerated and politically motivated. In fact, most of the interventions taking place in 1870 happened at the local and departmental level, and the state often tried to control *a posteriori* a number of initiatives which were not its own. *La sociale*, this mixture of old and new beliefs in a fairer state that would protect labourers and provide them with the means of decent living, was a central political aspiration during the whole war. Yet, when insurrections in its name were attempted on 28 September in Lyons; when Bakunin made some general declaration about the abolition of capital in Paris on 31 October; or when a motley crew of Blanquists attempted to highjack the national defence government to promote their more radical programme, it did not prove enough to win the day.

It is not only because the insurrections were particularly inept, but mostly because they did not strike a chord among guardsmen. On 18 March 1871, on the other hand, a riot became a revolution by accident and the political depth of *la sociale* was shown. What was different in September or October 1870 was that the republic seemed established along the lines of a new social compact. The war effort was to be rewarded after the victory, and representatives of the people were in power. In Lyons, for instance, members of the AIT were on both sides of the failed insurrection, and while the Croix-Rousse guardsmen had been taken to petition the town hall for a pay rise, they flatly refused to support an insurrection which seemed pointless.

The state had taken measures such as a moratorium on rents or debts, which postponed the full impact of the war on trade or private income; municipal authorities such as Lyons had abolished the hated imposition on goods entering the city, *l'octroi*. In Lyons, the municipal pawnshop had released all goods worth less than 20 francs – in effect, a massive handout to the poorer members of the community. Some, like Lyons or Marseilles, funded their generous work policies and the war effort by raising new taxes based on income or the value of capital or through long-term borrowings.[117] Even in religious matters, as we will see later, the most radical administrations of France had taken the symbolic measures desired of them by the left: secularising schools, expropriating congregations and targeting Jesuits. All these measures justified a dimension of trust and reciprocity. In other words, while the government of the 4 September revolution was moderate and rather timid, the lower echelons of the municipal administrations developed a programme later imitated by the Commune of Paris.

La sociale was at work largely because the state was so frail that it could not prevent it happening. The crisis of citizenship took place after the defeat, when the new peace order implied a return, a restoration to previous liberal economics. To re-establish normal economic exchanges meant the necessarily brutal withdrawing of the moratorium on debts, the abolition of new taxation and the restoration of old taxes, and the abolition of all democratic forms of relief through the National Guard. The conservatives' brutal policies reflected their belief in shock therapy and their hatred of what *la sociale* promised in terms of redistribution of wealth and private property. It is not insignificant that the new leader of the national assembly, Adolphe Thiers, was also the author of an anti-Proudhonist book defining property as the foundation of civilisation.[118] The problems and innovations of the 4 September revolution were the same: they were localised, municipal and thus easy to marginalise. It was only at the end of the war, when the social compact dissolved because it was no longer necessary to maintain a war effort, that guardsmen and radicals realised that it had been based on practice rather than texts, on gratuities rather than legislation, on handouts rather than rights.

4

MUNICIPAL FREEDOM AND WAR

To ignore the use made of communal resources would be to betray your own interests and your fellow citizens.[1]

The revival of provincial life was a beautiful spectacle for the partisans of decentralisation; everywhere there were public meetings organised, everywhere there were new centres of action, new committees organising defence.[2]

A war, any war perhaps, allows for a number of reforms under duress. Even the strongest state redirects its energy towards war ends and has to give back or renegotiate some of its grip on everyday life. In this sense, the war of 1870 went further because it was a war and a revolution and because the French state seemed on the verge of disappearing. The French state and civil service were deeply political and attached to the Second Empire. The Second Empire had singularly reinforced a number of infrastructures: the army, the civil service, especially the prefects, the police and education had been kept under special scrutiny, and these were therefore staffed largely by people convinced of their own importance and conscious of what they owed to the empire.[3] Many had played a direct political role.[4] Policemen and prefects had organised the monitoring of the opposition, organised elections and often taken on themselves the petty persecutions which embittered local politics.[5] Among the forces supporting the empire, the civil service was among the most conservative. It proved unable to prevent its collapse, but it remained uncertain about the longevity and viability of the regime that was to follow. Most prefects were thus revoked or resigned on 4 September,[6] some of them after stating one last time their fidelity to the departing regime.

At the level below, the police were always targeted, far more, it seems, than their military counterpart the *gendarmerie*, and high-ranking policemen exiled themselves. In many cities the republicans called for the abolition of state police and for their replacement by their own *sergents de ville*.[7] In Paris, where secret policing had gone to the worst excesses and where political spying had taken the most devious forms, a committee was set up to consider the abolition of the

59

préfecture de police which, together with a departmental prefecture, prevented Parisians from enjoying full municipal rights.[8] De Kératry's views were that

> It is not now a case of enacting theoretical decentralisation but [to promote] effective freedom in giving back to the magistrates the control of the metropolitan police [*police judiciaire*], to the ministry of the interior the national security [*sûreté générale*], to the mayor of Paris the municipal police and the management of the interests relating to it.[9]

The police prefects who rapidly followed each other, after de Kératry, Adam and Cresson, took an increasingly conservative view of reforms, and for the latter defended the existence of a 'beautiful administration'. The cult of the state, which has been noted by many historians, and the French liking of well-oiled administrative machines prevented the 4 September government from wiping the slate clean and rebuilding the system. The belief in expertise, which had been at the heart of the Bonapartist cult of success, remained in different forms under the republic.

To administer the country Gambetta decided to reform the superstructure and purge the posts of command by appointing new prefects with solid republican convictions and, if at all possible, some prior experience. Martin Nadaud, previously deputy of Creuse in 1848, was thus sent back to his native department as prefect. Gambetta chose friends and experienced republicans to become his war prefects. The nomination of prefects had always been a state decision based on political allegiance, but opponents perceived this sudden reform of the prefectoral corps as revengeful. Most importantly, many provinces were unwilling to receive the new prefects and wished to renegotiate the balance between local and national powers. The citizens of the new republic were not necessarily willing subjects of its administration. The exchange between governing and governed was fraught with doubts on each other's intentions and legitimacy.

Communes before *the* Commune

The administration of France had something colonial in its disdain for the people it governed. As an Haute-Vienne policemen put it, administrators had to negotiate with 'a feeble people, lazy and unintelligent, poorly fed, uncaring and excessively fearful ... above this mass an unenlightened bourgeoisie living off the meagre income of their landed property. In the midst of this, a powerful clergy.'[10]

The locals were deemed to be brutish, violent and uncivilised when they were rural, violent and riotous when they were urban. There is a large historiography of the fear of the dangerous classes across Europe, and while 1870 was not the apex of this unreconstructed bourgeois insecurity, it was the period during which a revival of 1830s anxieties was strongest.[11] These fears and contempt were manifested in the everyday administration of localities. Many small rural villages had absentee mayors nominated by the prefect who, while aware that his chosen administrators might not live in the village, preferred these bourgeois landlords or notaries to the less literate and familiar plebeian farmer or grocer. In terms of local democracy, French mayors enjoyed a status which made them closer to functionaries than to an elected representative of the people. Even so, some of the notables were not as docile as they should have been. The municipalities in the countryside were in a state of political limbo, constantly reminded of the prefectoral power that authorised or forbade whatever minor projects the village might have, constantly reminded that handouts depended on one man's good-will. In many respects prefects represented the emperor, embodied suzerainty and impersonated him in receiving, with varying degrees of luxury, the local conservative elite and in visiting the administered masses.[12]

The powers of this one representative of the government were more symbolic than real. It is clear that the prefects seemed more powerful than they really were and that they depended for their good administration and information on the goodwill of traditional notables, aristocrats or well-established families of notaries and landlords. In the departments, much of the local counter-power was to be found in the ranks of the departmental *conseillers généraux*. On the scale of the department, the *conseil général*, elected for nine years by universal suffrage, represented the main elements of a limited French decentralisation. In charge of limited budgets and responsibilities, these local assemblies of councillors, while devoid of debating rights, could nevertheless present a serious challenge to the prefectoral authority, if only by their force of inertia. In 1870 the departments saw a limited revival of the political roles of the *conseils généraux*. In some departments the prefects of the republic attempted to gain the support of the *conseil*. Georges Perrin, a journalist named as prefect of Haute-Vienne, and his successor Justin Masicault[13] thus extracted a loan of 1 million francs from the *conseil général*.[14]

As long as the recent prefects had enough energy or governmental support they were able to keep at bay the local notables, who mainly represented the rural areas rather than the urban centres.[15] Even though they were dissolved by an edict of Tours,[16] the *conseillers généraux* remained a power-in-waiting which played a part in the elections of February 1871. When the Thiers government of 8 February 1871 felt the need to fall back on solid conservative forces, the *conseils généraux* were there; the complete renewal of 1871 often demonstrated the long-term hold that notables still had on rural France. The structures of citizenship in the countryside were hampered by what French historians tend to call, nega-tively, the weight of old social hierarchies. In the more fluid social environments, where people could reinvent themselves more easily, the political game played by administrations was necessarily more complex and less stable.

The larger the city, the greater the resources given to the prefect and the more contested his attributions. As long as the politics seemed to be led from above, prefects could enjoy a free rein. When the police all but disappeared and when the state called to the citizens to reinvent their army and the values of citizenship, the prefects' attribution dwindled and the social contract seemed to be up for grabs. The war thus gave more power to the municipalities for the simple reason that the town halls were the first port of call for the conscripts, who were registered by their locality and, in the first instance, equipped at its expense. Guardsmen were even more intrinsically attached to their locality, which not only organised welfare relief for their families, as seen in Chapter 2, but also organised local elections for officers and often armed them and used them like a private army.[17] This increased role was an implicit consequence of the Niel laws of 1868. In a time when the state actually lost some of its power – for instance, its ability to give and provide resources – the municipalities found themselves better equipped than the improvised prefects. The fragility of the imperial construction is that of any organisation in which the flow of symbolic and monetary exchange becomes interrupted. When the prefects of the empire were withdrawn, and with them discretionary awards, handouts and favours, the power base of their successors, the republican prefects, was singularly eroded.

They could not depend on the police force, which either lay dormant or was thoroughly disorganised; they could not exchange or give much, and in effect depended entirely on the localities' goodwill to support national policies and plans. The poverty of any crude centralisation theory is that it does not account for the survival of a centralised nation state when it loses its top-to-bottom strength. Without repression, without bribes, the central power depends on the willingness of the periphery to support the existence of a symbolic centre, a locus upon which can be projected representations of nationhood or grandeur.[18] They were no longer the providers but the beggars of authority and power.

Luckily for the *Gouvernement de la Défense Nationale*, there was such a willingness in 1870. It largely embraced the national defence motto, and relied on the historical tropes of the nation in danger and the grandeur of France to support a war effort led by a handful of republican deputies and a conservative general. Yet this support was conditional and fragile. The legitimacy of their power was greater in Paris than anywhere else, and its representatives were made to feel that the times had changed and that they would have to negotiate with the locality. This exchange, centred on localities and local citizenship and taken here almost at its original meaning of belonging to a circumscribed city, is what makes 1870–1 such an important phase in the development of a modern French democracy within a centralised model. In this context, Gambetta's hope of reviving civic life was central to a renewal of the republican tradition:

> To establish free communes, the constitution of municipalities which are not under the exaggerated influence of the central power, enjoying a life of their own and able to initiate a renewal of France by renewing its public mores, has always been central to the fair demands of the democratic opinion which used to be expressed in the opposition … It is beyond doubt that the municipal councils elected last August in most

communes bear the mark of the old administration ... we want to ensure, within the limits of the constitution of the nation, the independence of the municipal bodies, so that activity and life circulate throughout all the parts of the social body.[19]

This emphasis on municipal and social bodies is common in the republican language, and reflected the revival of an organic representation of the nation tied to its political system of representation.[20] This position is one of the closest Gambetta ever expressed to the decentralist ideals of the Nancy programme of 1865. It was perhaps also the area of the revolution of 4 September 1870 which was most successful in spite of the government.

Lyons, Montpellier, Limoges and Tulle

A few instances may help the reader to comprehend the full scale of what took place. The four cities chosen were vastly different and yet carried the same administrative weight. Lyons, Montpellier, Limoges and Tulle were the prefectures of the Rhône, Hérault, Haute-Vienne and Corrèze departments respectively. The first two departments had shown a certain reluctance towards the Second Empire, and indeed the prefectures had voted against Napoleon III at the 1870 plebiscite; the last two headed more enthusiastically imperialistic departments but were also centres of dissent.[21] Lyons and Limoges were industrial cities specialising in weaving, shoemaking and porcelain respectively, while Tulle had a state armaments factory, and Montpellier was strictly speaking a university and administrative centre. In terms of size, Lyons dominated, with over 300,000 inhabitants. The great city of silk weaving also controlled a network of subsidiary villages and towns, where many of the looms had already been relocated.[22] Montpellier and Limoges (roughly 55,000 inhabitants in 1870)[23] were representative of the second rank of prefectures, while Tulle's limited size makes it representative of small French cities, then the majority. All of them possessed the same administrative infrastructure and diocesan authorities of some importance. Their stories in 1870 could hardly be more different.

Lyons prided itself on being the first city in France to proclaim the end of the empire, preceding even Paris; the committee of public salvation, organised by the ultra-republicans of the cities, united all the various movements of Lyonese imperial opposition. Hénon, the moral leader of the committee, was one of the few republicans of the assembly who since 1857 had defied the conservative majority.[24] Durand, one of the most influential councillors, was a socialist, and the members of the AIT who came to claim a share of power in the name of their organisation were originally well received. Andrieux, a Freemason[25] and anti-clerical leader of the period before the war, made a comeback from his cell in the Saint-Joseph prison to lead the judiciary.

There were deep divisions among this revolutionary committee. Some, like Durand or Crestin, were socialist revolutionaries inspired by the 1789 Revolution and Fourierist ideals. Andrieux had narrowed his social views to a strong anti-clerical demagogy. Richard[26] and other members of the AIT were obviously socialist, even if a little confused. Richard seems to have been particularly uncertain about his class loyalties, and his controversy with Véron, a journalist of the *Progrès*, during which they accused each other of being bourgeois, showed how sensitive the men of the left were about class labels.[27] As Paris would later do, the city established itself as a commune mainly as a reaction to a long period of state control during which the mayor and the whole council had been nominated by the prefect who dictated the whole municipal agenda.[28] This high level of scrutiny reflected the care of the empire and its fears that the great urban centres of Paris, Lyons and Marseilles might erupt in a riot at any time. Precedents from the 1790s, 1830s and 1840s comforted the state in the belief that such ideas in these metropolises were too 'advanced' or radical for their times. In exchange for this subjection, the state tended to over-provide in health and slum clearance schemes.

In fact, this fear of great unstable urban centres was widely shared, even among republicans, and Lyonese revolutionaries of September 1870 witnessed with some incredulity the arrival of Challemel-Lacour, sent by Gambetta as prefect with all powers. The first telegram announcing his arrival nearly precipitated a full-blown rebellion against Paris. After a more tactful second message, Challemel-Lacour was received in Lyons only to be held virtual prisoner of the committee of public salvation.[29]

The Committee knew, however, that their legitimacy was simply the fruit of necessity; they were not usurping the power of anybody since there was nobody there. Besides, their revolutionary right was established by simply being there and taking over a terrifying responsibility. They were also representing the underground work of sections organised from the Croix Rousse neighbourhood, high on the hills dominating Lyons, which since the beginning of the war had been planning a new commune.[30] Unable to reply to these arguments and wanting to solve the problem of democratic deficit inherent to any government born out of an insurrection (and this included the Paris government), the Lyonese committee of public salvation called for elections and was largely re-elected in the municipal council. In the words of the poster announcing the elections:

> Society was as endangered as the fatherland. Let us save the fatherland, but let us save society, which was nearing a disaster. Let us not fall again for the vagaries of state, Church and police, all administrations that have led us astray previously and which have shown their worth. Let us struggle against the bloody barbarians and a so-called civilisation without justice![31]

With this last manifesto, it ended its original direct mandate by calling for a thorough reform of political mores in France, principally targeting the state, including its administration and religion. The confusion of the two struggles, against invaders and against corrupting practices, served a municipal agenda.

From that period on the municipality legislated in all areas of finances, weapons, health and welfare without the approval of the prefect. The hapless *commissaire extraordinaire* could only ensure, with the help of Andrieux, that the Commune respected at least some of the forms of the previous jurisdiction and limited its intervention to areas congruent to local administration. Lyons wished to go much further, and indeed went as far as it could. In early October, the municipal authorities seriously considered coining their own silver and gold francs. Typically, this measure was meant to solve three issues simultaneously: it would affect the lack of cash, end jewellers' unemployment, and give greater visibility to 'the republic and the Commune in Lyons'.[32] Like the capital gains taxes decreed earlier, the measures were overturned on the grounds that they were infringements on the sovereign rights of the French state. The Lyons taxes were relatively small, in that they amounted to a direct contribution of 25 to 50 centimes per 100 francs of the capital and property owned.[33] The main intention was to find sources of income that would replace the hated town gate taxes of the *octroi*. Town gate taxes, which were a tax on consumption, affected primarily the greater number of poor people.[34] There was a debate on the issue of replacing the capital tax by doubling the local rates of taxes in order to avoid taking over some of the fundamental responsibilities of the state.

In Montpellier, the same issue had led the municipal council to issue bonds and borrow the money rather than encroach on the sovereign power of the state.[35] In Lyons, the radicals, led by Councillor Durand, won the crucial vote by a majority of one.[36] The Lyonese administration also attempted to release the cheaper goods pawned in the municipal pawnshops of the Mont de Piété[37] and to impose a moratorium on debts until a month after the end of the war.[38] Similar measures were taken only in the most radical arrondissements in Paris.[39]

As a consequence of the budgetary constraints imposed on the radical municipality, Lyons ended the war financially strained. It had only a disparate collection of weapons and guns to show for its war effort, and was severely criticised.[40] Over the town hall the red flag floated high, and Lyons lived under the Commune for nine months. During this period the red flag replaced and even eliminated the tricolour. An anecdote illustrates the emotional conflict between the colours of the revolution and the colours of the nation. On 23 September 1870, a self-appointed policeman in charge of the station of Vaise in Lyons removed three flags when 'the citizen herewith replied hastily that the red flag is the Prussian flag and that we seek to divide France with our red flag'. The enthusiastic policeman then stamped his report with a cap of liberty republican stamp.[41] The tricolour had lost the battle in Lyons, where the red flag reigned supreme except for a brief appearance of the black flag – a symbol of mourning and of the weavers' revolt – after the signature of the armistice and an enormous amount of political pressure on the municipal council.[42] The defenders of the tricolour were equally suspicious and the position of the Lyonese crowd towards the military was one of extreme defiance. On 6 September the *mobiles* invaded the military camps of Sathonay and imposed a release of all prisoners. Humiliatingly for the army officers in post, the soldiers lifted their rifle butts in the air and welcomed the guardsmen, who then imposed a red flag on the commanding officer; he had little choice but to congratulate the crowd on their manly behaviour and their patriotism.[43]

Some other officers had been forced to shout 'Long live the republic!' and many of the police officers of Lyons were arrested or had to go into hiding. General Espivent was among the men arrested and held in custody for a while.[44] He was followed by twenty-six informers, three magistrates, eleven priests and four Jesuits, and they were kept in the company of sixty-seven policemen arrested with the prefect on 4 September 1871. Most of the Lyonese prisoners stayed in prison for only a few days, and none more than twenty-four days.[45] Later, General Mazure was similarly challenged and entered into conflict with the Commune of Lyons. He replied that

> when I received the letter from the mayor of Lyons asking me to resign in the name of the council, I had to denounce to M. the prefect that this move from one of his subordinates was usurping legitimate powers. I consider that the respect of the hierarchy is one of the guarantees of order and liberty in any society.[46]

This letter was addressed to Hénon as an honourable man and not as the mayor of Lyons. The distinction undoubtedly projected Mazure's reluctance to recognise any legitimacy in his administratively inferior master.[47] Mazure failed – or refused – to accept that hierarchies had been turned on their head throughout the war. Republicans could not accept this haughty attitude.

Interestingly, what happened in Paris in March 1871 is not dissimilar at all. Even the more violent demonstration of deep anti-clericalism, a particularly lively rallying creed in Lyons, prefigured what happened in Paris. On 4 September, the seminary was invaded and the 'exercise room' was construed as a training room for some hideous but mysterious clerical plot. The first legion then took its quarters in the seminary and found 'the tibias of women ravished from their husbands, the skulls of mothers taken away from their duties'. The Grand-Guignol gore of these descriptions culminated in a sensational article, entitled 'The cutlass of the man in black', published in *Le Progrès*.[48] Later, the Carmelites were expelled and the convent became communal property on 9 October 1870. This anti-clericalism, which borrowed its sensational pathos from *Les Mystères de Paris* and gothic horror, lived on among radical circles and recurred during the Commune of Paris, when Raoul Rigault used the skeletons of a monastery crypt in Picpus, 'gasping for a last breath of air', for his propaganda. Beyond the anecdotal events, most Lyonese measures found their direct counterparts in the Parisian legislation. Many of the federalist claims made by Lyons were matched word-for-word in Paris, and even the social and political compositions of both cities' administrations was not deeply different. But there were two differences: first, Lyons did not challenge the existence of the French state to the same extent as Paris ended up doing, and second, the Lyons hinterland was more deeply affected than the region around Paris.

Lyons revolutionaries were scrutinised from afar with some puzzlement but they had considerable impact on surrounding villages and small towns.[49] Small villages and neighbouring towns near Lyons imitated the forms of revolutionary action. Vienne,[50] Tarare, Beaujeu, Villefranche-sur-Saône and many small villages created their committees of public salvation.[51] Many of them kept the red flag until after that of the Commune of Paris had fallen in the flames of May 1871. In the Rhône department, for instance, the village of Courzieux brought down its two red flags on 30 May 1871. The flags were hanging from the tree of liberty and the bell-tower of the church. At Saint Genis-les-Ollières near Lyons, at Marcy and Alix at some distance from Lyons, the flags came down on 29 and 28 May respectively.[52] After the announcement of the armistice, Lyons tried to pull its national weight one last time to convince Gambetta to lead a war party, forming a convention of urban municipalities established in Lyons. The programme included a number of points demanded by the club of La Rotonde in Lyons:

1   war to the last;
2   a *convention* government settled in Lyons;
3   a convention composed of delegates from the cities of the departments only;
4   a permanent commission of thirty members mandated by the people, and
     that no arrest could be made without the authorisation of that commis-
     sion.[53]

The council answered that the first three points were already the basis of its policy. The deputation led by Hénon travelled to Bordeaux and established links with radical cities such as Toulouse[54] and Marseilles and was, by early February, confident that it could turn the situation against the ex-government of national defence of the deputies of Paris.[55]

Disastrous reports in subsequent meetings of the municipal council squashed these hopes.[56] One of the salient aspects of this last-minute attempt to salvage the republican regime in the provinces was that it disenfranchised rural Frenchmen and recast citizenship as the right of city-dwellers only. The Lyonese were in this sense closer to their Parisian counterparts than to small-city dwellers, who were much more closely attuned to rural constituencies.

Viewed from the south of France, the revolution of Lyons inspired both fear and admiration.[57] The Montpellier administration was far more conservative. It debated lengthily and acrimoniously whether to support the republic before the Gambettist prefect replaced it with a more sympathetic committee.[58] The newly appointed group enjoyed only a short period of revolutionary enthusiasm, during which the prefect was often taken to task.[59] Under Bertrand, the administration of the city witnessed radical reforms such as the creation of secular primary schools to rival and compete with the congregationalist schools.[60] As late as August 1871, it tried to soften municipal pawn-shop rules and released the small items held in its stores.[61] The Montpellierans answered the Lyons committees of national defence and the *Ligue du Midi* with a cautious endorsement of the programme of national defence and local freedom.[62] While scrupulously organising National Guard elections, it did not object to demilitarisation.[63] After the departure of Bertrand on the issue of the Commune, it eventually followed Lyons in its effort to stop the war against Paris in the spring of 1871.

Limoges, a more radical city, was given a more experienced and respected prefect than Lyons, and he managed to reorganise local municipalities along democratic lines and balance internal opposition coming from the local elites and some resolutely pro-imperial sectors of bas-Limousin. In July 1870, Limoges had refused to pay lip-service to patriotism and had not sent a patriotic address to the emperor.[64] It contained many clubs, including one named the Popular Society for the National Defence, which involved the locals of the trade federations. In Limoges, as in other republican centres of some importance, the social question divided the republicans who limited citizens' rights to the declaration of 1789 and those who wished to include some of the rights to labour and fair wages expressed in 1848.[65] The election of a new mayor freed the city council from the shackles of prefectoral control. Limoges, like Lyons, attempted to borrow money by issuing bonds. Unlike Lyons, the government could afford to censor its patriotic efforts.[66]

The incidents that have been described as a thwarted commune of Limoges seem not to have been of that nature. What took place in Limoges was a demonstration against the war in Paris and generally against the assembly of Versailles. Soldiers were about to leave for Paris when the crowd attempted to stop them. The cavalry, brought in to clear the square, was left without a clear line of command; a few shots were fired and Colonel Billet was killed. The sense of shock was so deep that the army then found very little difficulty in re-establishing law and order. The clubs of the Popular Society and of the rue Palvézy were raided for deserters and closed down, and the National Guard was dissolved. What this incident shows is the reluctance, already found in Lyons, to engage in real street warfare. This cannot be explained purely in military terms, since in Limoges on 5 April the army hierarchy had lost control of its own soldiers.[67] The officers of the Cuirassier regiment of heavy cavalry denied any attempt to charge and pointed out that their colonel had not even worn his helmet.[68]

Tulle, on the other hand, presents an instance of royalist decentralisation, which centred its vision of local democracy on the values of religion and peace and order. The Baron Lafond de Saint Mûr, Bonapartist mayor of Tulle,[69] declared in the name of the council that 'the decentralisation of powers and notably the communal independence would be the best safeguard of local interests and against any coups of any origin'.[70] In the words of the royalist *Le Réveil de la Province*, 'The Commune is a family, it needs to be united, to maintain order and calm within if it wants to be strong and prosperous', adding that 'The weakened Commune, renouncing its authority, is discouraging, is the terror and the death of France. A terrible example of this dreadful situation is given to us by Lyons.'[71] The Lyons experiment served as a scaremongering counter-example, which hid the fact that the local monarchists had so little to offer. Tulle had voted in favour of the empire at the 1870 plebiscite, with 27,560 ayes to 1,296 nos.[72] Prefect Latrade, a republican journalist, found himself quite isolated in Tulle which, unlike Brive-la-Gaillarde, further south, did not have a republican leadership. Negotiating with the *conseil général*, the prefect could only manage to raise 500,000 francs with great difficulty.[73] From Tulle, the period seemed far less exciting and the war effort soon tired the rural economy of this fragile region. This reluctance for war was also to be found during the civil war, and the number of volunteers was ludicrously small.[74]

The limits of decentralisation

The obvious limits of decentralisation were to be found in the reluctance of many cities to follow the example of Paris and radically oppose local and national sovereignty. All cities of France enjoyed local elections, and indeed the Thiers government of February 1871 had to give more municipal freedom through the law of 14 April 1871, which allowed free elections of municipal councils from which the prefect could then choose a mayor for the larger cities.[75] The elections in early May returned moderate and radical municipal councils in most cities of France. This municipal freedom was moderated by the right of the government to choose the mayors from the elected councillors, but the law still gave more municipal freedom than any before. Even under Gambetta, the new men in post had removed a disproportionate number of mayors. In the Haute-Vienne, 153 mayors out of 201 had been dismissed.[76] To limit conservative votes, electors of February 1871 often had to walk long distances to the *chef lieu de canton*. The republicans, fearing rural voters, had hoped for large numbers of abstentions and a disproportionately high proportion of urban votes. In fact, their lack of faith in communal votes backfired, when groups of electors united by their journey voted together for peace and made individual viewpoints more difficult. When voting reverted to communes and local circumstances, the republicans achieved much better results.[77]

The April–May municipal elections had already indicated that the peace or war vote of February 1871 gave a distorted image of the strength of reactionary forces in France. To moderate this rise of the republican strongholds, the government had attempted to create sections, to enable the carving out of safe councillor seats. Some mayors reacted violently to the manoeuvre. In Villefranche-sur-Saône, the mayor protested against the law and the creation of sections which favoured conservative votes:

> It is materially impossible to create sections; first, there is not enough
> time; second, the prefectoral administration has undoubtedly been peti-
> tioned by the monarchist party. It looks like the bad old days of the
> empire … as for me, I will never accept the dismemberment of the city
> as long as I am the head of its administration.[78]

Prefect Valentin dismissed him on 27 April 1871. In Lyons, the application of
this law gave a stimulus to an attempted insurrection at the Guillotière.[79]

Even in Bordeaux, the seat of the royalist assembly before its return to
Versailles, the municipality proved to be conciliatory towards Paris.[80] The
municipal gains of 1870 were immense, and even Paris would come out of
the war with reinforced local administration, local politics and a platform
for its own brand of anti-clerical republicanism. The limits of decentralisation were thus revealed when decentralisation was presented as destructive
of national unity. Faced with the patriotic test, only a handful of people in
the most recently annexed regions of Savoy and Nice attempted to break
away from France. In all other places, different messages were sent,
stressing religion, anti-clericalism, traditional values or socialist ideals as
constitutive of French national identity, but always keeping clear of sepa-
ratist discourse.

It may be an exaggeration to see this period as symptomatic of a rejection of
centralisation. Indeed, centralisation survived, the centre was called to the
rescue, and the centre was still deemed to be important when its legitimacy and
power were at their lowest. There was a need and a call for the centre to exist.
What each city, newspaper or politically active Frenchman attempted to do was
to project a different type of French identity, to be applied to the whole of
France through the medium of centralisation. Everybody in France seemed to
be centralist for their neighbours, and there was real irony when Lyons
attempted to call for the centralisation of the war effort in Lyons.[81] In other
instances, the war seemed to offer the opportunity for political changes and
reforms along the lines of parochial *jalousie*. The behaviour of one town or city
allowed the hopes of rival communes to be revived. After the Laon disaster,
where the local people virtually forced the garrison to surrender, there were
voices in the rival Commune of Saint-Quentin to call for a redistribution of
administrative roles in the national structure, thus revisiting the administrative
quarrels of the first Revolution.[82]

> Laon has disgraced the country in general and the department in
> particular, it is not worthy of being the *chef-lieu* [residence of the prefect
> and important departmental representatives of the state]. *Now is the time
> to push forward on Saint-Quentin's behalf or, rather, the time will come after the
> peace and it needs preparing right now* … The opportunity is too good; our

honourable deputy is on good terms with the current government ... so all the circumstances are favourable.[83]

Paris

The decentralist debate in Paris also had important echoes, and it is impossible to understand the tensions that led to the Commune without looking at the changes that took place within besieged Paris. The first action of the government after 4 September 1870 was to give back local administration to the Parisians. The mayors were nominated in the first instance, and were chosen from among the strong republican figureheads of Paris.

The new mayor of Paris was the hapless Arago, who bridged the gap with 1848 history and belonged to the emblematic relics of this distant past. Each arrondissement soon took full municipal rights and organised its own guardsmen, health and food supply, its own police and its own policies. This freedom of each arrondissement led to a very fragmented political map: various shades of red coloured the city, with some areas very superficially republican. From the semi-rural and conservative XVI arrondissement of Henri Martin to the populous and boisterous XIX of Delescluze, the spectrum represented all possible political options. In the management of the siege, the mayors often distanced themselves from the government's centre-left management and, like Mottu of the XI or Clemenceau of the XVIII, promoted anti-clerical measures likely to undermine the Catholic support for the regime. Even within the municipalities of the arrondissement, some wished to return to the smaller units of the *quartiers* or districts. This small, organic and neighbourly dimension existed in practice in the division of each arrondissement into four (eighty for the whole of Paris). In the Parisian case the National Guardsmen defined themselves as belonging to a group originating from an area often not much larger than a few streets within a *quartier*. In the words of Charles Longuet and Edouard Vaillant, two of the young Turks who took an active part in the Paris Commune after 18 March, the districts had real potential for revolutionary self-government after 6 September.

> We all meet, each district determines something: these resolutions are passed on swiftly from one district to another, in a few hours the whole of Paris knows approximately the general decision, then, through delegates sent to the Commune, they tell the Power, which is only mandated. here is what I want.[84]

This aspiration to direct mandatory democracy led to the establishment of the central committee of the twenty arrondissements which, while moderately successful with the public or even the revolutionaries, stood like a watchdog of the *république sociale*.

Even if this theoretical importance of the districts never became a proper political counter-power, the municipal authorities nominated by the government and later elected maintained a closer bond with the local guardsmen. The various clubs were thus free to lobby the mayor and pass on their views:[85]

> Such was the role of the republican committee of the VI arrondisse-ment. Welcomed by the mayors and *adjoints* of the 4 September, the delegates elected by the republican meeting of the École-de-Médecine [sic] had the satisfaction of being the interpreters of the meeting to the municipality on a daily basis ... Since the mayors and *adjoints* have been elected, the committee's role towards the municipality cannot stay the same. Nevertheless, we must note that as long as the arrondissement does not have an arrondissement municipal council, it remains vital to make sure that the wishes of the republican opinion are made clear to the local authorities.[86]

The need to stay close to the grass roots, even if these were only a vociferous minority, explains much of the behaviour of the arrondissement mayors. The mayors attempted to manage the situation by resorting to the strategies of exchange sketched out in Chapter 3, which enabled them to give handouts and collect 'voluntary' contributions through the National Guard. The men went door to door to collect either funds or monthly payments from the suitably patri-otic bourgeois of, for instance, the VIII arrondissement. This muscular form of collection enabled the arrondissement to give a purpose to the National Guardsmen, calm their demands for inspections and requisitions, and bond the people in arms more closely to their rulers.[87] Only at the most local level could politicians find the support and small-scale power that was so vital in establishing a durable administration. When the mayor of the XI arrondissement crossed the borderline and practised secularist and anti-clerical policies, and when Clemenceau showed his own anti-clericalism, they went against the moderate desires of the coalition government.

This tension between municipal powers and state erupted into a real crisis when the guardsmen of Belleville, led by Flourens, attempted an insurrection on 31 October. The insurrection was bloodless and soon revealed the tensions existing between Blanqui and Delescluze, the latter wishing to obtain electoral legitimacy sooner than the former. In the confusion of this *journée de dupes*, the republicans demonstrated their lack of a coherent plan and the weaknesses which later plagued the Commune of Paris. To use Millière's phrase, the two govern-ments negotiated an electoral convention, leading to municipal elections and governmental elections. Edmond Adam, benign prefect of police, negotiated a settlement which allowed everybody out of the building without arrests. The government subsequently kept some of its part of the deal and sought popular support through a very successful plebiscite, the imperial electoral tool *par excellence*, and through municipal elections on 6 November.[88] The arrondissement elections did not lead to the establishment of a sovereign commune, as anticipated by the revolutionaries of 31 October, especially as Jules Ferry, who had led the evacuation of the town hall, exercised the two functions of prefect of the Seine and unelected mayor of Paris. The elections broadly confirmed the September nominees, but largely because they had broken away from the government. Without going into the details of policy, much of the Commune's action pre-existed the Commune and was enacted by the arrondissement mayors.

Decentralising the capital city proved difficult, since it put the government at the mercy of a private army from one side or the other. The conflict, which became violent in January 1871, thus set the Breton soldiers of Trochu against the guardsmen. The decentralisation was not simply the devolution of power to the communes of arrondissements but, within each arrondissement, to the guardsmen, who operated their little units like debating societies of citizens in arms. Guardsmen then considered themselves the best incarnation of democracy and used their weapons to reinforce their right to petition. In their address to the 'citizen prefect of Lyons' on 30 September 1870 immediately after the failed Bakunin-led insurrection, the guardsmen expressed their support in these terms:

> Rogue elements are few; they audaciously lie to the people; we must make them powerless so that they do not go to other cities, pretending to represent us, to sow the seeds of trouble and anarchy. The National Guard today offers you its powerful help to create mobilised battalions which will represent us against the enemy ... the National Guard is the whole city in arms. You have alongside you the municipal council, elected through the universal suffrage of this city; its advice will always be there for you, and when the election of the colonel of the national guard and of the *état-major* has completed the cogs linking you to every citizen, we will be able to walk like one man to the rescue of our country.[89]

The bond between citizen and state thus developed through the mediation of its elected council and of its National Guard, an experience limited to men only, and more precisely to valid and active men. These two counter-powers could make the whole work as one man, or they could watch and effectively control the central authority. In Lyons, Challemel-Lacour had to cope with the suspicion of both National Guardsmen and the council. In all accounts of the war, the guardsmen remained central, and this centrality of the guardsmen's experience is what later made the Commune of Paris build on National Guardsmen's organisations. When it came to the civil war, the battalions of the guard behaved like so many neighbourhood militias, and the Commune ended in the largely amorphous chaos from which it had arisen in March. Within the political experience of the Commune, the National Guard in Paris refused to let itself be demoted.

The guardsmen's central committee refused to disband, even after the Commune elections, and followed slightly different policies while controlling the most important human resource of the revolution. This chaotic situation showed

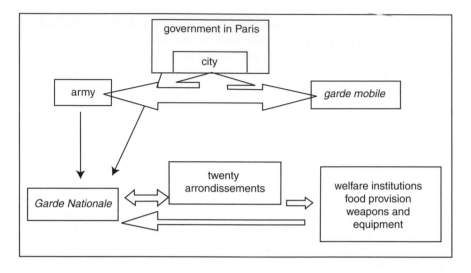

Figure 4.1   The French structure of command in 1870

the limitations of decentralisation when it reached the absurd level where juris-dictions overlapped and were muddled.

The diagram in Figure 4.1 shows the complexity and difficulty of a situation in which the *garde mobile* served almost as the Praetorian Guard of the govern-ment. Camped mostly outside Paris, it was almost immune to revolutionary aspirations, while the arrondissements, often in conflict with the city and the government, tried to control the National Guard through a series of welfare measures and initiative. The guardsmen themselves petitioned their mayors and the government on a regular basis. The thickness of the arrows represents the strength of this bond. Decentralisation had spawned a monster.

Through decentralisation, localities had their own armies with their own political and social dynamic, and the army ended up being a mix of disparate elements, including all guardsmen, over whom it had but little control and where the various elements could end up confronting each other. The dynamics of the insurrection of 18 March 1871 were there in September 1870. What kept this unstable structure in one piece for so long was the patriotic language, which postponed deeper political debates and papered over the cracks among republicans.

Fault lines in French politics

What all these tensions in the decentralist discourse revealed was an almost general reluctance to sink into civil war. As Chapters 6 and 7 will show, it was a slow process of brutalisation and alienation that led the French to civil war after the Parisian insurrection of March 1871. Why one neighbour should take arms against another is difficult to understand. Most readers will remember the collapse of multi-ethnic states of Europe in the 1980s, when ethnicity was used as a handy catch-phrase to conceal the most troubling elements of this neighbourly violence. Ethnicity, like class, is an historical construct of identity. It has no tangible existence beyond history, and in 1871 in France, class alone cannot explain the eruption of civil war violence.

The civil war erupted in Paris but not everywhere in the provinces, largely because many people in the localities did not see any need to take arms to obtain something they already had. In Lyons, the insurrection attempts of 23 March and 30 April were crushed rapidly by the combined forces of the guardsmen at the order of the municipality and the army. In fact, during both insurrections popular support did not materialise, and the municipality could defend its own record and demonstrate that, with the red flag flying over the town hall and the policies they were pursuing, the Lyonese already had their commune. When the guardsmen invaded the council room in Lyons to ask for a commune like that of Paris, Hénon remarked that 'Lyons already had a commune, that this commune had taken back many of the municipal powers, and that, if it remained, he was ready to grant some of the powers it could ask for, but without splitting away from the central power'.[90]

Crestin and Barodet then called for recognition of the movement in Paris against the wishes of moderate republicans who did not wish to become agents of sedition. Asked by national guardsmen themselves to take control of the National Guard, the army and the prefecture, the intruders took part in the political debate.[91] The proclamation of 23 March was also singularly modest in its aims to re-establish the full prerogatives that the Lyons municipality had enjoyed a few weeks earlier and arguably still enjoyed at that date.

> The Commune is for us the basis and the guarantor of the republic. We want the republic absolutely and by all means, and to ensure we obtain it for ever, we need an insurmountable moat and an invincible wall, we want the Commune! More fortunate and more enterprising than other cities, we already have established this right. The Lyonese Commune freely controlled its schools, suppressed the *octroi* and managed its taxes; but the municipal council has relinquished some of its powers ... the National Guardsmen are now under the control of a representative of the central government and of a general named by him.[92]

This proclamation had few echoes; the crisis of 23 March was short-lived, but it further undermined the commune. The final straw, which signalled that the municipal authorities were finally losing their grip on the city, came on 30 April, when the armed insurrection of the populous neighbourhood of the Guillotière shook the local government.[93] Here again the repression was swift, largely because the artisan neighbourhood of the Croix Rousse did not follow suit and because the National Guardsmen did not side with the insurrection.[94]

In Narbonne, as César's recent work shows, the bond of familiarity between republicans on both sides of the barricades was still strong[95] and sufficient to demonstrate to the insurrectionists their own isolation among the population.[96] The leader of the Commune of Narbonne, Émile Digeon,[97] decided to surrender after being promised an amnesty, which landed him and his friends in court. In fact, the jury of the tribunal of the *cours d'Assise* of Rodez, in the neighbouring department of Aveyrons, eventually recognised the amnesty as valid by letting most of the conspirators go free.[98] In Saint-Étienne, the prefect was murdered, albeit accidentally, while in the custody of an insane guardsman. In Limoges, a stray bullet killed an officer, but beyond a few isolated incidents there was no commune to talk about in either city in spite of the fact that both had a revolutionary tradition and enough weapons. Only in Marseilles did the army take violent revenge on a virtually harmless Communard movement.[99] Its leader, Gaston Crémieux, was the only provincial Communard to be executed, after a trial in 1871.[100]

This passivity in the defence of Communards' ideals has often been blamed on the mediocrity of local insurrection leaders. The argument developed in the rest of this book is precisely that the insurrection gesturing was exceptional and signified the breakdown of a common political culture, and the decay of social bonds and a public sphere. The Commune of Paris was, in many ways, out of touch with the rest of France. Lyons had gone further and faster than Paris, but other localities had found a different equilibrium and the war dynamic which was so rampant in Paris, largely after the siege, was not so important in the provinces. This does not mean that there was no club culture,[101] that political ideas were not discussed or that the Commune had a monopoly of socialist views. These movements, which have been far less studied and which reflect provincial reluctance to equip or staff the civil war Versailles army, show that even Périgueux and the highlands of Limousin rejected the logic of civil war.[102]

The deputation and the creation of the Third Party probably expressed the majority view at that particular time. Largely connected to the activities of the French Freemasonry, this attempted to calm the situation in March and early April 1871.[103] Local municipalities, down to the most humble, like Tarare, sent messages to Thiers expressing their main worry that the latter should proclaim the republic once and for all.[104] After the elections of 8 February the government only alluded to the type of government France might develop. In his opening speech, Thiers had mentioned that the 'great wounded soldier we call France' had to recover its senses before it could express a final constitutional choice. Provincial republicans imagined that this constitutional matter was, when added to the lack of municipal democracy in Paris, the main cause of the insurrection. Little did they realise that by late March the insurrection could no longer be appeased by constitutional concessions. The later excess of the Commune, as propagated by the Versailles government, managed to silence this Third Party and made a civil war inevitable. In the words of Thiers:

Negotiations were mentioned! I, subject to radicalism, complying with radicals, I listened to those who came to tell me: 'Don't shed rivers of blood, listen to us! We can negotiate; you will enter Paris, the government will sit in Paris but the army will not enter it!' I was indignant: 'The army will not enter it!' That is when I said: 'You talk of rivers of blood! But the army is France, it will enter Paris like the government before the government, the army must be everywhere, it will be there!' I faced cruel deeds. If there is one man to whom bloodshed is costly, it is me, I dare say … I, so complacent with radicalism and communism, I squashed … we squashed this hateful faction, and we have squashed it for a long time, I hope.[105]

Following this epic speech, Thiers was ousted from power in 1873 after the defeat of a Thierist candidate in the hands of Barodet,[106] leader of the radical Commune of Lyons in 1870–1.[107] The great difference, then, between the Commune of Paris and the radicals of France was not ideological. Indeed, many of the staff of the Commune of Paris had been active in the provinces beforehand, something that was apparent in the peculiar position of Paris towards centralisation. The Paris Commune had all the trappings of state power: it took the symbol of revolutions in France, not the parliament but the town hall: it controlled the Bank of France and the ministries, and mimicked much of its administration. The call to a federation of communes was belated and poorly relayed. It did not make much sense to provincials and it did not reflect the limited aspirations to managerial independence and local debating rights. More importantly, perhaps, it postulated war at a time when war had tired the defeated French. The capital of sympathy for the Parisians was immense in March 1871, and the Commune of Paris squandered it through the tone of its rhetoric and its early military operations. The historical language in which it shrouded its action, the creation of a committee of public salvation and the rest of Communard revolutionary paraphernalia had lost most of its currency value in the provinces, either because of overuse in 1870, or because it had awoken too many bad memories.

The men from the provinces who joined the Commune of Paris were either aspirational young men with a long experience of Paris, like Vallès or Lissagaray, idealists sickened by the pacifists, like Rossel, or more simply men like the simple National Guardsman Constantin, who had so much enjoyed his role in the National Guard that he did not want to surrender his lieutenant's commission. He travelled to Paris as a stonemason from his native Creuse, and when asked to join the Commune found it only natural to join the militia of the revolution.[108] The men of the Commune very often continued as National Guardsmen, because it was the National Guard that had become the substance of their existence and the best expression of their neighbourhood solidarity and welfare provisions. The men studied by Robert Tombs as cautious revolutionaries were probably representative of the majority. They had joined the Commune of Paris because the National Guard was part of it.[109] The Commune could only rely on these men when attacked. Considering the few casualties on the Versailles side during the conquest of Paris, one is forced to say that the Commune had failed to organise its military wing. Beyond its great significance as a largely but not exclusively working-class insurrection, the Commune of Paris had many failings. Lacking in original substance, lacking in military might or even comprehensive legislation, deficient in its practice of democracy, a parody in its historical language, it seems surprising that the Commune of Paris should have had such an enduring legacy as a practical example for future revolutionaries. It did so because of its historiography.

The Commune of Paris has generated a huge historiography, which has not been matched by a parallel interest in the French provinces; in fact, provincial Communards in exile were far fewer and quickly assimilated the Parisian culture.[110] Different political groups crystallised their views according to the *milieu* where they were refugees. In London, Lissagaray published the most authoritative account of the Commune, perhaps one of the few to reflect on the Paris–province chasm, largely because Lissagaray himself knew the situation in Toulouse so well. Lissagaray was not alone writing history in England: Vésinier also gave his *histoire*.[111]

In Switzerland, the Communards welcomed by the AIT divided their views and social circles between the Utopian socialists – among them Lefrançais – who mixed with the anarchists around Bakunin,[112] active mostly in Lyons,[113] and AIT followers of the London line.[114] In many respects the texts that issued from Switzerland remained more theoretical and attempted a retrospective definition of the programme of the Commune. Under the closest scrutiny of both French and Swiss police, the refugees fell into justified paranoia and distrust of each other, which soon made their exile even more unpleasant and prone to reverie.[115] Bakunin had been associated with Russian funds, and the general council in London accused him of being an *agent provocateur* made of the same stuff as his friend Albert Richard, who had recently visited Napoleon III in his English retreat. The split between the London council and the Swiss *Fédération Jurassienne* was a fundamental division over the means to achieve a revolutionary upheaval rooted in the experience of the Commune of Paris.[116]

The policeman writing from Lyons defined the anarchists as 'the most interesting faction of socialism in Switzerland, the one in which the French government will always find, ready to second us, the proper elements to divide demagogy.'[117] Lefrançais's *Étude sur le mouvement communaliste*[118] was thus more of an essay on socialism in action, which found some echo in B. Malon's *La Troisième défaite du prolétariat français* or in André Léo's work.[119] Malon had been well known since the strikes of Le Creusot, and his work and Léo's received their fair share of police attention. Besides these most influential texts, a multitude of Communard figures published anecdotal accounts of their time under the Commune weeks after they had had to flee.[120] The Commune was such a strange political animal that even its leading figures were uncertain how it had developed and how it could have ended, and because of this there was a craving for insiders' accounts and narratives which could counterbalance the caricatures issued in Versailles.[121] Within weeks of the defeat of the Commune of Paris, both sides of the conflict had recognised its historical importance and collected the documents of the period – posters, newspapers and other pamphlets – in order to establish a thriving market of Communard relics.[122] Right-wing observers such as Maxime du Camp joined in, and even newspapers such as *Le Figaro* published facsimiles of various Communard documents in their *Autographe* supplements. With the corpses of the insurgents only newly in their shallow graves or even still on the slabs of the morgue, the Commune was already part of the past, history to be written and memory to be overcome.[123] This publishing fad enabled the full range of Communard opinions to be aired and led to sectarian disagreements and entrenched hatred between the old comrades in arms.[124]

These divisions of the Communard *milieu* belong to a different historiography of the socialist movement, but they show that the Commune of Paris came out of fortuitous circumstances, political networks, half-baked revolutionary reveries and a rather mindless philosophy of action among the followers of Blanqui.

The third site of reflection was in New Caledonia, where the deported Communards re-wrote their history and sanctified their martyrs.[125]

One of the oddest developments of this historical thinking on the Commune of Paris and its inability to win over France was the tendency of a number of Communards to move towards authoritarian forms of government. Beyond the strictly socialist theories of a dictatorship of the proletariat which would solve the democratic deficit of minority radicalism, a number of Communards approached their enemies of yesteryear. Albert Richard and Gaspard Blanc[126] thus moved to England and met Napoleon III to offer their services, publishing Bonapartist neo-Communard books that combined the emperor's dreamy socialist view of his youth with a dictatorship of peasants and workers.[127] Blanc and Richard declared that socialism and democracy were irreconcilable, and lent their support to a socialist imperial restoration.[128] Jules Amigues and a number of Bonapartists followed the opposite route and defended the Commune against the monarchist assembly.[129] Later in the 1880s, Blanquists and Rochefort himself founded their hope of destroying a bourgeois conservative republic in the pseudo-gallant personality of General Boulanger. It seems that Thiers' panegyrists were not that far off the truth when they described his republic as being attacked jointly by the forces of radicalism and Bonapartism.[130]

All these moves and shifts, often taking place in the months following the destruction of the Commune, cannot simply be explained away by the madness of a handful of lost souls. The authoritarian tendencies of the Commune also had a very centralist side, and many Communards such as Raoul Rigault would have used centralist techniques like the police and the administration, preferring to use revolutionary forms to subjugate France.[131] The democratic processes, which had consolidated the Second Empire and the new Third Republic, were thus viewed with disdain or defiance, and Parisian leaders generated the splendid isolation which was fatal to their revolution.

One of the keys to the Communard psyche was the cult of poses and the glorification of revolutionary enthusiasm. Ideals had to fire up the citizens, and these ideals were to be fostered by the examples of earlier generations of revolutionaries, mediated by history. The end result was a movement based on a multitude of historical interpretations, historicist to the core and fragmentary in the expression of opinions and the conceptions of policies. This creative turmoil was not controlled at any level. The Communard citizens ran a *bateau ivre*, which mutated so frequently that it could be said there were several communes in the space of a few weeks. Adolphe Thiers and his conservative friends did not share this concept of citizenship based on enthusiasm, mainly because they objected to passions. For the conservatives of 1871, passions would arouse opposite political instincts and divisions. The paradox of this situation was that for many opponents of Bonapartism, deeply opposed to the rule of one man and his emphasis on unity, nothing could be worse than a political debate exacerbating divisions. In Thiers' words: 'When one is the slave of one's passions one should understand that they will provoke opposite passions.'[132]

At a more fundamental level, the concepts of citizenship as it existed and was practised during the Commune were those of an overwhelmingly powerful citizen ruler/citizen soldier – and this when the concepts of citizenship traditionally developed in the conservative practice of the French state were, to paraphrase Pierre Rosanvallon, those of a powerful citizen but weak *administré*.[133] The powerful citizen electors were also the citizen subjects of the state. Paradoxically, despite numerous protests against this overwhelming state, the administration held its sway, largely through the voluntary action of its constituents: the citizens. To return to Suleiman's definition of centralisation as the concentration of jurisdiction rather than effective power, the conflict between Versailles and the Commune, in legal terms, was irreducible and could not be appeased by any Third Party. It was fundamentally the conflict between a state which concentrated jurisdictional powers in the hands of a government representing the citizen electors, and citizen rulers who claimed to have jurisdiction over the state. The Communards claimed to maintain popular sovereignty and control through a universal and anarchical direct and mandatory delegation. Here was a government representing the nation and ruling, but facing citizens who claimed to be the nation ruling itself through direct and permanently renegotiable delegation of jurisdiction. Centralisation versus total decentralisation, state against non-state – such a conflict could be finally resolved only on the battlefield. For historians like Thiers or Henri Martin, this was a war against an opposite: the battle of the state that had made France against the anti-France:

> It [the Commune of Paris] is simply the complete radical renunciation of the values of the French revolution and its supreme motto, *The Republic one and indivisible*; it is the antithesis of the real federation, the one of 1790, and it is the annihilation of France.[134]

5

RELIGIOUS IDENTITIES AND CITIZENSHIP

Are you still singing the tired songs of 93? Where does the priest come from? Isn't he mostly the child of the worker or of the farmer? If the people are everything and not one party or another, I am one of them ... The priest is the glory of the people![1]

Religion and citizenship in France remained two separate categories in nine-teenth-century France, even though the Concordat of Napoleon I allowed for a more inclusive and instrumental definition of religion in French politics. Positivists could not reconcile the two concepts since they occupied the same spiritual space and each could only grow at the expense of the other.[2] The republican definitions of citizenship dating from the 1790s or even 1848 were openly theist and philosophical. Over the period 1848–70, this theism had lost much ground and competed with anti-clericalism. Anti-clericalism, aimed mainly at the Catholic clergy and more particularly at the religious orders like the Jesuits or the teaching orders, carried within itself the seeds of materialistic atheism which germinated in revitalised forms of French socialism.[3] Anti-clericalism embraced the notion that the state could not be sovereign if a large share of the population seemed to obey directives issued by a transnational entity such as the Catholic Church. This conflict between Roman Ultramontane churchmen and national sovereignty fed internal debates within the Church and among French theorists. At street level, Catholic organic and communal citizenship establishing duties attached to the fourth commandment, 'thou shall honour thy father and thy mother', was to a certain extent opposed to a rationalist but not necessarily individualistic republican balance of duties and rights.[4]

The religious debate became the great question of the first forty years of the Third Republic. In 1870 the debate had not yet been articulated in a definite manner, and this chapter investigates a number of dead ends, alternative concepts of citizenship and failed negotiations. In his speech of 24 May 1873, which signalled the end of his grasp on the republic,[5] Adolphe Thiers described the monarchists as the followers of a political nostalgia. In his words, the monarchy had 'for centuries, made the glory and prosperity of France; it would be strange if there should not be left in France some faithful followers of this political religion'.[6] The historian and statesman thus signalled in one concise formula that the monarchy belonged to the past rather than the future, and that its fate was associated with religion, indeed that it had all the strength and weaknesses of a creed. This reflection came three years into a period of great reactionary reform of the Catholic faith in France, and at a time when the Catholic Church seemed to turn its back on the values of citizenship.

Religion and citizenship

Definitions of citizenship varied considerably during the nineteenth century. When religion returned to the forefront of politics with the restoration of 1814–15 as the means of unifying state and altar, the Catholic Church never again enjoyed the monopoly which had made the culture of the *ancien régime*. Under the Second Empire, religion and citizenship were kept discreetly apart by a state keen to find support in all communities composing France and the French empire. This all-embracing policy led the empire to monitor as closely as possible the various churches, religions and even philosophical groups discussed in this chapter. This did not mean that the French state enjoyed an easy relationship with all of them. Indeed, the Catholic Church proved to be a difficult and demanding ally. Over the period 1851–70, the Church went through considerable theological and dogmatic reforms.[7] The new dogmas of the immaculate conception, the Syllabus of Errors and, even more controversially, the Vatican I council which settled on the pope's infallibility in dogmatic matters, centralised Catholicism on Rome.[8] This reinforcement of the centre in the Catholic Church was complicated and reflected a revival of religiosity using more exalted tropes and demonstrative expression of the faith.[9] Missions and pilgrimages became more common, and this revival of mysticism signalled the increased reluctance of the Catholic Church to embrace or even tolerate the modern materialistic world.

The infallibility debate raging in 1870 dealt with the role of the pope's decrees in Catholic theology and not on the personality of the pope as a man. In Kantorowicz's terms, it was a reinforcement of the power of the eternal pope rather than the mortal individual. This was lost on many faithful and lay people, who assumed, perhaps rightly, that the Church was gradually becoming even more of an absolutist institution. The debate within the Catholic Church was also very lively. The controversy between tenants of Rome's authority, the Ultramontanes, and the Gallicans who favoured a more episcopalian and consensual evolution of the Church turned to the advantage of the former. The French state could prevent the pope from intervening too brutally in the French Church's affairs, but it could not dictate the names of Gallican bishops to the pope. The situation was thus at a deadlock.[10]

Paradoxically, this intractable pope, Pius IX, had to rely on the French for the survival of the Papal State. In 1870, as a consequence of the war, the French army withdrew from Rome and the Piedmontese moved in to conclude Italian unification. Within the Bonapartist establishment there was the same break between agnostic and indifferent, Gallican, statesmen and Ultramontane reactionaries, who found their spokeswoman in the empress herself.

In France, the Catholic Church was in decline in spite of its greater visibility, and if it held sway in many rural regions it had lost the confidence of many urban centres. The bishops' docility towards local prefects had, for better or worse, associated the Church with the Bonapartist administration, and this will explain some of the hostility described later in this chapter. While the number of Catholics in 1866 represented 35,648,096 metropolitan French people out of a grand total of 37,386,161, there were also 1,561,250 Protestants – Calvinists of the south and south-west and Lutherans of the east of France – and 156,000 Jews. Another 20,000 belonged to minority sects, either breakaway cults of the Catholic Church or unrecognised Protestant denominations such as the Quakers.[11] Taking the greater France of France and Algeria, the second religion was Islam, with 2,778,281 people out of a total of 40,385,285.

It is necessary to take Algeria into consideration in 1870 because much of the 1870 crisis also occurred there, and because the Second Empire, more than any regime before or after, had integrated Algeria into a wider conception of France as a Mediterranean power. Algiers is, after all, closer to Marseilles than Lille by 200 miles.[12] It was also a central testing ground for French debates on citizenship and religious identity until 1962. The religious question, which was an implicit issue in France where citizenship and religion were not directly associated, was an explicit matter in Algeria, where religion at birth conditioned the status and citizenship of the inhabitants and the legislation to which they were submitted. The sectarian tensions that existed between the 92.8 per cent Muslims, 6.1 per cent Catholics, 0.9 per cent Jews and less than 0.2 per cent Protestants were considerable, and shaped almost entirely the identity of the colonisers and the colonised. The 1870 crisis would lead to an increase in these tensions.

Turcos and Orientalism at war

The Muslim past of France is not well documented, or even claimed or mentioned in the *Lieux de Mémoire* historiography of recent years. Whatever historiography there is of the Muslim past of France is limited to recent immigration.[13] This makes the Second Empire the pre-history of this French Muslim past. Quantitatively, the migratory moves from North Africa to France were negligible.[14] Qualitatively, the religious problem of Islam was not insignificant. Yet the confrontation within the French political space between French values and Islamic ones is both old – dating from *ancien régime* colonial enterprises – and significant, even though the French are now keener to be part of Western or even Northern Europe than to be seen to be a Mediterranean power.

The Algerian war of independence of 1954–62, which had many of its political roots in the early phases of the colonisation of the country, remains a difficult subject, left to war veterans of both sides. This silence reflects the fact that the conflict went beyond a decolonisation struggle and turned into a civil war on both sides of the sea. While 1870 is early to talk of a bilateral migratory flux, Algeria by then had become a destination of safe adventure and colonisation for French people and capital. Algeria had been colonised since 1830. During the first phase, cemeteries seemed to welcome more colonists than the cities, but recent improvements in the management of public health, the draining of the marshes and the increased access to Algeria's natural wealth had made the colony a more attractive proposition. Algeria had played an important role in internal debates in France since 1830, and the coup of 1851 would not have been possible without the use of troops normally garrisoned in North Africa. The inhabitants of Algeria featured in the Orientalist imagination of the French,[15] and the colonial wars had largely contributed to the shaping of the military culture prevalent in 1870, with all its weaknesses and qualities. Self-reliant officers and experienced *rezzou* soldiers were best suited to a war of devastating efficiency against less disciplined and less well-equipped people.

In the plains of Alsace and Lorraine, most of these adventurous qualities turned into carelessness and useless habits. The 1870 war saw the integration of the colonial empire to the war effort through the arrival and use of the 'Turcos', native soldiers recruited by the empire and later the republic to serve against the invading armies.[16] As the war became more desperate, the discourse on the great mass of Algeria, prefiguring the 'black power' imagery of the twentieth century, led some desperate journalists to hope that the war could be won using North African blood.[17] In fact, the sedentary *spahis*, *goumiers* and other irregulars refused to serve outside Algeria.[18] This notion that 'France has known how to associate with her men who love and respect her' enabled some idealistic journalists to make favourable comparisons between the North African colony and Prussia's satellites in southern Germany.[19] In spite of a figure of 35,000 volunteers, the fact remained that the population of Algeria was relatively small; the French relied entirely on bribes and conditional volunteering to raise troops in Algeria.

The mythologised Turcos were usually represented with the linguistic and sentimental tropes identified by Edward Said about occidental views of the Orient.[20] The Orientalist myth was particularly alive in military circles. Algeria offered a secure environment for social and political experiments, since much of its territory was in effect administered by the army. Constant skirmishes and raids allowed rapid promotion, and within the patronage networks of the French army colonial service was a ladder for ambitious men. Most senior officers of 1870–1 had served in Algeria in one capacity or another. Marshals Bazaine and MacMahon were two prominent examples of successful North African careers. Within the colonial forces, the *bureaux arabes* were the elite of this army and represented an opportunity for an alternative lifestyle and disproportionate devolved responsibility.[21] Their officers mingled with the locals, living with tribesmen, representing France and ruling like so many potentates. Through them the French favoured one family over another, one son over his elder siblings, and with a relatively small military presence the *bureaux arabes* were able to control large territories. Much of their lifestyle has been romanticised, although it seems clear that they had the leeway to enjoy a lifestyle impossible in provincial France. Fraternising with natives was allowed and even fostered. In West Africa, Faidherbe had even settled with a local woman in an illegitimate relationship unthinkable in metropolitan France.[22]

This 'French Raj' policy, which played on the divisions of traditional Algerian society, produced colourful stereotypes of the Algerian subject. The emperor himself had spent more time visiting Algeria than any other French territory and regularly invited leading Algerian leaders to Paris. Turco soldiers thus played a central role in the imperial imagery. Turcos were deemed to be childlike in their naivety, dog-like in their fidelity and savage in their bravery.[23] All these clichés of deep ingrained racism were relatively undifferentiated and hardly distinguished between Algerian and Senegalese soldiers.[24] They were also favourable, in the sense that all these demeaning terms were presented as a positive appreciation of sub-citizens learning at the table of civilisation.[25] They largely ignored the political realities of the French overseas departments in Algeria.

Algerians were born different from each other and the religion in which they were born submitted them to different legislation and authority. 'Colons' were answerable to the civilian authorities and enjoyed a separate lifestyle in segregated neighbourhoods and properties. The colons were themselves divided according to their origins. Maltese and Spanish immigrants were only slowly mixing with the French colons. Jews and Muslims were answerable to the military authorities, who ruled a form of protectorate respecting traditional community leaders, religious laws and policing.

This separate development policy was largely a pragmatic answer to the peacekeeping priorities of colonisation. Algeria was a vast country with many mountainous and desert areas, and could only be 'pacified' with the co-operation of the native population. Bugeaud had only managed to end armed resistance to the French by favouring one tribe over another, one member of a *Qadi* ruling elite over another. Even though the Algerian justice system of *Qadis* had lost much of its jurisdiction in favour of French criminal courts after 1841,[26] its autonomous existence and jurisprudence based on the *sharia* law remained a reality the colonist lived with. Islamic taxation was maintained and added to the French tax-load. In all these aspects – property law, elite rulings, petty justice, religious customs and laws – Algerian natives carried on living in the shadow of the French empire as they had lived under the Turks. There was a major difference, however, in that while the Turkish empire of old was a distant and feeble master the French were proactive, and some intended Algeria to become an integral part of France.

This was not a universal priority, however, and Orientalist and anti-Semitic settlers portrayed an idealised picture of willingly subservient and politically liminal natives opposed to the non-combatant Jew.

The Arab is the vital force of Algeria, he is our equal in self-denial and valour on the battlefield, besides he is the owner and worker of the land. The Arab will never claim [French] citizenship because that would be a denial of his nationality.[27]

There were some serious tensions in this colonial society. Much pressure came from the white settlers, who increasingly opposed the 'archaic' nature of this condominium and the division between civilian and military jurisdictions. They relentlessly demanded a simplification of laws and statutes, which would make Algeria fall within the common cradle of Roman law, individual ownership and judiciary.

Until 1870, the French army maintained a principality over the natives which was enshrined in Napoleon III's views of a Muslim kingdom twinned to and subsumed within the French empire.[28] There were many tensions between the colons, always eager to acquire more Arab land, and the increasingly dispossessed natives. Through the *Senatus Consulte* of 1863 and 1865, Napoleon III's Arabophile policies had guaranteed French citizenship to Arabs and Jews who desired it while preserving the religious and native status of the vast majority.[29] This legislation also marked a step to protect communal ownership from the colonist pressure on land.[30] It did not make all colonial subjects citizens, but it postulated their equality in rights with the French colons.

In spite of this legislation, the colonial establishment and the army promoted the cause of the hard-working colons against the 'indolent' and occasionally 'savage' natives. Recent detailed studies have pierced the myth of a benevolent army protectorate and have shown that there was a large amount of collusion between civilian and military elites to exploit and dispossess the colonised.[31] The imperial travel of 1865 had revealed the tensions between colonising and metropolitan administration and had led the imperial administration to consider two levels of citizenship, one at birth and one acquired. Full French citizenship would thus be acquired and would reflect assimilation in the social and political mould.

While all Arabs were French, and thus entitled to become civil servants or officers, they would require an administrative procedure to become fully French and obtain full citizenship rights. The same applied to the Jews or foreigners residing in Algeria for more than three years. In practice, renouncing the *sharia* or Mosaic laws was too great a price to pay for most devout Muslims and Jews.[32] The Catholic Church, led by Mgr Lavigerie's archbishopric of Algiers, entered a more active phase of conquest aiming at the full religious assimilation of the Muslim people, a religious crusade that entailed full citizenship. Only the Jewish French community wanted an enforced nationalisation of North African Jews. This law in fact accelerated the Mediterranean input of Spanish and Italian emigrants, who helped increase the colonial pressure for land.

A major agricultural crisis of 1866–9 and the localised famine that ensued had also increased political tensions in Algeria. During that period the colonial people, many of whom had been deported to Algeria for political reasons in 1848–51, associated themselves with the Republican cause, creating the specific politics of an ethnic minority and placing the colonial future at the heart of what Prévost-Paradol called *La France Nouvelle*. Republicans and colons advocated the French law approach, which would undermine tribal society and accelerate the decline of native culture. This assimilationism was cynically using the discrepancy between French law inherited from the Revolution, which had made all minorities part of the French nation, and French metropolitan policies, and protected the Arabs from the colonial enterprises. Assimilationists were also actively fostering the 'ethnic' divisions that French colonists defined between mountain dwellers (Kabyles), migrant Arabs and mixed Arab and Turk town dwellers.[33] The Kabyles were deemed to be well on their way to full assimilation, while the Arabs were held in contempt.[34] This ethnographic knowledge had produced a discriminatory policy towards the natives, which replicated in many ways the Turkish practices of favouring one tribe over another to maintain peace.[35]

In 1869 and 1870, the liberalisation of the empire witnessed the weakening of the Arab kingdom ideal, as it was defeated in parliament in March 1870 by an amendment of Favre, Gambetta and the members of the opposition. This first step led to a greater assimilation of Algeria to France and therefore a greater domination of the Arab people.[36]

In this increasingly tense situation, where the Arab people clearly lost ground on a daily basis, it is difficult to assess what the native population thought of their rulers prior to 1870. The sources we have at our disposal are few and were preserved when they ended up in the hands of *bureaux arabes* of the empire. As a result, historians have had lingering doubts of their validity as the Algerians' views on their rulers. In fact, it seems that the picture is more complex and that the suspicion of manipulation by the French may be overstated. The following document, coming as it did after the fall of the Second Empire, would have been ill advised, and it seems unlikely that the *bureaux arabes*, who were already endangered by the new republican order, would have committed themselves to such a demonstration of fidelity to the empire on 9 September.

> We have just learnt that the enemy has made the emperor prisoner. We beg you to tell the marshal [Palikao] to ask the Prussians to release him and maintain him on the throne. The Muslims of the three provinces [Algiers, Constantine, Oran] offer to pay the ransom. We also wish to tell you that what would be best for France would be peace.[37]

The letter was signed and sealed by three major leaders of Algeria: Mohammed Serif, Caid of Biskra, El-Hadj Mohammed El-Mokrani, and El-Hadj Ahmed Ben Sukkaz, who later led the insurrection against the French. Their interests were so interwoven with those of the French imperial administration that this message would be consistent with their uprising. The collapse of the empire was thus largely the end of a protective regime, even if a largely weakened one.

The Algerian debates on citizenship were to be made more central through the famous Crémieux decree.[38] Adolphe Crémieux, working in Tours with Gambetta, became the member of the national defence government concerned with Algerian matters, and his decree nationalised the whole Jewish community on 24 October 1870. The same decree gave a civilian administration to Algeria, jury trials (from which anti-Muslim Jews were excluded) and a governor, Henri Didier; it also allowed for municipal elections. Algeria began to resemble France, at least as far as the text of the law was concerned.[39] Its spirit was very different, and led to dramatic conflicts.

This nationalisation of the Jewish community, which forced the Jews to abandon Mosaic law, demonstrated to Muslim revivalists the dangers of assimilation and the risk presented by Crémieux's 'Jewish dictatorship'. This partly led to the 1870–1 insurrection against the French.[40] One of the great paradoxes of the situation in Algeria was that the arms-bearing community which served during the war in Turcos regiments was short-changed in favour of the most pacific minority of Jews, ordinarily town dwellers, merchants and craftsmen. In terms of the logic of exchange and recognition previously discussed in the context of the National Guardsmen of France, it becomes clear that a fundamental bond between subjects and rulers was broken. The feudal link between the great Arab leaders and Napoleon III was almost certainly overplayed by republican publicists, but the real link of vassalage between arms-bearing volunteers and colonial masters was challenged.

The Jewish community realised that service was now required, and many an anti-Semitic source stressed the parades of Jews through the streets of Algiers and the conflict to which they gave rise.[41] On 25 February 1871 a riot developed from an incident:

> A native child unloading a cart of building material was pushed around by a *tirailleur* [Jewish unit]. The child insulted the latter who replied with some insulting words on Islam… Couput, a wood merchant who witnessed the incident, blamed the behaviour of the captain of the Israelites, who had begun to hit the unarmed natives with their rifle butts; he then authorised the [natives] to come into his shop to equip themselves with batons.[42]

What had begun as an incident where, characteristically, the colonists and the Arabs united against the Jews, turned into a full pogrom. Two Jews were later assaulted by men dressed as Europeans, and the authorities chose to condemn two Muslim natives for the assault. Less than a week later, the pogrom was generalised across the market towns of Algeria.[43] The administration seized the opportunity to dissolve the battalion of Israelite *tirailleurs*[44] and press for removing the Jews' citizenship.

France has wanted to raise [the Jews] to the rank of French citizen, as a group, without understanding that this would cost us the love and esteem of the Muslims who alone have fought for us. The decree of 24 October is unconstitutional, it gives whole peoples the quality of French citizen which was not bestowed to the Arabs.[45]

This disingenuous telegram from the prefectoral office made its anti-Semitic point on behalf of the disenfranchised but idealised Arabs with a depth of hypocrisy common in Algerian matters.[46] On 21 July 1871, an aborted project to reverse the decision of 24 October 1870 fed further anti-Semitic passions. Within army ranks, there were repeated calls to avoid creating 'Jewish battalions in our army'.[47]

The Arab population undoubtedly opposed the assimilation of Jews into the French ruling community and often voiced their disagreement loudly, but it was the French anti-Semites who later emphasised this long-standing and often dormant ethnic conflict.[48] They, like Edouard Drumont, the author of *La France juive* (1886), praised the oriental myth of the noble Arab to better hate the vile Jew.[49] Anti-Semitism in Algeria took off remarkably well, and if it praised the Arab occasionally it also allied with Algerianism, the dream of an ethnic cleansing of Algeria, which expressed the desire of annihilating any Arab identity.[50]

Looking at the situation from an Arab point of view, the insurrection of 1871 was more a revival of Islamic identity against a set of legislative measures which threatened the *sharia*, the end of tribal laws and land-owning practices and the domination of the colonial invaders, including the much despised Jewish community. It was not only the last blast of religious violence: the financial situation was also crucial. The lifting of the moratorium on debts, which precipitated discontent in Paris after 18 March, also led Arab leaders to reach for their weapons. Many of the chief leaders on whom the imperial administration had relied for the relief of the tragic famine of the mid and late 1860s had borrowed large sums to maintain their almsgiving at the level required by their status. The military administration, led by MacMahon, had implicitly underwritten their debts.[51] By 1871, the collapse of the military domination of Algeria and the end of the empire meant that the underwriters proved unwilling to keep their word, and the bankers became increasingly nervous.[52] Many traditional leaders' fortunes were dented, while the Algerian republicans threatened their political status.

The departure of the protector Napoleon III and the *bureaux arabes* led to the full blown insurrection of Arab and Kabyle tribes in February and March 1871. The insurrection dominated large parts of Algerian territory and ended the colonists' dreams of an autonomous white Algeria. Administrators reported regularly on the growing unease arising from the distant echo of French defeats. The rumours that France might disappear or that the Prussians would make a landing in Algeria made colonial authorities aware of their vulnerable position in the absence of many of the army's normal garrisons.[53] Rumours of Turkish military activities in neighbouring Libya increased this unease.[54] The rebellion started in earnest in the spring and was militarily quite successful, with a full siege of Bougie, an important city on the northern coast, and the reduction of the French-controlled land to a narrow strip by the sea. The French colonists reacted to this threat by massacring the Arabs in their communes, and the war deteriorated further, with atrocities on both sides.

Republicanism and colonial racism united in anti-Muslim anti-clericalism which denounced El Mokrani, the French-appointed Bach Agha – the chief native leader – and the *Jihad* led by the Muslim Kh'ouân clergy.[55]

The violent repression of 1871 went in parallel with the repression of the Paris Commune. The French military returning from France created raiding *colonnes*, with the available soldiers including released prisoners from the penitentiaries. The three forces reached deep into the insurgents' territories and exacted terrible reprisals. This tradition of wars of destruction and raids was combined with the appeal for submission or *aman*, a traditional way of negotiating peace using compensations and fines to settle the dispute.[56] The army renewed its colonial tradition without any regard for the new political order it was protecting. The laws of European war did not apply, and neither did the French *Rights of Man and Citizen*.

The extreme left of the political spectrum was also the section most keen to dismiss the Arab people and condemn their traditions as the remains of feudal practices. In this, the left followed the great lines of anthropological thinking, which projected the historical heritage of Europe on to other people and societies. Arabs were thus no more than early feudal French victims of antiquated customs and barbaric religion. Delescluze, the leader of the Commune of Paris, had had some prison experience of Arab warlords held for rebelling against the French. He described them thus:

> The few dozen circumcised men, more or less sentenced, that the Gendarmerie brought to us over five months, were of the same mettle as the ones that they had left in Africa … as to their moral dignity they had none … their faces, lit by their fiery eyes, did not announce a lack of thought, but their features betrayed their sly ferocious nature, recalling that of the panther, always ready to leap on its prey.[57]

Delescluze did not belong to any bigoted racist coterie, and his usually moderate views made his opinion of Arabs all the more striking. The great irony was that the republicans of the Commune ended up in New Caledonia with the men of El Mokrani, and they eventually joined forces with the colonial forces to repress a Kanak revolt.[58] The limits of the republican message or of the values of equality and brotherly love could not be better summed up. The trial of 'the witnesses' that followed the repression of the insurrection took place in Constantine in 1873. Its proceedings led to widespread denunciation of the army. Republican lawyers, including Jules Favre, accused the army of organising the insurrection to maintain their protectorate.[59] This widely reported trial enabled major figures of the 4 September administration such as Jules Favre and Jules Grévy to invest in a sympathetic political platform and further associate republicanism with Algerianism.

Defending the chief leaders of the insurrection, Grévy and Favre attributed much of the blame to the army's *bureaux arabes*. The trial further denied the Algerians any autonomous political thinking or will-power. The main leaders of the rebellion perceived this conflict between military and civilians as a way of escaping punishment, and it worked: two-thirds of the accused were acquitted.[60] The *bureaux arabes* did not recover from this attack, and with them perished the last traces of official military paternalism. The trial and the repression of the insurrection also enabled a cynical advance of colonial interests. The *gouverneur général* thus reacted to a rumour that the president might declare an amnesty: 'This would be to lose the fruit of my labour over the last two years to reconquer for colonisation all the lands wasted on the indigenous people.'[61]

In destroying the tribal and clerical order of Algeria, the conservative republic abolished an *ancien régime* and balanced the repression of the left by a repression of the right, albeit native North African. As a consequence, assimilationism progressed through the enforced eviction of 500,000 hectares of land, the implantation of missions and mixed communal structures. This emphasis on a radical change of land-ownership rules enabled the rapid expropriation or piecemeal purchase of Arab land. The measure underlines the fact that the republican order was, of all the political systems of nineteenth-century France, the one which held individualism as central. By the late 1880s, 655,602 natives were administered by 'fully established communes' dominated by the colonists, while 2,164,190 were in the mixed administration communes. The latter, it was hoped, could be annexed to the fully established communes in order to enjoy full municipal rights – in other words, to complete the disenfranchising of the native people.[62] Algerian communal ownership was a screen protecting large pastoral wealth and the domination of feudal elites. In targeting traditional land ownership, the settlers wished to destroy the political and social grounding of native aristocrats. This practice was not uniquely the fruit of a specific colonial practice, however, as throughout France at the same period much of the communally owned land was carved out and redistributed.[63]

The image of the Turco, naive child of French colonisation, faded away. The Arab people, 5 per cent of the people of greater France, were denied any identity, becoming natives (*indigènes*), losing even the name of Algerians in favour of the colonists, who were reinforced by the implantation of Alsatian and Lorrain refugees who had left their homes in the German empire.[64] There is real irony in this displacement of citizens of an unwanted empire into another where they became, in turn, the exploiters.

Jewishness and French identity

The Jewish religious identity was therefore twofold: 156,000 Jews in the metropolis and 29,000 in the community enjoyed different levels of integration. The *consistoire*, a formal organisation of the Jewish community, gave official status to the metropolitan Jewish community, which, as Nord has clearly shown, enjoyed a well-established position in French society and some strength in eastern regions of France. The Jewish community had their elite and their openings in the Second Empire, but on the whole their support was for the republican values which had given them full citizenship. Major figures of the new republican administration were Jews – Camille Sée, Leven, Eugène Lisbonne, and Crémieux – and 1870 represented a breakthrough for republican Jews.[65] This does not mean that all Jews were republican or that the whole community was perceived as such. During the war, the *consistoire* made many important demonstrations of support, and in general the Jewish support for the war effort was well received. In Bordeaux, the prefect chose to emphasise the patriotism of the Jewish and Protestant members of the community the better to castigate the Catholic bishop.[66] The conservative paper *Salut Public* widely reported the activities of the rabbis and spoke in favourable terms of the Jews' efforts:

> Sir, I have just read in your valuable sheet of the 8th an article in which you report for your readers a letter written by one of our bankers in Paris and in which you mention in a most generous way the French Israelites. All Israelites will read with emotion these flattering words … Yes sir, the children of Israel know their duty towards the dear motherland, and when they would have sacrificed their fortune and life they would still be owing to her.[67]

This did not stop the same newspaper from blaming the Jews for the events in Algeria a few months later. The Crémieux decree aimed to follow the great revolution enfranchising Jews, but it also followed the many Jewish plans to integrate this isolated and largely illiterate community within the enlightened modern Jewish world. North African Jews were the 'natives' of French Jews, who considered them not a little unpolished.[68] The 1858 *Report on the Organisation of the Israelite Religion in Algeria* proposed to enshrine metropolitan influences in the organisation of the Algerian synagogues.[69] This assimilation of the Jewish community in France was not unanimous, but although there are anti-Semitic comments in the press and in historical accounts of the war these tend to be passing references.[70] The French army and the administration included many Jews, so that the 'Jewish question' which later poisoned the atmosphere of Third Republic politics[71] was not an 1870 phenomenon.[72]

The enemy within was then identified alongside racial stereotypes, which pre-existed but did not carry the same meanings. In fact, when internationalists and cosmopolitan revolutionaries were denounced, these terms, so often associated with Jews in the 1890s,[73] in 1871 referred mostly to the German, Polish[74] and other Hungarian members of the Paris Commune.[75]

Republican religions: Protestants, Freemasons and Freethinkers

A similar story could be told about Freemasonry. Freemasons in France had been reorganised under the empire. Prince Murat had thus been made the master of the majority obedience in France, the Grand Orient de France (GOF), while the Scottish rite was also subordinated to administrative and political control. The empire was well aware that much republican opposition found an opportunity to elaborate political and philosophical views in Freemasons' meetings, but it was able to intervene when groups pushed their revolutionary ideals too far.[76] While, in Louis Andrieux's words, 'in the provinces, Masonic lodges were the only place where beginners could find a free platform', their freedom was limited by the presence of spies and informers.[77] In Lyons, the Lodge of the Children of Hiram had been dissolved in 1859 for anarchism, and when in 1862 twenty-seven of its members reassembled in a new Lodge of Tolerance and Cordiality, they were subjected to the closest possible investigation. The lodge subsequently had to join the Scottish rite to avoid the censorship of the new Grand Master of the Grand Orient of France, Marshal Magnan. Police reports on some of the most prominent lodges in Lyons, those of the Friends of Truth and of Tolerance and Cordiality, give us some idea of their composition. The number of workers and artisans was seventeen and nine respectively: while the Friends of Truth had eight soldiers and only seventeen members of the petite and middle bourgeoisie, the more politicised Tolerance and Cordiality counted twenty-three middle-class members to nine workers.

We only have impressionistic views on the activities of the Freemasons, but the police claimed to give relatively precise data which, on the whole, showed that most Freemasons were liberals. The 'advanced' liberals formed a substantial minority, while there was a rump of Bonapartists.[78] The argument, supported by Nord, that the Freemasons served as a school of republicanism seems unassailable, but ought to be moderated by the small scale of its activities and recruitment.[79] There were many lodges, but most were small. In religious terms, the GOF in France remained largely theist until 1877, and many Freemasons cultivated a form of religiosity, which co-existed, with some difficulty with the Church's growing intolerance of these groups.[80] The whole Freemasonry movement had been excommunicated for a long time. The 4 September revolution was welcomed by Freemasons' institutions; indeed, many republicans were members of Freemason circles.

In Lyons, where the Freemasons had been particularly active, the ten lodges of 1861 had grown into an even larger number by the end of the empire. They provided the staff of the public salvation committee and much of the republican elite. Freemasons also had a number of supporters in the armed forces and thus

represented the centre of republican sociability. This explains the political attitude of French Freemasonry in 1870. When political differences were constantly
revived and made more acute, the Freemasons reacted as the broad church of
the new philosophy. This coming out into the open took place in any major
Freemasonry centre: in Paris, for instance, the GOF created its own ambulance,
which like Catholic or Protestant ambulances emphasised its role in French
society as a moral force. It also encouraged proselytising.

There was nothing conspiratorial about the Freemasons' omnipresence in
1870. Their lodges had been the welcoming places of republican thinking, and
their members often belonged to the Freemasons just as they later belonged to
political clubs like the rue Grolée in Lyons.[81] The report of the prefect of 1875
seems to prove that the Freemasons became more actively republican under the
republic than they had ever been under the empire:

> Under the empire, any lodge invested by the GOF could function
> without a special authorisation (ministerial circular of 12 November
> 1872). Since the fall of the empire, Freemasonry has escaped the very
> timid leadership of Marshal de Magnan and General Mellinet; it is now
> devoted to disorder, and provincial lodges have become the refuge of all
> the unhappy bourgeois radicals, barristers, doctors, teachers, busi-
> nessmen … In Villefranche, Jugny and Chassin, ex-members of the
> public salvation committee who had signed the most violent posters of
> the revolutionary periods, who had been tried and condemned in 1872
> for their affiliation to a secret society [have created] a lodge which is
> nothing but an electoral machine for the next elections.[82]

This message, sent in 1875 in the final years of the moral order, makes an
interesting point in that Freemasonry became far more republican under the
indecisive republic than it had been as a conspiratorial organisation beforehand.
The images projected on to the secret organisation thus tended to be myths
rather than reality.

During the Commune, Freemasonry had a fair number of brothers on both
sides of the barricades. The Parisian Freemasons openly called for a cease-fire
and were supported in this by other political and religious groups, including the
Catholic Church. Where they went further was in parading their banners on the
walls to call for an immediate cessation of the hostilities. When this failed,
leading Parisian Freemasons called for Freemasons to support the Commune.
Not surprisingly, given the intensely constitutional and devolved structure of the
organisation, this call did not ally the entire movement to the insurrection.

Characteristically, this association with the Commune did not condemn
Freemasons during the bloody week of May 1871. Indeed, the Masonic ambulance used its contacts on the Versailles side to preserve the rue Cadet
headquarters and patients.[83] Again, the Freemasons maintained their identity
through a broad understanding of citizenship, which bridged the divide among

republicans but gradually became more strongly associated with the anti-clerical and secularist definitions of the republic. Anti-clericalism in France had a long history even before the Revolution but, as René Rémond has shown, it developed greatly after the Revolution had fundamentally undermined the clergy's hold over the French. In many urban centres, anti-clericalism in 1870 was organised through campaigns for publicly funded and controlled primary schools,[84] secular funerals, the odd sausage feast on Good Friday, singing clubs poetically named 'L'harmonie Gauloise'[85] and openly secularist free-thinking clubs.[86] Some republican leaders, such as Andrieux in Lyons, even travelled to Italy for an anti-Synod radically opposing the Church's own. Freethinkers were often republicans, and their cult of citizenship and nationality was one of exclusive definitions denying the Catholic Church's sway over conscience. As the Catholic Church undertook to radicalise its anti-modern message in the 1860s, the anti-clerical message became more violent.

In North Africa, as seen earlier, anti-clericalism could also be used for exploitative purposes. In France it was used to attack the last symbol of *ancien-régime* values and kept alive some of the revolutionary rhetoric. In Lyons, for instance, *L'Antéchrist, Journal Anarchiste* clearly expressed its fundamental programme through its title and sub-title (*No more saviours!*) while it used the revolutionary calendar.[87] Denis Brack's newspaper *L'Excommunié* had a print run of up to 6,000 copies[88] while the *Catechism of Free Thought*, published shortly after the war, had a print run of only 500.[89] Anti-clericalism also reflected a long-term disaffection with practices, and the breaking down of ties which had been binding in a rural society. Religious observance had lost its relevance in an urban environment even for the most newly arrived. Furthermore, the chasm between priesthood and people had widened. The material dimensions of religion, the cost of religion and the constraint on politics and sociability all played an important part in the making of an almost equally sectarian anti-clerical church among French peasants and workers of the late Second Empire.[90] The clergy was fully aware of the enmities it might encounter in large urban centres. The bishop of Saint-Brieuc, wishing to go through Lyons, thought it advisable to write a letter to the prefect asking for a pass. He concluded his letter with the lines: 'what can alone save the republic is to convince France to respect all that is good and legitimate'.[91] In his mind, the Church was both good and legitimate, but these were precisely the two contentious points. Religious legitimacy, enshrined in the Concordat, was the target of the secularists, who almost without exception wanted a complete and thorough separation of Church and state. As for the good of religion, it was undermined by the gothic exploration of the obscure secrets of the monasteries and the dark mysteries of the Inquisition.[92]

Anti-clerical achievements in 1870 were far-reaching. For instance, many municipalities seized the opportunity to open new secular schools, sack congregationalist teachers, mobilise clergy into the National Guard and assess the value of clerical wealth in order to prepare for a separation of Church and state. Montpellier opened a secular school as late as 1 June 1871,[93] while Lyons secularised its local schools as early as 2 October 1870.[94] Even though some moderate republicans wished to distinguish secularism from atheism,[95] the campaign was deeply anti-clerical.[96] The religious congregationalist schools were closed down and the Jesuits' headquarters occupied, as were the buildings of many other religious orders.[97] The clergy did not remain passive to this attack: the congregationalists reopened their schools in neighbouring locations while giving practical support to the children who followed their ordained teachers. The municipal schools were led to protest that

> today this help [St Vincent de Paul, etc.] is going amiss, and in almost all our schools this has become the reason why parents are turning away and are continuing to give their children to the congregationalist schools, established in other locations at their own expense.
>
> This being the case, it is the duty of the municipality to respond and to replace religious almsgiving, which is granted at the cost of conscience, with a free legal distribution to the citizen children.[98]

But the battle for the citizen children had only just begun when it became obvious that counteracting religious involvement in a multiplicity of good causes, such as child welfare and help to the dying and the chronically ill, would be an onerous task. While the clerical versus anti-clerical struggle was overtly spiritual and political, its practical application led republicans either to concede defeat – renouncing the abolition of the orphanage founded by Empress Eugénie, for instance[99] – or to invest heavily and reluctantly in a social programme based on solidarity which flirted outrageously with socialism.[100]

Most prominent in this largely unofficial campaign were the religious orders that were perceived as taking their lead directly from Rome; they were therefore foreign to France and, as such, potentially the enemy. The fact that many of them had been reintroduced to France surreptitiously and outside the framework of the Napoleonic Concordat had left them without legal status. They were not *personne civile* or recognised organisations, and had in the hands of their enemies lost any right to the properties they enjoyed. The Lyonese anti-clerical forces therefore used the property laws to victimise the religious orders suspected of proselytism.[101]

Regular clergy suffered far less, both in the provinces and in Paris, even if the occasional seminary school was converted into barracks, as in Aix-en-Provence. Travelling ministers belonging to some distant foreign bishopric were nevertheless viewed as suspicious and were frequently arrested.[102] In Paris, some arrondissements went as far as possible in their anti-clerical policies. Like the Lyonese radicals, they made public demonstrations of the faith illegal: 'Considering that any religious rite on the public thoroughfares is nothing but ostentatious and provoking offensive behaviour, the committee of public salvation forbids any religious demonstration outside temples, churches, homes of any citizen and the burial sites.'[103] Mayors Mottu and Clemenceau of the arrondissements were very actively anti-clerical. Mottu secularised the schools and forbade religious activities in the open, while Clemenceau forbade the schoolteachers of his arrondissement to take the children in their custody to any religious service, as had been the custom.[104] Similar issues arose in Lyons at the same period.[105]

Radicals made anti-clericalism a symbol of their radical identity and, in the midst of a difficult siege, considered religious matters of the utmost importance. The Commune of Paris followed suit, and many of its activists pushed practical jokes and anti-clerical melodrama as far as possible,[106] using churches as clubs renewing revolutionary traditions, although they usually did not prevent the Sunday service from taking place.[107] Many parish priests were persecuted, but some enjoyed total impunity.[108] It is impossible to generalise the Communard experience. Some priests remained and even indulged in open club debates[109] while some of the most fearsome Communard leaders, such as Dominique Régère, a member of the Internationale and mayor of the Latin quarter V arrondissement, remained openly Catholic and even went through with the first communion of his son, Gontran. Tony Moilin, also politically radical, married his mistress, while some of the Communard funerals also involved a religious ceremony.[110] Ambulances and hospitals were forcibly secularised by the Commune, while education was thoroughly revised along philosophical lines. The Church was eventually separated from the Communard state, thus ending, albeit briefly, any link between religious beliefs and the state.

Some of this anti-clericalism was not atheistic. The Protestants, for instance, happily surrendered their schools to public curriculum reforms. Protestants, like Jews, belonged to the persecuted minorities of the *ancien régime* and welcomed the republic. Among the members of the government, a number of Protestants maintained this link between their faith and freedom of thought. The Protestant ambulances also served as a display of their philanthropically active minority. Again, as Nord noted, this whole group, even if still small, was most active and motivated by a sense of isolation. The Catholic Church opposed Protestant values, largely associated with Prussia, as anti-national, while the Protestant churches sought to demonstrate the strength of a social order built on their values as compared with backward-looking Catholic Europe.[111] This was a common belief among reformers, from Guizot to the most radical republican. The Commune of Paris did not have much to say about Protestantism, nor did the Communes in Lyons or Marseilles, yet the Protestant community emerged closely associated with the defeated cause through a number of figureheads such as Rossel.

Uneasy Catholics and the religious divide

The common enemy of all the previously discussed groups in 1870 was the Catholic Church. As mentioned above, it was in the midst of a crisis of its own when the war started. The Ultramontane tendency of the Church was constantly winning ground in the French episcopate, and this 'high church' ideology largely conditioned the political choices opened after the revolution of 1870. The revolution shocked the Church and led it to take a purely patriotic stance in the first instance.[112] The obvious calculation was that martyrdom could offer an alternative to republican cults of secular virtues and would satisfy the cravings of a more high-spirited Ultramontane church.[113] The bishops of Nantes and Angers thus sent their trainee priests to serve in the army: 'either they will fall martyrs for the motherland or they will serve religion in the best possible way'.[114] The archbishop of Paris organised his war chaplaincies[115] and many religious orders such as the Frères des écoles chrétiennes devoted themselves to ambulance work.[116] Other local priests spontaneously joined the forces going through their villages.[117] In the words of the primate of the Gauls, Archbishop Jacques Marie Ginoulhiac:

> Nobody ignores it here; since the beginning of our disasters your souls have turned with greater faith towards Mary; and we have been the voice of the diocese when we brought all our wishes and yours to her mother's heart. From all corners, under her blessed protection, came the answers to our calls to charity, penitence and prayer … an immense effort of charity was made to sustain and encourage the effort made by our country in the sacred interest of national defence. Public national workshops were organised, ambulances multiplied and gifts of all kinds came to alleviate war sufferings or to mend its aftermath. And, while our young men walk to war with the noble ardour that the greatest of causes inspires in them and with the example and encouragement of their fathers, girls, women, mothers of all ranks and conditions have become workers, servants, sisters of charity of our soldiers.
>
> The clergy, as you will know, dear brethren, did not stay behind in this patriotic movement. From the earliest days we offered our services as chaplains or servants in the army and hospitals. Some went to battle with our soldiers. Others were designated for the local ambulances … After all this, how is it possible, dear brethren, that some remain defiant, as if the Church could be anything but appalled by the brutality and political hypocrisy of our enemies, or as if it was reluctant to pay its share of the national duties? … our young legionaries take from a deeper feeling of religious truths the calm dauntlessness of old soldiers and the invincible ardour of martyrs.[118]

In this pastoral letter from the most important bishop in France, the many rhetorical figures are mixed and two major themes appear which are supported by the archives. First, the Church played an important role, and it did not hesitate to develop civilian forms of mobilisation. Second, it was obvious that this effort remained unrecognised and was judged suspiciously. In Lyons, home of the primate of the Gauls, the Church was most contested and attacked. As for the need for moral salvation in addition to a call to the values of citizenship, it reflects the hope that the new regime would place religious values at the heart of its discourse.

On the right, the Ultramontane media, led by Louis Veuillot, entertained the idea of a Catholic republican order even before the fall of the empire, stating in the influential Ultramontane newspaper *L'Univers*,

> Be Catholic and we will be republicans. What we said in a private conversation we are not afraid to repeat here loudly. We will even lower our conditions. We do not ask the republicans to be Catholics ... we will tell them simply: let us be Catholics and we will be republicans.[119]

This relatively moderate position had already been practised in 1848, but the enthusiastic support for the Second Empire or any authoritarian regime with religious values at its heart made such a declaration ring more than a little hollow.[120]

When Veuillot wrote, immediately after the defeat, 'I believe in the republic. Outside the republic there is nothing but dictatorships, all equally sterile and corrupt', he immediately added, 'France will heal and the republic will be the tool. This republic will be established by the clergy and the more intelligent members of the monarchist party; through her even the revolutionaries will become republicans.'[121] His vision of the republic opposed to the revolution was one of *res publica*, a common polity uniting all Frenchmen in a decentralised regional and self-governed society led by its spiritual and social elites. He had visions of a new aristocracy based on merit and duty, and dreamed of a constitution combining a sort of monarchy, a parliament and regional and communal counter-powers. It remained a fantasy which bore little resemblance to the 4 September republic but which expressed the wish to unite citizenship, regional autonomy, family values (required to obtain the vote), traditional hierarchies and religion in a coherent whole.[122]

While Veuillot remained on the extreme Ultramontane fringe of the Catholic party with little chance of ever becoming a supporter of a revolutionary regime, he nevertheless cautiously supported the government at the time of the plebiscite which followed the insurrection of 31 October.

> Voting for the government, in doing what I can to ensure that the majority be the largest possible, I will not act out of love for you, General [Trochu], or for your colleagues, although I greatly respect and trust you ... Up to now I have not felt secure, as I should be, in my rights and my honour as a citizen and a Christian. I have felt on my head and my heart the dirty feet of the scum, and I have despaired of the honour of the motherland ... Nevertheless, General, I will vote for you because you now sound better and more resolute in a long-expected manner. In your words, I still cannot find the Christian nor

even less the 'clerical' who would not ever abandon the Church's cause, but I can at least hear the general and the man of honour who does not want to betray the motherland.[123]

This support from the right-wing newspaper *L'Univers* was not entirely disin-genuous, but the government of 4 September knew it had to manage its relations with the Catholic forces and could not be dragged to the anti-clerical extremes of Lyons or Paris. Mottu was thus suspended while Challemel-Lacour tried to moderate the Lyonese republicans. In Paris, the liberal and Gallican Archbishop Darboy tried to manage open and honest relations with the government.[124] Trochu, the head of the government, was himself a Breton Catholic, chosen probably as much for his moderate views and religious credibility as for his limited military genius.[125] The Church, and Catholics in general, played a very subdued role during the war and were mainly in agreement with the republican government.

During the conflict, the Church made considerable investment in pastoral care for the soldiers and in besieged cities. It also played an important part in the ceremonies for the dead and wounded in Paris. Chaplains were almost alone in travelling between prison camps.[126] Darboy attempted to seize every opportunity to make the Catholic Church and the republic acceptable to each other. As

CÉRÉMONIE RELIGIEUSE DU JOUR DES MORTS, AU CIMETIÈRE DÉVASTÉ DU GRAND-MONTROUGE.

Figure 5.1   Religious ceremony on All Saints' Day in the devastated cemetery of Grand-Montrouge[127]

Figure 5.1 shows, traditional days such as All Saints' and all important religious festivals could be used to pass on this message. This engraving, like many others, stressed the central message of the crucifixion of Jesus Christ who, like beleaguered France in 1870, suffered for the sins of the past and the redemption of the future. This message was obviously available to all believers and fitted with the latest theology and vulgate catechism.

The Catholic military effort was also important and structured around Catholic values. The mercenary troops of the Vatican State had joined a *francs-tireurs* group of *Zouaves Pontificaux*, led by General Charette, a descendant of the famous Chouan royalist leader, adding to a diversity of Breton volunteers.[128] They fought under the sacred heart of Jesus, a recently revived symbol[129] at the heart of the mystical revival mentioned earlier.[130] The battle which led to the virtual destruction of this unit was also the occasion for a touching Catholic melodrama, during which the blood-stained flag was passed from one dying man to another. 'Please tell me in detail, if you know it, the story of the Zouaves' flag. We need such inspiring scenes, they will help us to bear the peace,' wrote Veuillot to Charlotte de Grammont.[131]

Arguably, the Gambetta government neglected the Breton volunteers, who stagnated in the camp of Conlie and were never properly armed. Even though the Catholic armed forces did not win the day, mystic forces were also called to the rescue.[132] The nun of Blois' prediction and a few apparitions of the Virgin Mary at Pontmain even lent a hand in the prophetic interpretation of the defeat.[133] Brother Hermann of the thirteenth century, the prophet Olivarius, the Orval prophecy of 1544, the visions of a Belgian nun[134] and the 'Sybillan oracles of Mlle Lenormand' were all reported in the press at some length.[135] The nun of Blois had the largest coverage. Interestingly, the nun of Blois who had verbally passed on her vision to her sisters some seventy years earlier was named Marianne, thus mixing republican imagery and exalted nationalistic mysticism.[136] Other virgins were crossing the country in the imitation of Joan of Arc, and more secular forms of mystical occurrences, such as new readings of Nostradamus, were summoned to cast a ray of light on a bleak situation.[137] The Catholic media lost its enthusiasm for these prophecies after the defeats of November 1870 except when they claimed that a royalist restoration would ensue from the defeat.[138] Catholic titles then took a resolutely pacifist outlook in January 1871.

Gambetta's last call for an inclusive definition of French historical identities remained unanswered:

> Frenchmen!
> Think of our fathers, who have left a compact and indivisible France; let us not betray our history, let us not cede our traditional property to the barbarians. Who will sign? It cannot be you, Legitimists, who are fighting so valiantly under the republican flag to defend the land of the old French kingdom; nor you, sons of the bourgeois of

1789, whose masterpiece was to weld together the old provinces in a permanent pact of unity; it cannot be you, urban workers, whose intelligent and generous patriotism always represents France in its strength and unity, like the initiative of a people with modern freedoms; nor you, finally, landowners, workers of the countryside, who have never bartered your blood in the defence of the Revolution to which you owe your ownership of the land and your title of citizen![139]

Instead, the Catholic Church and hierarchy sought more theological and moral consolations for the national defeat. This mystic recourse turned its back on negotiations with the republicans. When the lists supported by the conservative and Catholic press returned a solidly monarchist majority to the national assembly in the election of 8 February 1871, the break became final.

The new assembly, which was predominantly Orleanist and Legitimist, had received clerical support across France and led many clergymen to regard the revolution and the republic as finished, politically and socially. Mgr Dupanloup's letter, published in many newspapers, made this point clear and often appeared alongside the manifesto of the Legitimist pretender, the Count of Chambord. The Catholic Church seemed to be returning to its old royalist masters. Divisions among republicans comforted this choice. The Communard policies mentioned above attached the Church even more tightly to its traditional political anchor. It is in this respect an added irony that the hostages chosen by the Commune of Paris belonged primarily to the high clergy of Paris, the Gallican stronghold of the Catholic Church of France, and included Mgr Darboy. Darboy had been on the left of all the political debates of the period, and was the least effective hostage in the sense that he was more useful to his Ultramontane enemies dead than alive.[140] Indeed, those people who disliked him most later sanctified his martyrdom and used the massacres of various priests in the rue Haxo or in Mazas prison to justify the extremely violent repression of the Parisian uprising. His funeral was the most useful public service the Gallican priest had ever done his increasingly Ultramontane church.[141]

The 1870 crisis came at a moment when the Church perceived its loss of importance in French society and reacted using emotive language and mysticism. The reaction to the Communes of Paris and Lyons were triumphalist monuments, the Sacré-Coeur of Montmartre and the basilica of Fourvière, dominating both cities. These buildings were erected using private funds as two gigantic ex-votos, thanking God for the victory over the socialists and in expiation of the sins of modern France.[142] The Sacré-Coeur basilica occupied the site of the original Communard insurrection and stamped out any vestiges of the Communard Montmartre fort. In its reactionary attitude, the Church intended to show the way and to preach a return to Christian values to reconstruct France. Always pragmatic, the Church also went into the political arena and confronted the republicans in petty claims for damages or losses incurred during the war. The excesses of restoring moral order proved even more damaging.

Prefect Duclos in Lyons did more harm than good campaigning against secular burials, limiting them to before six o'clock in the morning in summertime and before seven in winter, and restricting any demonstrations or collections benefiting the secular schools associated with these extremely popular interments.[143] The prosecution of Freethinkers inspired ridicule, and the Church's political choices soon led to it being in a minority, fossilised in its sentimental opposition to the Republic. There were few Catholics who attempted, like Albert de Mun, to take the initiative on social matters.[144]

This period of 1870–7 was crucial in diminishing the importance of the Church in French politics and in radicalising and generalising anti-clerical views among the republicans and radicals to the point of Gambetta's 'Clericalism, here is the enemy!' The 1870–1 crisis was thus pregnant with heavy consequences for French notions of citizenship and religion. The revolt and destruction of Muslim traditional society asserted a politics of total assimilation opposed to the Muslim culture, a politics and a limited definition of citizenship which recent observers still find in modern French society, where the Muslim faith is second only to the Catholic Church.[145] Over the same period, the Catholic Church, which had a part to play in North Africa in the ideology of assimilation, lost its dominating role in French politics. How distant the spring of 1848 seemed to the men of 1870! Then, churchmen blessed and planted trees of liberty: in 1871, some presided over their felling. This evolution, and the dogmatic retreat to theocratic reaction against modernity, further antagonised Freemasons and Freethinkers of the republican left. Meanwhile, the traditional anti-Semitic and anti-Protestant views of the Catholic Church were applied to a denunciation of socialism and the Commune.[146] From the relatively elastic definitions of citizenship of the Second Empire, wanting in democratic practice but all-inclusive in religious terms, the new republic found its own base and practices narrowed down and expressing an exclusive and, in its own secularist terms, sectarian definition of citizenship.

6

THE ENEMY WITHIN

Traitors and spies, gender and age

> Women everywhere – great signal! When women are part of it,
> when the housewife pushes her man, when she takes the black flag
> flying over the pans to plant it amongst the cobblestones, it means
> that the sun will rise over a city in revolt.[1]

The processes of exclusion sketched out along religious fault lines in the definition of citizenship were not the only ones in French society. Beyond class and
beliefs, the French were divided on gender- and age-related issues. This chapter
is thus another step in understanding the divisions in French society.

The three sample groups selected here demonstrate the wide-angle approach
needed to consider citizenship and exclusion in history. Beyond class categories,
gender provides a much more trenchant instrument for dissecting French fears.
Age is also central to this narrative of fear. The first group, however, is structured
neither by age nor gender, but by difference and otherness: in Michel de
Certeau's terms, an alterity which did not invite further knowledge but rejection
and hatred.[2]

Traitors and spies: defining enemies

In 1870, France was seized by a mania of spies and traitors. German informers
supposedly led the enemy into French territory and guided them through the
most hidden paths. There is something odd in this presentation of France as a
dark and unfamiliar land, full of secret recesses and hidden secrets known only
to the residents and spies. French maps had been available since the monarchy,
and some of the most recent cartographic efforts provided easy and clear
reading. Detailed maps of French railways, roads, canals and other means of
transportation were widely available. Statistical analyses could give any geogra-
pher a clear idea of the size of the population as well as the resources available
to an army resorting to billeting and requisitions for its existence.[3] As for the
forts of Paris, the plans gave a great deal of detail, complete with the walks
Parisians customarily indulged in on Sunday afternoons, which had also been
available to German visitors to the Universal Exhibition of 1867. Secrecy
around weapons was also a straw issue, since all weapon details were known

from the first days of the war, including the notorious *mitrailleuse*, deemed a military secret.[4] There were few secrets in France in 1870, yet according to popular belief the Germans had entertained a crowd of paid spies in the midst of the unsuspecting French people. There was, of course, some truth in this, in the sociological sense that many Germans lived in France before 1870, forming the largest immigrant population along with the Belgians. At the onset of the war the French expelled most of the German residents, with the exception of the naturalised Germans, many refugees of 1848 and those whose children served in the French army. In spite of their 'assimilation' into the national community, they lived through difficult times. Since the French Revolution, subsequent regimes had solidified French identity into something difficult to obtain fully.[5] Even when they qualified as electors or soldiers, their foreignness remained attached to them like a shadow and brought suspicion or downright persecution.

Police files in small provincial archives narrate the ordeal of these people as they were forced to leave their homes to seek refuge deeper in France, as far as possible from the front line, where they were considered with much suspicion and kept under tight control. Intercepted letters signal only too well the zeal of the French police.[6] In a similar way, German commercial ships were held in harbour and detained as war catches.

German origins were defined by the foreign-sounding names and the heavy Teutonic accent, characteristics which would not make for good spying practice as they were shared with the natives of Alsace or neutral German-speaking countries, such as Switzerland or Austria.[7] The whole definition of what was Teutonic, alien and enemy was developed in the press, which also stressed the racial stereotypes defining the other.[8] A young man was thus arrested when, on the face of it, his suspect behaviour amounted to little more than excessive patriotism:

> He was offering tobacco and champagne to the mobilised [guardsmen] of Lyons who did not think they could accept them; he said he was the son of Edouard Frappe, businessman in Mulhouse, and that he was a member of the international society of this city [this could be either the Red Cross or the AIT]. He was carrying several armbands written in his own hand, the hat carried a blurred band and the hat did not fit the wearer at all. The suitcase was covered in foreign labels. A German one, especially, had been scratched off. This suitcase did not contain anything other than letters from the Frappe firm ... his handkerchief had the wrong initials. We suspect he is a spy or at the very least avoiding military service ... 23 years old, almost beardless, German looks and accent, speaks very fluent German.[9]

This racial definition of the heavy-featured, strong-boned, coarse Teutonic invader was more or less developed but omnipresent in the whole historiography and reports of the war. By extension, British people were often regarded as being

Germanic and Anglo-Saxon (an ethnic category the French still apply today, usually with negative connotations) and therefore natural racial allies to the Germans. The image of perfidious Albion and of the enemies of humankind was also deeply embedded in revolutionary memories and practices.[10]

In scientific terms the relevant evidence originated from Broca's racial anthropology, which differentiated races using cranial evidence and created a hierarchy of civilisation.[11] In Broca's philosophy, the paradox was that the French colonial troops did not correspond to civilised types. This racial element of definition was challenged by citizenship. Alsatians, French by citizenship and racially assimilated to the German group or naturalised Germans, presented strong counter-examples to racial theories of nationality. The French law of the land, which stated that being born in France also makes one French, opposed this blood definition of citizenship, which nevertheless attempted to compete and impose racial determinism.

Situations of warfare always stretched the assimilation ideals of French citizenship to the point of disappearing, to be replaced by so-called organicist and hereditary definitions. The spy or the enemy was to be found first and foremost among the nation of the other, among the recently arrived whose antecedents were unknown.

Beyond the more directly identifiable spies who obviously belonged to the enemy's nation, there were many other individuals who were isolated, redefined and threatened by French crowds. While this chapter and the following would not suggest that the situation of 1870–1 compares with the great fear of the French Revolution, there were some common points between the two great scares.[12] One notable point of comparison was the fact that the fear of spies spread to remote corners not directly endangered by the enemy's advance. The irrational aspects of some of the arrests point to a deep fear. A motley crowd dominated by guardsmen usually decided a spy's identity within a few minutes. Victims would then be dependent on the civic responsibility of the guardsmen, either being brought to justice or being lynched or beaten on the spot.[13] Travellers of indefinite origin were thus eminently suspect. In Meymac, a sleepy market town of Corrèze, an unknown woman suspected of spying was surrounded by 150 people and arrested.[14] Salesmen of foreign origin, or even French salesmen leaving foreign newspapers behind, unwittingly took their lives in their hands by looking different. The link was easily made between non-Frenchness and Prussian affinities. The local policeman of Lodève wrote:

> Considering the great events occurring in France, you will perhaps judge it necessary, Mr Mayor, to notify higher authority of the sojourn of this character who, if he is not of English nationality [sic], could be an emissary of that country or even worse, a Prussian spy.[15]

The culprit, a linguistically gifted travelling salesman, had left four copies of the *Pall Mall Gazette* in his hotel.

The police, often deeply associated with the imperial regime, returned to procedures originally developed against the republicans after the 1851 coup[16] and, in the immutable routine of administration, served the new regime with conspicuous zeal in the provinces.[17] This fear was not solely an administrative anxiety. It pervaded most social interactions. In the words of a journalist in Laon,

> Bitterness, suspiciousness, bad feelings abound. Conversations are dangerous. Words do not have their usual significance. We accuse each other in a manner one would be ashamed of if the circumstances did not explain all doubts and suspicions. *Le Courier de Saint-Quentin* publishes the complaints of a citizen accused of 'providing the enemy with information'.[18]

Clergymen were also often accused of carrying information or of using their clerical cloak to hide spying intent. A travelling priest from Savoy ended up sharing a prison cell in Limoges with two typographic workers tramping to find employment.[19]

More confusingly, the local baker in a rural province, such as Jules-Antoine Jaumet, the baker of Pont-Saint-Pierre (Eure, 850 inhabitants), could be tried and sentenced to death by the court-martial of the national guardsmen of the Landes for spying on behalf of an enemy he had never met.[20] Spies were denounced and followed in the smallest villages. Inhabitants of Treignac in Corrèze eyed any travellers with suspicion, and whisperings, repeated and amplified, soon led to a popular arrest. This spy mania threatened many individuals' livelihoods and endangered social order, yet the state and local administrations constantly reinforced the message. Gambetta, in a communiqué to the prefects which was widely reported in the local press, described the appearance and intents of Marshal Bazaine and his officers, requesting their immediate arrest if they were seen: 'Keep your eyes open. If you meet Bazaine or any member of his *état-major*, have them arrested and sent to Tours under strong surveillance.'[21]

Within the political language developed by republicans, the term 'Prussians within' (*prussiens de l'intérieur*) became increasingly useful in singling out their political opponents and negating their national identity. This rhetoric was to be found in Paris, but not in Paris alone, and many of the smaller newspapers of the provinces made similar use of the phrase.[22] This could then be turned against them; when, for instance, in Marseilles, General Espivent de Villesboinet declared that 'considering that the city of Marseilles is now occupied by foreigners in arms supporting an insurrectional and factious government', he had the right to enforce the rules of a regular engagement on the city.[23]

Traitors were also the men who attempted to escape their duty and avoid military service. Other soldiers commonly petitioned against exemptions. The young men of a village near Rochechouart, complaining about the exemption of a domestic servant of an aristocratic house, declared that wanting to leave this aristocrat his faithful henchman, he [the officer] declared Jean Veyretout exempt, to the surprise of all his comrades ... to shoot birds he can hold his gun very well, and we have seen him hunt and we have gone hunting with him ... If the squire Jean Veyretout does not come with us, we the young men undersigned will refuse to go. To avoid any disruption in Saint Martin, make Jean Veyretout leave with us, and we will not spare our blood for the defence of the father-land, which needs us, and everybody will leave happily, thinking that the nation needs its children and will also know how to reward them.[24]

Similar letters abound and show how divisive conscription remained, especially when the memories of previous wars showed that the rich rarely lost their sons in battles. Clergymen were also denounced, and any form of nepotism and support coming from the established authorities was denounced by the comrades of reluctant conscripts.[25] Jealousy and fear fed this distrust of all who contributed to the defeat through their inaction, and there were many ways of denouncing the uselessness or cowardice of one's neighbour. Infirmities were called into question and the crippled regarded as malingerers.

This angst and these conspiracy theories prevailed to explain socialist uprisings and social unrest. Bakunin was thus linked to the Russian chancellery while Gaspard Blanc, a member of the AIT, was denounced as a Prussian spy in Lyons. Blanc and Richard's offer of service to Napoleon III in 1871–2 was later recast as a conspiracy. Andrieux also saw a Bonapartist hand in the March and April trouble in Lyons. This emphasis on the possible links between Communards and Bonapartism was also reinforced by the activities of the maverick conspirator, Jules Amigues.[26]

Secret societies were accorded an inflated importance, and the AIT was consequently regarded as responsible for the Lyons agitation and the Paris Commune where, in fact, it remained a minority force. Freemasons were also denounced and isolated by reactionary authors such as Maxime du Camp. The paradoxes of republican citizenship were made blatantly clear when Valentin, the prefect of the Rhône in 1871, was revealed to be a Freemason and a member of the AIT, and when it became clear that Andrieux, *procureur de la République*, was himself a Freemason and close to many of his new political enemies. The political situation matured so fast in 1870–1 that this anxious denunciation of the other became a way of stating to oneself one's own position in society. This pattern was repeated in every incident of the war, when names were spontaneously and anonymously forwarded to the police authorities by witnesses who were often perpetrators of the drama they blamed on others.[27]

The accusation of treason followed the same pattern. Napoleon III was thus a traitor king by the fact of his own ignominious defeat, and Marshal Bazaine was made to bear the shame of the army, regarded as a traitor for his unwillingness or inability to break the siege of Metz, where he surrendered in October 1871.[28]

The trial of Bazaine illustrates the need to find a scapegoat of some importance: 'we are convinced that the conduct of Marshal Bazaine, who had already contributed to the catastrophe of Sedan, had a nefarious influence throughout the war and was the principal cause of French defeat!' claimed the prosecution, led by General Pourcet.[29]

The surrender of Metz led directly to the Paris insurrection of 31 October. In many ways it was rightly perceived as dubious and as signifying that some members of the military were happier negotiating with the enemy than with republicans. As a result, the Bonapartist army was under suspicion, and in many places the generals of the old army were held under house arrest or even in custody. In Lyons, the prefect arrested General Mazure, and a crowd of up to 10,000 people followed his arrest.[30] In Grenoble, the commander of the place was also arrested. In Paris, the soldiers often challenged their officers, while in the north the Bonapartist Bourbaki found it impossible to establish his authority. The deep anti-militarism of the republican party had been reinforced by the disastrous defeats of the summer of 1870 and by the obvious reluctance to fight a revolutionary war, which went against accepted procedures and routines.

This hatred was reciprocal, and traitors and defectors were denounced in the new republican army. In Paris, professional soldiers ritually humiliated the cowards among the volunteers of Belleville and paraded them through the streets.[31] The volunteers of Belleville and most 'advanced' soldiers had the opposite perspective, and saw in the many inept commands, unprepared battles and sudden and contradictory moves the evidence that their officers betrayed and attempted to bleed the revolution to death. Within the army in the provinces, Gambetta took it upon himself to reinforce military discipline and presided over the execution of a number of deserters. In Mongré, a Jesuit college near Villefranche-sur-Saône, a number of soldiers were thus sentenced to death. These anecdotes reveal the tensions between the army and the National Guard (*mobile* and *sedentaire*) who shared a common defiance for each other, and little else, a lack of trust which appears throughout the historiography accounts; all accounts consider at some point whether the army or the revolutionaries were right in considering the other inept or untrustworthy. What this meant was that the war was conducted as an exercise in divisive representations.

It is the nature of defeat to apportion responsibility and guilt, but the French were perhaps defeated first and foremost by themselves in the way they conducted the war. Gambetta's name was not enough to maintain the coherence of disparate groups in the same uniforms. Even his best and most ardent generals, such as Chanzy, only narrowly escaped public lynching by Communard crowds. The enemy was within as well as without. A logical extension of this narration of the defeat was to include degeneracy theories and to blame the French defeat on a qualitative decline of the French nation.[32]

Threatening citizens: women and war

Anxieties were not restricted to the enemy without or within, however. Wars enable a challenge to any form of hierarchy, particularly when some of the official and social chains of command break down. The argument has been made repeatedly that women, in Britain especially, gained political and social emancipation through their First World War effort.[33] This view has been severely undermined, but similar arguments about other sections of society still hold sway in historical narratives,[34] and tend to imply that wars are a test enabling people to demonstrate their relative social worth and thus push forward an egalitarian agenda. This argument has mostly been deployed in Western Europe about the First and Second World Wars, or more recently about the emancipation of Eritrean female warriors. It implies that in times of war society is more receptive and gender politics are open, offering new opportunities and rewards. It makes patriarchy singularly unfit in times of war, while other evidence seems to show that patriarchal modes of politics are reinforced through war.

The crisis of 1870 could have given rise to a similar narrative, yet it did the reverse. The year 1870 is now commonly perceived as a major setback in the feminist history of France, or even of Europe.[35] The French history of women's rights is long but peculiar in its 'stop–go' spasmodic developments.[36] Before 1870, revolutionary rights and activism had tended to be thwarted in the years of the revolution themselves or immediately afterwards.[37] The great activity of Flora Tristan, George Sand and others in 1848 had a short trail, and there is little evidence of a long-term impact during the Second Empire.[38] In 1869, John Stuart Mill's essay on the subjection of women had also been published in France and had stirred the issue of equality and suffrage, but to no avail. This does not mean that many women did not have some power: some prominent women were at the centre of French politics. The empress had real influence over Imperial politics, as did Princesse Mathilde over the literary elites of France. Female suffrage was not a prominent issue in imperial politics. So it was, therefore, that 1870 represented the fall of a political order unfavourable to women and, with the new republic, the rise of a more open political order, which nevertheless did not pay the full dividends of much female activism.[39] Post-war feminists struggled to make themselves heard in spite of significant inroads in education.[40]

Women's roles in times of war were limited to the extreme beyond the dubious honour of being the archetypal victims and martyrs, often confined to the domestic sphere violated by ruthless enemies. The first part of the war revived and channelled women's work in the middle- and upper-class networks of charitable and philanthropic activity. Women's committees in each department organised bazaars and street collections. With the help and usually the close supervision of male counterparts and administrators, these committees played an important role in their own ways in redistributing some wealth in goods and cash to the families of the men in uniform.[41]

In social terms these groups were mostly the reflection of provincial social life and were thus headed by the prefect's wife and a selection of the most established aristocratic names. The Catholic Church lent its support in most places, except in predominantly Protestant areas where the reformed churches had a similar influence. The type of help given during the first few months of the war was not qualitatively different from that distributed in peacetime, but it was significantly more important in terms of the volume of goods and wealth.

The Red Cross, with its somewhat confused organisation, offered more scope for innovation. Ambulances needed a whole human infrastructure to support the medical effort. For each man involved, there were perhaps five or six women. Gathering *charpie*, recycled items of clothing destined to become dressings, items of bedding, beds and even room-dividers, was a logical extension of homework and domestic chores.[42] Together with the increasing involvement in the management of the ambulances, much fund-raising and direct provision of funds came from women. Within the hospitals, laywomen became nurses, a radical change for French medicine which usually relied on nursing religious orders or deaconesses for nursing duties.[43] Nun-nurses, being devoted and underpaid, provided an ideal and expendable workforce strengthened by the strong revival of monastic orders, which was a prominent feature of the Catholic revival of the nineteenth century.

Women as diverse as Sarah Bernhardt[44] and Louise Michel,[45] the *Comédie Française* actress and the socialist activist, joined Red Cross ambulances. Both embraced the secular version of a sacred vision of womanhood. Sacred ideals built largely on religious tropes and on representations of physical frailty and the responsibility of motherhood.[46] This idealised vision of femininity was at the heart of religious representations, and the recently enacted dogma of the immaculate conception had been echoed vigorously by the Catholic Church, which saw in Mary, the weeping Mother of God, a sentimental and appeasing representation of mercy and love.[47] This Marian cult had a real impact in France in the 1860s; Lyons, for instance, started illuminating windowsills and houses on 8 December, a tradition continued to this day. Mary had also manifested herself in visions throughout the century, most famously to the exalted nun Bernadette Soubirous of Lourdes, but also in 1870 in Pontmain.

In 1872 and 1873 she manifested herself at various shrines.[48] Mary had acquired greater visibility almost than Christ and was deemed to be more accessible than her Son. Church *ex-votos* addressed to her still adorn the walls of many churches and demonstrate her intermediate status between sainthood and divinity. She incarnated the new 'pastorale of love' which dominated mid-nineteenth-century Catholic theology.[49] As a *pietà*, Mary was naturally the symbol of carers and nurses, and had even been picked up as a useful symbol by conservative feminists.[50] Ambulance work was thus placed under the highest protection, but it was severely limited geographically: women mostly nursed in their own homes or in neighbourhood ambulances.

It would be tempting, therefore, to dismiss this kind of involvement as a simple and limited intervention within the realm of the domestic.[51] In fact, the detail of the operations of such ambulances reveal the women's appropriation of the ambulances themselves and of the noble cause, the war aims and even the soldiers. Patriotic examples set out by ambulance workers had their importance and acquired high media importance, especially in besieged Paris. The soldiers coming into the ambulances could literally be appropriated by their nurses who could, if they wished, select their favourite patients for treatment at home.[52]

In many instances, women created the ambulances themselves. As a propaganda tool, ambulances conveyed more than simple feminine values and were deeply reflective of a class order. Dmitrieff and other socialist women like Louise Michel well understood the relevance of philanthropic work when they created an ambulance service, which grew in importance during the Paris Commune as a symbol of revolutionary femininity in action.[53] The *Comité central de l'Union des femmes pour la défense de Paris et les soins aux blessés* established a political programme which simultaneously promoted feminine citizenship and socialism through sacrifice and the protection of the wounded.[54] They relied on the established paradigms while making grand claims for a universal republic, which they intended to defend 'giving like their brothers their blood and their life for the defence and triumph of the Commune, that is the people!'[55] This was a role recognised and supported by radicals. Clemenceau went as far as being a character witness for Louise Michel after her arrest. Considering his own delicate position as the mayor of the XVIII arrondissement, where the insurrection had begun, it was a characteristically courageous act. In giving a good reference, he nevertheless hinted that Louise Michel could be excused her Communard behaviour on the grounds that her mental faculties were limited by the characteristics of her sex:

> This woman has greatly helped the local people during the siege of Paris by distributing foodstuffs and items of clothing. She belonged to the relief society of the XX arrondissement. She was in charge, with Mrs Paul, of the distribution of help in the XVIII. She was sometimes deranged: for instance, I have seen her cry and lament because she did not receive the quantity of food and clothes that she wanted to distribute.[56]

The secularisation of schools and hospitals in the more radical corners of the 4 September republic and during the Commune of Paris also provided many opportunities for female work, and volunteers abounded. More directly relevant to the war effort, some women volunteered to create *franc-tireurs* units; these, like *les Amazones* in Paris, led by a man, and even those formed in remote corners such as Saint-Quentin, gathered more ridicule than support.[57] The fact that soldiers were not in short supply undermined this militarisation *à outrance*. As pointed out earlier, conservatives feared that the militarisation of men and women had led to their greater freedom from the shackles of domestic life, giving them to the revolution.[58] In spite of municipal soup kitchens and basic provisions for paupers, women were not enfranchised, and many had to provide for their entire family.

Factory work, especially in the making of ammunitions and more difficult and intricate assembly work, soon became a reserved area of female war effort in various cities of France. Unemployed seamstresses and silk workers turned into war workers, among whom revolutionary language and ideology flourished. The women involved in the industrial war effort soon became the vanguard of political struggle in Lyons and Paris. All this work was not rewarded directly by the government. The legislative programme of the 4 September government, while rich in democratic reforms of the National Guard and measures in favour of ethnic minorities, remained silent on women. Similarly, the Commune of Paris, like other radical movements, subordinated women's agenda to the national reform of the political world.[59]

It was, however, the tremendous revolutionary work of women during the various political moments of turmoil which later undermined the sanctimonious and saintly imagery deployed through charitable and humanitarian work. The Commune of Paris had a number of women in its ranks, many firing occasionally or helping their soldiers with some Dutch courage – the *cantinière* – or tending to the wounded. They were often portrayed as the harbingers of drunkenness and debauchery in Versaillais sources. The reality was much more prosaic, and the Commune tended towards Puritanism rather than debauchery.[60] Prostitutes were severely repressed by the Commune of Paris, and in the provinces the revolutionaries thought it necessary to reorganise the medical services under police regulation.[61] In Paris, some voices denounced sexual exploitation and proclaimed the abolition of prostitution, but this was never the majority view,[62] and Raoul Rigault, chief of the Communard police, reorganised his services to mimic the imperial police force.[63] In Lyons, the regulation was depoliticised and, as previously, the prostitutes fell under the responsibility of sanitary services.[64] Only the more radical Councillor Durand challenged the law and asked for both male and female partners to be locked up until cured. The radicals responded by asking for the incarceration and penal control of the prostitutes, forgetting, by the time the vote came round, his emphasis on shared responsibility. The myth of the revolutionary orgies has no grounding at all in the remaining evidence.

Representations and realities are more difficult to disentangle when we deal with the role of women in revolutionary activities. Women did get involved, and it was women rather than men who began the insurrection of 18 March 1871. In Chapter 7, the brutalisation of French politics will be analysed in more detail, but it is significant at this stage to stress the role women played in all insurrections, or at least the role that contemporary eye-witnesses attributed to women in all insurrections. These accounts tend to stress female guilt and describe women as the firebrands of most acts of collective violence, although they were rarely taken to court and prosecuted successfully.

There was an important gap between representation and prosecution. In Narbonne or Lyons,[65] women were designated as being the most venomous in their cries and display of hatred:

The women, eager to deserve their noble name of women of Sparta given to them by Digeon, had joined the insurrection in large numbers. It was not only to bring food to the soldiers or to care for the sick that they occupied the town hall; they were the keenest to shout cries of war and death and to prepare the means of defence. The prosecution observes that they played the most dreadful role in the insurrection.[66]

In Lyons, 'women more than half-drunk were throwing pepper dust in the eyes of the policemen'. Pepper was a relatively common weapon which, with the kitchen knife and other domestic tools, served to demonstrate that while violence made women come out in the open, they belonged, even in the weapons they used, to the domestic sphere.[67]

The workers of the ammunition factory, wearing their mourning dresses and following a black flag, led the Arnaud affair, to be detailed later. Women petitioned and gathered in clubs in Lyons[68] and Paris; the major institutions of republican thinking such as the Freemasons might be closed to them, but they developed their own public meetings and even their own newspapers.[69] This political participation was vilified very early on, and the *pétroleuse* myth of incendiary and sexually ambiguous death squads of Communards fitted perfectly in an imagery of revolutionary excess in which women always represented the extreme and most objectionable tendencies.[70] The *pétroleuses* followed the *tricoteuses*, revolutionary harpies of 1793–4 sitting contentedly at the foot of the scaffold, knitting peacefully within a few feet of a flood of blood.

The myth in many ways predated the Commune of Paris and revolutionary women were already tarred with the same brush. The women of Lyons had already been described in these violent terms when the Commune of Paris, which ended in the fires of 1871, added the incendiary element to the picture. Incendiaries and arsonists had been codified in the Napoleonic code as murderers and were liable to the death penalty. Arsonists were thus criminals in civil terms, irrespective of gender, and were not simply political criminals.

The pictures published during or immediately after the civil war illustrated this desire to demonise women as the most dangerous element of the revolution. The series of 'types' of the Commune published by *Le Figaro* mixed lifelike portraits of known Communards, drawn from photographs, and archetypal caricatures.[71] The pictures in Figure 6.1 thus represent almost the whole range of female activities.

These four pictures illustrate the role of women in almost chronological order. In the first instance, the woman is inciting the club; it is she, not a priest, who preaches to the men in the background, probably a reference to the club of Saint-Sulpice. The second picture of a woman on the barricade, brandishing a firebrand and a red flag in a pose reminiscent of the famous Delacroix painting or the *Marseillaise* group of statues by Rude on the Arc de Triomphe, is a cliché of 1871, as it had been of 1848. The third and fourth pictures represent

LE CLUB A L'ÉGLISE

LA BARRICADE

PÉTROLEUSES DE LA RUE DE LILLE

EN ROUTE POUR VERSAILLES

Figure 6.1   The women of the Commune: The *clubbiste*; On the barricades; The *pétroleuses*;
On the road to Versailles

115

women in defeat. In the third, women, dressed in their working-class attire, are shiftily looking around with their menacing cans of petroleum spirit. These are the *pétroleuses*, working-class women in the class war of envy, destroying what they cannot keep.[72] The fourth picture, entitled 'On the road to Versailles', is an unflattering portrait of a working-class matron whose resolute air betrays her undefeated spirit, and thus her guilt. In the background, younger women lower their heads in shame. This matron is the veteran revolutionary mythologised in 1871.

The paradox of such caricatures, of course, was their reversibility.[73] To the violent women of the Commune were counterposed the cruel and degenerate *bourgeoises*, the trollops and whores of Versailles. Communards walking through a crowd of violent women and men remembered mostly the spit, stones and sticks women used to humiliate and wound them. Lissagaray thus devoted a whole chapter to women of the Commune simply to sanctify them and compare them to the prostitutes and *semi-mondaines* of the middle and upper classes. It seemed that even the most polished radical accounts could not break away from the stereotypes of the 'unclean androgyny, born in the mire of the empire, the Madonna of the pornographers'.[74]

Many retrospective accounts of the Commune re-emphasised women's role and, reflecting on the last days of the First Internationale and Second Internationale, they highlighted the revolutionary role of women when freed from clerical influence. Female religious attendance and the use of Christian imagery had made any hopes of enlightening women distant to many ardent republicans. Women were deemed to be under clerical and familial influence, subject to superstition and tradition. Through the anti-clerical rhetoric, this argument was to stick to the feminist cause for the duration of the Third Republic.[75]

What Michel and many socialist women had proposed to counter this argument, in which they believed themselves, was to educate and train women in specific secular institutions, schools and professions. During the conflict itself, the most advanced republicans voiced their concerns that the government might rely on women to make defeat acceptable. 'The people, tired of an aimless resistance, discouraged by the laments of unnerved women and the cries of hungry children, would leave the bourgeois the right to demand the surrender of Paris.'[76] In this portrayal of women as the objective allies of reactionary class structures and shameful surrender, Millière reflected a deep-seated contempt among revolutionaries and republicans, who tended to use a rhetoric referring back to the gender stereotypes of the revolutionary period, explored by Dorinda Outram.[77] Manhood, virility and manly behaviour were central to republicans' self-image and reinforced stereotypes.

At the end of 1871, women's political equality seemed more remote than ever before, especially considering the depth of suspicion coming from both sides of the political spectrum. Increasingly pathologised, hysterical women of the left seemed to be the reverse side of the submissive, clerical creatures of the right.[78]

They were a threat to any political order, and few were the men ready to support their cause when in power.

Odd citizens: veterans and children of the war

To the major myth of a female-led resistance was added that of boys and old men.

> It does not seem to me that we defended well; at the barricade of rue Lepic there were either very old or very young people, almost children; rue de l'Abbaye, at the corner of café Sergent, I saw a bunch of women go by, rifles on their shoulders, *cartouchières* at their sides, their skirts lifted.[79]

The revolutionary legend has recently focused more on the women of the Commune because gender historians, feminists and socialists could reclaim these women in the grand narrative of their struggle for gender equality. Children and old men, who were probably as much if not more a part of this struggle, have been neglected because no one cared to champion them except in the most sentimental terms.

Yet the war, and later the civil war, again offered the opportunity for the aged and under-aged to express their political or patriotic concerns. Veterans were rapidly organised and called to arms.[80] The army suffered from a severe shortage of qualified NCOs and officers. Old men, retired soldiers, were called back to action and led National Guard units to the battlefield. More numerous were those who trained sedentary National Guards to march and use whatever weapons they had. Political veterans such as Martin Nadaud or Etienne Arago served the 4 September republic as remnants of older political agitation and assured the transmission of a republican tradition from 1830 and 1848 to 1870, jumping over years of exile and absence. In these terms, the ultimate glorified veteran was Victor Hugo, triumphing over his old enemy and by then adorned with the whitest patriarchal beard. The old guard placed their own men in the positions of importance, and attempted to infiltrate the administration and army with republican ideals which had been utterly forbidden over the previous twenty years.[81]

This high-profile use of 'experience' disguises the more down-to-earth forms of political and war mobilisation practised by the various volunteers; in Paris, these became watchmen, observing the skies for the next shower of bombs, or police and amateur firemen. For instance, the *Corps civique de sécurité du IX arrondissement* asked to be entrusted with six separate but major responsibilities: surveillance, fire warning, census, enquiries relating to home help, municipal collections, and the distribution of foodstuffs. In fact, most of these activities fell into the hands of the *conseil de familles* of the National Guard, but this unit succeeded in serving in a more limited capacity.[82] Wearing a uniform, these units united the old and the new: they patrolled Paris and defined sectors, sections and blocks of buildings in a fine surveillance grid. They could even have a political role. Treillard, who later became the head of the Assistance Publique, thus used his veteran guardsmen of the Luxembourg quarter to petition the government on pressing matters and revolutionary issues.[83] In the VI arrondissement, similar organisations wanted to act to arrest 'the shopkeepers who exaggerate; the beggars; the criminals; the people who demoralise the citizens; the deserters; the women … who would be a source of scandal and would provoke public disorder'. They also wished to

> protect individuals; to close public places at the legal hour; to protect public fountains [from poisoning]; to arrest suspects and drunken soldiers; to disperse the public singers and musicians who would disturb public rest and would insult the national grieving; and to prevent fires.[84]

This extensive civic role was in practice shared between the 170 veterans of the VI arrondissement and the new body. Some of the fears their programme expressed belonged to the stock of ancient public myths. The poisoning of fountains by enemies of the people was an old recurring fear from the great cholera epidemics of the past, while the puritanical insistence on morale and public mourning was new.[85] The most common position given to the older men who wished to prove their patriotic feelings and protect the republic they had so often seen fail, was that of observer, sitting on house roofs and watching for fires or suspicious characters.[86] These older men were the link with the revolutionary past of Paris.

Children played an opposite role, in the sense that they were deemed to be the future, nurturing the memory of the defeat and preparing revenge. Besides being steeped in revolutionary matters, children were locked out of schools for much of 1870–1 and witnessed the war. They also suffered disproportionately high casualties from the shelling of Paris in January 1871.[87] Projects for various children's brigades were abandoned, and the sedentary National Guards often opened their ranks to admit the younger members of the community as their drummers or musicians. This association of the old and the new was often described as doubly negative when it came to the propagation of revolutionary ideas. The old corrupting the young and the young enthusing the old seemed an ultimately lethal combination. For the under-age National Guard, service automatically granted citizen's rights[88] to bear arms and to vote.[89] The friendly behaviour of some was thus immediately denounced as a corrupting influence and was linked to excessive drinking. Young boys also seemed to take a prominent and symbolic role in demonstrations of the extreme left. During the Arnaud affair, boys were handed the weapons to deliver the final shots (they did not work) and it seemed as if they were chosen to give the mercy shot for symbolic reasons.

Neither youth nor old age was sufficient to protect Communards during the arrests and massacres of May 1871. The tropes of the white-haired revolutionaries had been developed since the Revolution, and Blanqui, the leader of the revolutionary vanguard since the 1830s, was by 1870 an old man, nicknamed *le vieux* by his faithful followers. Delescluze, who was probably the nearest approximation of a leader of the Commune, was an old and broken man in 1871. Age did not save him from the bullets, and prison was not spared the eternal prisoner Blanqui.[90] During the repression of Paris, particular documentary insistence was put on the veterans of previous uprisings, whose crime in 1871 seemed amplified and dramatically worsened by their previous deeds in 1848 and 1851. Killing old men would only have been a crime if their murderers had recognised in them any spark of humanity. The political murders of 1870 had the chilling modernity of systematic dehumanisation. The old were not necessarily the wise, and if the Revolution of 1793 was senile, putting it down was almost an act of mercy.

In terms of youth, the revolutionary wars of the 1790s had seen some cross-dressing and much under-age volunteering, as indeed was the case in 1870, but Victor Hugo's *Les Misérables* had made of Gavroche, the streetwise revolutionary boy, a stereotype of all revolutionary boyhood. It is interesting that gender restrictions applied in the sense that boys rather than girls were later arrested and detained. The emphasis was on the playfulness of childhood, a picture contradicted by the evidence of a harsh and often miserable life which only qualified as childhood through an almost absurd comparison with middle-class younger days.[91] In the fire of May 1871, the children of the Commune were depicted using a new term which would later haunt the criminal literature: 'juvenile delinquent'.[92] As the seeds of unrest, the violent and arm-bearing youth of the revolution, as a gang of degenerate and already hardened criminals, the children of the Commune received little compassion from their executioners. When some of them were spared it was on sentimental grounds, as a whim. Communard and socialist anecdotes played on the sentimentalisation of these executions against nature. The story of the little boy who pleads to take his watch back to his mother and is thus released amidst laughter, only to return a moment later to be shot with his comrades, belongs to the same stock of sob-stories developed in any civil war. The more honest narrators of the Commune thought this one hard to swallow, and issued counter-accounts stating that the boy had been sent to a *maison de correction*.[93] Children did fight in places, however: in the Place du Trône and in the XI arrondissement, prisoners released by the Communards took to the barricades, shooting randomly and ineffectively.[94] The virtues of courage, self-sacrifice and suicidal idealism projected on to the children of the Commune became exemplars of what the Commune could have achieved, and turned these victims into allegories of forthcoming new dawns. The small number of children held in custody after the repression of the Commune, 435 in 1872, reflected the embarrassment of the army authorities with this type of political opponent.[95] If we take the sample of child prisoners held in the Cherbourg hulks on 7 October

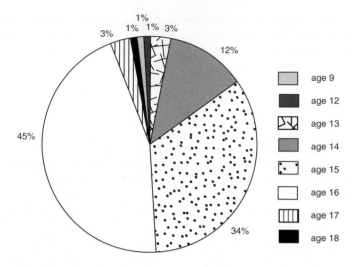

Figure 6.2 Age structure of the children held on board the hulk boat *Tilsitt* in Cherbourg.[96]

1871 (Figure 6.2), we get a fairer idea of who these children were in terms of age, profession and family background.

Of these, half had lost either their mother or their father, and 11 out of 163 were orphans. In terms of social origins, all but possibly 3 were working class, and 98 per cent were in employment of one kind or another. The grouping around the age of 16 is explained by the fact that many of the older children thought they were 16 or used the ploy to avoid harsher prisons. Significantly, most of the arrests were made in June, July and August 1871, after the end of the Commune, on denunciations. Few were arrested during the conquest of Paris, giving credence to the belief that many were executed. We have some photographic evidence of this. Those who were arrested during the bloody week of May were mostly found among the wounded in hospital.[97] The judicial authorities found these little prisoners difficult to deal with:

> Experience has shown that these children, on whom we find it difficult to collect evidence, have at the beginning of their captivity told each other about their acts and participation in the insurrection, and that these are the only ways to get them out of the complete silence they currently maintain.

The children of the Commune were almost invisible and were only arrested because whole neighbourhoods were detained or because someone held a grudge against a little Communard spy. Some of the prisoners, like Georges Denicher, 15, were singled out for their sad adult vice of alcoholism. The reports stressed the family connections of the prisoners and claimed clear evidence of their possible reintegration in society:

> Victor Pinson, 15 years old, placid temperament but light-headed, has worked twelve to fifteen days on the fortifications with his stepfather who was also arrested, sent to Brest and later released when the charges were abandoned [*non lieu*]. Took the 1f. 50 and the foodstuff. Corresponds actively with his mother, who seems to be well disposed.[98]

The emphasis on the 1f. 50 and foodstuff serves to indicate that Victor was indeed a National Guardsman, taking full advantage of adult rates and wages. Ultimately he was released. The role of the forty-eight young Communards kept in Versailles is better known. Some of them were serving in the regular Communard units, while others were taken on to the barricades by their mothers. A few were distinguished for early release. Notes comment on their 'very good behaviour', 'good temper', 'from a good family', 'father and mother separated … receives visits', in spite of their military record in the 112th Battalion. Dissident children, on the other hand, were unwittingly risking their fate. One, aged 10, was thus 'the smallest but the most evil'. In most cases, the family was blamed and attempts were made to hand them back.[99]

When they were not executed in the heat of the action, old men and young boys were treated very differently from their 20- to 50-year-old comrades, and the courts were usually lenient. The boys were thus often returned to families which, for the most part, they had left for an apprenticeship or an independent life years before.[100] Middle-class judges and juries imposed their own notions of childhood on them and often freed them on bail or shortened their prison sentence.[101] Most of their behaviour was addressed in terms of education, influence and heredity. While the latter category offered but little hope, the former allowed the exertions of pastoral care, religious education or re-admission to an idealised and estranged family. Even though these young men returned to their place of birth, they remained under the eye of the police. The orphans were disposed of in Church-sponsored institutions, such as Abbot Roussel's training and reformatory school near Paris.[102]

Processes of exclusion

The representations of youth, old age and gender were not class-free, and nor were those of otherness. The processes of exclusion narrowed down the definition of citizenship to the core of male, law-abiding citizens of fighting age. This is particularly revealed in the preparations for the siege of Paris and the later rationing process. The siege of Paris focused attention on the useful citizens, and calls were made to evacuate *les bouches inutiles*, redundant stomachs who would eat food better reserved for the army.[103] Suspected foreigners, prostitutes and criminals, paupers and invalids were thus evacuated. When they remained, the old and the young especially suffered from rationing. The bulk of the doubled mortality rates could be explained by the sudden inability of the old to keep reasonably warm and by children suffering from malnutrition.

There was, therefore, a dual process in the war effort: one which gathered energies and channelled money, time and enthusiasm in increasingly efficient ways, and another which channelled some of the conflict's violence back against the traitors and the useless elements of society. In practice, adult male citizenship was not such a stable category during the civil war. The age qualification for active citizenship could be challenged and extended to include male children as young as 9 or 10 and older men, but the gender qualification proved more resilient.

In Certeau's terms, the first group analysed in this chapter is relatively unproblematic in the sense that their otherness was official, that the foreigners were recognisable as foreigners while travellers obviously did not belong. The alterity of women, of children and of old men when they sided with a political cause was more difficult: it simultaneously fed the civil war and was a result of it. The women's question challenged the most central tenets of French concepts of citizenship based around the family, of which women were but the passive, stabilising and procreating part. The *ouvrières* explored so anxiously by Jules Simon, a minister of Thiers in 1871, were ten years earlier the antithesis of respectable femininity.[104] The same women-in-arms presented an alienating and frightful challenge to middle-class observers.[105] A paradox here is that this image of revolutionary violence was central in the iconography of recent French history in all historical depiction of the revolution and on French monuments such as the Arc de Triomphe. The recently revived Marianne, like paintings by Delacroix, demonstrated that women possessed an iconic importance in all revolutionary movements, even if, as David Barry argues, this role was essentially passive and meant to be silent.[106]

We must not ignore the romantic image of the Commune as an emancipatory revolt. Parisian revolutionaries often objected to women on several grounds, and the struggle of leading female Communard leaders was an uphill battle. The religious dimension of the gender characterisation of women meant that the last bastion of reactionary forces of Paris was the women protesting against the use of the church of Saint-Sulpice as a club.[107] Children, often active workers themselves, also fell below a threshold of age and maturity, while old men, past productive age, lost much of their importance, social status and even gender attributes in the working or rural classes. The politicisation of all these groups demonstrated to conservative observers that the revolutionary moments were a time of saturnalia, *carnivalesque* in their grotesque subversion of conventions and rules. The correction of this subversive world was to be effected by a thorough repression and a concentration on education, control and protection.

The education of girls leapt forward after 1870 but in many places remained the prerogative of convent schooling. Margadant's study of female education stresses the subordinate role given to *mesdames les professeurs* under the Third

Republic.[108] The professional schooling of young delinquents, the non-political category in which most children Communards surviving the Commune were placed, also expanded, while old age was increasingly protected through pensions and coercive institutions. The spirit of freedom which had inspired these women, boys, and elderly citizens, the unelected representatives of an unspoken two-thirds majority of French people, did not die easily, however. The women who returned from New Caledonia carried on an uphill struggle for their rights. Twentieth-century feminists were able to reclaim these voices from the past and obtain some of the rights they called for. Arguably, children and aged citizens are waiting for them still.

7

THE BRUTALISATION OF
FRENCH POLITICS

Such are our social wars, and we have only just begun.[1]

This chapter represents the culmination of the reflection on exclusion and repression elaborated in the three or four previous chapters, and makes use of recent developments in the theory of brutalisation. The brutalisation of French politics works directly in reference to the work of Norbert Elias and his followers Roger Chartier and George Mosse.[2] 'Brutalisation' has been used as a concept to describe the rising tolerance of warriors to the war atrocities they commit. The concept revolves around the idea of atrocity and postulates the sacredness of human life and the deep political and cultural implications of any systematic use of violence. These liberal values were at the heart of the civic culture of France in the 1860s, and while there had been instances of extreme violence in the June Days of 1848, or in 1851 during the coup of Napoleon III, 1870 represented to many French people a peak of political violence. Taken in isolation, it could either be described as regression to the distant past of the wars of religion and the St Bartholomew massacres, or a sinister warning of what was to come. Robert Tombs has systematically considered the war effort of the Thiers government against the Commune and concluded that this was one of the first instances of truly systematic political slaughter in modern Europe.

Although convincing in broad terms, this analysis neglects the general process of brutalisation, the distance between victims and perpetrators, and the gradual acceptance of the necessity of this systematic violence limited to Paris. To chart this rise in violence and to narrate the decline of French political polity, this chapter examines in detail a number of case studies which were all deemed exemplary or typical in their own ways. It does not represent a comprehensive survey of political murders. There are other cases that deserve attention, such as the killing of the prefect of Saint-Étienne by a guardsman. In this case there were allegedly a number of macabre rituals desecrating the body, and some sources went as far as accusing the guardsmen of cannibalism.[3] The incidents investigated in this chapter all achieved mythical status and distorted the historiography of political violence in 1870. Many narratives of this brutalisation borrowed tropes and images from the pre-existing rhetoric and imagery of crime.

This chapter argues that these crimes were not presented in isolation and that this violence was not depicted as sporadic. The first two incidents of Hautefaye and Lyons fitted within a specific genre of political writing and representation of social dangers and threats, and it is only because they could be integrated so well into this literature that they acquired such national importance.[4] These violent incidents facilitated the gradual discrimination and dehumanisation of the social enemy, a feature that was replicated at the origins and at the end of the Commune of Paris. The following examples of rural and urban political violence will show within which parameters one can read the repression of the Commune of Paris: on the one hand the rural class violence of Hautefaye, and on the other the internecine violence between revolutionaries and republicans. The first instance signalled the unreliability of rural France and its potential for violence if given too much latitude; the following case, the Arnaud murder, demonstrated to republicans that the immediate danger posed by revolutionaries was even greater than that posed by reactionaries. Taking these two instances, we can read the logic of the brutalisation of the Paris Commune and understand more fully the Parisian exception.

Despite the eruption of this violence in many places and despite the crude usage made of these incidents, it remains striking that a full civil war did not erupt. In most places, republicans managed to keep open a dialogue between the forces of government and revolutionaries.

Repression, murder and politics

Political violence in France since the Revolution was much deplored but remained a constant trait of an unstable country in search of a satisfactory constitution. The massacres of the Terror featured in all accounts of the Revolution, while the extensive anti-revolutionary purges of the White Terror of 1814 had left deep scars in the southern regions of France. Since 1830, however, massacres had been less spontaneous and more often the result of harsh military reprisals and repression during uprisings. In Lyons in 1834 and Paris in 1832, 1848 and 1851,[5] the army had killed dozens of individuals in the heat of full-scale military operations.

The use of the military in peace-keeping missions was a blunt instrument of repression which created martyrs, famously so in February 1848, and which could backfire badly when the soldiers lifted their rifle butts in the air to signify their unwillingness to shoot 'the people'.[6] During the Second Empire the army and policing system had been reinforced, and spying on secret societies was pushed to such extremes that the government often had only to choose the time of arrest. The type of opposition violence developed against the empire became far more *ad hominem*, and Napoleon III was the target of several assassination attempts, some of them plotted abroad and involving Mazzinians and British radicals.[7] This level of terrorist violence had its importance, and the many assassination attempts aimed at Louis-Philippe, and before him the successful murder of the Legitimist heir to the throne, had had immense political consequences.

Robert Nye has also shown that ritual violence on political grounds took the form of duels among equals, generally upper- and middle-class men, which were most often tolerated by the police.[8] The famous death of Armand Carrel at the hands of Émile de Girardin had left a deep impression in the press, where a culture of insults and duelling had grown.[9] In this context, the killing of Victor Noir by Pierre Bonaparte, remote cousin of the emperor and black sheep of his noble family, enabled Rochefort to wage an important campaign against the imperial family of murderers.[10] People as different as Michel Foucault and Roger Williams have also noted the importance of some crucial criminal stories in the late 1860s. The Troppmann affair, in which an ambitious and deluded young man slaughtered a whole family, had made an impact as a reflection of barbarity under the cloak of civilisation.[11] The Troppmann story was also to be found in different guises in the *feuilletons* published by much of the conservative press during the 1870 war.[12] *The Parricide*, by A. Belay and J. Dantin, thus played on heredity and violence, on social status and crime. Its central features were the ambivalence enabling a criminal in middle-class clothing to escape punishment for a while, and the confusion between a degenerate bourgeois and a member of the dangerous classes.[13] This particular *feuilleton*, found in at least three local newspapers, also featured a Jewish fence character and played on most of the common fears of urban criminality Louis Chevalier describes in Paris in the 1840s.[14] The notion that crime lurked beneath polished habits, that civility was a cloak of vice, was universally shared, and if the middle class viewed with suspicion their obsequious social inferiors, working-class writers and speakers stressed the superficiality of upper-class respectability. This tension existed in the works of socialist writers, who often took the moral high ground to denounce upper-class immorality and vices. To this class-related perception of the fragility of civility was added a clearly geographic distinction between urbane behaviour and coarse rurality.

The French felt strongly that citizenship and cities were cognate, and thus that the countryside and rural politics belonged to an earlier age of human development. This was a theme repeatedly evoked by leading republicans such as Gambetta.[15] The sentimental work of George Sand, which turned French peasants into romantic good savages, had only served to reinforce this view.[16] The paradox, of course, was that the reported levels of violence pointed to exactly the reverse. The cities were infinitely better policed and repressed than the countryside, which the military police or *Gendarmerie* controlled almost entirely with very few men, but crime rates were part of an urban set of representations. Political repression affected mostly urban centres, and the rural insurrections of 1851 remained an anomaly.[17] In 1870 a number of political cases had shown that the liberal empire intended to use its teeth, and the raids and arrests of members of the workers' Internationale in the spring of 1870 were meant to demonstrate the new government's vigour against secret societies.[18]

With the war, security measures of the empire were reinforced but also weakened by the arming of the National Guard. The 4 September republic weakened the policing apparatus further: it was then perceived as a creature of the empire, and for a short while attempted to devolve policing to local authorities.[19] In Lyons the revolutionaries reformed the police apparatus by hiring a multitude of politically reliable agents, some of whom had an unchecked criminal past. The Lyonese also published the secret police files and tried to shame their opponents. Some of these liberalising measures backfired, but the emphasis on accountable policing lingered on well after 1870, even though the Third Republic was not a golden age of human liberties and justice.[20]

Bonapartist cannibals: Hautefaye

The first great criminal story of the war was the murder of Hautefaye, which has been analysed by Alain Corbin in the *longue durée* tradition.[21] Hautefaye, in the Dordogne, near southern Limousin, was a small village of strong Bonapartist traditions. The local elite was royalist, moderately Orleanist, and therefore suspect to the villagers. The whole incident took place over a few hours during which the young Alain de Monéys d'Ordière came to the village feast, was denounced as a republican – and therefore a spy or a Prussian – was beaten up, sadistically killed and roasted on a spit.[22] As Corbin pointed out, the clear intent of Monéys' murderers was to reduce their victim to the level of an animal.[23]

The press reports inaccurately described the murder as uniting local men, women and children in a mix that is a feature of the description of popular violence in 1870. The men were accused of doing most of the beating and actual physical damage, while the women and children were blamed for subverting their normal subservient position in society by leading the criminal procession and inciting the men to more violence. In fact, there was no unanimity and the murderers had to fight against a few brave souls defending the young man. If there were children, women were not mentioned in the prosecution.

The killing of a German spy, as this young man was improbably described, was not in itself an isolated incident, and a number of well-known cases of public drowning and stoning took place in Paris later with little public outcry. Only the conservative press made the link between the violence that had existed in Paris in the early days of the siege and the Hautefaye murder, to better contrast the outrage about Hautefaye with the oblivion covering up the atrocities of Paris. 'Will the cannibals of Paris be punished, will they even be prosecuted? It is most unlikely.'[24] The theme was to recur during the days of the Commune and in the build-up to its destruction.

What seized the imagination and made the Hautefaye story and subsequent trial a gory *feuilleton*[25] was the roasting of the corpse and its antiquated anti-aristocratic politics.[26] In terms of timing, the Hautefaye story occupied provincial *faits divers* over most of the Franco-Prussian war and served as a stark reminder of rural reactionary violence.[27] Socially located between urban unrest and rural barbarity, the bourgeoisie and the elites felt acutely threatened.

The central feature of the Hautefaye incident was the roasting and alleged cannibalistic scenes. Debunking the myth, Corbin has dismissed cannibalism, in this case limited to talking of human fat as if it were pig fat.[28] This seems the most plausible explanation, especially since most violence deployed in 1870 referred directly to one tradition of killing or another. Mentions of cannibalism were not universal, and it is significant that the local press only mentions the sick joke of one of the participants of the murder that 'it was a shame that such nice fat should be lost'.[29]

The fact that these men and women were Bonapartist supporters eliminating a class and national enemy in a ritualised way was not emphasised so much as the manner in which the killing took place. The slow agony of the victim, also a pattern of many popular executions, reinforced the feeling that society was facing the barbarity of the rural *rustre*, uneducated men forming the plebeian mass. The rural threat to a civilised exchange of views and reasoned argument was paradoxically felt by the imperial regime in the first instance. These were its supporters, and the citizens who gave the Second Empire its rural majority and its democratic credentials. The barbarity of the incident undermined universal suffrage applied to uneducated rural folk. The republicans were defiant of the rural masses, and the Hautefaye incident fitted with their representation of rural brutality. If people reacted with horror, it was less because the incident was incongruous, as Corbin states,[30] than because the murder fitted with dark representations of rural France. News of the execution of the Hautefaye cannibals came on 10 February, days after the elections of the reactionary assembly by the rural masses.[31] For republicans, other rustic barbarians were camping within Paris. The soldiers of Trochu, Breton *mobiles* speaking little or no French, were similarly perceived in Paris as the praetorian guard of the Catholic general and as the perpetrators of such senseless violence as the *fusillade* of 22 January.

Even though Gambetta and urban democrats addressed the peasant and rural masses on a regular basis, they had real and deep-seated contempt that these men who lacked education and the means of civil exchange should share fundamental values and modes of thinking. The same was not true in the Arnaud case, and one could argue that Hautefaye, which confirmed pre-existing fears, had less impact than the later story, which divided the left and shattered some of their democratic ideals.

Street chaos and the murder of Arnaud

The Arnaud story has to be put in the context of the Commune of Lyons.[32] The Lyonese republicans, holding the town hall and prefecture since September, had allowed a very vibrant democratic culture to emerge. Even though guardsmen exercised their petitioning rights on a regular basis and the AIT had attempted unsuccessfully to take over the town hall in September 1870, this democratic culture worked reasonably well, in the sense that most conflicts between republicans were resolved through debates in the public sphere.

The Lyons public sphere, in the Habermasian sense, had been revived by a multiplicity of newspapers, pamphlets and public meetings in clubs,[33] street gatherings and frequent posters and announcements. The deliberation of the town hall had been made public for the first time and even the secret discussions were released into the open a short while afterwards. The vibrant political culture of the left which dominated the city had been validated and revived during the elections. The new municipality reflected this diversity and allowed for very different views and class attitudes to exist within the same government. Members of the AIT could rub shoulders peacefully with a Jacobin anti-clerical like Andrieux, old 1848 Utopians like Hénon, or Hebertist extreme revolutionaries like Crestin. The petitions also allowed for this political diversity, and the following letter, signed by 7,000 guardsmen, referred to 1793 or 1792, depending on the political tone of a particular group, without undermining the fundamental message:

> We hope that the help that we provide, together with your energy and that of the French people, will lead to a peace based on the great ideas of our fathers of 93 [92 in all but eight surviving petitions]. The Republic does not negotiate with enemies which occupy its territory.[34]

This soft unanimity, which gelled on issues such as anti-clericalism, the right to work and national defence, was severely undermined by the Arnaud incident.[35]

The Arnaud story began with a revival of club culture led by discontent members of the Lyonese extreme left, such as Denis Brack, who, while ideologically very close to the ruling power, disagreed on the practice of revolutionary action. Class politics in the Lyons area were not at the origin of this crisis.[36] Arnaud was a leading Freemason, officer elect of the National Guard, father of three and small employer of two, a well-established local republican who had been in the town hall on 4 September; he was a well-known and well-liked man. His death was largely the fruit of a failed insurrection. After the conflicting accounts of a military defeat at Nuits, a gathering of radicals proclaimed the universal republic at the Valentino club. On the morning of Tuesday, 20 December, a revolutionary meeting at the Valentino gave rise to much passion, and a resolution was passed declaring that the guardsmen of the neighbourhood and the women of the ammunition factory were to be called and that the Croix Rousse people ought to walk to the town hall to make themselves heard and support the revolution. In many ways the original plans for the demonstration were what has been called by sociologists a '*cortège identitaire*', a demonstration of identity rather than class.[37] When Arnaud refused to lend his support to a demonstration he considered subversive of revolutionary aims, he removed himself from his own community. As the public grew more riotous, Arnaud was pushed and beaten, and when he tried to defend himself he was accused of murdering the people.

Here versions vary: he was either pushed or fell backwards after tripping on a kerb. Once on the ground, he was or was not stabbed with a bayonet. Arnaud attempted to take out his sabre, failed, was increasingly distressed; pushed, in tatters, he pulled out his handgun and shot into the air. The distant crowd heard the shots, and a rumour spread that a woman and child had been hit. 'He fired at the people!' became the rallying cry of this crowd. Accounts differ on the existence of a trial at the Valentino, but soon after he was sentenced to death. Then began an odd procession, which took him before guardsmen who presented arms, past the local arrondissement town hall to a secluded square, the *clos jouve*, where he was put against a wall and shot.

The event contributed to the fragmentation of republican unity, and Arnaud, that good republican, anti-clerical, Freemason and patriotic father, became a martyr to the dangers of revolutionary excess. Beyond this political analysis, one could relate the murder to other crimes committed by the 'mob'. Through the Arnaud crisis, it is possible to find the resurgence of old psychotropic explorations in 'crowd *mentalité*'.[38] The discourses of horror and repulsion in the 1830s explored by Louis Chevalier and the analysis of the literary response to the Commune of Paris by Lidsky were revived and set in place, respectively.[39]

There is no denying that the story was harrowing. People he knew well, many of whom were his neighbours and even acquaintances, killed Arnaud. The crowd that pushed him to his death was his community. Arnaud had to die, not for political reasons, but because it was believed that he shot at the people and refused to recognise the people's sovereignty.[40] It is probably significant that, in their defence, some of the perpetrators compared his execution with that of the guardsmen of a Lyonese battalion executed at the college of Mongré near Villefranche-sur-Saône. In Mongré the firing squad had 'instinctively in unison missed the target. The condemned raised the blindfold and said, "I am not wounded." An immense emotion arose among thousands of men and cries of "Mercy!", forbidden and punishable by death in such circumstances, were then heard.'[41] In spite of this pleading, the Mongré execution carried on.[42] Similarly, Arnaud pleaded for his life until his death and some voices were heard in his favour, but as in Mongré the executioners were convinced that they were enacting an important judicial decision.

The incident, like all legal cases, appeared in various lights and different versions through the deposition of the suspects arrested by the *procureur de la république*, Andrieux. Himself a familiar figure in the neighbourhood, Andrieux led his enquiry from the house of the local apothecary, his friend Francfort,[43] and, oddly, did not – or did not wish to – implement the arrest of his old friend Denis Brack.[44] Brack was seen in Lyons for another three weeks before he was forced to leave.[45] The leaders of the Valentino club were arrested immediately after the events and designated as the culprits from the early days, but they were not major figures of radical republicanism in Lyons. They belonged to the crowd in many ways. Deloche, the second tallest of the crowd at 170 cm and the only one wearing distinctively petit-bourgeois clothing such as a grey hat and gaiters, was identified as a leader almost by virtue of his clothing. His clothes enabled a more consistent set of witnesses to identify him at every stage of the tragedy.[46] At the trial in Riom, miles away from Lyons, where radicals hoped to obtain the liberation of the accused, the other suspects clearly chose to blame Deloche and isolate him. Socially, Deloche was one of a handful of suspects who had no professional contacts with the other accused.

Deloche's defence was to blame the National Guard for not acting to protect Arnaud. Cornered by a multitude of witnesses who gave him the role of leader in the murder, he ended his defence arguing that his mind had been overtaken by the frenzy of the crowd: 'If my body has done anything, my mind was not there.'[47] A friend of Arnaud's who had known him ten years also mentioned 'emotion' as the reason why he could not save him. Burnier declared, 'If I said "to death" it was only to imitate the others.'[48] It seems strange, if this heated and riotous atmosphere had such a hold on the suspects, that Deloche still found the self-control to ask the crowd whether Arnaud should be killed when he had reached the *clos jouve*.[49] The same Deloche, a few instants later, was seen trying to shoot Arnaud at close range.

This emphasis on mob psychology seems to have been superimposed on the events retrospectively by the suspects themselves, following the lead of the newspapers. It fits with the great clichés of psychology, and might well have been construed as a possible form of defence in a country where such categories of crime as *crimes passionels* led to frequent acquittals.[50] In fact, the defence seems to have worked, for most of the suspects were released.

Other suspects rationalised the murder of Arnaud in very different ways, however, and did not attempt to play the mad crowd scenario. Poquet, a guardsman, thus declared that

> I believed he was being sentenced according to a law and that this case was similar to that of my brother-in-law, who had been sentenced to death by the court martial of the 1st Legion in Villefranche – what confirmed that view was the behaviour of the guardsmen at the arrondissement town hall when we passed them: they presented arms and beat the drums, which convinced me that everything was legal. I thought I was doing something worthwhile shooting the commandant.

This way of seeing the assassination as an execution fits well with the findings of specialists of urban violence, who tend to argue that calls to justice and legal concepts are central to most riots.[51] In spite of this logical argument, however, the suspect declared a few minutes later that his emotion was such that he could not recollect the names or faces of any other member of the execution squad, save, perhaps, Deloche's grey hat. The cause of the execution seems to have been the widespread belief that Arnaud had shot at 'the people'. By shooting at the people, he had betrayed all networks of solidarity and friendship. Not one of his men, friends and neighbours wanted to recognise him. In this sense, the two shots fired in the air were fatal.

At the trial, the captain of the 4th Company of the guard stated: 'The squadron was in two minds. Some of my men said that Commandant Arnaud had shot at the people. Some of my men were ready to intervene but the others refused, saying "he is only getting what he deserves".' Some accounts gave estimates of a 3,000-strong crowd at Arnaud's execution, a crowd large enough to intimidate the handful of armed men of the town hall.[52] Besides, there seems to have been a relative consensus on Arnaud's fate, and Deloche was seen the same evening drinking with the men of Arnaud's squadron.[53]

Andrieux, who knew Arnaud and indeed many of the accused, singled out the leaders of the Valentino club for trial and sought some plausible murderers. Table 7.1 analyses the results of Andrieux's arrests which, much like Hautefaye, were meant to set an example and be representative of the guilty community.

The sentences were not particularly heavy except for two of the accused. Some commentators could not explain how Denis Brack managed to stay in Lyons for several weeks before absconding to Switzerland. Andrieux and Brack knew each other well and they had belonged to the same circles, meetings and lodges. Andrieux had been the president and Brack the vice president of the *Société coopérative d'enseignement laïque*. In 1868 they had commemorated the revolution of 1848 together, in 1869 they had collaborated on the stillborn newspaper *La Fédération*, and in 1870 they had been seen repeatedly sharing the same club platform on 30 April and 3 May.

Andrieux had also defended Brack when *L'excommunié* was prosecuted.[54] There was in Lyons an old bond of comradeship that did not want to die.

When Andrieux chose an expiatory victim, the man he chose was Deloche, a bogeyman of the extreme left, and a secondary figure although he might have belonged to the AIT.[55] As to the execution itself, Andrieux himself believed that the actors of the drama thought they were applying the 'people's own version of martial law'.[56] This belief must have weighed heavily on all radicals-turned-prosecutors and law and order defenders. Their entire education in revolutionary events led them to consider past similar actions as legitimate and justified by the dramatic events. The 'defeat of Nuits-St-Georges', in fact a marginal victory, had enflamed the people of Lyons, and the massacre that ensued fitted in with the supposedly spontaneous instances of the earlier revolutions. This time, however, the revolutionary tropes were not bar-room rhetoric but flesh-and-blood and uncontrolled violence.

The Arnaud incident had immense impact. Across France, the local press reported in amazement the *affaire Arnaud* which fitted so well with the trial of the Hautefaye affair and provided a perfect urban equivalent.[57] It came as the first

Table 7.1   Arnaud's executioners (2nd Conseil de Guerre, 8e Division Militaire, tribunal de Riom, 7 –18 March 1871)

Accusation	Age and gender		Profession		Origins		Sentence	
Enticement to civil war	10–20	1M	Weaver	7	Lyons	5	Not guilty	7
	20–30	1M	Policeman	1	Rhône dep.	2	Deportation	1
	30–40	2M	Journalist	1	Other dep.	3	*Absentia* deportation and prison	
	40–50	2M	Textile worker	1				
	50–60	3M						1
	60+	1M					*Absentia* death	1
Enticement to civil war and murder	40–50	1M	Weaver	2	Lyons	2	Not guilty	2
	50–60	2M	Builder	1	Other dep.	1	Prison (one month)	1
Enticement, violence and outrage	20–30	1F	Weaver	1	Lyons	1	Not guilty	1
Enticement and murder	10–20	2M	Weaver	5	Lyons	8	Not guilty	8
	20–30	3M	*Chauffeur*	1	Rhône dep.	5	Prison (five years)	2
	30–40	4M	Cabinet maker	1	Other dep.	1	Death	2
	40–50	4M	Textile worker	4	Unknown	1	*Absentia* death	2
	50–60	2M	Juvenile	1			Parental care	1
			Unknown	3				
Enticement and accomplice to murder	10–20		Weaver	5				
	20–30	4M	Cabinet maker	1	Lyons	8	Not guilty	12
	30–40	6M, 1F	Textile worker	5	Rhône dep.	1	Prison (five years)	1
	40–50		Public writer	1	Other dep.	3		
	50–60	2M	Unknown	1	Unknown	1		
	60+							
Enticement and accomplice to murder and illegal arrest	30–40	1M	Weaver	1	Lyons	1	Not guilty	2
	40–50	1M	Textile worker	1	Other dep.	1		
Total: 44 accused	10–20	7%	Weavers	46%	Lyons	58%	Not guilty	74%
	20–30	20%	Textile workers	23%	Rhône dep.	23%	Prison (five years)	9%
	30–40	33%	Other artisans	7%	Other dep.	14%	*Absentia* deportation	2.5%
	40–50	18%	Tile makers	9%	Unknown	5%	*Absentia* deportation and prison	2.5%
	50–	20%	Other	8%			Death	5%
	60	2%	Unknown	7%			Absentia death	5%
							Parental care	3%

murder of a republican by republicans. Soon after his death, the organisation of Arnaud's funeral became a national concern. Crémieux's governmental condemnation of the murder had made the assassination a national crisis.[58] Locally, Prefect Challemel-Lacour reasserted his trust in the National Guard but also seized the opportunity to use imperial legislation against the Lyonese clubs. Arnaud's funeral was probably one of the most significant secular funerals since the revolution.[59] Gambetta headed a large crowd of guardsmen and Lyonese people who followed the coffin through the streets of Lyons to its final resting-place. The crowd was estimated, somewhat generously, at 150,000 people, which would make it the largest demonstration of the period.[60] The black flag of mourning was flying at half mast over the town hall, in company with the tattered red flag of September.[61]

Using the black flag as a symbol of mourning and weaver revolt was also the intention of the crowd which had killed Arnaud, and the funeral of Arnaud set a precedent, which was used again on the occasion of the armistice.[62] On 3 March 1871, Mayor Hénon announced that the black flag would rise again to replace the 'proud flag of the nation in danger and of resistance to the last' in 'sign of mourning for the mutilated motherland'.[63] The red flag was brought down with finality.

Beyond the symbolic mourning, the municipal council meeting a few hours after the death of Arnaud was

> deeply impressed by the fateful event of the day. We speak of the moving details of the horrible drama which ended with the murder of brave Commandant Arnaud.
>
> His death was heroic. Falling under the blows of his murderers, his last words were a cry saluting the republic he loved and of which he was a worthy defender. The entire municipal council is united to the sufferings of his unfortunate family and the administration makes the following proposition, initiated by Citizen Maynard, a friend of the victim:
>
> The Municipal Council, considering that Commandant Arnaud, of the 12th battalion of the National Guard, had been cowardly murdered while doing his duty and attempting to maintain the threatened public order, decides:
>
> Art. 1   that the city of Lyons will adopt the three children of Citizen Arnaud;
> Art. 2   that a lifelong pension will be given to his widow and a temporary one to his children;
> Art. 3   that the funeral of Commandant Arnaud will be paid for by the city and a plot of land will be given in perpetuity [for his grave].[64]

To some extent, what Arnaud came to represent was the end of an age of innocence where the shared memories of a republic under the empire could still bind together the most divergent views and political aspirations. The death of Arnaud was untimely, as the republican war came to a difficult point in the harsh winter. The people involved – children, women behaving in a ritualised manner, the men mimicking military discipline – were all threatening far beyond the Arnaud incident. The type of subversion they represented was a true test of republican ability to maintain a social order compatible with the conservative majority. The sentences were not executed in Lyons, and Andrieux carefully removed Deloche to Riom to have him executed. The sentencing of Arnaud's murderers and the events of 18 March 1871 were announced in the same issues of the newspapers on 21 March.[65] What happened in Lyons was civil war on a small scale but, unlike in Paris, both sides instinctively used the same political register and referred to the same ideals. A different type of regime might have reacted differently, and indeed did after the conservative elections of 8 February.

Institutional violence and the end of the Commune

The Arnaud incident undoubtedly played a part in the radicalisation of French politics in 1870–1. Paris and the Parisians had, moreover, followed a separate collective trajectory from the rest of the French and, even more than the Lyonese, had developed their own political discourse without an equivalent on the government side. The trauma of the siege cannot be overstated and undoubtedly played a part but, seen from without, the Paris Commune fitted into a typology of violence framed by the murders of Hautefaye and Lyons.

The Commune of Paris started in an incident strongly reminiscent of that of Lyons. The crowd of women who stopped a dismally organised attempt at weakening the Parisian guardsmen by removing their artillery from the hill of Montmartre were closely akin to their Lyonese counterparts: working women with a significant minority of politicised leaders. After the 18 March execution of Generals Lecomte and Thomas for what was almost an exact repetition of the Arnaud killing, the Parisians found themselves led by the National Guard, which reluctantly surrendered its sovereignty to an elected Commune.[66] At this stage, the violence of 18 March became the breaking point between the Versailles government and Paris. The elections to the Commune had been an attempt to create a non-insurrectional and legitimate negotiating force. The Third Party, analysed by Nord[67] and many others, was playing an important part in trying to mend the body politic.[68] Yet it failed in Paris. The call for a pacific solution on 27 April 1871 smacked of desperation:

> To the National Assembly we say: what do you hope for? Is your purpose to take Paris by force? You could only enter the city, in any case, by walking on heaps of corpses and among charred ruins under the curses of orphans and widows. You would only find before you a shadow of a city. And in the aftermath of such a victory, what would your moral authority be in the country? Open your eyes – there is still

time. Recognise that a city defending itself with such heroism against the whole French army is motivated by something other than passions and blind restlessness. It protects a right, proclaims a truth …

To the Commune we would say: beware! By going further than your original remits you are alienating rightful and sincere minds. Go back to the municipal issues. On those grounds you are right and just – do not use weapons liberty disapproves to defend liberty. Do not suppress newspapers … end arbitrary arrests! Stop forced enrolments … enough blood has been spilt! You have the right to sacrifice your own life and your memory; you have no right to endanger democracy to an irretrievable defeat.[69]

Signed by Barodet, Crestin, Ferouillat, Outhier and Vallier, who were all on the left of the Lyons municipal government, this call remained unanswered. The representatives of Lyons later wrote a report which described their experience in Versailles and Paris to the municipal council:

[in Versailles] Paris is literally considered a cave where there is no safety for goods or people. We must say, to be truthful, that we have enjoyed the most complete freedom there … We have interrogated the petit bourgeois, the small shopkeepers, the small businesses, which suffer cruelly, as well as the world of the publicists, the men of the professions and political circles. Here is the result of our enquiry. Paris is not with the Commune, and it rejects its excesses and reproaches its lack of programme and, when it came out, the vagueness or exaggerated character of its formulas. But let it be clear: it is even less with the assembly as long as it contests its municipal freedoms … we were received by the executive commission of the Commune and we have found there, we must say, the same position as in Versailles, the same will to carry on the struggle to the last, the same resistance to conciliatory ideas.

The Lyonese councillors, who had not pushed their political investigation to the extreme of asking the opinion of the poor or working-class supporters of the Commune, in despair gave the executive committee of the Commune of Paris a bleak assessment of their military position. Going back to Thiers, the provincial politicians found the statesmen adamant that the law of 14 April on municipal freedom had gone far enough in the direction of decentralisation, and that only a few cities shared any feelings with Paris.[70] Other private forums, such as the *Commission de conciliation du commerce, de l'industrie et du travail*, attempted to define a space for negotiation.[71]

Yet while the Lyons representatives shared their time equally between both sides and attempted to reconcile the ultra-left republicans with the reactionary government of the contested republic, they could not achieve the results obtained in Lyons in September or Narbonne in April.[72] Similarly, most of the

Communard movements of France were nipped in the bud, not because excessive force was applied but because there was enough trust and common ground to enable the moderate republicans to disarm or disband the ultras on both sides. The trials which followed the violent incidents were usually tolerant and relatively understanding of the circumstances. The murderer of the prefect of Saint-Étienne was thus dismissed as insane,[73] and the people arrested in Limoges after the death of a cavalry colonel were sent for a maximum of three years' imprisonment, the death penalty being reserved for the leader, who had not been arrested. Condemnation *in absentia* was largely symbolic. Sentencing the leaders of an insurrectional National Guard unit to penalties ranging from one to a maximum of three years in jail was remarkably lenient.[74] The 1871 period of civil war was a victory for the Third Party, the party of conciliation everywhere but in Paris.

In Paris, two distinct wills were preventing the Third Party from acquiring much influence. The Third Party leaders, the mayors elected on 6 November 1870, the radical deputies Adam and Ranc, the Freemasons and other public figures had all been associated with the 4 September republic, and they had lost much of their credibility with the defeat. Their *Ligue d'union républicaine des droits de Paris* had only minor successes, such as the armistice which enabled the people of Neuilly to vacate their suburb when it became a front line.[75] The Versailles government lacked any republican credentials and the peace national assembly seemed on the point of restoring a monarchy. Within Paris there were serious divisions which led to the marginalisation of several strata of republican elites. The violence, exerted within the Commune itself, which singled out various military leaders for trial was of a kind which undermined the unity of the movement, and as it became more fractured its ability to negotiate on anything rapidly diminished.

The civil war started with the death of a Dr Pasquier, who on approaching Communard lines was shot without warning. The death of a man wearing the Red Cross armband was used for propaganda purposes by the Versailles army, which started a series of executions at the first engagement against the Communards. This parallel increase in the threshold of violence became self-justifying. The Commune replied to the killing of Flourens with the law of hostages, which mainly targeted moderate republican figures of 4 September, personalities of the economic elite of the Second Empire and clerical leaders and members of congregations.

The killing of defenceless Communards was made easier for the army, many of whom had returned embittered from harsh German camps, by the fact that the enemy was denied military status in spite of the posturing of the Commune's most able generals, Drombrowski and Rossel. In fact, the anti-militaristic culture which prevailed throughout the Commune was the undoing of its military apparatus, but also vindicated Versaillais' views that Paris was in a state of chaos threatening the rest of France. More rare but indicative of an unstable political order was intra-Communard violence.

The best-known example of intra-Communard violence was the killing of a young officer named de Beaufort. In spite of his aristocratic name, Beaufort had joined the Communards, only to be executed by them on 24 May 1871.[76] His elegant uniform, posturing and a vague threat addressed to a National Guard unit meant that, when recognised in the last few days of the Commune, he was promptly beaten up and executed in a rapid tragedy reminiscent of the Arnaud affair.[77] Even Delescluze and other Commune leaders could not save him. He had been branded a traitor and a spy, and to such accusations, combined with class hatred, there was no answer. In the pro-Communard historiography there is still controversy about Beaufort, who was later accused of treason by most Communard historians.[78] The prosecution of his executioners by Versailles and the vague rumours of a letter to Versailles forces sealed his posthumous fate. The prosecution described the murder thus:

> The crime committed in the most revolting circumstances began the series of murders committed in the Roquette neighbourhood in the last few days of the Parisian insurrection. Through [this murder] the insurrection revealed all the signs of the cruelty, hatred and savagery associated with all the assassinations of the hostages.[79]

Beaufort had been reclaimed as a conservative victim of internecine Communard violence and was made the precursor of a long series of atrocities. In fact, radicals and Communards did not want to challenge the principle of popular sovereignty. In the words of Lissagaray: 'The blind justice of revolutions punishes in the first-comers the accumulated crimes of their caste.'[80]

The real peak of violence was reached in the notorious bloody week of May 1871 when the army entered Paris through an abandoned gateway. The conquest of Paris was marked by the most systematic arrests of political opponents in French history until Vichy. The police used their detailed knowledge of some neighbourhoods to identify their targets. The army, equipped with blurred photographs and descriptions of Communard leaders whose portraits had been well distributed in the press during the second siege, seem to have enjoyed a free rein in pacifying Paris. Within the violent actions that took place, among the turmoil and chaos of the civil war, it is still possible to define more precisely the intents and aims of this repression. If we look at the nature of the Versailles rhetoric, we will find that it is almost a literal transcription of the discourse produced during the war against the invading Germans. This quotation, extracted from a leader of *Salut Public*, was directly applicable to the Communards:

> The barbarians ... because arson is a duty prescribed to the soldiers by their leaders. They have even turned it into a judiciary punishment ... as to pillage, it is an innate instinct among the Teutonic race, as is pilfering and limitless gluttony and indescribable dirtiness. As to their

bloody cruelty, it is now proverbial in this war of extermination. How many slaughters of defenceless individuals did the press report?[81]

Similar rhetoric and tropes were applied to the Communards and contributed to making Parisians alien to the Versailles forces and to Frenchmen. In another article, published in March, on the insurrection led by Bakunin and Cluseret in Lyons in September 1870, the metaphors were more specific:

The Henry IV room was found in a dreadful state ... It was there that they deliberated, it was there that they ate, it was there that the members of the committee, disturbed by the blue wine [low-quality wine] and the *charcuterie*, found relief in all sorts of ways. Along the wood panelling can be seen the long marks of wine dejections. They rested their heads against the wall and vomited one after the other, these people who claimed to be the delegates of the people of Lyons. Elsewhere the excretions were of another sort ... they left traces similar to the Prussians.[82]

The metaphor of lowly dejections and drunkenness recurred throughout the period, to describe revolutionaries who were simultaneously identified as the excretions of society and the producers of coprophiliac politics and scatological thoughts. Reduced like the invaders to the levels of lowly bestiality, Communards and revolutionaries in general did not belong to the political landscape. By stressing their alterity and their bestiality, their murder became possible along the sadly familiar lines of the dehumanisation and barbarisation of warfare. There were a number of incidents where no prisoners were taken, where arguably soldiers caught up in the heat of the action slaughtered the enemy, and other opportunities when the wounded enemy seemed to provoke retaliation upon themselves.[83]

Yet what is striking and new in May 1871 are the executions on both sides, which took the appearance of rational and ordered measures or of structured riotous events such as the Arnaud murder. On the Communard side, a number of priests held in the political prison of Mazas were shot, while some personal revenge was taken against a few well-known enemies of yesterday. Thus Raoul Rigault, the Commune's repressive arm, avenged the death of his friend Sapia by killing the individual he reckoned to have been responsible. A number of Dominicans and nuns, locked in a small cell of rue Haxo, were later executed in the street in a scene reminiscent of a popular riot. These executions were later evoked in photomontages[84] which, while highly implausible in ballistic terms (the last row would be shooting the first's heads), conveyed a feel for the human tragedy; see Figure 7.1.[85]

The conservative press, even now, still occasionally recalls this story,[86] and the stoic manner in which these priests and nuns went to the slaughter made them martyrs, the victims of socialism: a new type of martyrdom, much needed in the

Figure 7.1   Massacre of sixty-two hostages on 25 May, rue Haxo. Photomontage
Trémelat, published by Josse, 1871

Source   *L'Invasion, le siège et la Commune*, Stusi, 1901, p. 313

coming struggle against socialist thoughts. The Commune had tried to exchange
Archbishop Darboy (Figure 7.2) for Blanqui, but Thiers feared the leadership of
the old revolutionary more than he cared for an isolated Gallican priest.

Versaillais executions became systematic in the last few days of the war when
the army set up its tribunals and execution centres in various headquarters of
the capital. There were many blind executions, where suspects of a red neighbourhood were sentenced to death together for their collective guilt. There were
also a number of executions based on photographic evidence, which meant
death to many look-alikes of Vaillant, Vallès and others. When Rigault was
arrested, he was shot within minutes and his corpse was left on the pavement
without any ceremony. Paradoxically, this haste meant that the authorities were
not entirely sure that they had executed the right man. The list of suspects
published in August 1871 contained his description, and his entourage was kept
under scrutiny for years after his death.[87] The violence was there, but there was
something eminently more sinister in the orderly queues of men and women
who had to wait in silence for their ineluctable execution. People arrested on
denunciations, wearing old remnants of uniforms, with powder-dirty hands or
speaking careless words, were sentenced to death by a mock tribunal of some
sort.

In the end, the Versailles government, which never commented on the repression, covered up the charred remains of the dead and hid the extent of the

Figure 7.2   Archbishop Darboy
Source   *L'Autographe*, 11 November 1871

massacre.[88] Censorship eventually covered any reporting of the acts of the Commune and of the repression. It is a measure of this repressive violence and mindless repression that police files were left open on Raoul Rigault and a number of leading Communards who had been well identified and shot. In the provinces, much of the proscription routines of the Second Empire had been revived, and suspects were listed and identified. Republicans had their files revived from the ashes, and travellers were systematically subjected to the most intense scrutiny.[89]

The violence of Parisians against Parisians was exacerbated by the physical damage of civil war, during which the rue de Rivoli burnt, the town hall and

(Parisian) archives were reduced to cinder, and the *Legion d'Honneur* chancellery and the Tuilerie palace were torched. Even today, historians disagree as to who started the fires. The use of lighting gas and petrol must have made arson or accidental damage equally easy in a situation of open warfare. When the Communards were taken in long columns of prisoners through Paris and all the way to Versailles, they were victimised on their way. They were later locked in camps such as the training camp of Satory, where they stayed for weeks awaiting trial. Those who survived were then dispatched to terrible prisons such as Fort Boyard in the Atlantic Ocean,[90] and later deported to New Caledonia in the south Pacific.[91]

What remained of the brutalisation of French politics were, on the one hand, martyrs on both sides, and, on the other, a deep split between republicans and socialists. The sense of political affiliation between first-generation politicians and socialist children was gone for ever. The accusations of murder and gratuitous violence also never faded away. The Commune was simultaneously reaching mythical dimensions in the socialist and anti-socialist literature. In Paris, the whole period became a political embarrassment, a source of quarrels. Alongside the September massacres of 1792, the massacres of May 1870 were hidden under the false excuse of the heat of the moment or the rightful indignation of over-zealous executioners.[92] There was probably less fighting than Versailles claimed. The Communards did not defend themselves very well, and they were not, for the most part, shot in the heat of the struggle. They were executed lined up against a wall with their hands tied behind their backs.

One of the side-effects of this intense violence was the lack of qualified workers in the years that immediately followed the war, and historians have long insisted on the irony of a bourgeois order finding difficulties in obtaining decent artisans to cater for its needs. Another dimension, more sinister in its implied cold calculation, was the fact that the civil war acted like a slum-clearance campaign in some of the ancient revolutionary hotbeds at the very heart of the capital city. A good example of this could be found in the I arrondissement, where the municipality estimated that the arrondissement had almost been swept clean. Between 1866 and 1872, the population of the arrondissement declined from 81,598 to 73,482, and the population of less well-established people living in rented furnished accommodation (*garnis*) declined brutally from 5,189 to 3,579, a 32 per cent decline.[93]

This repression haunted the Third Republic and later regimes, which swept the issue aside and, up until 1971, ignored any effort to commemorate this particularly atrocious period of French history. There were always some defenders of the Commune who apportioned the blame to the Versailles side only. In the reactionary years at the beginning of the Third Republic, the *conseil municipal* played such a role. The *conseil municipal* of July 1871 had acquired much of the municipal freedom the Parisians pined for in 1870. It then looked back at traitors of the past, such as Provost Étienne Marcel, who had organised the revolts of the Parisians against the regent of France in 1358, and found in him a defender of local freedom. In the Commune of Paris they saw a series of missed opportunities, and tried to rehabilitate this revolutionary moment by building a monument to the memory of the deceased. A good example of this reworking of recent history would be the work of a radical like Dr Louis Fiaux, who had been active in the National Guard during the war.[94] He was later very active in the municipal council of Paris, denouncing Ferry as a public enemy[95] and rewriting the history of the Commune as a full-blown civil war.[96] Yet the Commune had not been a full-blown civil war, in the sense that most of France watched passively, and if the Communards ended up dehumanised by warfare and political terror, the violence of the conflict remained geographically limited and did not acquire fuller class dimensions.

The Franco-Prussian war and the Commune eventually led to the establishment of the Third Republic, but at the heart of the new regime this original sin of repression remained and reasserted the absolute force of the state. A paradox of this repression has been that it made a republican conservatism possible, and thus enabled many conservative elites to join in. A side-effect of this original sacrifice was that republicans could not look with pride to the founding moments of the republic. The Third Republic, haunted by ghosts of its own making, had to define itself as a progressive movement breaking away from its past, breaking away from the tradition of revolutionary nostalgia which had been the nemesis of previous republics.

8

THE FRENCH STATE IN QUESTION

A nation, therefore, is a great solidarity, made of the feeling of the sacrifices already made and of the further ones, one is disposed to make.[1]

The Weber hypothesis and French unity

The French historiography over the last two hundred years has tended to assume French identity and then seek out the factors which helped it crystallise and function within the European political space. The recent *Lieux de Mémoire* collection of the 1980s and 1990s thus first proposed a selection of sites and imaginary loci of national identity, and then explained how the various elements hung together.[2] This 'historiographical turn' in French historical circles focused on the ways memory and space interconnected to form a relevant geography book of identity, conducive to ceremonies and practices of identity. It sought to understand how they were gradually integrated into an archive of the French nation, a living memory of what it is to be French.[3] At the core of this introspection and historiography were the founding figures of the French historical profession and a return to the fundamental tropes of national identity developed during the Third Republic between 1871 and 1914. In many ways this reflected the impact of Weber's work on this crucial period.

Eugen Weber, writing in the 1970s and largely inspired by the insights of social anthropology, postulated that national identity could not be taken as fact but rather as a progressive evolution structured by the integration of smaller *terroirs*, peasants' living space, within a wider national geography.[4] Transport and schooling thus played a part in the creation of a French melting-pot. His particular point of view led him to regard Frenchness and assimilation as symbiotic and necessary corollaries of each other.[5] In other words, a French-Breton, hyphenated identity made as little sense to Weber as it did to the pedagogic authorities of the Third Republic, who tried to reduce illiteracy and local cultures simultaneously in most linguistic areas of France. One of the central impediments to the recognition of any hyphenated identity in France was the holistic attitude of historians and intellectuals who tend to regard France, the French, culture, and so forth, as indivisible autonomous entities.[6]

Since the 1970s, the general pattern of Weber's narrative has been challenged in its chronology (the French state has used French as its administrative and authoritative tongue since 1518),[7] and in its simplistic and top–bottom sociology.[8] William Brustein, for instance, took a structuralist stance to demonstrate the correlation between regional modes of production and political identities while he argued for the close mapping of modes of ownership and voting patterns.[9] This somewhat mechanistic interpretation of local political culture still presents the advantage of undermining any pedagogical determinism, where people had to be educated, reaching Frenchness and republicanism as their literacy rates increased.[10] The fact that local languages were often used to explain French to schoolchildren demonstrated a slightly less violent repression of local cultures than that assumed by the many regionalist movements of France.[11] Recent studies tend to stress that the partially depreciative concept of '*petites patries*' – small motherlands, affective territories of homeliness, akin to the German *Heimat* – was integrated into many strands of French politics during the Third Republic. Poincaré and his own conservative republican tradition used this nostalgia intensely to find the political roots of the republic in traditional France. On the left, Jean Jaurès, himself a Provençal and Occitan speaker, sought to reclaim regionalism and regionalist culture for the left.[12] The *terroir* or the *petites patries* could only function as parts of the nation.

Other ways of relating to the nation existed, as Caroline Ford has shown, which for instance used religion as a medium. For a long time historians did not recognise religion as a medium of national consciousness or of citizenship, because religion does not belong to the usual tools of French modernisation.[13] Yet it functioned that way, too. It is also unclear that reasoning in Breton or Lemouzi would predispose to 'reactionary' politics. The vitality of politics in the 1846–52 period seems, indeed, to point to the opposite.[14] To reverse the usual proposition on integration, it remains to be demonstrated that cultural imperialism is unequivocally beneficial. When it comes to assimilation in France, cultural prejudices die last.

In Weber's account, 1870 took on a particular importance, mainly because it set the Third Republic on the assimilationist lines mentioned earlier concerning Jews in Algeria and because it reinforced a feeling of inferiority in education and conscription.[15] The great military service legend, which supposedly returned more literate young men who were thus more nationalistic and more used to notions of hygiene than when they had left, only started with the reforms of the 1880s. Meanwhile, the 'black hussars of the republic', modest schoolteachers fighting at the same time alcoholism and illiteracy, regionalism and religion, date from the Ferry reform on education of 1882 at the earliest.[16]

In fact, Third Republic hagiography, always keen on promoting the new order, greatly overestimated the nature of the problems in order to triumph more easily against inflated odds.[17] Illiteracy among the insurgents arrested in Lyons and Paris was not high, and up to 86 per cent of the conscripts serving in 1871 in a non-French-speaking department like Corrèze could read and write some French.[18] If basic education had a central political meaning in 1870, it was by no means the preserve of a tiny minority. Religious schooling and local enterprise had answered the needs of many areas.[19] More importantly, historical works on literacy have undermined the link made between literacy rate and republicanism.[20] The same works also rightly show that anti-clericalism was not a preserve of the republican left until 1870, and that Bonapartism could also flirt with anti-Church feelings.[21]

Also striking in 1870 is the manner in which an impotent state without armies, administrations willing to serve the government, funds or even a wealth of popular support managed to survive a difficult war and invasion and a civil war. Such was the constancy of the French state that, even defeated, it was never vacant. Illiterate soldiers did know something about their own Frenchness. Historians relying on literary sources are building on sand. Descriptions of the backwardness of the rural troops used near Paris used ancient literary tropes, and witnesses described the surface of things, mainly using prejudices as analytical tools. In 1870 the striking factor that kept France together was the desire for unity and even for centralisation.

This does not mean that this entire chapter will be a celebration of French unity already achieved and pre-existing the Third Republic. Indeed, some of the centrifugal forces had their opposites.[22] In Nice, a handful of Italian nostalgics tried to reunite the city to Italy in 1870. In Algiers, the rise of a committee of public salvation started a communal reorganisation of the colony and aimed at a much more aggressive domination of the territory by republican French citizens, even briefly considering breaking the link with the metropolitan power. There were talks of turning Algeria into an English protectorate. In this movement can be found some direct claims for independence which illustrate the processes described by Benedict Anderson about South America: the independentism of an ethnic minority isolated among the mass of 'natives' whose rights they intend to negate.[23] The Arab insurrection of 1871 pushed the independentists back towards France and its military apparatus, and invited them to revise their views and promote French assimilation. This fear led the white settlers to refuse an autonomous constitutional settlement in 1872 and 1873.[24] The periphery called for the centre to make Algeria more French and thus the native Algerians more foreign on their own land.[25]

Within France, the rise of local elites and local democracies, often dominated by radical leaders, unsurprisingly threatened the conservatives who had been the most fervent decentralists before the war. The evolution of the Commune of Lyons and the *Ligue du Midi* seemed to mean an in-depth reform of French administrative centralisation and the possible creation of a federal nation. Their political leaning created some real anxieties among royalists and conservatives. As an outcome of the war, one finds that the municipal reforms, the powers granted to the elite-dominated *conseils généraux*, and ultimately the second chamber, satisfied most partisans of administrative decentralisation.

Also striking is the fact that very few Frenchmen rebelled against the war effort. Most places were already fully aware of the state and its prestige. Napoleon III's tours and the politics of great works had had an impact on rural populations. In many families, migrants and poor labourers had gone to the city to earn some cash and knew more about the rest of France than commonly thought. Since much of this travelling was done on foot, the perception of the size and diversity of France was often a very real and physical experience. In Paris, billeted hosts might complain that their lodgers, natives of various corners of France, argued over the dinner table as to the superiority or qualities of their respective regions, but these Frenchmen were still able to communicate.[26] Even though soldiers competed on regional terms, they wore the same French uniform and had a notion of what France was. Besides, closer investigation reveals similar rivalries between soldiers of different neighbourhoods of Paris.[27] Tensions within a nation still reveal its existence, and the remarkable fact that a handful of deputies were able to proclaim a new republic using the prestige of their title of deputies of Paris revealed the almost unanimously accepted centrality of Parisian politics. They asserted anew the essential superiority of Paris over the provinces.[28] Even the Lyons contest soon limited itself to an autonomous management of the Commune.

Desires for centralisation

The desires for centralisation were thus overpowering in 1870–1. The federalist approach failed to touch a raw nerve during the Commune, mainly because the state gave the communes of France the amount of freedom and the political support which was later to characterise the Third Republic. When the president of France invited the thirty-odd thousand mayors of France to a banquet in Paris for the Universal Exhibition of 1900, he celebrated the terms of local democracy and its direct bond with the nation.[29] The reform of April 1871 on the election of municipal councils and the election of mayors in most urban centres represented the amount of freedom most desired in France.

Beyond this debate on local citizenship, a diversity of functionaries and state servants looked back to the centre for direction because middle management was not adequate.

The prefects who had most freedom in the management of their political region had been purged, and most prefectures were now in the hands of appointees of Gambetta. Their prestige was much diminished by their obviously political appointment and their relative lack of expertise. New prefects were not always welcome. Radicals such as the Lyons revolutionaries first attempted to reject them:

> [The council] could not so abruptly accept a prefect imposed brusquely and without consultation. It would have been to abdicate, to recognise the vacuity of the power they had just received and to betray their mission. What? The men acclaimed by Lyons, the men mandated by

this great city which had been the first of all to rebel, had to withdraw humbly before an unknown character because messieurs the deputies of Paris, representing Paris alone, had taken for themselves the power to decide![30]

Yet in the end, and after a renewal of the electoral bond between the council of Lyons and the people of Lyons, they eventually accepted the prefect and turned towards Gambetta and the central power he incarnated to provide the necessary leadership. The practice of communal democracy provided administrative boundaries to any forms of decentralisation and renewed the validity of the revolutionary reorganisation of the French political and administrative space. The tensions of 1870–1 around the rights and duties of the communal authorities in most of France demonstrated that, after eighty years, the *ancien régime* regions had been totally superseded by departmental and parochial forms of identity. The contests between some prefectures and sub-prefectures for the revolutionary leadership in the department occasionally renewed the debates of the revolutionary period explored by Margadant or the parochial politics developed in Alain Corbin's work.[31] On the whole, they implicitly accepted the importance of being the centre of an administrative unit mimicking at the local level the centralisation of the nation. Even though decentralisation was a lively political discourse dominating the public sphere of 1870–1, its boundaries and anchoring points were those established by administrative centralisation, and it never freed itself from this politico-geographic construct. The spatial organisation of France was unchallenged, and even the more extreme Legitimists did not consider a return to the provinces of old, except possibly in imagination or through the use of antique racial denominators opposing the races of France.

Centralisation remained at the heart of their discourse, in the sense that the organic metaphors that they used to project France as a social body remained anthropomorphic and required a head, whether Paris or Versailles, where the government would be. The ties of a royalist organisation of France, either in the fantasy of Louis Veuillot's 'republic for all' or the more traditional royalist revivalism, would have been stronger and more direct than what the early Third Republic had created. The Lyonese revolutionaries who, as we have seen throughout this book, represented a radical alternative to the revolutionary discourse emanating from Tours or Paris, expressed the following views:

The primitive organisation of the departments which placed the administration in the hands of the people has been replaced by the current organisation, which puts the whole department under the administrative and political authority of the prefect, emissary of the central power, whose interests he must espouse and whose whims he must satisfy.

We want to react against this centralist spirit and also against the anti-republican tendencies that we believe are not thought through.

Nevertheless, I am not a federalist; I have always opposed this form of government ... but while rejecting the federal system I am nevertheless the partisan of the independent commune. We all agree on this point, we only begin to disagree when we attempt to follow on the consequences of the communal independence. This disagreement exists because we do not live in the shadow of republican institutions and because, on the contrary, it is the monarchist institutions which rule social relations and institutions ... The true republican institution is the commune, widened on its basis, serving to organise public services useful to the citizens and with an assembly at the top, revitalised from below and regulating [life] in the common interest.[32]

This report centred on the vexed question of the police, which, of all institutions, seemed the worst instrument of centralist power. It announced their replacement by the municipal police, which later led to the joint existence of two police corps in French cities. In accepting the role of the department and of the commune as fundamental basic units of the state, and in placing the assembly as the culmination of a political life constantly flowing up and down the pyramid, the Lyonese decentralists were simply giving new vigour to the old administration. This is an objective to be found in the establishment and running of the institutions of the Third Republic.

The army, traditionally a subservient arm of the state, did not contest the revolution and obeyed. The non-state-funded bodies such as the doctors, who saw themselves as belonging to the French state by serving the nation's health, turned instinctively back to the centre and, when faced with the political option of the Commune, chose to serve the government in Versailles rather than obey the Communards. This centralisation of thought reflected the organisation of knowledge in nineteenth-century France, where most of the secondary and provincial seats of expertise – Montpellier in the case of medicine[33] – had sunk into marked decline.[34] The career structure of the medical elites led them to Paris, but it was strengthened by the way information travelled. The flow between Paris and the provinces firmly reinforced the image of France as a centralised nation.[35] More figuratively, the hygiene literature produced since the 1830s and the sanitarian discourse on healthy individuals and the state reinforced the importance of regulatory authorities similarly controlling bodies and social body.[36] This form of centralisation was more absolute and ran deeper than anything the Third Republic would be willing to deliver. The recent work of Murard and Zylberman, inspired by this hygienist literature, reflected these frustrated centralising aspirations based on authoritarian ideas of efficiency, which existed in theory but not in administrative practice.[37]

Looking at other important conveyor belts of the state reinforces this analysis. The notaries, for instance, were among the better-known representatives of the state in rural France in the sense that they recorded sales and inheritance, and negotiations between neighbours and even within families. Beyond this administrative role they also lent funds, provided mortgages and invested savings. Locally they had often been chosen as mayor under the Second Empire, and were often elected after 1870. They were not and are not civil servants in the modern sense. They owned their office, but regardless of this they contributed to the maintenance of the state and anchored its existence economically and administratively in daily life.[38]

When radicals promoted local autonomy, the conservative press, previously noted for its regionalism, called for the repression of excessive local democracy, for the protection of the freedom of their press and against local taxation. Within even the most rebellious cities such as Lyons or Algiers, there were people defending the boundaries between autonomous commune and sovereign state, and attempting to limit the legislative initiatives of the most enthusiastic provincial councils. The appeal of a centralist state for the administered deserves more attention.

What the state could offer uniquely was prestige, power, rewards and career investments on a much bigger scale. The Second Empire had manipulated its investment strategies to engineer its electoral successes and had conditioned local development to compliance. Notables could invest their family educational capital in the state and in many ways become the new meritocratic elites.[39] Beyond the change of regime, there is again more social stability than one would expect.[40]

Also, the state could reward through highly symbolic gestures. For instance, the *Légion d'Honneur* was a superb tool to honour and attach individuals. The status the red ribbon gave to the recipient assured his or (more rarely) her notable position. In most non-military cases it confirmed an acquired social position. Civil service, a stable waged employment involving limited physical effort and an assured retirement, was also a reward worth reaping. At another level, smaller privileges such as the authorisation to keep a tobacconist's shop, or, for the local press, the privilege of publishing lucrative legal announcements, could provide a substantial and vital income. The state was thus an institution of patronage, which symbolically and materially consolidated precarious income-based class perceptions. Over the whole of the nineteenth century, the state had been incarnated by one individual, since 1848 by Napoleon III, but in 1870 the government argued for a faceless regime, the exact opposite of the cult of the emperor.[41]

This vacuum of image was soon filled by the statesmanly profile of Gambetta, on whose youth and energy most of the attention was focused. With him some of the regal and caesarean customs of the French state returned in an atomised form. Instead of one emperor, the Third Republic created hundreds of representatives of the sovereign state in its deputies. The deputies and their government promptly realised the benefits of regal patronage. Some earlier puritanical views were renounced. For instance, the government of national defence had intended to limit the *Légion d'Honneur* to the military. Under pressure to find an inexpensive way of rewarding services, the republicans reverted to a more generalised use of the *Légion d'Honneur*.[42] Similar compromises took place else-where as republicans had to rely on established social networks. In the humanitarian sector of the war effort, even regional efforts created a superstructure covering areas of decision-making and selection which were implemented in the name of co-ordination and rationalisation. The latter term is particularly important in this desire for centralisation. The central state was deemed to be the most rational way to redistribute aid across the country and manage the war effort. In many ways, the national organisation of war relief was a blueprint for a centralised state in most conflicts. In 1870 France, it reflected the structures of society.[43]

The sum of all the interests vested in centralisation shows that the state was wanted, and that even when Paris was cut off from the rest of France the symbolic centre remained and was wanted as the nexus of political and social interchange. After February 1871, Paris again cut itself off from the French body politic by taking a radical political trajectory different from that of the rest of France. Much has been made of this, and the following section seeks to give a more balanced picture of French attitudes towards the Commune.

Frenchmen against the Commune

There is a tenacious legend that makes the massacres of May 1871 the great revenge of the provinces after a hundred years of Paris-led violence and revolution. This myth was born in the last days of May 1871 and grew from localised but real deep-seated hatred of Paris among provincial elites.[44] Provincial French people did not understand the Commune and did not have the means of following its developments. The provincial press had to distribute and circulate the Versailles images of the Commune of Paris. The *Journal Officiel édition de la Commune* had been swiftly suppressed by the police, which severely limited its distribution, and soon there was only state-controlled material in circulation.[45] Information about the Commune was distorted through the medium of state censorship and proclamations. The few newspapers taking a pro-Communard view, such as the *Droits de L'homme* published by Jules Guesde in Montpellier, were censored and their editors prosecuted.[46]

The circulation of Communard emissaries was also limited. Martin Johnson thus tracks the number of contacts a Corrézian envoy could have had: nineteen people in tiny mountain villages, like Viam on the edge of the miserable Millevaches plateau, and small market towns like Treignac. Besides, even when reached, the interlocutors of the Communard showed limited understanding of the Commune's views.[47] The more important emissary sent to Lyons bearing a message from Felix Pyat, Vaillant, Delescluze, Varlin, Tridon, Malon and Ranvier, left on 17 April and arrived five or seven days later, after a long journey that took him through Switzerland. Because of the risks involved, few of these individuals ever reached their destination. When they arrived, they depended on local radicals for their reception. Far from exporting the revolution like Carnot or major heroes of an earlier age, the emissaries of the Commune were power-less and weak, often arrogantly out of touch and certainly never as welcome as a reading of Parisian Communard evidence might lead one to believe.[48]

In Lyons the emissary met with lukewarm support. Writing in 1872 from the Prison St Paul, where he was being held, Gaston Caulet du Tayrac described his surprise at the casual meeting in the back room of a wine merchant on 25 or 26 April 1871.[49] He reported in a letter smuggled out of prison and possibly aiming to discredit Councillor Durand among the radicals of Lyons:

> Citizen Durand, who seemed supported tacitly by his colleagues in the meeting, declared that if it was a movement that we wanted to achieve he did not believe it possible. He asked the commission what was its influence and what were its means of action, and finished by saying that it was not his style to accept such enterprises without taking some share in its direction. He added, I think, that in any case there were negotia-tions to reconcile Paris and Versailles, and that a movement in Lyons could only complicate the situation.
>
> I rose immediately and declared abruptly that to dream of an agree-ment between Paris and Versailles was no longer possible after the savage executions ordered in cold blood by the reactionary generals. The moment had come when citizens could not be allowed to hesitate any longer, and those who did not take sides could only be considered as the enemies of the cause of the revolution.[50]

Addressing the municipal council, Caulet du Tayrac was received with a mixture of resentment and suspicion. He raised his voice in an authoritarian way, to which the old Hénon retorted that he must leave and that he would have been arrested if he had not given him his protection. Barodet, who had led the mission to Paris and Versailles in the hope of bringing the enemies to the negoti-ating table, stated:

> I do not believe that M Caulet du Tayrac is a real delegate of the Commune of Paris, especially considering that his conversation and his pretensions went against what the members of the Commune of Paris had told me when I went there.[51]

It had become clear that the radicals of the provinces had not followed the Parisians, and that the few committees gathered by the more militant members of the AIT like Gaspard Blanc had little support and credentials. The revolu-tionary committee of the proletarian neighbourhood of la Guillotière, at the heart of the failed insurrection of the end of April 1871, was thus leaderless and lacklustre, heterogeneous and containing a diversity of artisans. On its central committee there were two wig-makers, a sculptor, five clerks, two wine dealers, a physician, a railway worker, two locksmiths, a printer, a shoemaker, a gardener, a hatter, a clockmaker, a cabinet maker, etc. Crucially, it contained no weavers, and it failed to arouse the Croix Rousse radicals.[52] Gaspard Blanc was later made the scapegoat of the failed insurrection of 30 April. Historians have blamed Blanc, when in reality the insurrection had no chance of winning without the heavyweights of Lyonese democracy and the support of the national guardsmen of the traditional silk-weaving neighbourhoods.[53]

The Commune of Paris had failed to send a clear programme of national relevance until late in the civil war, and, a little like Bakunin's declaration calling for the abolition of capital, its declarations remained more theoretical than practical. The Commune thus failed to pass on its message, largely because its message was constantly in the making and was never a fixed and definite manifesto. When the declaration to the French people came, it was almost anodyne. It contained the claims for the republic, communal autonomy in matters of budget and expenditure extended to the police, magistrates, teachers and administration – all things Lyons had enjoyed for months in 1870. The purges they called for had already taken place, and censorious Communards within the walls of Paris already challenged the sacrosanct freedom of speech. The message came at a time when the Commune itself was turning its back on these ideas.[54]

The provincials as a whole failed to understand the Commune of Paris. They had some good reasons: the municipal freedoms had been acquired, war to the last was no longer an option, and besides, even the Commune of Paris negotiated with the Prussians. As late as 27 May, the municipal councils of the smallest urban centres like Brive-la-Gaillarde could not comprehend why it had become so difficult for the assembly and Paris to agree on municipal franchises and the guarantee that the republic was established.[55] Socialism was not the most central part of the Commune ideology, and there was little directly applicable in the Parisian message. Congresses were attempting to unite the moderate voices and provide a negotiating middle ground to both Versailles and Paris. There was an attempt to form a 'congress of the patriotic league of republican towns' in Bordeaux, which, like local agitation, was severely repressed.[56] Local prefects were ordered from Versailles to ensure that their mayors and municipal powers would not contribute to this new assembly.[57] A congress in Moulins united the representatives of up to fifty republican provincial newspapers which attempted to promote the same conciliatory message.[58]

The more successful congress of Lyons attempted to push forward a middle-ground political settlement. The participation of the congress was hotly debated in many municipal councils desiring an immediate cease-fire. In Montpellier, the municipal council debated the legality of sending an address to the government. This was forbidden by the law of 5 May 1855 but justified in recent practice. They also debated the opportunity to send representatives in Lyons. In the end the vote gave a twenty-four to seven majority for an address, and a smaller majority of eighteen to twelve for sending representatives in Lyons.[59] The congress of Lyons was moderate, and thus made the reasonable but unseasonable suggestion that the end of the war between Versailles and Paris should be followed by dissolution of the national assembly on the signature of the peace treaty. They also wanted the Commune of Paris to be dissolved and elections in Paris to follow, while national elections would create a constituent assembly. Representatives from sixteen departments signed this moderate manifesto, which demonstrated better than any speech how distant provincial politicians were from both Versailles and Paris.[60] This memorandum reflected other local initiatives. The Montpellier address stressed the need to reinforce 'national unity, [building on] an indestructible basis of municipal freedom in their broadest sense in order to bring back energy and activity to all the parts of the social body and to give a new life to the whole country'. They also called for a universal law for all communes, the proclamation of the republic and an amnesty.[61]

The report, presented by Ferouillat to the municipal council of Lyons, led the Lyonese radicals to distance themselves from the Commune of Paris. This was much to the satisfaction of Thiers who at that stage could not have entertained fighting a war in the provinces as well as in Algeria and in Paris.[62] The Lyonese believed in a peaceful settlement and 'to that conviction I [Thiers] owed the inaction of the great towns – that is to say, the safety of France and society'.[63] In other corners of the country even the efforts of the provincial communes were not understood, and the more traditional conservatives roundly condemned the insurrectionists. To *La Nation Française*, a moderate newspaper of Limoges, the whole negotiating position of the Lyonese and Bordeaux municipalities or of arrondissement mayors appeared a betrayal:

> We are surprised that members of the national assembly are still fostering the dangerous illusion that an honest government could find some grounds for a conciliation with the worst possible kind of insurrectionists … this petition from the communes is nothing more than a counter-revolution of sorts. March is to September [1870] what June was to February [1848]; the first attempt is political the second is social or communal; in the end it is the same attempt, it is the same riot, it is the same crime.[64]

The position was thus to separate social republicans from political republicans, the state of laws of the republic from the dreams of a redistribution and demagoguery. In Limoges, after the limited bloodshed of early April, the republican bourgeois had clearly decided to accept that Thiers was a guarantor of a republic built on the minimal common denominator. Soon afterwards, the municipal elections conceded by Versailles across France provided the first real test of the national political leaning. In effect, the elections of the assembly had been an oddity; they were pushed on in a real hurry after less than a week of campaigning and on a simple war or peace message. This confusion had returned a monarchist assembly, but many of these rural notables were simply the most prominent, stable and powerful men in their areas. Their elections demonstrated nothing truly political in the sense that they embodied business, landholding, good sense and clearly non-political issues. Four hundred monarchists dominated an assembly of 645 deputies.[65] A staggering 230 members of the assembly belonged to the aristocracy, and 63 per cent had never been elected to a national assembly and ignored its rules. After many years during which the Bonapartist vote had often been an anti-notable vote, voting for notables was the only alternative to returning a Bonapartist.[66] Some of them had been elected because they had been successful war leaders or because they had shown the right example by giving generously to charity.[67]

Besides the lack of clarity of the campaign, the royalists had fought the elections better than the republicans, who often presented rival lists of very similar political colour. In Corrèze, the analysts point out that with fewer candidates they matched the Bonapartist and royalist vote combined.[68] The elections at the municipal level were fought on an entirely different ticket. The mayors or communes had for the most part either been elected illegally, as in Lyons, or been nominated by Gambetta's prefects after the great purge of autumn 1870. They belonged, for the most part, to the republican fold. The elections provided a test of the vigour of the roots established over this chaotic year. While the results are difficult to interpret nationally, the urban centres of some importance gave a clear majority to the republicans and radicals. Lille, Nantes, Le Havre, Châlon-sur-Saône, Rouen, Agen, Douai, Périgueux, Le Mans, Grenoble, Saint-Étienne, Angers, Melun, Montauban, Albi, Limoges, Montpellier had all elected municipal councils dominated by the left. Some of these reflected the activities of energetic prefects, others a long-established tradition, but in most cases it enabled the more advanced republicans to claim that

> The assembly seems far too keen on feeding on itself, on its own importance and the exaggerated idea of its power. The truth is that it wanted to ask the country for a vote of confidence, and that the country replied with a negative vote.[69]

In the rather diverse Haute-Vienne department studied by Corbin, which combined pockets of deep radicalism and even deeper conservatism, the elections returned a number of men as either mayors or *premiers adjoints* who were classified later by the prefect (see Table 8.1). The prefect used makeshift categories born out of his own contacts with them. Some were thus described as 'political nullity'.[70]

Given that Thiers, the conservative leader, would bring together the conservatives and the moderate republicans as well as the 'men of order', if not the Bonapartists, the balance of power in Haute-Vienne was tipping in favour of the conservative republic by 123 (131 including radicals) to 69. If we do not include conservatives and moderate republicans, the balance of power is more indecisive, with 66 conservatives, 55 republicans and 69 monarchists of various tendencies. We cannot create a national figure from such local results, and local elections tend on the whole to reflect local issues. The elections of spring 1871

Table 8.1   Political inclinations of mayors and adjoints
in the Haute-Vienne department in 1871

Conservatives	15
Conservative liberals	35
Monarchists	35
Legitimists	27
Orleanists	7
Men of order	26
Bonapartists	25
Moderate republicans	47
Radicals	8
Non-political figures	78

showed, however, that a three-way political balance had appeared. This led Thiers to steer his numerous followers and admirers in the direction of a conservative republic. The moderate republicans had to pay for this alliance, and the price was the abject submission of Paris. For the divided monarchists, the need to unite was never so pressing, nor so infuriatingly slowed down by the intransigent principles of the dynasts of the competing Bourbon branches.

Even if we accept that the royalists maintained a wide rural hinterland, the results of the elections of May 1871 were undoubtedly a major blow to the monarchist party. This was followed by the by-elections of 2 July 1871, when 99 republicans were elected out of a grand total of 114 deputies.[71] Towards the end of the period of this first assembly, republicans and a Bonapartist revival simultaneously threatened the monarchists. The monarchist party, so prone to self-delusion, saw its majority eroded continuously in the thirty-eight further by-elections, at the end of which it represented only 46 per cent of the assembly.

From the elections of 1871 it became clear that the monarchists had lost support in urban centres. The loss of urban France to the republicans was certainly a blow, but it was not a fatal blow in the sense that the conservative Versailles assembly simply repeated the empire's loss of ground in urban and industrial environments. If we consider the symbolic importance of cities in the national public sphere, however, this loss was irretrievable. In a country focusing its cultural identity on great urban centres and on Paris, the loss of both Paris and the major urban centres to the cause of conservative politics would condemn the monarchists to a ruralist and nostalgic discourse.[72] This discourse then fed the concept of the war of France on Paris. Closer inspection of the evidence available shows that even in the small communes of France the conservatives did not have the hold on local politics their rank or local history could have entailed. The mayor of Lubersac reported with some glee that

> all these young men bring back to the countryside the conviction that
> their leaders, royalists or Bonapartists, were kind to the invader because
> they hated the republic and ordered retreats at the time to win.

Following the good cattle markets of this month, the peasants are no longer cursing the republic. Many of them, shaken in their Bonapartist fetishism by the sarcasm of their sons, are starting to think things through and regret having elected reactionaries [at the February election].[73]

From 1871 to 1876, the rural masses of the centre and east of France would thus drift towards the republic.[74] The slide from Bonapartism to republicanism would not be abnormal in the sense that Bonapartism rested on a revolutionary heritage and called on similar values. Martin Nadaud's father was thus a fiery Bonapartist who ended up being buried in a secular ceremony wearing his red cap of liberty.[75]

When the logic of civil war brought increased destruction and violence on both sides, the Versailles government managed to censor the reports of its own losses and atrocities and blackened the image of the Commune. Yet this propaganda, though well relayed by the press, did not send Frenchmen in their thousands to the slaughter of the class enemy. Parisians were often born elsewhere, and if many of the leaders of the Commune came from outside Paris there is no reason to believe that its supporters did not as well. The recruitment drive of the Versailles army was slow, and some areas gave pathetically low returns of volunteers.[76] In the Creuse department, the newly appointed prefect told all his contacts and colleagues that he 'faced an inertia and obstructiveness that made me despair'.[77] Recruitment was made more difficult at this early stage because people were still evoking the possibility of restarting war against the German empire.

Considering the migrating patterns of the Creuse stonemasons and their many Parisian contacts, recruiting men to fight the Parisians proved to be an almost impossible task. In Corrèze the mayor of Meymac reported, 'There is among us an unanimous disapproval of the political divisions in the capital city, yet this feeling, I must say, has not provoked the patriotic volunteering hoped for by the government of Versailles.' In Ussel the sous-préfet reported that there were no volunteers, and added that the 'reasoning they have is this: why should I go to defend an assembly composed of men hostile to the Republic? Why help their work in restoring a monarchy?' In Lubersac the mayor reported,

> Most of our citizens do not understand why the assembly with an ever-expanding army would need volunteers . mobiles and soldiers recently demobilised were saying on Sunday among the crowds of naïve listeners: 'We were not allowed to fight the Prussians, we won't fight against the French.'[78]

The workers of Périgueux, who had but little contact with the Commune of Paris and belonged to the region that had produced the Bonapartist 'cannibals' of Hautefaye, managed to enrol the support of their local National Guard to prevent the Versailles army using the armoured trains they had built. Children and women gathered and threatened the army officer and paraded a banner bearing the motto: 'Long live the republic! Down with civil war!'[79] Eventually, order came back to Périgueux largely because both sides avoided each other.

In Bordeaux, small demonstrations similarly worried the conservatives but did not seriously threaten public order.[80] On the other hand, the negotiators of the Third Party received the approval of many communes of France.[81] The civil war imposed itself on Paris but not on France, and it is another demonstration of the strength of the French state as an ideal that it survived this episode.[82]

The repression of the Commune left a state of emergency in many areas, including Lyons, which was later used to repress political dissent and to comb the population in a search for the elusive Communards. It did not lead to a dictatorship, and even the moral order phase of the new regime between 1873 and 1875 could not erase the experience of the democratic upheaval of 1870. The episode of the Commune constitutes an anomaly in the sense that the government used the state's might to crush a number of people who, for the most part, did not want the end of the state but wished simply to fix its democratic constitution. Furthermore, their central aim was to extend the state's prerogatives and widen its action and rulings to the social sphere. There was scope for negotiation, and only the assembly's dogmatic rejection of the republic and the wish of Adolphe Thiers (a native of Marseilles) to impose the sovereignty of the central government led to the bloodshed.

New Frenchmen?

The wars of 1870–1 were epoch-making in many cultural and political ways. That they contributed to produce new Frenchmen is more debatable. One of the key results of 1870 was the loss, often referred to as an amputation, of Alsace and northern Lorraine. In a country defined by *jus solis*, the citizenship conferred by birth on the land, a territorial loss had a deep impact on French citizenship. Alsatian refugees who had to choose nationality were installed in numbers in Algeria, which was then integrated further into the national fabric. The war also changed the outlook of many people in the provinces. Yet were the returning soldiers new Frenchmen? Or was the French national identity still an amorphous mass waiting to be worked on by the schools, commercial networks and military service of the Third Republic?

In 1870 the national identity had been strengthened against the Germans, and Germany then became the counter-image of France in a manner that had no precedent. Claude Digeon, in a masterful analysis of generations of French literary figures, defined this as the German crisis of French. Pushing this analysis further, Allan Mitchell sought to demonstrate the influence of Germany in French social and political reform.[83] On the former issues, the French did not move at the German pace of reforms and indeed, on issues like health, seemed to move at the more ponderous British rate of change. The latter touched a raw nerve.[84] It was to Germany that gymnasts and university reformers pointed as an example, which paradoxically remained repulsive and yet worth emulating.[85] It is also from Germany that the French army borrowed much of its institutional and training reforms.[86] New Frenchmen were therefore mirroring the German invader in some respects.

There are, however, many flaws in the narrative of Eugen Weber. Some, like Peter Sahlins working on the Spanish border or Timothy Baycroft on the Flemish north of France, have showed conclusively that the peasants did not become Frenchmen at the rate anticipated by the American historian. Both stress that the understanding of national borders enabled people to conceptualise the national space better in relation to the locality.[87] Other analyses might point out that the centralist perception that Frenchness is made of cultural and linguistic hegemony might be misplaced.[88] The soldiers of 1870 did not all speak French, and the military service they endured during the conflict did not lead to a greater acquisition of the language; indeed, some rural volunteers of Brittany, that most resilient religious and cultural enclave, were receiving their orders in Breton.[89]

They served nevertheless, and the head of the government who made so much of his own Breton regional identity was proud and probably relieved to depend on such solid troops. Other diaries and accounts describe the travels of Béarnais through France, mingling with the locals of Burgundy in spite of language difficulties.[90] Why did they fight if they did not believe in something called France? In other instances the regional and the national were not dissimilar idioms.

The *Ligue du Midi* and other organisations for national defence discussed in this book were all calling to the republic one and indivisible, but the unity was made of diversity and self-rule. The year 1870 could have led to a different realisation of national identity based on the sense of a looser federalism centred on municipal good governance, yet it did not. If we separate the French language from the 'fact' of being French, living in a space called France but comprising many competing boundaries, localities, departments, bishoprics, *rectorats*, arrondissements, military regions, judiciary sections, to name but a few, we would probably agree that the French were conscious of their national identity through practice and social interaction. This process, marked in daily life in time of peace, was exacerbated in time of war.[91] The issues of language and literacy as the cement of national unity belong to the pedagogic Utopianism of Abbot Grégoire.[92] National identity came from a common narrative identifying the enemy and the ally. In spite of this disclaimer, there is no doubt that this narrative was reinforced in schools and periodicals, pamphlets and stories. It was made even more central in 1870, when the defeat fixed French borders which did not match the historical geography of the nation.[93] The lost territories were thus to be recovered. In this imaginary political geography, the loss of Alsace-Lorraine was always meant to be temporary.

To a certain extent the war served as a school of national identity. It is a credit to the resilience of the French administration and the ideas of the French state that the state survived both the war and the civil war with its attributions and prestige almost unaffected. The negotiations on the margins of its jurisdiction should not distract from this. The French state still had a lot to offer to the French citizen, whether Francophone or not. Much of what it could deliver was not tangible or physical but symbolic and honorific.[94]

9

UNION AND UNITY

The Third Republic

> Beyond this fatal concept of the state ... there is another equally
> dangerous concept [sic], it is the concept of Unity and of
> Centralization. People have confused UNITY with UNION –
> here is the whole mistake. *There is strength in Union – there is despotism
> in Unity!*[1]

This final chapter considers the legacy of 1870–1 for the evolution of the practice of citizenship in France. It begins by looking at the role of the elector in
what had become *de facto* a decentralised administration of a centralist state. This
reflects the powers of the citizen in a bartering political order, and expresses the
deep impact of republican practices over the 1870–1 period while not denying
that the political heritage of 1870 was not entirely claimed. In fact, it is the
contention of this book that the practice of citizenship in times of war and civil
war, and in a political vacuum, cannot be entirely consistent and narratively
coherent with the periods that precede and follow. The debates on communal
freedom and decentralisation had their corresponding counterweight in a desire
for centralisation, but all had the elector-citizens at their heart, and this
remained a feature of the French parliamentary system of the Third Republic.

The second part of this chapter deals directly with the central argument of
the second part of this book on the decline and brutalisation of French politics
in the period leading to the Paris insurrection. Looking at the aftermath of the
wars, it considers how 4 September republicans and Communards were reintegrated into the political fabric, even though their political enterprise had been a
failure. This mending of the French political fabric was never complete or
universally accepted, but it functioned well in rapidly historicising the events of
1870–1 and in converting them into a national founding myth which concluded
with the necessity of the Third Republic. This political use of history did not
bury all the issues raised in 1870–1, and much of the social compact established
in 1871 came to haunt the conservative democracy.

There were remnants of the social and political compact of the war in the
administration of the Third Republic, however, and these played an important

part in the republicanisation of France, which is considered in the concluding section of this final chapter.

Overwhelming electors?

The Commune of Paris was perhaps one of the most wasteful experiments in democracy, yet not all the lessons of municipal citizenship and freedom had been lost. As soon as the warring abated, the debates on municipal democracy resumed, and the law of 10 August 1871 picked up a number of conclusions from the commission of decentralisation mentioned in Chapter 2. That it could do so a few weeks after the extermination of the Paris Commune proves that, in the end, the civil war had become dissociated from the central issues of local government and direct democracy.[2] In spite of this divide, the parliamentarians revising the status of the commune as local authority took another thirteen years to agree to the full range of ideas promoted in 1870.

Another layer of this local communal power and a remnant of the mandatory democracy of 1870 could be found in the Senate, created in 1875 and established against the desires of the more autocratic parliamentarians like Thiers. This rather unpopular institution fulfilled an important mission throughout the history of the various republican regimes established since then.[3] The Senate represented the rural interests first and foremost, and even more than the chamber of deputies allowed the electors to obtain tangible rewards for their support. The fact that this second-degree electorate was limited to the *grands électeurs*, councillors of the town councils and *conseils généraux*, made this flow of gifts and rewards all the more effective. Similarly, some historians have seen in the patronage networks established by deputies of the Third Republic and in the flow of rewards that sustained their grass-roots support a symbol of the regime's corruption. Some went as far as suspecting the subterranean influences of secret societies.[4] Some of the exchanges between political figures and the public took the shape of a collusion of interests between liberal businessmen and moderate republicans. There was corruption, and some of this behaviour was obviously criminal.[5]

On the other hand, one should not be too hasty in condemning the Third Republic. Recent historical accounts of the troubled relationship between politics and money have made the analysis more complex.[6] Undeniably, it is difficult to draw the line between patronage and corruption, and historians of eighteenth-century Britain are familiar with this debate.[7] The exchange of favours and the very direct request made to the deputies to be nothing but the spokesmen of their constituents reflected a wish to maintain direct mandatory democratic practices. The deputies had to cultivate their constituency and practise the art of demagoguery, but also defend their constituents' wishes. To add to these rural metaphors, they had to find some roots in the locality. In the words of Machelon, 'more than a legislator the republican deputy wanted to be a go-between, a negotiator, commissioned and intervening on behalf of electors or his ward'.[8] The radicals especially emphasised the defence of the citizens against the powers of the faceless state.[9] This went against any real party discipline or parliamentary organisation. In the words of Siegfried, the republican deputy of the Third Republic acquired special status and his position in the state changed the nature of the government:

> He alone in the republic is directly responsible to the people, and holds a direct delegation of the sovereign masses. Now with the constituency system, which is the truly French way of voting, the Member of Parliament really owes nothing to his party, for as it did not create him it cannot depose him ... Thus the political system rests on a local foundation, in fact a polyarchy of constituencies where the deputy is absolutely at his best if he happens to be personally a local man, in which case he becomes the plenipotentiary of the districts to Paris. [He] should ... always remain a provincial endowed with a mission.[10]

Some were more effective than others, but it meant that the chamber of deputies and the Senate were the protectors of local peculiarities and the promoters of local developments. Some of these peculiarities and local interests somewhat undermined the grand plans of the central administration, and historians, sitting comfortably among the papers of the central institutions, have been reflecting the central administrators' frustrations. Some, writing on the history of public health, are still indignant that the Parisian experts' efforts could be thus squandered and wasted on rustic minds and resilient local customs.[11]

Surely one could suggest that a nation where the centre has free rein is no longer a democracy? The truth of the Third Republic freedom can be found in this constant negotiating between a strong but cash-starved administration and a weak political leadership, which gave the deputies a great deal of leeway to intervene on behalf of their electors. In the absence of a clear political party system, this mechanism maintained the electors at the heart of the political debates. In the words of constitution specialist Gooch,

> the extreme centralization of the French organization gives to the French executive ... a position of immense potential force. A powerful legislature, however, is unwilling to see this potentiality fully realized in practice. Consequently the weak position of the government appears in a more pronounced light through a marked discrepancy between potentiality and reality.[12]

This may not be very noble or grand, but it worked, and this murky state of affairs allowed French people to defend themselves from a centralist state, which they constantly begged to intervene in their local disputes. Even the short-lived 'great ministry' of Gambetta (from November 1881 to January 1882), dominated by southern provincial deputies, was only a shadow of what it could have been had the fractious and anarchistic tradition of the Commune not lasted.

After the bloodbath: enemies and reconstruction

One might say that it was a high price to pay for such small results as the acquisition of a conservative republic allowing moderate local freedom. The second half of this book has highlighted the forms of violence developed during the war and the civil war. In the final analysis, the republican idiom developed during the empire as a language of opposition was not viable, and the sacrifice of the left was necessary to win over conservative French men and women. In many ways this could overstate the facts. The violence was the product of two factions competing for central power, and not the result of a national desire for civil war.

Another piece of evidence that the Commune was far less a final catastrophe for French revolutionaries was that their return to French politics was relatively swift. They were readily welcomed back among the ranks of the republican left, especially the radicals, whose woolly programme had been narrowed down to rabid anti-clericalism combined with the vaguest social vestiges of the Communards' social aspirations. As Nord has noted, much remained between them, and the republicans exerted themselves to help the victims of Versailles or obtain their amnesty.[13] In terms of a grand narrative of class-consciousness, sociologists like Gould and historians like Yves Lequin perceived the revolution of 1870 as a misfit.[14] The revolution did not give rise to pure political organisations based on class, and some of the urban structures which enabled and maintained the existence of the National Guard and provided the basis of its power went directly against the concept of class. That this should be the analysis even in the recent historiography only shows how rigid and dogmatic the concept of class had become. The revolution of 1870–1 may not have been the culmination of a major factor in the making of a class, but revolutions in general are far more complex than a simplistic Marxist view entails. Besides the fact that, according to Jacques Rougerie, up to 57 per cent of Parisians lived on the product of industrial labour and that there may well have been stronger class components than Gould allows for, the issues are elsewhere.[15]

The issues were diverse and class did play a part. But it was class in the city, class in the neighbourhood, class embedded in the historical discourse of national identity, class as a constitutive element of identity, but neither the most important nor the most vibrant dimension of the revolutionary self. In the same way that the historical heroics and dramatic drum-rolling of war can resonate more strongly than a latent and deeper attachment to the nation and its land, the revolution of 1870 was built on historical narrative and bathed in a language of class and citizenship which remained mainly conceptual rather than practical. To find any depth of Communard thinking, one has to read texts written after the events. Even the most immediate account was still distant from the sources emanating from the Commune itself. In exile, the revolutionaries of 1870–1 matured rapidly. Their ideas and socialism replaced the vacuum left by their defeat. The rhetoric had been intoxicating, but in many instances it had only been circumstantial and disjointed. The socialism of the Communards was retrospective rather than prospective.[16] It did not lead the Commune, and indeed, the Commune was leaderless.

Communards returned nevertheless, and they rebuilt themselves in the post-war polity. Some of them followed the logic of their action and became more socialist in thoughts and deeds than they had been during the Commune. Others remained on the fringes of the socialist groups, and some, like Louise Michel, went into terrorist activities, to be faced by their associates from before the war. Andrieux, Paris Prefect of Police thanks to Gambetta, thus fostered the terrorist groups of Michel and kept his secret agents busy in the same way that, under the Second Empire, the prefect of Lyons had kept his records up to date on Denis Brack and on Andrieux himself. His spies within Michel's group kept him informed. He went as far as being a real *agent provocateur*, financing the anarchist paper *La Révolution Sociale* in 1880 in order to attract them and incite them to commit crimes. The old Communards of 1880 could only manage to cause slight damage to a statue of Thiers. This was a great sadness to the Gambettist policeman, who would have been equally pleased to arrest the old Communards and to see the old enemy's effigy destroyed.[17] Many republicans of yesteryear were now lifelong enemies. These divides had taken place during the war, and this political experience lasted throughout the republic. The pre-1870 Utopia was now dead, and the citizens of the new republic were now enemies. Louise Michel remembered nostalgically:

> One day on the step of the town hall [of Paris], Jules Favre held us all in his long arms, Rigault, Ferré and me, calling us his dear children.
>
> As for me, I knew him for a long time; he had been, like Eugène Pelletan,[18] the president of the society for primary education, and in rue Hautefeuille, where the classes took place, we were shouting 'long live the republic' well before the end of the empire.
>
> I was thinking about all this in these days of May in Satory, by the bloody puddle where the victors washed their hands, the only water prisoners could obtain, lying out under the rain in the blood-laden mud of the courtyard.[19]

The republic as a political idiom of inclusiveness could only live in opposition. With the 4 September republic the tensions within republican ranks became stronger than the bonds that had united the liberal middle-class professionals and the power-hungry members of the bohemian underclass like Vallès or Michel. This group portrayal of Rigault, Ferré, Michel and Favre, while unlikely – Favre would have needed immensely long arms – presents a truly moving image. Rigault was shot by the side of the hotel where he lived, Ferré was executed after his arrest, Favre, as a member of the Thiers government, persecuted the Communard refugees across Europe, asking for their prompt extradition as early as 26 May 1871.[20]

The return to politics had not been easy for the republicans of the government forces either. Republicans were now deeply split, and most of their divisions dated from the wars. Clemenceau and his associates created the radical group, which kept some links with the Communards. Gambetta and the remnants of the national defence government coalesced into the opportunist group and the *Union Républicaine*.[21] In the early years of the Third Republic it is difficult to talk of parties in the English or American meaning of the word, and French politics remained dominated by groups and looser electoral coalitions for much of the first thirty years of parliamentary democracy.[22] These looser forms of politics enabled the return of Communards to the fray, since there was no machinery to exclude them. Some Communards moved to the radicals, some stayed among the socialist minority, many disappeared without trace.[23] Others, like Rochefort, became the enemies of a democracy unable to deliver on the social front and joined the ranks of the Bonapartists or authoritarian figures like General Boulanger. Finally, one has to wait for the Dreyfus affair to see the French political card game reshuffled afresh.[24]

In the background of the Dreyfus affair, one of the lingering memories of the 1870–1 period was obviously the loss of the war itself and the loss of Alsace-Lorraine.[25] The issue of the *revanche* has led many historians into a frenzy of denouncing French politicians as the harbingers of the great catastrophe of 1914.[26] Jean Jaurès was himself convinced that the French had played the trick of Ems back on Germany. Many historians dispute that the *revanche* mattered at all during this inter-war period which lasted nearly two generations. Indeed, historians like Bertrand Joly have a point, in the sense that many politicians repressed the issue so far back in their minds that they hardly ever mentioned it or seldom cared to think a new war possible.[27] Republicans were only too aware that the monarchists would denounce them as warmongerers if mention were made of the *revanche*.[28] The *revanche* lived on in a subterranean way.

School inspectors and writers to the *Revue Pédagogique* complained loudly that the education system had failed to impress on the young the meanings of major historical and national dates or figures. Among a sample of conscripts of the 5th Corps d'Armée (Lyons region) 'more than half could not say anything about Joan of Arc, three-quarters did not know the meaning of Bastille Day and nearly two-thirds did not know a thing about the war of 1870'.[29] The choice of terms reflects a natural tendency to whinge about the state of the nation and puts an interesting choice of historical terms forward: Joan of Arc, recently beatified and reinvented as a bellicose incarnation of the pre-Marianne nation, Bastille Day, and 1870. The equation of the three made for a potent brew that may not have been palatable to the average young man, many of whom had left school much earlier. The *revanche* teaching may well have been less efficient than manuals and textbooks lead us to believe, but it remains the case that 1870 was put on the same footing as 1789 and Joan of Arc. It is also true that the great propagandists of a new conflict, like Juliette Adam[30] or Déroulède, were preaching in the desert and the popularity of General Boulanger owed more to his anti-parliamentarian banter than to the perspective of a new war on Germany.[31] Indeed, the recent analyses of Boulanger's rhetoric point to its contradictions and purely domestic use.[32]

Thiers had been a pacifist, and the following generation of pragmatic politicians could hardly dream of a situation in which France could attack and win over an enemy twice her size. France in 1870 was occupied and was to remain occupied for three more years, a German occupation the French have tended to ignore historically. In many parts this occupation was lived as a continuation of the war, with the occupying forces remaining billeted in private houses for up to three years.[33] Many real republicans were also repulsed by the thought of initiating a war.[34] The organisations set up to foster a *revanche* spirit soon lost their political integrity and had to find strange bedfellows with the royalists, the old Communards and the remnants of the Bonapartists. Never powerful, the *revanche* parties became even faintly ridiculous while peace dragged on and the French colonial empire expanded in Africa and Indochina.[35]

The *revanche* was not, however, the purely contemplative exercise Joly describes, nor can we so easily deny any correlation between the Dreyfus affair and the traumas of 1870. The two stories were constantly correlated and juxtaposed. Within the pages of the illustrated supplement of *Le Petit Journal* one could find on the first page the famous scene of Dreyfus standing, his clothes in tatters and his sword broken, with the legend 'the traitor', and in the following pages one could read a war narrative of 1870. In fact, for the year 1895 when the affair first came to light, Dreyfus was represented twice and had two short articles about him, while the Franco-Prussian war was mentioned in thirty full-length articles and referred to in five full-size pictures. Many of the remaining full-size pictures referred to the army and its role in Madagascar and to the Russian alliance.[36]

The many thousand articles and books published over this recent period of history demonstrated the desire to remember, to remember to forget, or to make sense of the defeat. The inflated prestige of the army, in spite of its recent humiliating defeat and bloody civil war victory, came largely from a desire to repress the recent past. Repression does not mean silence, however. Public space and collective landscape were re-shaped using the terminology and names of the 1870–1 period.

The proliferation of historical monuments and the multiplication of new boulevards named after the period of 1870–1 reflected the desire to establish a collective civic landscape around the events of 1870. New names and statues were often the fruit of nationwide campaigning, so that the civic landscape and the national became intermingled and confused. Monuments of the glory of Belfort by Bartholdi in Paris and Belfort were funded by national subscriptions. The memorial of the battles of Nuits-St-Georges in 1872 joined the monuments built in memory of Coulmiers or Mars-la-Tour.[37] Later, many departments erected one single monument to commemorate the dead of the department.[38] In all of these, the memory was one of sacrifices and expiatory defeats.[39] It cannot be denied that they were primarily acts of remembrance and grief, but they were also the result of negotiated settlement within the locality, which centred on the war and its traumatic effects. One would search in vain for examples on such a scale for earlier wars.[40]

While the collective was the subject of acts of remembrance, the individual was seldom singled out. Veterans of the war were only awarded the pensions to which they were entitled after a lengthy struggle by a number of aristocratic campaigners.[41] On the other hand, the veterans whose stories and anecdotal evidence were to fill the vacuum left by the absence of a national epic narrative were not honoured by the state. A form printed in the 1890s by the French administration explicitly stated that there was no military medal for the veterans of 1870. The same form continued to be used until 1911, when a bill offering such a medal was debated to be eventually voted in in 1912. The search for the survivors had begun when the war put an end to this modest honouring of a previous generation. After the disruption of the First World War, the archives show that it was the 1930s before all the veterans of 1870 received the medal they were entitled to as a private recognition of war sufferings.[42]

A more liminal memory of the civil war was kept afloat among radical circles by other alternative forms of memory calling for radical monuments, such as the one to the memory of Blanqui which led Louise Michel to speak in the now legendary Croix Rousse neighbourhood, or the monument to Raspail.[43] Reintegrated into national politics, the Commune of Paris eventually began to enjoy a revival of interest and a mythology that enabled its survivors to make a living from their lectures and memoirs. Their original writings had become collectibles when the ashes of Paris were still smoking. Communards had achieved the status of living legends, but this only reflected their irrelevance to the new polity.

Even the more humble Barodet, leader of the radicals of Lyons in 1870 and whose election led to the fall of Thiers, had his posthumous hour when, in 1910, the young mayor of Lyons, Herriot,[44] declared,

> if it has been possible to say of a statesman that he was the liberator of the territory [Adolphe Thiers], one could say that Barodet was the liberator of the Commune by the authority, craft and energy he used to free it from the heavy burden weighing upon [the city].[45]

Barodet was thus reconciled in death with Thiers, the arch-enemy. In 1873, Thiers' friends had described him in rather more colourful language: 'Barodet, he's a *stiffy*! Barodet blows your mind fifteen feet away, as your friend Père Duchesne would say.'[46] The man of the Commune of Lyons was described as 'a keen patriot exempt of any attachment to the revolutionary clans' by the prefect who dipped his pen deep in the revisionist ink of Third Republic myths.[47]

Republicans appropriated Thiers himself. The old statesman was soon recognised as the embodiment of a conservative republic. In one particular incident towards the end of his life, the deputies of the left and centre turned towards him to honour the repressor of the Commune. This famous session of the assembly took place on 17 June 1877 and was immortalised dramatically by two tremendous group portraits by Garnier and Ulmann, reproduced throughout France (Figure 9.1).

The mnemonic landscape of the *année terrible* came to dominate the civic landscape in many often literal ways and it is often in this physical record of the wars of 1870 and 1871 that one finds the longest lasting expression of alternative views on citizenship. The Catholic Church was particularly efficient in erecting monuments to its own glory and vision of the recent past. The Montmartre[48] and Fourvière (1891)[49] basilicas answered in monumental style and dwarfed any secular monuments radicals could muster.

Even if we take into account the large number of historical variables between 1871 and 1914, it cannot be denied that the conflicts of that year served as reference point in any political discourse. In social terms the fundamental questions asked in 1870 remained the questions that the Third Republic was attempting to answer up until 1914. The action of the conservative republic was originally reactionary, and the Third Republic witnessed a regression of the mutual societies and trade unions in the immediate aftermath of the war.[50] In terms of rights and benefits, the republic did not prove generous.[51] The republican cause was built up in adversarial terms on the purely political ground of the right-wing

Figure 9.1   The Liberator of the Territory (17 June 1877), J.A. Garnier, 1878

republicans around Ferry and Gambetta.[52] The social ground only became political when the republicans realised that it was the natural battlefield for a struggle against the Catholic Church. This realisation occurred mostly in the local context and within the remit of the municipal franchise.[53] The Paris council or the Lyons council thus spent the early years of the un-republican republic plotting their ultimate victory over school and hospital provisions.[54]

In narrative terms, the war and civil war anchored the discourse and fixed the language of Third Republic politics. Writing retrospectively, the historian Edgar Quinet stated optimistically that 'the republic only has to live on [*se laisser vivre*] to grow and increase'.[55]

The key issues of the relationship between citizenship and religion continued to plague the political debate. The great debate on the separation of Church and state haunted the first thirty years of the republic to the exclusion of many other pressing social issues, but it claimed other victims on its way. The Dreyfus affair revolved on the issue of religious identity and citizenship, and the poor Dreyfus, the Alsatian Jew, was emblematic of these questions raised in Chapter 5.[56] In North Africa, anti-Semitism had a dramatic importance which reflected the same dynamics. The North African French citizens, most recently implanted, felt the need to exclude one of the oldest and most isolated communities of the region, and many turned anti-Semitism into a political system. One can see the scars of the war in these two surges of anti-Semitism. In France, the need to identify a traitor, an internationalist agent, accidentally focused on Dreyfus at a time when French racialist definitions of citizenship were popularised by Drumont, elected deputy of Algiers in 1898.[57] In North Africa the tensions between the Arabs and the colonisers found some relief in the isolating of a common enemy, the Jews. The new order of the republic was not one of fully inclusive citizenship; the idealism of the origins was denied by compromises, and as the republic moved on it turned its back on its shameful origins while never freeing itself from the debates arising in 1870–1.

The long *constituante*: assembly politics and the making of the Third Republic

After the 8 February elections, the assembly seemed the instrument of a rural counter-revolution. In fact this was misleading. It is true that the assembly was dominated by the great names of small places. But the restoration of a Bourbon, Bourbon Orleans or Bonaparte faced too many hurdles to be possible in the long run. The Bonapartist cause was of course impaired by the fresh memory of Napoleon III's military disaster, but it managed to create a party for the first time in its history and it was not without some local roots itself.[58] The royalist cause, which also had some deep roots in many places, was if anything more plagued by internal rivalries than any other faction.

The problems of the royalist cause were twofold. First, they disagreed on the potential monarch, and the debates on an Orleanist or a Legitimist candidate revealed a chasm between two ideologies which made Orleanists closer to republicans than to Legitimists. Second, the assembly had not been elected to re-establish the monarchy but to sign a peace treaty. In the words of the moderate republican newspaper *Le Corrézien*,

> We have not lost our memory and we perfectly remember the period preceding the elections of February. At that time, did one deputy, one single one, declare clearly in his manifesto that he was the partisan of such or such form of government? Which candidate declared, 'Elected, I will ask for the restoration of Henri V'?[59]

The restoration of Henri V was made impossible by the expectations it raised. Over the forty-one years between Charles X and 1871, nearly twice as long as the period between 1789 and 1814, the Legitimists had retreated into an ideal world fed on Chateaubriand's romanticism and exalted mysticism.[60] The drive of Ultramontane religiosity was strongest in 1871, immediately after the invasion of Rome, the Syllabus of Errors (1864) and the dogma of the infallibility of the pope.[61] It was a renunciation to the world, which inspired the pretender himself but also excluded the monarchists from achieving their dream of a terrestrial Jerusalem.[62] Their dream society belonged to a fantasy past, and they showed no real inclination to negotiate with the present day to rule in earnest.[63] The hierarchy of their peers did not support the few active Catholics involved in working-class politics.[64] The repressive moral order of the monarchist rule did not generate the support anticipated, and the legitimist political and social doctrine was in a dead end similar to that of the Catholic Church.[65] One had to wait for *Rerum Novarum* and the papal lead of 1891 to see things change among some Ultramontane Catholics and for them to attempt to play a meaningful part in French politics and a renewal of Christian democracy.[66] Interestingly enough, the leading move towards recognition of the republic came from the archbishop of Algiers, Lavigerie, who was at the heart of the conflicts over religion and citizenship in the newly assimilated colony.

The Orleanist house, on the other hand, lacked the legitimacy of history, the prestige and ideologically the substance to make it a distinctive force on the liberal right of French politics. The great betrayal of Thiers, who seems to have accepted that a restoration was impossible, showed the way towards authoritarian republicanism.

This stalemate led to a finely tuned balance of powers for the period 1871–3 between an amorphous assembly majority, regularly weakened by the loss of its aged members, and a composite executive led by Thiers. Thiers included in his ministers a number of old republicans of the centre left, such as Jules Simon and Jules Favre. Lacking real support on the right, he sought allies from the left. This strange equilibrium of a government in contradiction with many of the assembly's desires reflected the constitutional vacuum in which both operated. Between 1871 and 1875 or even 30 January 1879 (the day Jules Grévy, an old republican, replaced the monarchist president MacMahon), the national assembly became the longest serving and most understated constituent assembly. In fact, the Third Republic did not benefit from a single constitutional set of laws but from the aggregation of rules and practices. Thiers was thus first a head of the executive; he then assumed the title of president of the republic during the repression of the Commune (granted officially on 31 August 1871).

Thiers subsequently lost his right to address the assembly at length on 13 March 1873, and soon afterwards had to resign on 24 May 1873. The following presidency was given to the lacklustre Marshal MacMahon for a seven-year term, which was to allow the monarchists to restore the Bourbons. In 1875 the Senate was created and, after the narrow vote of the Wallon amendment, the rules guiding the relationship between the president and the parliament created a constitution.[67]

In 1871, the only solid institution was the head of the executive who was simultaneously a deputy, the head of government and the head of state. Thiers could be all this because of his experience, his age and his ambiguities. The regime could have evolved towards a presidential rule in the American style, but it did not. In 1876, the elections returned a moderate republican majority. Between 1876 and 1879 royalist hopes waned and the powers of the president declined accordingly, until MacMahon decided to resign to be replaced by a powerless figurehead. By 1879 the Third Republic had mutated into a purely parliamentary regime marked by relative political instability (many ministries followed each other) and great administrative stability. While the presidents of the council (prime ministers) fell in rapid succession, some people remained in power in the same function through a series of crises: for instance, Freycinet remained at the Ministry of War for five years. The policies of some departments of state remained constant under several governments.

Jaurès's paradoxical argument that 'the Commune saved the Third Republic' has some truth in it. The scare of a united republican force driven to the despair and left-wing excesses of the Parisian revolution offered Thiers the space he needed to sell his conservative version of the republican form of government to the provincial French.[68] The Parisians had been sacrificed while the Lyonese and the many other provincial radical republicans had been saved from a full-blown civil war they would probably have lost.

The 1870–1 wars were probably the funeral of revolutionary myths in France, as François Furet has argued.[69] The citizens of 1870–1 had not managed to reinvigorate the armies of the revolutionary age, they had lost the war and the most radical among them had been defeated in Paris. In the provinces, on the other hand, the revolution had found some space and rooted itself. The republicans had dissociated themselves from the revolutionary myth because it was an almost exclusively urban myth and France was rural. Republicans and republican historians came to celebrate the rural virtues expressed by George Sand to the extent of minimising the real value of education and book learning.[70] In fact, having won over the cities, the modernist

Third Republic had to become rural and even 'ruralist' to survive, choosing its emblems in an agricultural iconography.[71] Socialist authors like Guesde, denouncing the 'rural justice' of the rustic republic, were misjudging entirely the political realities of a country where 70 per cent of the citizens were living in small rural communes. What happened in 1870 made obvious a number of central mechanisms in the republicanisation of the country around the existing processes of universal male suffrage inherited from 1848 and the Second Empire.[72] Citizens were not all from cities, and rural communes were also communes worthy of notice and work. The Commune ideals, separate from the specific evolution of Paris in 1871, lived on, and had enabled political renewal locally through the medium of National Guards, help committees and *ligues*. The countryside and the small communes of France were not a desert of political imagination.

Fraternalist ideology and mutual help also existed in the rural backwaters, and from this experience followed the realisation, even at a very prosaic level, of what the state actually was and of how the state and the nation fitted together in symbiosis.[73] The state was an abstract concept much more widely shared than had been thought hitherto, and the French understood how to reward those who participated in its strengthening. The republic – even the repressive, conservative, almost anti-republican regime of 1871–6 – ultimately by simply being a republic, created citizens working within the republic.[74] The regime gradually removed its competitors from the political field. A dreamt empire or monarchy belonged to the past, and the republic took great care to project itself into the future, turning its back on the past. Through the practice of local elections, visits by deputies and senators, the exchange of honour and help, and the sociability of the republic, the citizens became republicans almost by default. The republic created republicans.

APPENDIX 1
Chronological landmarks

July 1870

After a short crisis over the Spanish succession, the weakened government of the Liberal Ollivier was pushed to declare war on Prussia and thus on most of its German allies. This phase, improperly named the Franco-Prussian war in much of the historiography, can be divided into two sequences, the imperial war that ended in defeat in Sedan and the revolutionary war which ended in February 1871. The first sequence is marked by bloody battles and high casualty rates on both sides, while the second is noticeably more patchy with a number of key sieges, including that of Paris, and battles and skirmishes which only dented the circle of iron around Paris.

July 1870: imperial war phase

15	French mobilisation.
16	German mobilisation.
19	Declaration of war.

August 1870

2	East: French attack of Sarrebrücken.
4	East: French defeat of Wissembourg.
6	East: French defeat of Froeschwiller (or Woerth).
8	East: retreat on Metz. Reorganisation of the National Guard.
9	Paris: fall of the Ollivier government. General Palikao forms a new conservative government.
10	East: beginning of the siege of Strasburg.[1] Mobilisation of French males 25 to 35.
14	East: French victory of Borny.
16	East: battle of Gravelotte.
18	East: Bazaine's army moves to Metz, battle of Saint-Privat.
20	Paris: General Trochu arrives in Paris.
21	East: beginning of the siege of Metz.

September 1870

1   East: battle of Sedan.
2   East: Napoleon III surrenders.

Revolutionary war phase

This phase of the war was marked by its military improvisation and relatively unsuccessful attempts at matching the invaders in the battlefield, and by the administrative and governmental confusion. The government of 4 September was proclaimed in Paris and soon decided to split in two, setting a delegation in Tours in the event of a full-scale siege. This delegation was singularly reinforced by the arrival in October of Gambetta, who created the mechanics of a war dictatorship relying on regional initiatives and negotiating with the municipal movements around the country.

4   Paris: revolution, Gouvernement de la Défense Nationale proclaimed, arrival of retreating armies. Creation of a *Commission des barricades*, led by Rochefort. Committees of vigilance and Central Committee of the arrondissements.
4   Lyons: Commune proclaimed at the Hôtel de Ville.
6   France: freedom of the press.
10   Paris: organisation of the *guardes mobiles* into an army of 100,000 men.
11   Paris: city, National Guard *sédentaire* and gendarmerie, 200,000; battle-field and fortress, army and *mobiles*, 200,000.
11   Tours: *délégation* of the French government settles in.
13   Paris: organisation of Paris into nine sectors.
15   Paris: first 'red poster'. This red poster stated radical revolutionary aims for the first time.
17   Paris: arrival of German troops near Paris. *Guardes mobiles* obtain the right to elect officers.
19   Paris: siege of Paris begins.
19   Marseilles: creation of the *Ligue du Midi*.
20   Paris: end of postal and telegraphic communications. *Défense à outrance* becomes the doctrine. Creation of the Paris court martial. End of peace talks at Ferrières. During these peace talks the government was first given the German war aims regarding Alsace-Lorraine and war compensations. The conditions were not accepted by the French foreign minister, Jules Favre.
22–3 Paris: skirmish of Villejuif.
24   Paris: symbolic closure of theatres.
24   Tours: organisation of the first Armée de la Loire.
27   Paris: first balloon leaves Paris.
28   East: surrender of Strasburg.
30   Paris: battle of Chevilly.

October 1870

7	Paris: departure of Gambetta in a balloon.
8	Paris: demonstrations in favour of the Commune.
9	West: arrival of Gambetta in Tours, negotiation with Garibaldi.
10	West: defeat near Orléans.
11	France: mobilisation of parts of the National Guard *sédentaire*.
13	West: loss of Orléans.
13–14	Paris: battle of Bagneux.
20	Paris: battle of the Malmaison.
20	North: the Bonapartist General Bourbaki forms the northern army.
26	Paris: Flavigny brings half the 500,000 ff of British aid to Versailles. Reopening of the Comédie Française, great ceremony at the Panthéon reminiscent of 1793 (organised by Dr Bertillon, mayor of V arrondissement).
28	East: Marshal Bazaine surrenders Metz. Thiers comes back from his European tour. The old politician had attempted to drum up some support from the great powers and had found a frosty reception in all major capital cities.
29	Dijon: Garibaldian defeat.
30	Paris: loss of le Bourget; the surrender of Metz becomes known.
31	Paris: Commune insurrection, led by Dorian, Blanqui, Delescluze, Félix Pyat, Bonvallet and Flourens, fails. This attempted insurrection was very short-lived and poorly supported in spite of gaining control of the police prefecture, the town hall and most of the sitting government. A negotiated settlement put an end to the crisis.
31	Dijon: German invasion.

November 1870

1	Paris: plebiscite for 3 November.
2	Paris: Ernest Cresson re-establishes the Préfecture de police services. Mobilisation of all men aged 21 to 40.
2	Burgundy: German army moves down to Beaune.
3	Paris: governmental plebiscite: 562,000 yes, 62,000 no. Clément Thomas becomes commander-in-chief of the National Guard.
3	Tours: edict asking for the creation of one gun battery per 100,000 inhabitants, paid for by each department, within two months.
4	Paris: arrest of Pyat, Ranvier, Razoua, Mottu, Millière, etc. Women petition for the Commune.
5	Paris: elections of arrondissement mayors.
5	Burgundy: Garibaldian victory of St Jean de Losnes.
6	Paris: reorganisation of the army.
7	Refusal of the armistice. Twenty-two departments invaded, twenty-one fortresses attacked, ten besieged, eleven captured.

8	Paris: mobilisation of the National Guard in active units. East: surrender of Verdun.
9	Orléans: battle of Coulmiers, victory of the Loire army, Van der Tann retreats from Orléans.
12	Paris: snow.
25	Provinces: creation of instruction camps.
27	Paris: renewed censorship on news coverage of military operations. North: defeat of Amiens.
28	Paris: offensive on Champigny. Provinces: defeat of Beaune-la-Rollande.
30	Paris: retreat after the battle of Champigny.

December 1870

2	Provinces: defeat of Loigny. Paris: $-18°$ Celsius, end of the Champigny battle. North: northern army defeated, 1st German army moves towards Rouen.
4	Paris: reorganisation of Parisian armies. West: Orléans lost.
6	Tours: creation of two Loire armies, Bourbaki's and Chanzy's.
7–9	Provinces: battle of Beaugency.
9	Tours: German offensive on Tours. The delegation leaves for Bordeaux.
12	Provinces: creation of the Armée de l'Est.
14	Paris: reorganisation of the army in Paris into thirty regiments; rationing of meat, adulteration of bread. East: Montmedy and Phalsbourg surrender.
20	Provinces: creation of centres for the convalescent wounded and sick.
21	Paris: battles of Le Bourget, Montretout, Buzenval; temperatures of $-24°$ on the walls and $-15°$ inside Paris.
27	Paris: shelling of Parisian walls begins.
28	Marseilles: end of the *Ligue du Midi*.

January 1871

2	Mézières surrenders.
3	North: French victory of Bapaume.
5	Paris: night-time shelling of Paris.
7	Paris: 'red poster' calling for the Commune. The second red poster was the most important in the sense that it was widely perceived as setting the agenda for a new Communard revolution.
11	Le Mans: defeat. East: Bourbaki moves towards Belfort.[2]
12	West: retreat from Le Mans to Alençon and Evreux.
15	West: skirmishes on the Loire. Paris: the forts are being flattened. East: Bourbaki attacks German positions near Belfort.
16	West: fall of Alençon. German army moves in behind Bourbaki.
17	Paris: hospitals bombed. First bombs on the right bank of the river.

18   East: retreat of Bourbaki. German empire proclaimed in Versailles.

19   Paris: battles of Buzenval and Montretout. Le Flô becomes general-in-chief.

21   Paris: breakaway from Mazas, insurrection in the XX arrondissement; Vinoy becomes the general of the Paris armies. Burgundy: attack of Dijon defended by Garibaldi.

22   Paris: insurrection of the XX arrondissement finishes.

23   Paris: clubs are closed, left-wing newspapers like *Le réveil et le combat* are censored. Burgundy: battle of Dijon continues.

24   East: Bourbaki in Besançon. Paris: Central Committee of the National Guard meets. Favre negotiates with Bismarck.

25   West: Second Armée de la Loire moves towards Caen. East: retreat of Bourbaki.

26   Paris: convocation of the mayors of Paris. Ceasefire.

27   East: Bourbaki attempts to commit suicide.

28   All of France but the east: armistice. East: retreat of Bourbaki's army towards Switzerland.

31   State of provincial armies: Faidherbe 100,000; Second Loire 140,000; Brittany 30,000; Bourbaki's 80,000, retreating towards Switzerland.

February 1871: the Versailles–Paris–Algeria conflicts

The war had ended in February, and yet it continued in the east of France, from which the government had no news, hoping for a last-minute breakthrough. Instead, the badly devised armistice led to the destruction of the second largest French army. Immediately after the cessation of hostilities, the elections of 8 February were organised on a purely war or peace platform. The majority returned to the National Assembly was conservative or even monarchist. The situation in Paris did not improve rapidly and the measures announced by the government on the end of the National Guard, the end of the moratorium on rent and debts fuelled discontent. The fact that the new government had left open a possible restoration of the monarchy as well as a bungled attempt to disarm the National Guard led to growing resentment and an armed insurrection which found support in the National Guard Central Committee.

1   Paris: food riots at Les Halles. East: Bourbaki's army become refugees in Switzerland.

3   Paris: railways reopen.

5   Paris: food arrives under police surveillance.

6   Bordeaux: Gambetta resigns.

7   Paris: end of requisitions, *boucheries municipales* maintained.

8   France: general elections.

9   Bordeaux: war council in which only General Chanzy believes in continuing the war.

11   Paris: riot in Belleville.

14   Bordeaux: opening of *Assemblée Nationale*.

15   Dismantling of the armies of the Loire and the north.

16   Bordeaux: Grévy president of the Assembly.

17   Bordeaux: Thiers *chef du pouvoir exécutif*.

20   Paris: Thiers in Paris to negotiate peace.

21   France: announcement of the dismantling of the National Guard, reconstitution of the army.

22   France: liberation of volunteers.

24   Paris: commemorative demonstration in honour of 1848.

26   Paris: anti-Prussian demonstration of demobilised National Guard. Versailles: peace preliminaries.

28   Paris: evacuation of second sector by regular troops.

March 1871

1–2 Paris: 30,000 Germans enter second sector, Champs Elysées.

9   Algeria: *Jihad* declared against the French.

10   Bordeaux: anti-republican agitation in the lower chamber, Versailles chosen as the new seat of Parliament. End of the moratorium on rent and debts announced.

11   Paris: Vinoy suppresses six republican journals, including *Le Vengeur*, *Le Cri du peuple* and *Le Mot d'ordre*. The insurrectionists of 31 October are sentenced to death in their absence.

15   Paris: general assembly of the National Guard Committee.

17   Paris: order to take away the guns of Paris, Provence: Blanqui arrested.

The Paris Commune began in an improvised riot and execution which could have been of moderate significance had it not been for the government's hurried departure from Paris and the rapid organisation of the National Guard into a provisional government. The Commune then mutated twice, first through municipal elections and then through a return to the historical precedent of the revolutionary commune and the creation of a Committee of Public Salvation.

18   Paris: commune insurrection when the army fails to remove the guns of Montmartre. Generals Lecomte and Thomas are executed by their own men.

19   Paris: Central Committee announces municipal elections for the Commune.

21   Versailles: occupation of the Mount Valérien fort. Paris: pro-government demonstration.

22   Paris: violent pro-government demonstration repressed by the National Guard.

22   Lyons: failed Communard insurrection.

23   Marseilles: Communard insurrection.

24   Toulouse, Narbonne, Saint-Étienne: Communard insurrections lasting

at most a few days.

26   Paris: municipal elections. Le Creusot: short-lived Communard insurrection.

28   Paris: Commune proclaimed.

April 1871

2   Paris: separation between Church and state.

3   Paris: Communard offensive defeated, death of Flourens.

4   Marseilles: end of insurrection. Versailles: Duval executed.

6   Paris: law on hostages.

8   Algeria: *Jihad* in full sway.

11   Paris: *Union des femmes pour la défense de Paris et les soins aux blessés.*

13   Paris: decree on destruction of the Vendôme column.

16   Algeria: Fort National besieged until 12 May.

19   Paris: Communard programme: *Déclaration au peuple Français.*

21   Versailles: conciliatory visits from the Freemasons. Paris: new municipal butcheries.

24   Versailles: organisation of municipal elections throughout France.

May 1871

1   Paris: Committee of Public Salvation. The Jacobin majority seems to be taking yet more power in the Commune of Paris. Cluseret sacked and replaced by Rossel.

5   Algeria: death of El-Mokrani.

6   Versailles: Thiers rejects any conciliation.

7   Paris: decree on pawning.

8   Versailles: Thiers' ultimatum.

9   Versailles: Fort d'Issy occupied.

10   Paris: Rossel resigns, replaced by Delescluze. Frankfurt: peace treaty between the new Reich and France.

11   Paris: Thiers' house pulled down.

13   Versailles: fort of Vanves occupied.

16   Paris: Column Vendôme pulled down.

17   Paris: decree on pensions to include common-law wives and children.

18   Paris: censorship of ten newspapers. Versailles: vote on Frankfurt Treaty.

21   Versailles: troops enter Paris.

22   Paris: west of Paris occupied.

23   Paris: Montmartre taken; Dombrowski shot; first fires.

24   Paris: Hôtel de Ville burnt; Darboy shot with five other hostages; Quartier Latin falls. Mass executions of Communards taken prisoner.

25   Paris: death of Delescluze.

26   Centre of Paris occupied, mass massacre of hostages.

27   Belleville falls, Père Lachaise and east fall.
28   Last barricade rue Rampenneau.
29   Fort of Vincennes surrenders.

July 1871

1   Retaliations in Algeria.

August 1871

13   End of conflict in Algeria.

November 1871

28   Executions of Communards: Rossel, Ferré.

January 1872

16   Great requiem in Notre-Dame.

May 1872

3   Deportations of Communards to New Caledonia.

May 1873

24   Parliamentary defeat of Adolphe Thiers.

May 1880

23   Commemoration at the *Mur des fédérés*.

July 1880

11   Amnesty of all Communards.

APPENDIX 2

Detailed breakdown of the French war effort by departments

Department	Gardes Nationaux mobilisés[1]	Corps-francs[2]	Male population	Male population 20–40[3]	Total population[4]	%age of male population in age group
Ain	9,111	2	181,185	72,474	369,767	13
Aisne	Occupied	3	276,652	110,661	564,597	
Allier	7,200	4	174,651	69,860	356,432	10
Alpes, Basses	4,000		71,720	28,688	146,368	14
Alpes, Hautes	3,000	1	61,299	24,519	125,100	12
Alpes Maritimes	6,000	9	95,343	38,137	194,578	16
Ardèche	11,074	2	190,379	76,151	388,529	15
Ardennes	2,000	16	161,264	64,505	329,111	3
Ariège	6,000	1	123,406	49,362	251,850	12
Aube	Occupied	8	128,764	51,505	262,785	
Aude	8,000	1	138,966	55,586	283,606	14
Aveyron	12,000	1	193,979	77,591	395,877	15
Bouche-du-Rhône	15,500	7	248,484	99,393	507,112	16
Calvados	9,500	9	235,686	94,274	480,992	10
Cantal	4,500	1	117,856	47,142	240,523	10
Charente	7,000	2	185,749	74,299	379,081	9
Charente inférieure	8,300	3	235,719	94,287	481,060	9
Cher	5,354	3	158,462	63,385	323,393	8
Corrèze	6,072	2	151,957	60,783	310,118	10
Corse	4,503	1	123,915	49,566	252,889	9
Côte d'Or	Occupied	3	188,228	75,291	384,140	
Côte du Nord	17,500	2	308,051	123,220	628,676	14
Creuse	6,500	3	132,327	52,930	270,055	12
Dordogne	9,930	4	245,826	98,330	501,687	10
Doubs	10,000	4	145,177	58,070	296,280	17
Drôme	8,500		160,075	64,030	326,684	13
Eure	Occupied	8	195,343	78,137	398,661	

Department	Gardes Nationaux mobilisés[1]	Corps-francs[2]	Male population	Male population 20–40[3]	Total population[4]	%age of male population in age group
Eure et Loir	Occupied	3	142,323	56,929	290,455	
Finistère	13,950	5	307,379	122,951	627,304	11
Gard	12,558	4	206,832	82,732	422,107	15
Garonne	10,025	4	237,199	94,879	484,081	11
Gers	8,732	4	146,476	58,590	298,931	15
Gironde	16,000	7	326,924	130,769	667,193	12
Hérault	11,500	1	200,601	80,240	409,391	14
Ille et Vilaine	17,878	2	286,615	114,646	584,930	16
Indre	6,228	1	132,326	52,930	270,054	12
Indre et Loire	6,500	10	158,550	63,420	323,572	10
Isère	14,000	4	283,096	113,238	577,748	12
Jura	10,800	1	146,046	58,418	298,053	18
Landes	4,331	1	147,411	58,964	300,839	7
Loir et Cher	Occupied	4	131,824	52,729	269,029	
Loire	17,223	2	253,625	101,450	517,603	17
Haute Loire	9,302	3	149,705	59,882	305,521	16
Loire inférieure	17,317	7	284,301	113,720	580,207	15
Loiret	Occupied	1	172,850	69,140	352,757	
Lot	5,090	2	144,815	57,926	295,542	9
Lot et Garonne	5,500	2	162,711	65,084	332,065	8
Lozère	4,331		67,309	26,923	137,367	16
Maine et Loire	12,000	4	257,745	103,098	526,012	12
Manche	11,098	4	289,796	115,918	591,421	10
Marne	Occupied	4	188,894	75,557	385,498	
Haute Marne	Occupied	3	126,665	50,666	258,501	
Mayenne	10,453	2	183,832	73,532	375,168	14
Meurthe	Occupied		210,035	84,014	428,643	
Meuse	Occupied		149,714	59,885	305,540	
Morbihan	12,660		238,387	95,354	486,504	13
Moselle	Occupied		218,763	87,505	446,457	
Nièvre	7,658	4	163,078	65,231	332,814	12
Nord	Disputed	13	638,656	255,462	1,303,380	
Oise	32,000	2	196,694	78,677	401,417	41
Orne	7,354	16	207,441	82,976	423,350	9
Pas-de-Calais	17,009	3	354,925	141,970	724,338	12
Puy-de-Dôme	11,209	3	282,440	112,976	576,409	8
Pyrénées, basses	6,854	2	213,947	85,579	436,628	14

Department	Gardes Nationaux mobilisés[1]	Corps-francs[2]	Male population	Male population 20–40[3]	Total population[4]	%age of male population in age group
Pyrénées, hautes	6,887	3	117,687	47,075	240,179	15
Pyrénées orientales	3,500	4	89,063	35,625	181,763	10
Rhin, bas	Occupied	9	283,359	113,343	578,285	
Rhin, haut	Occupied	7	252,743	101,097	515,802	
Rhône	13,500	10	324,621	129,848	662,493	10
Haute-Saône	Occupied	2	155,419	62,167	317,183	
Saône et Loire	11,186	3	285,247	114,098	582,137	10
Sarthe	7,300	8	228,416	91,366	466,155	8
Savoie	8,000	1	134,769	53,907	275,039	15
Haute Savoie	6,000	3	131,073	52,429	267,496	11
Seine	At siege	59	957,293	382,917	1,953,660	
Seine-inférieure	22,711	19	387,094	154,837	789,988	15
Seine et Marne	Occupied	5	172,632	69,053	352,312	
Seine et Oise	Occupied	3	251,405	100,562	513,073	
Deux Sèvres	8,250	2	161,120	64,448	328,817	13
Somme	Occupied	3	280,596	112,238	572,646	
Tarn	8,800	4	173,280	69,312	353,633	13
Tarn et Garonne	3,300	2	113,950	45,580	232,551	7
Var	7,318	4	154,607	61,843	315,526	12
Vaucluse	7,500	4	131,445	52,577	268,255	14
Vendée	8,500	5	193,890	77,556	395,695	11
Vienne	6,000	4	157,793	63,117	322,028	10
Haute Vienne	5,994	3	156,601	62,640	319,595	10
Vosges	Occupied	4	203,587	81,435	415,485	
Yonne	Occupied	3	181,449	72,579	370,305	
Alger	No data	7			974,491	
Constantine	No data	10			1,402,027	
Oran	No data	4 including Algerians		622,606		
Total					40,386,005	

184

NOTES

1 Introduction: citizenship, wars and revolutions

1 Simon E. Baldwin, *The Relations of Education to Citizenship*, New Haven, Yale University Press, 1912, pp. 27–8.
2 Katherine Auspitz, *The Radical Bourgeoisie: The 'Ligue de l'Enseignement' and the Origins of the Third Republic, 1866–1885*, Cambridge University Press, 1982.
3 This is no less than a form of colonialist discourse turned inwards to the working class. On the colonialist discourse on education see Robert Aldrich, *Greater France: A History of French Overseas Expansion*, Macmillan, 1996, pp. 212–15.
4 For instance, see recent instances: R. Mosher *et al.*, *Preparing for Citizenship: Teaching Youth to Live Democratically*, Westport, Praeger, 1995; Patricia White, *Civic Virtue and Public Schooling: Educating Citizens for a Democratic Society*, Teachers' College Press, 1996; Lynn Yates (ed.), *Citizenship and Education*, Bundoora, Victoria, La Trobe University Press, 1995; Orit Ichilov, *Citizenship and Citizenship Education in a Changing World*, Woburn, 1998.
5 This goes against well-established concepts of citizenship predating the French Revolution; see Richard Vernon, *Citizenship and Order: Studies in French Political Thought*, University of Toronto Press, 1986, pp. 15–33.
6 Richard Vernon, *Citizenship and Order: Studies in French Political Thought*, University of Toronto Press, 1986, pp. 125–7.
7 Pierre Rosanvallon, *Le Sacre du citoyen, histoire du suffrage universel en France*, Gallimard, 1992, pp. 330–90.
8 This was the central message of the texts published around 1870–1 by Ernest Renan; see 'La Réforme intellectuelle et morale de la France', *Qu'est-ce qu'une nation?*, Imprimerie Nationale, 1996, pp. 143–57.
9 Jacques Rancière gives central importance to Michelet's work in *Les Noms de l'histoire*, Le Seuil, 1992, pp. 110–19; Ceri Crossley, *French Historians and Romanticism: Thierry, Guizot, the Saint-Simonians, Quinet, Michelet*, Routledge, 1993, pp. 186–93.
10 Roger Bellet, *Jules Vallès*, Fayard, 1995.
11 Jules Vallès, *Le Bachelier*, Maxipoche, 1998, pp. 81, 211–12.
12 Jules Vallès, *Oeuvres complètes: Souvenirs d'un étudiant pauvre, le candidat des pauvres, lettre à Jules Mirès*, Éditeurs Français Réunis, 1972, pp. 323–5.
13 See Rachael Langford, *Jules Vallès and the Narration of History: Contesting the French Third Republic in the Jacques Vingtras trilogy*, Bern, Peter Lang, 1999, pp. 145–57; Priscilla Parkhurst Ferguson, *Paris as Revolution: Writing the Nineteenth Century City*, University of California Press, 1994, p. 192.
14 Jules Vallès, *L'Insurgé*, Maxipoche, 1998, p. 156.
15 SAT LY36. Examinations sat on 4 May, *Rédactions dirigées par les gardes nationaux*.

185

16 And there is no denying its usefulness in the context of democratisation campaigns. See Lucy Taylor, 'Textbook citizens: education for democracy and political culture in El Salvador', *Democratization*, 6 (1999) 3, pp. 62–83.

17 Roy Porter (ed.), *Rewriting the Self: Histories from the Renaissance to the Present*, Routledge, 1997.

18 Michel de Certeau, Luce Giard and Pierre Mayol, *L'Invention du quotidien*, 2 vols, Gallimard, 1994, vol. 1, pp. 270–5; Michel de Certeau, *L'Écriture de l'histoire*, Gallimard, 1975; also in Philip Hansen, *Hannah Arendt: Politics, History and Citizenship*, Cambridge, Polity, 1993, pp. 66–7.

19 Louis Veuillot, *Paris pendant les deux sièges*, 2 vols, Victor Palmé, 1871, vol. 2, pp. 111–12, 267.

20 Jean-Yvan Thériault, 'La citoyenneté entre narrativité et factualité', *Sociologie et Sociétés*, xxxi (1999) 2, pp. 5–14, p. 9.

21 T.H. Marshall, *Citizenship and Social Class*, Pluto, 1992; Dean Hartley, *Welfare, Law and Citizenship*, Harvester Wheatsheaf, 1996; John Scott, *Poverty and Wealth: Citizenship, Deprivation and Privilege*, Longman, 1994, pp. 145–54; Ian Culpitt, *Welfare and Citizenship: Beyond the Crisis of the Welfare State?*, Sage, 1992; Martin Bulmer and Anthony Rees (eds), *Citizenship Today: The Contemporary Relevance of T.H. Marshall*, UCL Press, 1996; Lydia Morris, *Dangerous Classes: The Underclass and Social Citizenship*, Routledge, 1994, pp. 44–7; Maurice Roche, *Rethinking Citizenship: Welfare, Ideology and Change in Modern Society*, Cambridge, Polity Press, 1992, pp. 11–37.

22 Gershon Shafir (ed.), *The Citizenship Debates: A Reader*, University of Minnesota Press, 1998.

23 This was inevitably also a site of conceptualisation: Adrian Oldfield, *Citizenship and Community: Civic Republicanism and the Modern World*, Routledge, 1990, pp. 127–30, 145–50. Pre 1789, citizenship existed primarily within this framework. Charlotte C. Wells, *Law and Citizenship in Early Modern France*, Johns Hopkins University Press, 1995, p. xiii.

24 See Pierre Rosanvallon, *Le Sacre du citoyen, histoire du suffrage universel en France*, Gallimard, 1992, pp. 307–24.

25 Norbert Elias, *La Société des individus*, Fayard, 1987, pp. 52–3, 216.

26 See the work of Sophie Duchesne, *Citoyenneté à la française*, Presses de Sciences Po, 1997, pp. 11–5.

27 Guy Thuillier, 'La bureaucratie en France aux XIXe et XXe siècles', *Economica*, 1989, pp. 425–34. The interaction between state and citizen is, of course, mediated through state-controlled institutions such as the administration, which grew and reformed ceaselessly throughout the nineteenth century, and other semi-autonomous bodies, such as the notaries or the *corps médical*: Ezra N. Suleiman, *Private Power and Centralization in France: The Notaries and the State*, Princeton University Press, 1987; B. Taithe, *Defeated Flesh: Welfare, Warfare and the Making of Modern France*, Manchester University Press, 1999, ch. 6. Thuillier's view of the Commune's non-administration is not inaccurate. In fact, there is strong evidence that the administrative cogs of the state apparatus were broken by Versailles, but the Communard state had a relatively ambiguous role to play in the power struggle between the Jacobins, intent on reconstituting and running everything, and the National Guard, whose institution had taken many roles belonging to the state.

28 Jules Le Berquier, *Administration de la Commune de Paris et du département de la Seine*, Imprimerie et librairie administrative Paul Dupont, 1861.

29 Sophie Duchesne, *Citoyenneté à la française*, Presses de Sciences Po, 1997, pp. 130–5.

30 Charles Tilly, 'The emergence of citizenship in France and elsewhere' in C. Tilly (ed.), *Citizenship, Identity and Social History, International Review of Social History*, supplement 3 (1995), pp. 223–36.

31 Amédée Fauche, *Montereau-Faut-Yonne, Journal de l'occupation prussienne*, Montereau, L. Zanote, 1871, p. 64.

32 The Bismarck legend for Machiavellian plots was not straightforwardly organised by the German statesman, and many diplomatic papers show that the Reich tried to dispel the myth by demonstrating to the British and Russians that the French had gone into war in an act of folly; see, on the war scare of 1875, E.T.S. Dugdale (ed.), *German Diplomatic Documents, 1871–1914*, 4 vols, Methuen, 1928, vol. 1, pp. 6–19; Georges Dethan, 'Le Quai d'Orsay de 1870 à 1914', in Philippe Levillain and Brunello Vigezzi (eds), *Opinion publique et politique extérieure, 1870–1915*, Università de Milano/Collection de l'école française de Rome 54, 1981, pp. 168–75.

33 This would certainly be the perspective gained from anti-French sources: for instance, E. Dunsany, *Gaul or Teuton? Considerations as to Our Allies of the Future*, London, Longman, Green, 1873.

34 Pierre Deluns-Montaud *et al.*, *Les Origines diplomatiques de la guerre de 1870–1871, recueil de documents publiés par le ministère des affaires étrangères*, 10 vols, Gustave Ficker, 1910–15.

35 Lynn M. Case, *Franco-Italian Relations, 1860–1865: The Roman Question and the Convention of September*, Philadelphia, University of Pennsylvania Press, 1932; *L'Empereur Napoléon III et l'Italie*, Paris, E. Dentu, 1859; F. Dupanloup, *Lettre à M. le vicomte de la Guéronnière*, Charles Douniol, 1861; M. Poujoulat, *Réponse à la brochure de M. de la Guéronnière*, Charles Douniol, 1861.

36 Paul Gaulot, *La Vérité sur l'expédition du Mexique d'après les documents et souvenirs de Ernest Louet, payeur en chef du corps expéditionnaire*, 3 vols, P. Ollendorff, 1889–90; Nancy Nichols Barker, *The French Experience in Mexico, 1821–1861: A History of Constant Misunderstanding*, Chapel Hill (NC), University of North Carolina Press, 1979.

37 Jean-François Lecaillon, *Napoléon III et le Mexique: Les illusions d'un grand dessein*, L'Harmattan, 1994.

38 W.E. Echard, *Napoleon III and the Concert of Europe*, Baton Rouge, Louisiana State University Press, 1983, and *Foreign Policy of the Second Empire: A Bibliography*, New York, Greenwood Press, 1988.

39 Gustave Rothan, *Souvenirs diplomatiques, l'affaire du Luxembourg, le prélude de la guerre de 1870*, Calmann-Lévy, 1882.

40 Albert de Broglie, *Mémoires du duc de Broglie*, Calmann-Lévy, 1938, pp. 325–8.

41 Vincent Benedetti, *Ma Mission en Prusse*, H. Plon, 1871; Albert Sorel, *Histoire diplomatique de la guerre franco-allemande*, 2 vols, H. Plon, 1875.

42 M. Bernard-Griffiths and Paul Viallaneix (eds), *Edgar Quinet, ce juif errant*, Clermont Ferrand University Press, 1978.

43 Baron Eugène Stoffel, *Rapports militaires écrits de Berlin*, Garnier Frères, 1871.

44 Richard Holmes, *Road to Sedan: The French Army 1866–1870*, Royal Historical Society, 1984, pp. 73–86; Jacques Dumont de Montroy, *Napoléon III et la réorganisation de l'armée de 1866 à 1870, la loi Niel mutilée du 1 février 1868*, published by the author, 1996; Jean Casevitz, *Une Loi manquée: la loi Niel 1866–1868, l'armée française à la veille de la guerre de 1870*, Presses Universitaires de France, 1959.

45 Robert Nye, *Crime, Madness and Politics in Modern France: The Medical Concept of National Decline*, Princeton University Press, 1984.

46 Napoleon's illness was public knowledge. Jules Simon, *Souvenirs du 4 Septembre, origine et chute du second empire*, Calmann-Lévy, 1876, pp. 280–3, 345–6.

47 Nancy Nichols Barker, 'Napoleon III and the Hohenzollern candidacy for the Spanish throne', *The Historian*, 29 (1967), pp. 421–50; W.A. Smith, 'Napoléon III and the Spanish revolution of 1868', *Journal of Modern History* (1953), pp. 214–24.

48 Theodore Zeldin, *Émile Ollivier and the Liberal Empire of Napoleon III*, Oxford, Clarendon Press, 1963, p. 145; Émile Ollivier, *The Franco-Prussian War and Its Hidden Causes*, Isaac Pitman and Sons, 1913.

49 Stéphane Audoin-Rouzeau, *1870, la France dans la guerre*, Armand Colin, 1989, pp. 19–32.
50 On the bourgeoisie and the *Garde Nationale* see Georges Carrot, 'La Garde Nationale 1789–1871, une institution de la nation', thèse de doctorat de 3ième cycle, Université de Nice, 1979.
51 Thomas J. Adriance, *The Last Gaiter Button: A Study of the Mobilisation and Concentration of the French Army in the War of 1870*, Westport, Greenwood Press, 1987.
52 Louis Garel, *La Révolution lyonnaise depuis le 4 septembre*, Lyon, Association Typographique, 1871; for a reactionary view see Durand-Auzias, 'Le 4 Septembre à Lyon', *Revue Hebdomadaire*, 3 September 1910, pp. 20–38.
53 L.J. Trochu, *L'Armée française en 1867*, Amyot, 1867. This book was a pessimistic litany of failings but it by no means predicted the defeat of 1870.
54 M. d'Aiguy, *Quel gouvernement la France se donnera-t-elle?*, Lyons and Paris, Félix Girard, 1871.
55 *Le Bonapartisme condamné par l'Armée: protestations des officiers français internés en Allemagne contre la restauration impériale*, Librairie Internationale, A. Lacroix, Verboeckhoven et Cie, 1871.
56 Pierre Lévêque, *Histoire des forces politiques en France 1789–1880*, Armand Colin, 1992, pp. 259–88.
57 See Philip Thody, *French Caesarism from Napoleon I to Charles de Gaulle*, Macmillan, 1989, pp. 48–74; René Rémond, *Les Droites en France*, Aubier, 1982.
58 *Le Conciliateur, journal des intérêts de la Creuse*, 8 September 1870.
59 See Chaâbane Harbaoui, 'Le Statut rhétorique du "Peuple" et de la "Révolution" dans le discours de Michelet', in Christian Croisille and Jean Ehrard, *La Légende de la Révolution*, Clermont Ferrand University Press, 1988, pp. 379–92.
60 See the right-wing views of Marie-Madeleine Martin, *Histoire de l'Unité française: l'idée de patrie en France, des origines à nos jours*, Paris, Presses Universitaires de France, 2nd edn, 1982, pp. 339–44.
61 Édouard Fleury, *Éphémérides de la guerre de 1870–71*, Imprimerie du journal de l'Aisne, Laon, 1871, pp. 6–7.
62 Edmond Béraud, *Gambetta dictateur*, Poitiers, H. Oudin, 1881; H.R. Blandeau, *La Dictature de Gambetta*, Amyot, 1871; Léonce Dupont, *Tours et Bordeaux, souvenirs de la république à outrance*, E. Dentu, 1877.
63 See Jean El Gammal, 'La guerre de 1870–1871 dans la mémoire des droites', in Jean François Sirinelli (ed.), *Histoire des droites en France*, 3 vols, Gallimard, 1992, vol. 2, *Cultures*, pp. 471–504.
64 This improbably exact figure comes from H. Durangel, *Rapport présenté par le chef de la division administrative générale et départementale à M. Jules Cazot, secrétaire délégué du ministère de l'intérieur*, Organisation des gardes nationales mobilisés, Bordeaux, & Émile Crugy, 1871, pp. 6–7.
65 ADHV, 1 M 158, examen des actes du gouvernement provisoire, 23 January 1872; reply of 16 February 1872.
66 Sudhir Hazareesingh, *From Subject to Citizen: The Second Empire and the Emergence of French Democracy*, Princeton University Press, 1998.
67 Louis Greenberg, *Sisters of Liberty: Marseille, Lyon, Paris and the Reaction to the Centralized State*, Cambridge (Mass.), Harvard University Press, 1971.
68 Riciotti Garibaldi, *Souvenirs de la campagne de France 1870–71*, Nice, La Semaine Niçoise, 1899; Robert Middleton, *Garibaldi, ses opérations à l'armée des Vosges*, Garnier Frères, 1872 and Brussels, C. and A. Vanderauwera, 1871.
69 Allegations of corruption marred this international army. Incompetence and the odd crook explain most of the misdeeds exposed in Louis Philippe de Ségur, *Les Marchés de la guerre à Lyon et à l'armée de Garibaldi*, H. Plon, 1873.

70 For instance, Gustave Flourens, *Paris Livré*, A. Lacroix, Verboeckhoven et Cie, 1871.

71 Général Antoine Eugène Chanzy, *La Campagne de 1870–1871, la deuxième armée de la Loire*, H. Plon, 1871, reprinted Gautier, 1895; Arthur Clinquet, *Le Général Chanzy*, Léon Chailley, 1883.

72 John Patrick T. Bury and Robert P. Tombs, *Thiers 1797–1877*, Allen and Unwin, 1986, and (no author) *Monsieur Thiers: d'une république à l'autre*, Published, 1998.

73 For instance, in Corrèze, all but one of the five candidates were on at least two or three of the five lists published in the local press.

74 *Le Salut Public*, 15 February 1870.

75 *Le Corrézien*, 9 March 1871.

76 See M.A. Thiers, *Occupation et Libération du territoire, 1871–1873, correspondances*, 2 vols, Calmann-Lévy, 1903; the terms of the Frankfurt Treaty, at least in their general outline, were known well before the cessation of the hostilities, especially the surrender of German-speaking territories on the German border. Robert I. Giesberg, *The Treaty of Frankfurt: A Study in Diplomatic History, September 1870–September 1873*, Philadelphia, University of Pennsylvania Press, 1966, pp. 17–42. The French public got to know the text of the treaty, which was reproduced in many local and national newspapers. For instance, *Le Corrézien* (Tulle), 18 May 1871.

77 Gambetta suffered a breakdown and retired to Spain for the whole of spring 1871. John Patrick T. Bury, *Gambetta and the National Defence: A Republican Dictatorship in France*, Longman, 1936, and *Gambetta and the Making of the Third Republic*, Longman, 1973; H.R. Blandeau, *La Dictature de Gambetta*, Amyot, 1871.

78 For instance, Eugene Kamenka, *Paradigm for Revolution? The Paris Commune, 1871–1971*, Canberra, Australian National University Press, 1972.

79 Philip G. Nord, *The Republican Moment: Struggles for Democracy in Nineteenth Century France*, Cambridge (Mass.), Harvard University Press, 1995.

80 Alain Dalotel *et al.*, *Aux origines de la Commune: le mouvement des réunions publiques à Paris, 1868–1870*, François Maspéro, 1980.

81 Martin Philip Johnson, *The Paradise of Association: Political Culture and Popular Organization in the Paris Commune of 1871*, University of Michigan Press, 1996, p. 19.

82 See, for instance, the November manifestos of the Club positiviste and the Club républicain et socialiste du XIIIe arrondissement, reproduced in *Les Révolutions du XIXe siècle*, 10 vols, Paris, EDHIS, 1988, vol. 6, ff. 12 and 13.

83 Martin Johnson thus quotes unquestioningly from the parliamentary enquiries, which attempted to create evidence when they could not find any. Martin Philip Johnson, *The Paradise of Association: Political Culture and Popular Organization in the Paris Commune of 1871*, University of Michigan Press, 1996, p. 19.

84 David Harvey, *Consciousness and the Urban Experience: Studies in the History and Theory of Capitalist Urbanization*, Oxford, Blackwell, 1985, pp. 63–220.

85 Roger V. Gould, *Insurgent Identities: Class, Community and Protest in Paris from 1848 to the Commune*, Chicago University Press, 1995, pp. 135, 153–4.

86 David P. Jordan, *Transforming Paris: The Life and Labour of Baron Haussmann*, University of Chicago Press, 1995, pp. 185–210, 291–4; Priscilla Parkhurst Ferguson, *Paris as Revolution: Writing the Nineteenth Century City*, University of California Press, 1994, pp. 115–25.

87 David H. Pinkney, *Napoleon III and the Rebuilding of Paris*, Princeton University Press, 1958.

88 W. Scott Haine, *The World of the Paris Café: Sociability among the French Working Class*, Johns Hopkins University Press, 1996, pp. 162–3, 219–25. It is Haine's contention that the repression of the Commune, far from crushing the neighbourhood café political culture, helped invigorate it (p. 207); Carol E. Harrison, *The Bourgeois Citizen in Nineteenth-Century France: Gender, Sociability, and the Uses of Emulation*, Oxford University Press, 1999, pp. 6–9.

89 Gay Gullickson, *Unruly Women of Paris: Images of the Commune*, Ithaca, Cornell University Press, 1996.
90 M.F. Crestin, *Souvenirs d'un lyonnais*, Imprimerie Decléris, 1897, p. 66.
91 Stéphane Audoin-Rouzeau, *1870, la France dans la guerre*, Armand Colin, 1989.
92 John F. Merriman, *The Red City: Limoges and the French Nineteenth Century*, Oxford University Press, 1985; A. Corbin, *Archaisme et Modernité en Limousin au XIXe siècle, 1845–1880*, 2 vols, Limoges, PULIM [1975], 1998.
93 Daniel Pick, *War Machine: The Rationalisation of Slaughter in the Modern Age*, New Haven, Yale University Press, 1993.
94 Louis Appia and Gustave Moynier, *La Guerre et la charité, traité théorique et pratique de philanthropie appliquée aux armées en campagne*, Geneva, Cherbuliez, 1867. Gustave Moynier was particularly active then: *Notes sur la création d'une institution judiciaire internationale, propre à prévenir et à réprimer les infractions à la Convention de Genève*, Geneva, Comité International, 1872; 'Notes sur la création d'une institution judiciaire internationale, propre à prévenir et à réprimer les infractions à la convention de Genève', *Bulletin International*, III (1872), pp. 122–34; *La Convention de Genève, ou la guerre Franco-Allemande*, Soullier et Wirth, 1873; *Les Dix Premières Années de la Croix Rouge, comité international de secours aux blessés militaires*, Geneva, Fick, 1873; 'La Convention de Genève pendant la guerre Franco-Allemande de 1870', *Bulletin International*, IV (1873), pp. 51–104; *La Croix Rouge, son passé, son avenir*, Sandoz et Thuillier, 1882; *Essais sur les caractères généraux des lois de la guerre*, Geneva, Eggimann, 1895. For a critical appraisal see John F. Hutchinson, 'Rethinking the origins of the Red Cross', *Bulletin of the History of Medicine*, 63 (1989), pp. 557–78; *Champions of Charity: War and the Rise of the Red Cross*, Oxford, Westview Press, 1996.
95 Even though the work of Clausewitz was very imperfectly known by 1870.
96 François Furet, *La Révolution 1770–1880*, 2 vols, Hachette, 1988.
97 On positive revision of patriotism, see Maurizio Virolli, *For Love of Country: An Essay on Patriotism and Nationalism*, Oxford, Clarendon, 1995.
98 James F. McMillan, *France and Women 1789–1914: Gender, Society and Politics*, Routledge, 2000, pp. 124–7.
99 Prosper Olivier Lissagaray, *The Paris Commune of 1871*, New Park Publications, 1976; Gay Gullickson, *Unruly Women of Paris: Images of the Commune*, Ithaca, Cornell University Press, 1996.
100 Étienne Balibar, *Droit de Cité*, Éditions de l'Aube, 1998, pp. 50–3.
101 Alain Corbin, *The Village of Cannibals: Rage and Murder in France, 1870*, Cambridge (Mass.), Harvard University Press, 1992.
102 Eugen Weber, *Peasants into Frenchmen: The Modernization of Rural France, 1870–1914*, Stanford University Press, 1976.
103 Odile Rudelle, *La République absolue, aux origines de l'instabilité constitutionelle de la France républicaine 1870–1889*, Publications de la Sorbonne, 1982; Claude Nicolet, *L'Idée républicaine en France, essai d'histoire critique*, Gallimard, 1982.

2 Total war, civil war and 'modernity'

1 E. Renan, *Qu'est-ce qu'une nation?*, Imprimerie Nationale, 1996, p. 186.
2 Stig Förster and Jörg Nagler (eds), *On the Road to Total War: The American Civil War and the German Wars of Unification, 1861–1871*, German Historical Institute (Washington D.C.) series, Cambridge University Press, 1997.
3 There were some exchanges between the two, the best example being Cluseret, one-time leader of the Communard army. See Philip M. Katz, *From Appomattox to Montmartre: Americans and the Paris Commune*, Harvard University Press, 1998.

4 Colonel Lonsdale Hale, *The 'People's War' in France, 1870–1871*, Hugh Rees, 1904; Richard D. Challener, *The French Theory of the Nation in Arms, 1866–1939*, New York, Columbia University Press, 1965.

5 ADR, 1 M 118.

6 ADR, 1 M 118, *Réunion présidée par Bastelica dans la salle de l'Alhambra* (9 September 1870).

7 This confusion was to be found in the United States as well; Philip M. Katz, *From Appomattox to Montmartre*, pp. 98–114.

8 H.J. Schroeder (ed.), *Disciplinary Decrees of the General Councils*, Herder, 1937. There is much debate on the intention behind the atrocities endured in Andersonville. Wintz was executed for a violation of Article 59 of General Order 100.

9 Raymond Aron, *Penser la guerre, Clausewitz*, 2 vols, Gallimard, 1976; Christopher Bassford, *Clausewitz in English: The Reception of Clausewitz in Britain and America, 1815–1845*, Oxford University Press, 1994; Peter Paret, *Clausewitz and the State, the Man, His Theories and His Times*, Princeton University Press [1976], 1985.

10 Daniel Pick, *War Machine: The Rationalisation of Slaughter in the Modern Age*, New Haven, Yale University Press, 1993.

11 See the editors' introduction in Stig Förster and Jörg Nagler (eds), *On the Road to Total War*.

12 *Rapport présenté par le chef de la division administrative générale et départementale à M. Jules Cazot, secrétaire délégué du ministère de l'intérieur*, Organisation des gardes nationales mobilisés, Bordeaux, Émile Crugy, 1871, p. 2.

13 AVdP, VD6 1222/1, *Dispense des services ordinaires des ouvriers boulangers et de l'imprimerie impériale* [sic], 28 September 1870.

14 Decree of 29 October 1870.

15 AVdP, VD6 1711 3, *Oeuvre Nationale des Orphelins de Guerre*.

16 ADHV, 4 R 78, decree of 29 October published 2 November 1870.

17 Charles de Freycinet, *Souvenirs, 1848–1878*, Delagrave, 1912.

18 ADC, R 106, for instance 30 January 1871.

19 For instance, ADHV, 2 R 175. To be fair, some of this enthusiasm calmed down as the war went on. In Mas Léon, a small commune near Limoges, the primitive rifles were not used after the departure of the mobilised soldiers, 'the bad weather preventing the National Guard from meeting'.

20 ADR, 1M 118, *Conseil municipal à Huis Clos*, session of 18 October 1870, 22 October 1870, 27 October 1870.

21 ADR, 1M 118, *Conseil municipal à Huis Clos*, session of 14 October 1870.

22 *Rapport présenté par le chef de la division administrative générale et départementale à M. Jules Cazot, secrétaire délégué du ministère de l'intérieur*, Organisation des gardes nationales mobilisés, Bordeaux, Émile Crugy, 1871, p. 17.

23 Jean-Jacques Becker, *The Great War and the French People*, Leamington Spa, Berg, 1985, p. 3. *Comment les français sont entrés dans la guerre*, Presses de la Fondation des Sciences Politiques, 1977.

24 B. Taithe, 'Rhetoric, propaganda and memory: framing the Franco-Prussian war', in B. Taithe and T. Thornton, *Propaganda: Political Rhetoric and Identity, 1300–2000*, Sutton, 1999, pp. 203–22.

25 AVdP, VD6 760 6, *Ordres du capitaine de la première compagnie*, 12th Bat.

26 Gustave Flourens, *Paris Livré*, A. Lacroix, Verboeckhoven et Cie, 1871, p. 103.

27 André Corvisier (ed.), *Histoire militaire de la France*, 4 vols, Presses Universitaires de France, 1992, vol. 2, pp. 559–62.

28 ADHV, *Rapport à monsieur le ministre de l'intérieur*, 19 April 1872.

29 This particular incident took place in a notoriously Bonapartist stronghold in Haute-Vienne in Saint-Yrieix and in Chateauneuf-la-forêt. The conscripts physically

assaulted the recruitment officers and destroyed everything in sight. *Le Courier du Centre* (Limoges), 14 November 1870. Later, many men from these areas attempted to avoid being mobilised for active service. *Le Courier du Centre* (Limoges), 29 December 1870. See also the reports of the prefecture ADHV, 4 R 177, 12 November 1870, 14 November 1870 about the events in Perilhac, St Genec and Chaplot.

30 Edmond Thiebault, *Riciotti Garibaldi et la 4ème brigade, récit de la campagne de 1870–1*, Godet Jeune, 1872.

31 A. Martinier, *Corps auxiliaires cré ès pendant la guerre 1870–1871; vol. 1, Garde Nationale Mobile*, Edmund Dubois, 1896–7, p. 28.

32 For a detailed breakdown of sources and figures see Appendix 2.

33 A. Corbin, *Archaisme et modernité en Limousin au XIXe siècle, 1845–1880*, Limoges, PULIM [1975], 2 vols, 1998, vol. 2, pp. 937–43.

34 The story of Hoff recurs in all the media. See the summary in L. Louis-Lande, *Récits d'un soldat, les fusiliers marins au siège de Paris, un invalide, le Sergent Hoff, la Hacienda de Camaron [sic]*, H. Lecène et H. Oudin, 1886.

35 See, for instance, ADHV, 2 R 183, *Oeuvre des orphelins de la guerre*; 2 R 182, *Répartition du fond de secours*.

36 Ch. Bauquier, *Les Dernières campagnes dans l'Est*, Lemerre, 1873, pp. 8–10; Louis Philippe Antoine Charles de Ségur, *Les Marchés de la guerre à Lyon et à l'armée de Garibaldi*, H. Plon, 1873.

37 ADHV, 2 R 175, *Francs tireurs de la Haute-Vienne*.

38 B. Taithe, 'The Red Cross flag in the Franco-Prussian war: civilians, humanitarianism and war in the "modern" age', in R. Cooter, S. Sturdy and M. Harrison (eds), *Medicine, War and Modernity*, Sutton Publishing, 1998, pp. 22–47.

39 Henri Monod, *Rapport du comité évangélique auxiliaire de secours pour les soldats blessés ou malades, 1870–1871*, Sandoz and Fichbacher, 1875, p. 7.

40 Félicien Court, *Louis Ormières, 1851–1914, et l'ambulance du Grand Orient de France en 1870–1871*, Imprimerie Nouvelle, 1914; and 'Louis Ormières', *Bulletin du Grand Orient de France*, 26 (1870), pp. 380, 392.

41 Alain Gérard, 'Action humanitaire et pouvoir politique: l'engagement des médecins Lillois au XIXe siècle', *Revue du Nord*, 332 (October–December 1999), pp. 817–36.

42 ASSAT, box 63/1. *Répartition des hôpitaux et ambulances de la ville de Paris*.

43 ADC, R244, 26/10/1870. *Utilisation des établissements publics*, letter, 20 September 1870, from Toy-Viam.

44 ASSAT, box, 62/1. *Note à monsieur le médecin en chef [Larrey], Murno, Intendant Militaire de la 1ère division*, 7 January 1871.

45 For a fuller account see B. Taithe, *Defeated Flesh*, ch. 7.

46 Léon Boulanger, *Compte rendu des travaux du Comité de Secours de la Sarthe*, Le Mans, 1871, pp. 36–8.

47 H.A. Wauthoz, *Les Ambulances et les ambulanciers à travers les siècles*, Brussels, Lebègue, 1872, p. lx; I. de Crombrugghe, *Journal d'une infirmière pendant la guerre 1870–1871*, H. Plon, 1872, p. 10; J. Jurgensen, *Le Soir du combat, récit d'une infirmière, poème*, Geneva, Durafort, 1871; P. and H. de Trailles, *Les Femmes en France pendant la guerre et les deux sièges de Paris*, F. Polo Libraire, 1872.

48 A similar process emphasising German atrocities took place in 1914–15. J. Horne and A. Kramer, 'German "atrocities" and Franco-German opinion, 1914: the evidence of German soldiers' diaries', *Journal of Modern History*, 66 (1994) 1, pp. 1–33; R. Harris, ' "The child of the barbarian": rape, race and nationalism in France during the First World War', *Past and Present*, 141 (1993), pp. 170–206.

49 Alfred Michiels, *Histoire de la guerre franco-prussienne et de ses origines*, Alphonse Picard, 1871, p. 68b.

50 *The Times*, 15 September 1870, reported the first massacre of civilian population by the Bavarians. Émile Alexandre Gavoy, *Étude de faits de guerre: le service de santé militaire en 1870, hier, aujourd'hui, demain*, Paris and Limoges, Henri Charles Lavauzelle, 1894, p. 21. Simultaneously the Germans published reports of the attack on a German ambulance in Bazeilles. Dr Weill, manuscript report, ASSAT, box 64/30, *à Stuttgart*, p. 9. A meeting in Brussels in 1874 attempted to solve the vexed question of the status of irregular warfare. P. Karsten, *Law, Soldiers and Combat*, Westport, Greenwood Press, 1978, pp. 22–3; also F. Christot, *Le Massacre de l'ambulance de Saône-et-Loire, 21 Janvier 1871*, Lyons, Vingtrinier, 1871.

51 J.C. Chenu, *De la mortalité dans l'armée et des moyens d'économiser la vie humaine*, Hachette, 1870, p. 50.

52 J.H. Plumridge, *Hospital Ships and Ambulance Trains*, Seeley, Service and Co., 1975, p. 86. Adapted wagons modified to accommodate stretchers had been exhibited at the 1867 exhibition; P. Casimir, *Les Pages douloureuses de la guerre*, Niort, L. Favre, 1872, p. 101. The evacuation of the Niort hospital took place on 25 December 1870. Some unfortunate soldiers reached the terminus or the Spanish border.

53 ADHV, 4 M 66, report on the arrival of a hundred wounded soldiers, 21 October 1870.

54 François Prosper Jacqmin, *Les Chemins de fer pendant la guerre de 1870–1871*, Hachette, 1872.

55 On the subject of smallpox, see Bertrand Taithe, *Defeated Flesh: Welfare, Warfare and the Making of Modern France*, Manchester University Press, 1999, pp. 53–7. AVdP, VD6 0968/2, *Commission d'hygiène*.

56 *Le Courier du Centre* (Limoges), 17 January 1871.

57 Louis Garel, *La Révolution lyonnaise depuis le 4 septembre*, Lyons, Association typographique, 1871, p. 19.

58 Patrick H. Hutton, *The Cult of the Revolutionary Tradition: The Blanquists in French Politics, 1864–1893*, Berkeley, University of California Press, 1981.

59 Fernand Rude, 'Bakounine en 1870–1871', *Cahiers d'histoire*, 24 (1979) 4, pp. 75–83.

60 Maurice Moissonnier gave a classic Marxist account in *La première internationale et la Commune à Lyon*, Éditions sociales, 1972.

61 See Fédération Révolutionnaire des Communes (26 September 1870) poster, *Les Révolutions du XIXe siècle*, 10 vols, Paris, EDHIS, vol. 10, *Affiches, feuilles volantes, documents divers*, 1988, p. 30.

62 *Le Salut Public*, 1 October 1870.

63 *Le Salut Public* (Lyons), 2 October 1870.

64 Étienne Arago, *L'Hôtel de Ville de Paris au 4 Septembre et pendant le siège, réponse à monsieur le comte Daru*, Paris, Hetzel, 1871.

65 P. Lay (ed.), *Lettres d'un homme [Victor Desplats] à la femme qu'il aime pendant le siège de Paris et la Commune*, Jean-Claude Lattès, 1980, p. 201; the treacherous U-turn of October 1870 haunted Ferry's subsequent career. Louis Fiaux, *Jules Ferry, un malfaiteur public*, Librairie Internationale, 1886.

66 Col. Comte de Meffray, *Les Fautes de la Défense de Paris*, A. Lacroix, Verboeckhoven et Cie, 1871, pp. 11–14.

67 Odile Rudelle, *Jules Ferry; la république des citoyens*, Imprimerie Nationale, 1996, vol. 1, pp. 20–1, 23b–42.

68 Jules Favre, *Gouvernement de la Défense Nationale du 30 juin au 31 octobre 1870*, H. Plon, 1871.

69 Ernest Cresson, *Cent jours à la Préfecture de Police, 2 novembre 1870–11 février 1871*, H. Plon, Nourrit, 1901.

70 Louis Fiaux, *Histoire de la guerre civile de 1871*, Charpentier, 1879, p. 69.

71 Marc César, *La Commune de Narbonne (mars 1871)*, Perpignan, Presses Universitaires de Perpignan, 1996; see chapters 4 and 8 for a discussion of Lyons.

72 I will return in a later chapter to the breakdown of civility, which led to the brutalisation of French politics.
73 E. Schulkind, *The Paris Commune of 1871: The View from the Left*, New York, Grove Press, 1974, pp. 197, 200, 266–80.
74 Stig Förster, and Jörg Nagler (eds), *On the Road to Total War*, p. 10.
75 The First World War benefits from the modernist literary movement to help qualify it as the eponymous war of modernity. Modris Eksteins, *Rites of Spring: The Great War and the Birth of the Modern Age*, Bantam Press, 1989; Trudi Tate, *Modernism, History and the First World War*, Manchester University Press, 1998.
76 William MacCormac, *Notes and Recollections of an Ambulance Surgeon*, J.A. Churchill, 1871, p. 112.
77 Ernest Saint-Edme, *La Science pendant le siège de Paris*, E. Dentu, 1871.
78 See, for instance, Émile Zola, *La Débâcle*, La Pleiade, reprinted 1990; Alphonse Daudet, *Les Contes du Lundi* [1873] reprinted Maxipoche Classiques Français, 1995.
79 Pierre Vaisse, 'La représentation de la guerre dans la peinture officielle avant et après la défaite de 1870–1871', in Paul Viallaneix and Jean Ehrard (eds), *La Bataille, l'Armée, la Gloire, 1745–1871*, 2 vols, Clermont Ferrand, 1985, vol. 2, 581–90.
80 Louis Nathaniel Rossel, *Mémoires et correspondance de Louis Rossel*, preface by Victor Margueritte, with a biography by Isabella Rossel, P.V. Stock, 1908; Édith Thomas, *Rossel 1844–1871*, Gallimard, 1967; Jules Amigues, *Louis Nathaniel Rossel, papiers postumes recueillis et annotés par Jules Amigues*, Lachaud, 6th edn, 1871.
81 J.M.G. Roberts, *The Paris Commune from the Right*, English Historical Review, Supplement 6, Longman, 1973.
82 Eugene Schulkind, 'Socialist women in the 1871 Paris commune', *Past and Present*, 106 (1985), pp. 124–63; Gay Gullickson, *Unruly Women of Paris: Images of the Commune*, Ithaca, Cornell University Press, 1996.
83 See, for instance, Bram Disjkra, *Idols of Perversity: Fantasies of Feminine Evil in Fin-de-Siècle Culture*, Oxford University Press, 1986.
84 See AVdP, VD6 730 256, *Don patriotique de l'Angleterre à la France*. Also see B. Taithe, 'De la supériorité de l'Angleterre sur la France? Regards sur la France dans la crise de 1870 et naissance de l'humanitaire', in K. de Queiros Mattoso (ed.), *L'Angleterre et le Monde, XVIIIe–XXe siècle, l'histoire entre l'économique et l'imaginaire, hommage à François Crouzet*, Paris, L'Harmattan, 1999, pp. 311–39.
85 Robert I. Giesberg, *The Treaty of Frankfurt: A Study in Diplomatic History, September 1870 –September 1873*, Philadelphia, University of Pennsylvania Press, 1966.
86 Léonce de Cazenove, *La Guerre et l'humanité au dix-neuvième siècle*, Armand de Vresse, 1869, 2nd edn 1875.

3 The crisis of citizenship and *la sociale*

1 Jules Vallès, *L'Insurgé*, Maxipoche, 1998, p. 75.
2 A good introduction to these issues is to be found in James Vernon (ed.), *Re-Reading the Constitution*, Cambridge University Press, 1996, pp. 9–21; Patrick Joyce, *Visions of the People*, Cambridge University Press, 1991; Gareth Stedman-Jones, *Languages of Class: Studies in English Working Class History, 1832–1982*, Cambridge University Press, 1983.
3 Bernard Ménager, *Les Napoléons du Peuple*, Paris, Aubier, 1988, pp. 121–67, 188–9.
4 Louis Girard, *Problèmes politiques et constitutionnels du second empire*, 2 vols, Paris, CDU, 1964–5.
5 Odile Rudelle, *Jules Ferry: La république des citoyens*, Imprimerie Nationale, 1996, pp. 234–5.
6 Bernard Ménager, '1848–1871, autorité ou liberté', in Jean-François Sirinelli, *Histoire des droites en France*, 3 vols, Gallimard, 1992, vol. 1, *Politiques*, pp. 89–147.

7 Alistair Cole and Peter Campbell, *French Electoral Systems and Elections since 1789*, Aldershot, Gower, 1989, pp. 45–7.

8 Even rigged results are more complicated than it appears; see Frédéric Bluche (ed.), *Le Prince, le peuple et le droit, autour des plébisicites de 1851 et 1852*, Presses Universitaires de France, Paris, 2000.

9 Political parties were obviously not modern parties as such. Electoral committees since 1864 had been the temporary expression of political coalitions. Raymond Huard, *La Naissance des partis politiques en France*, Presses de Sciences Po, 1996, pp. 125–37.

10 See the very interesting instances of prosopography undertaken by Éric Anceau, *Dictionnaire des députés du second empire*, Presses Universitaires de Rennes, 1999.

11 The propaganda aimed at rural voters by the urban leadership of the left remained insensitive to rural preoccupation and focused most of its attention on conscription. Charles Delescluze, *Aux habitants des campagnes*, poster reprinted in *Les Révolutions du XIXe siècle*, 10 vols, Paris, EDHIS, vol. 10, *Affiches, feuilles volantes, documents divers*, p. 21.

12 A. Gérard, 'Le Thème de la Révolution/religion dans l'historiographie républicaine de Michelet à Mathiez', *Recherches Institutionnelles*, 5 (1982), 12–25, p. 15.

13 *Le Conciliateur, journal des intérêts de la Creuse*, 3 November 1870. The *Conciliateur* was originally a Bonapartist local sheet but it had become a moderate supporter of Nadaud and Gambetta during the war.

14 Frédéric Robert, *La Marseillaise*, Les nouvelles éditions du pavillon, Imprimerie Nationale, 1989, pp. 76–80.

15 Louis Garel, *La Révolution lyonnaise depuis le 4 septembre*, Lyons, Association typographique, 1871, pp. 37–8.

16 Michael Howard, *The Franco-Prussian War: The German Invasion of France, 1870–1871*, New York, Dorset Press, 1961, reprinted 1990; Richard Holmes, *The Road to Sedan: The French Army 1866–1870*, Royal Historical Society, 1984; François Roth, *La Guerre de 1870*, Fayard, 1990.

17 Ludovic Halévy, *Notes et souvenirs 1871–1872*, Calmann-Lévy, 1889, p. 25.

18 This was a return to 1830s and 1848 practices. Alain Corbin, *Le Monde retrouvé de Louis François Pinagot, sur les traces d'un inconnu, 1798–1876*, Flammarion, 1998, p. 269.

19 *Nouveau manuel de la Garde Nationale, règlement du 16 mars 1869, revu et mis en ordre par un officier d'État-Major, adapté pour les Gardes Nationales Mobilisés*, Hachette, 1870; *Organisation de la Garde Nationale*, Librairie Administrative Dupont, 1870.

20 ADCr, 1 M 199.

21 Henri Durangel, *Rapport présenté par le chef de la division administrative générale et départementale à M. Jules Cazot, secrétaire délégué du ministère de l'intérieur*, Organisation des gardes nationales mobilisés, Bordeaux, Émile Crugy, 1871, p. 4.

22 Edmond Fuzier-Herman, *La province au siège de Paris – Garde Mobile du Tarn*, Paris, Librairie Militaire de J. Dumaine, 1871, p. 24; Le Marquis de la Rochethulon, *Du Rôle de la garde nationale et de l'armée de Paris dans les préparatifs de l'insurrection du 18 mars, rapport spécial fait à la commission d'enquête*, Léon Techener, 1872, pp. 6–9.

23 Sutter-Laumann, *Histoire d'un trente sous (1870–1871)*, Paris, Albert Savine, 1891, p 70. Sutter-Laumann was a radical journalist and poet who wrote *Les meurts de faim*, 1888, and *L'ironie du Sort*, 1892, both published by Albert Savine.

24 E. Razoua, *Petit manuel du Garde Nationale républicain*, Chevalier, 1870 (September).

25 A. Bougeard *et al.*, *Des Districts!!!*, 6 September, 1870, reproduced in *Les Révolutions du XIXe siècle*, 10 vols, Paris, EDHIS, 1988, vol. 6, pp. 1, 3.

26 *Le Salut Public*, 6 October 1870.

27 SAT LY 36, organisation of the IV arrondissement.

28 Sudhir Hazareesingh, *From Subject to Citizen: The Second Empire and the Emergence of French Democracy*, Princeton, 1998, p. 12.

29 Sophie Duchesne, *Citoyenneté à la française*, Presses de Sciences Po, 1997, pp. 84–8.

30 ADCr, 1 M 198, 6 November 1871, Martin Nadaud to the National Guard and the *francs-tireurs*.

31 Many similar proclamations imitate the emphatic style of Gambetta's own text. This represents the last golden age of republican rhetoric.

32 Edmond de Goncourt, *Paris under Siege from the Goncourt Journal*, Ithaca, Cornell University Press, 1969; Charles Jacob Marchal (de Calvi), *La Guerre de 1870, formule du Communalisme*, Pau, Imprimerie Véronèse, March 1871.

33 *Le Réveil de la Province*, 11 September 1870.

34 Victor Desplats, a bourgeois isolated in Paris, commented with some dismay on his young brother-in-law's enthusiasm for National Guard service. Pierre Lay (ed.), *Lettres d'un homme à la femme qu'il aime pendant le siège de Paris*, Jean-Claude Lattès, 1980, pp. 87 and passim.

35 Anti-democratic feelings existed among the left. G. de Molinari, *Les Clubs Rouges pendant le siège de Paris*, Garnier Frères, 1871, pp. 160–1.

36 This picture comes from a compendium of good illustrations of the war published in 1871 under the name *Les deux sièges de Paris, album pittoresque*, Au bureau du journal *L'Éclipse*, 1871.

37 P. Lay (ed.), *Lettres d'un homme [Victor Desplats] à la femme qu'il aime*, p. 59.

38 Roger V. Gould, *Insurgent Identities: Class, Community and Protest in Paris from 1848 to the Commune*, Chicago University Press, 1996.

39 Sutter-Laumann, *Histoire d'un trente sous*, p. 276.

40 AVdP, VD6 791, VIII. This was particularly used in some arrondissements, such as the VIII in Paris. Judith F. Stone, *The Search for Social Peace: Reform Legislation in France, 1890–1914*, State University of New York Press, Albany, 1985, p. 27; Sophie Duchesne, *Citoyenneté à la française*, p. 173. This was theorised by Léon Bourgeois's solidarism in the 1890s

41 *Le Salut Public*, 29 December 1870.

42 Some mutual societies were actually created this way: *Société de Secours Mutuels pour les Accidents du Siège*, AVdP, Vbis 1H3 7, *Procès verbal du conseil de famille*. On mutual societies, a recent discussion can be found in Carol E. Harrison, *The Bourgeois Citizen in Nineteenth-Century France: Gender, Sociability and the Uses of Emulation*, Oxford University Press, 1999, pp. 130–9.

43 AVdP, VD6 791. F, *Instruction générale*, pp. 5–12.

44 AVdP, Vbis 1H3 7, *Procès verbal du conseil de famille*, 22–24 September.

45 Charles-Aimé Dauban, *Le Fond de la société sous la Commune* [1873], Slatkine-Megariotis Reprints, 1977, p. 21.

46 M.F. Crestin, *Souvenirs d'un lyonnais*, imprimerie Decléris et fils, 1897, p. 86.

47 *Organisation de la Garde Nationale Sédentaire – lois, décrets, circulaires et instructions, deuxième édition revue et augmentée des décrets et dispositions parues depuis le 4 septembre*, Dupont, 1870, pp. xiv–xv.

48 Jeanne Gaillard, *Paris la ville*, Lille, Université de Lille III, H. Champion, 1976, p. 320. Survival rather than comfort was the norm; R. Fuchs, *Poor and Pregnant in Paris*, New Brunswick, Rutgers University Press, 1992; A. Pain, *Des Divers Modes de l'Assistance Publique*, Baillière, 1865.

49 B. Taithe, *Defeated Flesh: Welfare, Warfare and the Making of Modern France*, Manchester University Press, 1999, ch. 3.

50 AMM, H3 186 and 'Délibérations du conseil municipal', 57 D1.

51 M.F. Crestin, *Souvenirs d'un lyonnais*, imprimerie Decléris et fils, 1897, p. 83.

52 AVdP, VD6 791 F.

53 AVdP, VD6 1711, VIII arrondissement, *Conseil de famille de la Garde Nationale*.

54 AVdP, Vbis 1H3 7, *Procès verbal du conseil de famille*, 18 November 1870.

55 AML, 4 M1 10005, *Procès verbaux du conseil municipal de Lyon*, 2 February 1871.

56 M.E. Denormandie, *Le VIII arrondissement et son administration pendant le siège de Paris*, Garnier Frères, 1875, pp. 77–85.

57 ADC, R 106. The defence committee of Corrèze was created 17 September 1870 and the municipal committees to distribute help date from 23 September 1870 in Corrèze.

58 This was carried on under the Commune. In spite of dismissive comments from historians of administration, the Commune attempted to carry on a statistical and social mapping programme. AVdP, VD6 730 256, 30 April 1871.

59 M.E. Denormandie, *Le VIII arrondissement et son administration pendant le siège de Paris*, Garnier Frères, 1875, p. 56. *Étrennes* given on 31 December were a way of exchanging gifts with neighbours, friends and employees. Some workers such as concierges depended heavily on these 'gifts', which were no less than a statutory part of the wages.

60 Jean-Luc Marais, *Histoire du Don en France de 1800 à 1939, dons et legs charitables, pieux et philanthropiques*, Presses Universitaires de Rennes, 1999.

61 Text of the report to the parliamentary commission of 24 June 1871, reproduced in Odile Rudelle (ed.), *Jules Ferry: la république des citoyens*, Imprimerie Nationale, 1996, p. 242. Text of the report to the parliamentary commission of 24 June 1871.

62 ADR, 3 M 1705, *Élections municipales du Vème*, Lyons, 14 September 1870.

63 ADR, 3 M 1329, *Élections du 5 juillet 1871*.

64 ADR, 3 M 1328, *Élections du 8 février 1871*.

65 ADR, 3 M 1328, *ibid.*

66 Alan R.H. Baker rightly reminds us that we must at all costs avoid gross generalisations about the French peasantry. Alan R.H. Baker, *Fraternity among the French Peasantry: Sociability and Voluntary Associations in the Loire Valley, 1815–1914*, Cambridge University Press, 1999, pp. 5–6.

67 The royalist myth of the Vendée and Chouannerie was then very much alive; Geoffrey Cubitt, 'Memory and fidelity in French Legitimism: Crétineau Joly and the Vendée', *Nineteenth Century Contexts, an Interdisciplinary Journal*, 21 (2000) 4, pp. 593–610.

68 Priscilla Parkhurst Ferguson, *Paris as Revolution: Writing the Nineteenth Century City*, University of California Press, 1994.

69 This is, however, not a completely new theme; see, for instance, François Burdeau, *Liberté, libertés locales chéries!*, Paris, Éditions Cujas, 1983, pp.157–213; Sudhir Hazareesingh, *From Subject to Citizen: the Second Empire and the Emergence of French Democracy*, Princeton, 1998, pp. 195–213.

70 Brigitte Basdevant-Gaudemet, *La Commission de décentralisation de 1870: contribution à l'étude de la décentralisation en France au XIXe siècle*, Presses Universitaires de France, 1973, pp. 10, 27–55.

71 ADC, *Le Réveil de la Province*, published in Tulle, was a Catholic weekly which made clear that it was a Limousin newspaper established against the information provided by Paris.

72 *Ligue d'Union Républicaine des droits de Paris, Armistice de Neuilly, rapport des délégués, les révolutions du XIXe siècle*, 10 vols, Paris, EDHIS, vol. 7, *Projet de Loi Municipale*, pp. 2, 8.

73 *Ligue d'Union Républicaine des droits de Paris, Armistice de Neuilly, rapport des délégués, les révolutions du XIXe siècle*, 10 vols, Paris, EDHIS, vol. 7, *Fédéralisme. Projet de traité entre Paris et Versailles*, Association typographique, May 1871, p. 2.

74 Louis Garel, *La Révolution lyonnaise depuis le 4 septembre*, Lyons, Association typographique, 1871, p. 10.

75 This, for instance, was one of the objectives of the society for the defence of human rights founded in Lyons; *Les Révolutions du XIXe siècle*, 10 vols, Paris, EDHIS, vol. 10, *Affiches, feuilles volantes, documents divers*, 1988, p. 46.

76 Jeanne Gaillard, *Communes de province, Commune de Paris 1870–1871*, Flammarion, Question d'Histoire, 1971; A. Olivesi, *La Commune de 1871 à Marseille et ses origines*, Rivière, 1950, pp. 83–149; Raymond Huard, *La Préhistoire des partis, le mouvement républicain en bas languedoc*, Presses de Sciences Po, 1982, pp. 250–5; Louis Fiaux, *Histoire de la guerre civile de 1871, le gouvernement et l'assemblée de Versailles, la Commune de Paris*, Charpentier, 1879, pp. 227–34.

77 Raymond Huard, *La Naissance des partis politiques en France*, Presses de Sciences Po, 1996, p. 148.

78 See the call for the *Ligue de l'Est* signed by Edmond Ordinaire, prefect of the Doubs, in Besançon. *Ligue de l'Est pour la défense de Besançon*, reproduced in *Les Révolutions du XIXe siècle*, 10 vols, Paris, EDHIS, 1988, vol. 8, p.1; Ch. Bauquier, *Les Dernières campagnes dans l'Est*, Lemerre, 1873, pp. 11–21.

79 Louis Garel, *La Révolution lyonnaise depuis le 4 septembre*, Lyons, Association typographique, 1871, pp. 60–61.

80 Ch. Bauquier, *Les Dernières campagnes dans l'Est*, Lemerre, 1873, pp. 11–12.

81 *Le Salut Public*, 1 October 1870.

82 ADR, 1 M 118, *Réunion presidée par Bastelica dans la salle de l'Alhambra*, 9 September 1870.

83 *Procès verbaux du conseil municipal de Lyon*, pp. 94–5. This was the position of Ferouillat of the town council, who was behind the central committee for defence based in Lyons.

84 *Les Révolutions du XIXe siècle*, 10 vols, Paris, EDHIS, vol. 10, *Affiches, feuilles volantes, documents divers, Ligue du Midi*, p. 36, their emphasis.

85 *Ligue du Sud-Ouest, Comité de Salut Public, commission exécutive*, 10 October 1870, *Les Révolutions du XIXe siècle*, 10 vols, Paris, EDHIS, vol. 10, *Affiches, feuilles volantes, documents divers*, p. 32.

86 AOM, *Le Colon*, 3 November 1870.

87 *Le Corrézien*, 18 October 1870.

88 *Le Réveil de la Province*, 13 October 1870.

89 *Le Réveil de la Province*, 5 November 1870.

90 *Le Réveil de la Province*, 22 November 1870.

91 Andrew R. Aisenberg, *Contagion: Disease, Government and the 'Social Question' in Nineteenth-Century France*, Stanford University Press, 1999.

92 R. Magraw, *Workers and the Bourgeois Republic*, 2 vols, Blackwell, 1992.

93 Maurice Moissonnier, *La Première internationale et la Commune à Lyon, 1865–1871*, Éditions Sociales, 1972, p. 65.

94 *Troisième procès de l'Association Internationale des travailleurs à Paris*, Les grands procès politiques, Paris, Armand le Chevalier, 1870.

95 Un bourgeois républicain, *Histoire de l'internationale (1862–1872)*, Londres/Paris/Bruxelles, n.p., Combe et Vande Weghe, 1873.

96 Oscar Testut, *L'Internationale*, E. Lachaud, 1871, p. vii.

97 Not to be confused with a central committee of defence established by the municipal council of Lyons in the session of 17 September, which intended to centralise defence in the south of France. *Procès verbaux du conseil municipal de Lyon*, 17 September 1870.

98 ADR, 4 M 288, poster of the proclamation of 9 October 1870.

99 A small insurrection also took place in Marseilles on 1 November 1870. A. Olivesi, *La Commune de 1871 à Marseille et ses origines*, Rivière, 1950, pp. 118–24.

100 Ellen Furlough, *Consumer Cooperation in France: The Politics of Consumption, 1834–1930*, Ithaca, Cornell University Press, 1991.

101 SAT, LY108. *Association des ouvriers de metallurgie; société coopérative des fondeurs de fer*.

102 G. de Molinari, *Les Clubs rouges pendant le siège de Paris*, Garnier, 1871.

103 To his credit, Gould mentions it once for Paris. Roger V. Gould, *Insurgent Identities: Class, Community and Protest in Paris from 1848 to the Commune*, Chicago University Press, 1995, p. 156.

104 ADHV, 1 M 158, *Examen des actes du gouvernement provisoire*, 23 January 1872; reply of 16 February 1872.

105 *Le Salut Public*, 29 December 1870.

106 Amédée Fauche, *Montereau-Faut-Yonne, Journal de l'occupation prussienne*, Montereau, L. Zanote, 1871, pp. 65–6.

107 M. du Camp, *La Charité privée à Paris*, Hachette, 1885, p. 2; A. Fleury, *De l'Assistance Publique à Paris*, Rousseau, 1901.

108 ADHV, 2 R 183, *Oeuvre des orphelins de la guerre*; 2 R 182, *Répartition du fond de secours*.

109 Anxieties on food and the political meanings of food are explored in B. Taithe, *Defeated Flesh*, pp. 104–12; Madeleine Egrat, 'La Boulangerie Parisienne sous le second empire', *L'Actualité de l'Histoire*, 14 (1956), pp. 12–29.

110 AVdP, VD6 730 256, *Extrait du bulletin de l'Académie des Sciences*, T xxxv, p. 669. Printouts of this text were distributed in the I arrondissement. A. Husson, *Les Consommations de Paris*, Guillaumin, 1856.

111 AVdP, VD6/1586/3, *Histoire du fonctionnement des services ordinaires et extraordinaires du huitième arrondissement durant le siège*, 1874, p. 75. Charles Joubert and Arnauld de Vresse, *De la Défense de Paris pendant le siège au point de vue de l'alimentation*, Arnauld de Vresse, 1871.

112 *Les Deux sièges de Paris, album pittoresque*, Au bureau du journal *L'Éclipse*, 1871.

113 AVdP, VD6 1222/3, *Requisitions illégales*, 19 December 1870.

114 Étienne Arago, *L'Hôtel de Ville de Paris au 4 Septembre et pendant le siège, réponse à monsieur le comte Daru*, Paris, Hetzel, 1871, pp. 328–9.

115 AVdP, VD6 721/13, *Recensement numérique de la population indigente de la Ville*; AAP 542 Foss 47, *Caisse de bureaux de bienfaisance*.

116 AMM, D 52, V, *Correspondance au préfet*, 4 November 1870.

117 AML, 4 M1 10005, *Procès verbaux du conseil municipal de Lyon*, 26 January 1871.

118 A. Thiers, *De la Propriété*, Paulin, L'Heureux, 1848.

4 Municipal freedom and war

1 R. Poincaré, *Ce que demande la cité*, Hachette, 1912, p. 2.

2 Ch. Bauquier, *Les Dernières campagnes dans l'Est*, Lemerre, 1873, p. 4.

3 Vincent Wright, 'Les Préfets de police pendant le second empire: personnalités et problèmes', in Jacques Aubert (ed.), *L'État et sa police en France (1789–1914)*, Geneva, Librairie Droz, 1979, pp. 83–102, pp. 90–1.

4 Local studies are now sufficiently abundant, and all tend to prove the importance of prefectoral and civil service staff in the shaping of a quiet if not mute local democracy. See, for instance, on the functioning of a provincial *préfecture* and *conseil général*: François Igersheim, *Politique et Administration dans le Bas-Rhin (1848–1870)*, Presses Universitaires de Strasbourg, 1993, pp. 357–77; P.M. Jones, *Politics and Rural Society: The Southern Massif Central c. 1750–1880*, Cambridge University Press, 1985, pp. 220–3.

5 Bernard Ménager, *La Vie politique dans le département du Nord de 1851 à 1877*, 3 vols, Atelier National, reproduction des thèses, Lille III, 1983, vol. 1, pp. 123–223.

6 On prefects, see Bernard Leclère and Vincent Wright, *Les Préfets du Second Empire*, Fondation Nationale des Sciences Politiques, 1973. The prefects of France received increased powers under the misnamed decree of decentralisation of 24 March 1852.

7 AML, 4M1 10003, *Procès verbaux du conseil municipal de Lyon*, session of 17 September 1870. The problem seems to have been finding volunteers to take on the hated

function of police *commissaire*. Also see the session of 17 November 1870 and 19 November 1870 on the abolition of the state police.

8 See Benjamin F. Martin, *Crime and Criminal Justice under the Third Republic*, Louisiana State University, 1990, pp. 48–63.

9 Quoted in Louis Fiaux, *Jules Ferry, un malfaiteur public*, Librairie Internationale Achille Le Rey, 1886, p. 35

10 ADHV, 4 M 24, *Rapport à Monsieur le préfet du commissaire de police de Saint Yrieix*, 3rd term of 1870.

11 J. Merriman, *Consciousness and Class Experience in Nineteenth-Century Europe*, New York, Holmes and Meier, 1979; A. Corbin, *Time, Desire and Horror: Towards a History of the Senses*, Cambridge, Polity Press, 1997.

12 Leclère and Wright, *Les Préfets du Second Empire*, p. 46.

13 ADHV, 2M13.

14 ADHV, 1 M 158, *Examen des actes du gouvernement provisoire*, 23 January 1872; reply of 16 February 1872.

15 See Louis Girard *et al.*, *Les Conseils Généraux en 1870: étude statistique d'un personnel politique*, Presses Universitaires de France, 1967, pp. 171–80.

16 Ch. Bauquier, *Les Dernières campagnes dans l'Est*, p. 12; Sudhir Hazareesingh, 'The Société d'Instruction Républicaine and the propagation of civic republicanism in provincial and rural France, 1870–1877', *Journal of Modern History*, 71 (1999) 2, pp. 271–307, p. 301. Hazareesingh makes the point that this was one of the least inspired moves of the Gambetta dictatorship. It was in harmony with the radical purge of mayors, judges and functionaries undertaken under the dictatorship.

17 AMM, H3 186 and *Délibérations du conseil municipal*, 57 D1, 14 September 1870.

18 R. Tombs (ed.), *Nationhood and Nationalism in France*, HarperCollins, 1991.

19 *Le Courier du Centre*, 23 September 1870, circular from Gambetta.

20 Mary Poovey, *Making a Social Body: British Cultural Formation, 1830–1864*, University of Chicago Press, 1995, pp. 76–115.

21 François Goguel, *Géographie des élections françaises sous la troisième et la quatrième république*, Cahiers de la Fondation Nationale des Sciences Politiques, 159, Armand Colin, 1970, pp. 16–18. Hérault and Rhône voted less than 55 per cent in favour of the referendum, Haute-Vienne voted more than 65 per cent, and Corrèze 75 per cent. Jacques Gouault, *Comment la France est devenue républicaine: Les élections générales et partielles à l'assemblée nationale de 1870–1871*, Cahiers de la Fondation Nationale des Sciences Politiques, 62, Armand Colin, 1954.

22 Pierre Léon, *Géographie de la fortune et structures sociales à Lyon au XIXe siècle (1815–1914)*, Centre d'Histoire économique et sociale de la région lyonnaise, 1974, pp. 14–15.

23 Louis Pérouas, *Histoire de Limoges*, Privat, 1989, p. 196.

24 Jules Simon, *Souvenirs du 4 Septembre, origine et chute du second empire*, Calmann-Lévy, 1876, pp. 255–62.

25 Andrieux was a member of the Lodge of Perfect Silence, ADR, 4 M 263, *Associations politiques*.

26 The members of the AIT in Lyons' committee were Albert Richard, Palix, Placet, Taccussel, Doublet, Charvet and Lombail. Other members of the committee were card-holding members, but the above mentioned were added on behalf of the AIT as official representatives. Doubts about Richard led to his name being removed early on. Louis Garel, *La Révolution lyonnaise depuis le 4 septembre*, Lyons, Association typographique, 1871, pp. 26–7.

27 *Le Salut Public*, 6 October 1870.

28 A. Hodieu, *Du Principe électif à appliquer à la ville de Lyon pour la nomination de son conseil municipal*, Lyons, 1864.

29 *Comité de Salut Public de Lyon, Procès verbaux*, Lyons, Association Typographique, 1870.

30 Louis Garel, *La Révolution lyonnaise depuis le 4 septembre*, Lyons, Association typographique, 1871, pp. 24–5.
31 *Les Révolutions du XIXe siècle*, 10 vols, Paris, EDHIS, vol. 10, *Affiches, feuilles volantes, documents divers*, p. 24. The date of this edition of the poster is not accurate: the text was not published on 4 September but on 15 September.
32 *Le Salut Public*, 4 October 1870.
33 Comité de Salut Public, *Procès verbaux des séances*, Lyons, Association Typographique, 1870, session of 12 September. The taxes were set twice under the committee of public salvation and later under the elected municipality.
34 *Le Salut Public*, 15 October 1870.
35 AMM, H3 186 and *Délibérations du conseil municipal* 57 D1, 3 October 1870.
36 AML, 4 M1 10003, *Procès verbaux du conseil municipal de Lyon*, 23 October 1870.
37 ADR, M 4/100. Thierry Halay, *Le Mont-de-Piété des origines à nos jours*, L'Harmattan, 1994, pp. 104–5.
38 *Le Salut Public*, 26 October 1870.
39 AVdP, VD6 1711 3, *Dégagements gratuits du Mont de Piété*.
40 This enterprise was severely criticised later; there is a damning indictment of its budgetary amateurism in the report of the royalist Comte de Ségur. Louis Philippe Antoine Charles de Ségur, *Les Marchés de la guerre à Lyon et à l'armée de Garibaldi*, Henri Plon, 1873, pp. 128–30. Ségur obviously hated everything Lyons stood for in 1870–1. Crooks like Malewski or Lutz thus embezzled much of the funds put in their hands to recruit *francs-tireurs* and equip them. *Le Salut Public*, 15 January 1871.
41 ADR, 1 M 118, *Rapport de l'agent de la gare de Vaise*.
42 AML, 4 M1 10005, *Procès verbaux du conseil municipal de Lyon*, 21 February 1871.
43 Rapport du major du camps de Sathenay, 06 September 1870. ADR, 1 M 118.
44 Comité de Salut Public, *Procès verbaux des séances*, Lyons, Association Typographique, 1870, session of 5 September.
45 ADR, 1 M 118, *Liste des personnes arrêtées à Lyon*.
46 AML, 4 M1 10003, *Procès verbaux du conseil municipal de Lyon*, 30 September 1870.
47 In French administrative hierarchy, generals precede mayors.
48 *La Comédie Politique*, 26 November 1871.
49 *Le Courier du Centre* (Limoges), 3 October 1870.
50 *Le Salut Public* (Lyons), 8 November 1870.
51 ADR, 4 M 223.
52 ADR, 1 M 118.
53 AML, 4 M1 10005, *Procès verbaux du conseil municipal de Lyon*, 31 January 1871; 1 February 1871.
54 On Toulouse, see Ronald Aminzade, *Ballots and Barricades: Class Formation and Republican Politics in France, 1830–1871*, Princeton University Press, 1993, pp. 216–23; Armand Duportal, *La Commune à Toulouse, simple exposé des faits*, Imprimerie Générale Paul Savy, 1871.
55 *Le Salut Public*, 3 February 1871.
56 AML, 4 M1 10005, *Procès verbaux du conseil municipal de Lyon*, 3 February 1871; 18 February 1871.
57 For the feeling of fear, see ADC, R 520, *Dépêches télégraphiques*.
58 AMM, H3 186 and *Délibérations du conseil municipal* 57 D1, 17 September 1870.
59 AMM, H3 186 and *Délibérations du conseil municipal* 57 D1, 16 September 1870.
60 AMM, H3 186 and *Délibérations du conseil municipal* 57 D1, 18 January 1871.
61 AMM, D3/2, 15 August 1871.
62 AMM, H3 186 and *Délibérations du conseil municipal* 57 D1, 20 September 1870.
63 AMM D3/2. The last election was organised on 25 May 1871.
64 See A. Corbin, *Archaisme et modernité en Limousin au XIXe siècle, 1845–1880*, 2 vols, Limoges, PULIM [1975], 1998.

65 Louis Pérouas, *Histoire de Limoges*, Privat, 1989.
66 *Le Courier du Centre* (Limoges), 28 November 1870.
67 *La Nation Française*, 6 April 1871; 7 April 1871.
68 *La Nation Française*, 8 April 1871.
69 Michel Lidove, 'Le Département de la Corrèze et la fondation de la troisième république', *Bulletin de la Société des Lettres, Sciences et Arts de la Corrèze*, 68 (1964), pp. 6–14.
70 ADC, 1D44, 19 February 1870.
71 *Le Réveil de la Province*, 15 September 1870 and 22 September 1870. The Lyons example is inspired by the Lyonese paper *La Décentralisation* of the same political inclination, and refers to the events of 28 September in Lyons.
72 *Le Corrézien*, 6 May 1870.
73 *Le Corrézien*, 26 November 1870.
74 The number of volunteers for the whole of Corrèze seems to have been fewer than twenty. Only one man had come to enrol in Tulle by 30 March.
75 Jacques Girault, *La Commune et Bordeaux (1870–1871), contribution à l'étude du mouvement ouvrier et de l'idéologie républicaine en province au moment de la Commune de Paris*, Éditions Sociales, 1971, p. 149; Éric Bonhomme, 'Bordeaux et la défense nationale', *Annales du Midi*, 223 (1998), pp. 319–42.
76 ADHV, 1 M 158, *Examen des actes du gouvernement provisoire*, 23 January 1872; reply of 16 February 1872.
77 Jacques Gouault, *Comment la France est devenue républicaine*, pp. 42–3.
78 ADR, 3 M 1477.
79 ADR, 4 M 223.
80 Éric Bonhomme, 'Bordeaux et la Défense Nationale', *Annales du Midi*, 223 (1998), pp. 319–42, p. 341.
81 'Compte rendu d'une séance tenue par le comité de défense de Lyon', *La Décentralisation*, 3 October 1870.
82 This pacifism is carefully occluded from the official history of the city: Michel Bur (ed.), *Histoire de Laon et du Laonnois*, Toulouse, Privat, 1987, pp. 234–5.
83 Édouard Fleury, *Éphémérides de la guerre de 1870–71*, Imprimerie du journal de l'Aisne, Laon, 1871, p. 12, quoting the *Glaneur de Saint-Quentin*.
84 A. Bougeard, Brière, Dassis, Dourle, E. Dupas, Hamet, Leclerc, Leverdays, Lupin, Longuet, Maillard, Marchand, Martel, Vaillant, *Des Districts!!!*, 6 September 1870, reproduced in *Les Révolutions du XIXe siècle*, 10 vols, Paris, EDHIS, 1988, vol. 6, ff. 1, pp. 2–3.
85 G. de Molinari, *Les Clubs Rouges pendant le siège de Paris*, Garnier Frères, 1871, pp. lv–vi, 9, 42–8.
86 Tony Moilin *et al.*, *Rapport du Comité Républicain du VIe arrondissement* (club de l'école de médecine, 5 December 1870), reprinted in *Les Révolutions du XIXe siècle*, 10 vols, Paris, EDHIS, 1988, vol. 6, ff. 15, pp. 3–4. Dr Tony Moilin played an important part in the sanitary services of the Communard army and a minor role in the council of the XII arrondissement during the Commune and was executed after a summary trial on 28 May 1871, italics in original.
87 M.E. Denormandie, *Le VIII arrondissement et son administration pendant le siège de Paris*, Garnier Frères, 1875, p. 100. The VIII arrondissement proceeded through this strong encouragement to public charity and did not create ambulances as such, relying instead on the more established public and private networks of almsgiving.
88 For the insurrection's point of view, see Jean-Baptiste Millière, *Le 31 octobre. Compte rendu au 208e bataillon de la Garde Nationale par le Commandant Millière*, Paris, Association générale typographique, November 1870, reproduced in *Les Révolutions du XIXe siècle*, 10 vols, Paris, EDHIS, 1988, vol. 6, ff. 9, pp. 12–13.

89 ADR, 1 M 118, *Adresse de la garde nationale de Lyon au citoyen préfet, investi des pouvoirs civils et militaires.*

90 ADR, 1 M 118.

91 AML, 4 M1 10005, *Procès verbaux du conseil municipal de Lyon*, 22 March 1871.

92 ADR, 1 M 118, proclamation of 23 March 1871, signed by Bouvatier, Perrare, Perraton, Colonna, Garel, Poncet, Blanc, Tissot, Micaud.

93 ADR, 4 M 223, *Acte d'accusation sur les évènements du 30 avril 1871.*

94 ADR, 4 M 288, *Insurrection de la guillotière.* Andrieux had become the bête noire of the extreme left since the repression of the Arnaud incident.

95 Much more so than the more dramatic interpretation given by Christopher E. Guthrie, 'The battle for the Third Republic in the arrondissement of Narbonne', *French History*, 2 (1988) 1, pp. 45–73.

96 Marc César, *La Commune de Narbonne (mai 1871)*, Presses Universitaires de Perpignan, 1996, pp. 160–71.

97 Christopher E. Guthrie, 'Émile Digeon and socialism in the Narbonnais', *French History*, 12 (1998) 1, pp. 43–67.

98 *Proclamation de la Commune à Narbonne. Compte Rendu Sténographique du procès d'Émile Digeon et de ses 31 coaccusés*, n.d., n.p., reprinted in *Les Révolutions du XIXe siècle*, 10 vols, Paris, EDHIS, 1988, vol. 8, ff. 15, pp. 105–11.

99 A. Olivesi, *La Commune de 1871 à Marseille et ses origines*, Rivière, 1950, pp. 151–4.

100 *Affaire du mouvement insurrectionnel du 4 avril 1871 à Marseille*, T. Saurat, Marseilles, 1871.

101 The club culture of most urban centres seems to have arisen in the early days of the 4 September republic. See for instance Édouard Fleury, *Éphémérides de la guerre de 1870–71*, Imprimerie du journal de l'Aisne, Laon, 1871, p. 16.

102 In Périgueux the workers refused to let the trains go. *Le Corrézien*, 15 April 1871.

103 See, for a regional example, Bernard Ménager, *La Vie politique dans le département du Nord de 1851 à 1877*, 3 vols, Atelier National, reproduction des thèses, Lille III, 1983, vol. 3, pp. 1002–5; Philip G. Nord, 'The Party of Conciliation and the Paris Commune', *French Historical Studies*, 15 (1987) 1, pp. 1–35.

104 ADR, 1 M 118, address of 2 May.

105 A. Thiers, *Discours de M.A. Thiers, le 24 mai 1873*, Paris, Degorce-Cadot, 1873, pp. 15–16.

106 Barodet had been one of Gambetta's strongest supporters in the municipal council of Lyons, and in January 1871 had gone to Bordeaux with Hénon and Vallier to ask Gambetta to lead a last-ditch effort to continue the war. ADR, 1 M 118, 29 January 1871, *Le Conseil municipal de Lyon constitué en comité de salut public.*

107 Alan Grubb, *The Politics of Pessimism: Albert de Broglie and Conservative Politics in the Early Third Republic*, Newark, University of Delaware Press, 1996, pp. 105–6.

108 ADCr, 1 M 106. The notary of his village and his many friends vouched for his good character.

109 R. Tombs, 'Prudent rebels: the Second Arrondissement during the Paris Commune of 1871', *French History*, 5 (1991) 4, pp. 393–413.

110 André Bastelica, *Appel aux français, lettre d'un proscrit*, Geneva, 1876.

111 P. Vésinier, *Histoire de la Commune de Paris*, London, 1871.

112 M. Bakunin, G. Léo and G. Lafrançais, *Simples questions sociales*, Saint-Imier, Propagande socialiste, 1872.

113 M. Bakunin, *La Révolution sociale ou la dictature militaire*, Geneva, 1871.

114 A. Claris, *La proscription française en Suisse, 1871–72*, Geneva, 1872.

115 ADR, 4 M 288, *Rapport de Monsieur le Commissaire spécial de Fresnay, l'Internationale en Suisse et surtout à Genève*, 25 March 1872.

116 A. Claris, *Les Ennemis de l'internationale démasqués au congrès de la Haye*, Brussels, L. Verrycken, 1872, pp. 86–114.

117 ADR, 4 M 288, *Rapport de Monsieur le Commissaire spécial de Fresnay, l'Internationale en Suisse et surtout à Genève*, 25 March 1872, p. 4.
118 G. Lefrançais, *Étude sur le mouvement communaliste à Paris en 1871*, Neuchâtel, 1871.
119 B. Malon, *La Troisième défaite du prolétariat français*, Neuchâtel, 1871; see also André Léo, *La Guerre sociale, discours prononcé au congrès de la Paix à Lausanne*, Neuchâtel, 1871. André Léo was in fact Léodile Champseix (1832–1900), a novelist whose novels, *Le Divorce* and *Le Mariage scandaleux*, had received some critical attention. She led the Société de revendication des droits de la femme in 1868 and was the editor of the relatively moderate Communard journal *La Sociale*; she was also a member of the Comité de vigilance des citoyennes de Montmartre before emigrating to Switzerland with B. Malon.
120 For instance, M, Vuillaume, H. Berenger and L. de Marancour, *Hommes et choses du temps de la Commune*, Geneva, 1871; G. Jeanneret, *Paris pendant la Commune révolutionnaire de 1871*, Neuchâtel, 1871.
121 V. d'Esboeufs (Vergès), *La Vérité sur le gouvernement de la Défense nationale, la Commune et les versaillais*, Geneva, 1871.
122 J. Lemonnyer, *Essai bibliographique sur les publications de la proscription française ou catalogue raisonné d'une bibliothèque socialiste, communaliste et de libre pensée*, Versailles, Au Palais de l'Assemblée Nationale, 1873.
123 Similar attitudes prevailed at the end of Napoleon I's reign: Stuart Semmel, 'Reading the tangible past: British tourism, collecting and memory after Waterloo', *Representations*, 69 (2000), pp. 9–37.
124 For instance, see V. d'Esboeufs, *Le Coin du voile, trahison et défection au sein de la Commune*, Geneva, 1871.
125 The Caledonian deportation had few other activities. Jean Maitron (ed.), *Henri Messager, lettres de déportaion, 1871–1876*, Le Sycomore, 1979, pp. 295–366.
126 Gaspard Blanc had been crucial in the AIT of Lyons with Palix, Chol, Richard and Places. He was the secretary in charge of the correspondence. His police file, ADR, 4 M 290, contains the manuscript minutes of the AIT commissions.
127 Bernard Ménager, *Les Napoléon du peuple*, Paris, Aubier, 1988, pp. 282–4; Albert Richard's views were against a bourgeois democracy valuing wealth before social justice; see his views in his *Aux Français. Simples appréciations d'un révolutionnaire*, Lyons, December 1870, reproduced in *Les Révolutions du XIXe siècle*, 10 vols, Paris, EDHIS, vol. 10, *Affiches feuilles volantes, documents divers*, 1988, ff. 42.
128 *L'Égalité*, 15 February 1872. They were then expelled by the *Section de propagande et d'action révolutionnaire socialiste de Genève* of the Jurassian sections. Albert Richard eventually came back into local French politics. *L'Empire et la France nouvelle*, Brussels, n.p., 1872.
129 Amigues belonged to the left-wing fringe of the Bonapartist movement and was a fervent decentralist. Sudhir Hazareesingh, *From Subject to Citizen: the Second Empire and the Emergence of French Democracy*, Princeton University Press, 1998, p. 64. Jules Amigues, *La France à refaire: la Commune*, Lachaud, 1871.
130 Alfred de la Guéronnière, *M. Thiers et sa mission*, E. Dentu, 1871, p. 8.
131 Charles Prolès, *Les Hommes de la révolution de 1871, Raoul Rigault, la préfecture de police sous la Commune, les otages*, Chamuel, 1898.
132 A. Thiers, *Discours de M.A. Thiers, le 24 mai 1873*, Paris, Degorce-Cadot, 1873, p. 23.
133 Pierre Rosanvallon, *L'État en France de 1789 à nos jours*, Le Seuil, 1990, pp. 71–4.
134 Henri Martin, previously mayor of the XVI arrondissement of Paris, quoted in *Le Corrézien*, 3 May 1871.

5 Religious identities and citizenship

1 Abbot Delmas, speaking in the club of St Anselme in April 1871. Abbé G. Delmas, *Un Prêtre et la Commune de Paris en 1871, récits historiques,* Josse, 1873, p. 126.
2 This is particularly obvious in the work of Durkheim; Richard Vernon, *Citizenship and Order: Studies in French Political Thought,* University of Toronto Press, 1986, pp. 174, 180.
3 While there are still numerous arguments as to the cause of dechristianisation in nineteenth-century France and debates on the results of revolutionary anti-clericalism, the recent historiography emphasises how spatially segregated religious practice had become after the Revolution. Michel Vovelle, *Religion et révolution, la déchristianisation de l'an II,* Hachette, 1976; Louis Pérouas et Paul D'Hollander, *La Révolution Française, une rupture dans le christianisme? Le cas du Limousin (1775–1822),* Naves, Les Monédières, 1988; Paule Lerou and Raymond Dartevelle, *Pratiques religieuses, mentalités et spiritualités dans l'Europe révolutionnaire (1770–1820),* Brepols, 1988.
4 Sophie Duchesne, *Citoyenneté à la française,* Presses de Sciences Po, 1997, p. 170; Yves Déloye, *École et citoyenneté. L'individualisme républicain de Ferry à Vichy: controverses,* Presses de Sciences Po, 1994. Duchesne and Déloye tend to overemphasise the individualistic tendencies of the republican model of citizenship. What the crisis of 1870 demonstrated was its communal dimension.
5 The crisis of 24 May 1873 was one of the most momentous of the assembly's existence. It signalled the end of a strange alliance of radicals and conservatives to maintain the French republic before the advent of a proper constitution. In the short term, it signalled a change in politics and a drift towards neo-monarchist policies. See Alan Grubb, *The Politics of Pessimism: Albert de Broglie and Conservative Politics in the Early Third Republic,* Newark, University of Delaware Press, 1996, pp. 73–117.
6 A. Thiers, *Discours de M.A. Thiers, le 24 mai 1873,* Paris, Degorce-Cadot, 1873, p. 7.
7 Albert de Broglie, *Mémoires du duc de Broglie,* Calmann-Lévy, 1938, pp. 354–8.
8 Jean Maurain, *La Politique écclesiastique du Second Empire de 1852 à 1869,* Paris, Félix Alcan, 1930, p. 886.
9 Ruth Harris, *Lourdes: Body and Spirit in the Secular Age,* Harmondsworth, Allen Lanc, 1999.
10 J. Maurain, *La Politique écclesiastique,* pp. 876–901. Ernst Hartwig Kantorowicz, *The King's Two Bodies: A Study in Mediaeval Political Theology,* Princeton University Press, 1957.
11 Quakers obtained some recognition following their humanitarian work. Xavier Long, *Rapport au sujet de la répartition des secours faite par la société anglaise des Amis, Quakers, aux victimes innocentes de la guerre en France, 1870–1871,* n.p., 1872.
12 The two countries still entertain a confused relationship of interdependence. See Étienne Balibar, *Droit de Cité,* Éditions de l'Aube, 1998, pp. 73–89.
13 Noiriel, for instance, chose to entitle the first section of his book *Non-lieu de mémoire;* Gérard Noiriel, *Le Creuset français: histoire de l'immigration, XIXe–XXe siècle,* Éditions du Seuil, 1988, pp. 15–67. Yet his insistence on using a well-defined sociological framework undermined his perspective on the earlier period; pp. 71–8; also see David Assouline and Mehdi Lallaoui, *Un Siècle d'immigrations en France,* 3 vols, Syros, 1996, vol. 1, *Première période 1851–1918, de la mine au champ de bataille,* p. 68.
14 Émile Temmime, 'La politique française à l'égard de la migration Algérienne: le poid de la colonisation', *Le Mouvement Social,* 188 (July 1999), pp. 77–89, p. 78.
15 On this see Peter Dunwoodie, *Writing French Algeria,* Clarendon Press, Oxford, 1998, pp. 42–67.
16 Balkacem Recham, *Les Musulmans Algériens dans l'armée française (1919–1945),* L'Harmattan, 1996, p. 10. Created on 10 December 1841, *Tirailleurs Algériens*

regiments were composed of volunteers; in some cases, like the *Spahis* or *Goumiers*, the light irregular Algerian cavalry, soldiers had a right to refuse to serve far away from their homes.

17 *Le Salut Public*, 11 October 1870.
18 AOM, F80 1682, 24 January 1871.
19 *Le Salut Public*, 29 November 1870.
20 Edward W. Said, *Orientalism*, 1st Vintage Books ed., New York, Vintage Books, 1994. Reverse exoticism also existed, and the wealth of exchanges through the Mediterranean is only now coming to light; see, for instance, Susan Gilson Miller (ed.), *Disorienting Encounters: Travels of a Moroccan Scholar in France in 1845–1846: The Voyage of Muhammad As-Saffar*, University of California Press, 1992.
21 Kenneth J. Perkins, *Qadis, Captains and Colons: French Military Administration in the Colonial Maghrib, 1844–1934*, New York, Africana Publishing, 1981, pp. 14–45. See John M. MacKenzie, *Orientalism, History, Theory and the Arts*, Manchester University Press, 1995, for a revisionist account of the historiography of orientalism.
22 Hans-Jürgen Lüsebrink, *Les Troupes coloniales dans la guerre: présences, imaginaires et représentations*, Images et Colonies, BDIC-ACHAC, 1993.
23 Alice L. Conklin, 'Colonialism and human rights, a contradiction in terms? The case of France and West Africa, 1895–1914', *American Historical Review*, 103 (1998) 2, pp. 419–43.
24 Myron Echenberg, *Colonial Conscripts: The Tirailleurs Sénégalais in French West Africa, 1857–1960*, Portsmouth (NH), Heinemann, London, James Currey, 1991, pp. 10–15. Created in 1857, *Tirailleurs Sénégalais* were mostly involved in the nascent West African French empire, but their image was regularly exhibited when the empire wished to demonstrate its scope.
25 Many of the memoirs representing Turcos used the same normative clichés, which also stressed the comradeship of shared strong coffees in mixed race units. L. Armagnac, *15 jours de campagne, août–septembre 1870, étapes d'un franc-tireur parisien de Paris à Sedan*, 6th edn, Hachette, 1889, p. 76.
26 Kenneth J. Perkins, *Qadis, Captains and Colons*, pp. 92–7, 100.
27 Dr Amédée Maurin, *L'Humaniste, les cent jours de l'Algérie*, Algiers, Typographie de l'Association Ouvrière, 1871, p. 13.
28 Neil MacMaster, *Colonial Migrants and Racism: Algerian in France, 1900–62*, Macmillan, 1997, pp. 22–7.
29 J. Bowlan, 'Polygamists need not apply: becoming a French citizen in colonial Algeria, 1918–1938', *Proceedings of the Annual Meeting of the Western Society for French History*, 24 (1997), pp. 110–19.
30 A. Sainte Marie, 'La province d'Alger vers 1870, l'établissement du Douar Commun et la fixation de la nature de la propriété dans le cadre du Senatus Consulte du 22 avril 1863', *Revue de l'Occident Musulman et de la méditerranée*, 9 (1971), pp. 37–61.
31 For a later period, Alice L. Conklin, 'Colonialism and human rights, a contradiction in terms? The case of France and West Africa, 1895–1914', *American Historical Review*, 103 (1998) 2, pp. 419–43, p. 419.
32 Robert Attal, *Regards sur les juifs d'Algérie*, L'Harmattan, 1996; J.A. Clancy-Smith, *Rebel and Saint: Muslim Notables, Populist Protest, Colonial Encounters (Algeria and Tunisia 1800–1914)*, Berkeley, University of California Press, 1984.
33 This myth of the racial differences is well dissected in Patricia M.E. Lorcin, *Imperial Identities: Stereotyping, Prejudice and Race in Colonial Algeria*, I.B. Tauris, 1995, pp. 146–73.
34 François Joseph Gastu, *Le Peuple Algérien*, Challamel Ainé, 1884, pp. 6–10.
35 Raphael Danziger, *Abd al-Qadir and the Algerian Resistance to the French and Internal Consolidation*, New York, Holmes and Meier, 1977.

NOTES

36 André Masson, 'L'opinion française et les problèmes coloniaux à la fin du Second Empire', *Revue Française d'histoire d'outre-Mer*, 69 (1962), pp. 366–437.
37 AOM, 11 H26–27, letter and translation 9 September 1870.
38 Albert Tissier, *De l'Application du décret du 24 octobre 1870 sur les israélites indigènes de l'Algérie*, Algiers, Adolphe Jourdan, 1891, pp. 7–9.
39 Jean-Charles Jauffret, *Parlement, gouvernement, commandement: l'armée de métier sous la IIIème, 1871–1914*, 2 vols, SAT, 1987, vol. 2, p. 656.
40 R. Ayoun, 'Le Décret Crémieux et l'insurrection de 1871 en Algérie', *Revue d'Histoire Moderne et Contemporaine*, XXXV (January–March 1988), pp. 61–87.
41 *Le Messager, Journal d'Alger*, 3 March 1871.
42 AOM, 1 H28, *Correspondance politique*, 25 February 1871.
43 AOM, *Rapport du commissariat central d'Alger*, 2 March 1871. Thirteen Jews were hurt, one Muslim was killed and 272 people were arrested in one day in Algiers.
44 AOM, *Rapport au ministre*, March 1871.
45 AOM, 1 H28, *Correspondance politique*, 1 March 1871.
46 Michel Ansky, *Les Juifs d'Algérie du décret Crémieux à la libération*, Éditions du Centre, 1950, pp. 38–44.
47 Guy Pédroncini (ed.), *La Défense sous la troisième république*, vol. 1, *Vaincre la défaite, 1872–1881*, SAT, 1989, p. 56.
48 See the *Proposition de loi présentée à la session de 1899 par Marinand, Drumont etc. pour l'abolition du décret du 24 octobre 1870*, AOM, F80 174, *Culte Israélite*.
49 Pierre Birnbaum, *'La France aux français', histoire des haines nationalistes*, Éditions du Seuil, 1993, pp. 260–3.
50 Pierre Hebey, *Alger 1898: la grande vague antijuive*, Paris, Nil Eden, 1996.
51 AOM, Ih4 F80 1726, *Agence Havas*, 25 April 1873. Text of the agency distributed to the French media. Also the correspondence between El Mokrani and Germé, 8 April 1871, AOM, F80 1682.
52 AOM, 11 H26–7, Constantine, 11 December 1870 telegram from Sétif on the debts of Caid Sabi Ben Beddar.
53 AOM, 11 H 26–7, report from Constantine on 25 October 1870.
54 AOM, 11 H 26–7, report from Constantine on 29 November 1870.
55 AOM, 2H73, *Rapport sur l'insurrection de 1871 dans la province d'Alger*, 22 January 1872.
56 Colonel Robin, *L'Insurrection de la Grande Kabylie en 1871*, Henri Charles Lavauzelle, 1900, pp. 518–20; Louis Rinn, *Histoire de l'insurrection de 1871 en Algérie*, n.p., Algiers, 1891, AOM, 3XI Rinn papers.
57 Charles Delescluze, *De Paris à Cayenne, journal d'un transporté*, Paris, Le Chevalier, 1872, pp. 164–6.
58 G. Mailhe, *Deportations en Nouvelle Calédonie des Communards et des révoltés de la Grande Kabylie (1872–1876)*, L'Harmattan, 1994.
59 Colonel Robin, *L'Insurrection de la Grande Kabylie en 1871*, p. 529.
60 AOM, Ih4 F80 1726, *Note sur le procès de Constantine*, 12 April 1873.
61 AOM, Ih4 F80 1726, *Gouverneur général au ministre*, 5 March 1873.
62 AOM, Ih4 F80 1726, *Note sur la question de l'internement des indigènes Algériens non-naturalisés français*, 1887.
63 Nadine Vivier, *Propriété collective et identité communale, les biens communaux en France, 1750–1914*, Publications de la Sorbonne, 1998, pp. 253–92, 296–9. Communal land still exists in remote areas of Massif-Central areas, and is often owned not by the commune but by the sections, hamlets or groups of houses.
64 To be fair, more Alsatians had moved to Algeria before 1870 than after, but the state made a point of relocating some of the 120,000 refugees to Algeria by giving a large proportion of recently confiscated land for colonisation. Fabienne Fischer, 'Les Alsaciens et les Lorrains en Algérie avant 1871', *Revue Française d'Histoire d'Outre Mer*, 84 (1997) 317, pp. 57–69, p. 58.

207

65 Philip Nord, *The Republican Moment: Struggles for Democracy in Nineteenth Century France*, Cambridge (Mass.), Harvard University Press, 1995, pp. 87–8.

66 Jacques Girault, *La Commune et Bordeaux (1870–1871), contribution à l'étude du mouvement ouvrier et de l'idéologie républicaine en province au moment de la Commune de Paris*, Éditions Sociales, 1971, p. 89.

67 *Le Salut Public*, 10 October 1870.

68 Simon Schwarzfuchs, *Les Juifs d'Algérie et la France (1830–1855)*, Centre de recherches sur les Juifs d'Afrique du Nord, Jerusalem, Ben Zvi, 1981, p. 83.

69 AOM, F80 174, *Culte Israelite*, ordinance of 9 November 1845 on the *consistoire* of Algeria, report of Béquet, *Rapport au conseil de gouvernement, organisation du culte israélite en Algérie*, Imp. du gouvernement, 1858. Béquet proposed that four out of seven representatives on the *consistoire* should be 'French' and that the rabbis should be chosen from among French clerics.

70 Rev. P. de Damas, *Souvenirs de guerre et de captivité (France et Prusse)*, G. Téqui, 1883, p. 123.

71 See the controversial book by Pierre Birnbaum, *Le Moment antisémite, un tour de France en 1898*, Fayard, 1998, p. 193, on the association of 1870 and anti-Semitism. For a critique of Birnbaum, see Éric Cahm, *Société Internationale d'histoire de l'affaire Dreyfus*, 6 (1998–9), pp. 47–9. Interestingly, Birnbaum neglects to mention Algeria except in his discussion of Marseilles, pp. 175–210.

72 The role of Jews in French administrations should not be overstated; the chances of a Jewish magistrate, for instance, could be limited, at least geographically, by the known anti-Semitism of some areas such as Alsace or Algeria. Jean-Pierre Royer, Renée Martinage and Pierre Lecocq, *Juges et notables au XIXe siècle*, Presses Universitaires de France, 1982, pp. 148–61.

73 Pierre Birnbaum, *'La France aux français', histoire des haines nationalistes*, Éditions du Seuil, 1993, pp. 106–9.

74 A. de Bellina, *Les Polonais et la Commune de Paris*, n.p., 1871.

75 David Assouline and Mehdi Lallaoui, *Un Siècle d'immigrations en France*, vol. 1, pp. 101–11.

76 This is part of the central argument of Philip Nord, *The Republican Moment*, pp. 13–17.

77 Louis Andrieux, *À Travers la République*, Payot, 1926, p. 24.

78 ADR, 4 M 263, *Associations politiques*. Correspondence of 17 July 1862, 24 November 1863, 3 March 1869 to the Ministry of the Interior.

79 Philip Nord, *The Republican Moment*, pp. 17–20.

80 On the relationship between GOF and Church, see, for instance, J.M. Mayeur (ed.), *Libre Pensée et religion laïque en France, de la fin du Second Empire à la fin de la Troisième République*, Strasbourg, Cerdic Publications, 1980.

81 ADR, 4 M 295; Charles Roche, *La rue Grolée*, Lyons, Lepagnez, s.d., 1872.

82 ADR, 4 M 263, *Associations politiques*, prefect to the minister, 24 August 1875.

83 Félicien Court, *Louis Ormières, 1851–1914, et l'ambulance du Grand Orient de France en 1870–1871*, Imprimerie Nouvelle, 1914; *Bulletin du Grand Orient de France*, 26 (1870), pp. 380, 392.

84 This is not the place to discuss in depth the emblematic value of education in the contest between Catholics and their anti-clerical opponents. Since the Falloux laws of 1848, the Church had enjoyed some important privileges in the provision of primary and secondary education. In the early 1880s the school issue was revived; it again became a festering source of dissent and contributed powerfully to the anti-republican stance among Catholics. See Jules Simon, *Dieu, Patrie, Liberté*, Calmann-Lévy, 1883, pp. 115–92; Mona Ozouf, *L'École, l'église et la république (1871–1914)*, Cana/Jean Offredo, 1982.

85 ADR, 4 M 289, file of Pierre Gangeret; *Gauloise* is a double entendre, signifying Gallic and rude. All the members of the choir were said to be members of the AIT.

86 ADR, 4 M 289, Andrieux's file.

87 *L'Antéchrist, journal anarchiste: assez de sauveurs comme ça*, 26 Brumaire, an 79, no. 5.

88 Françoise Bayard and Pierre Cayez (eds), *Histoire de Lyon du XVIe siècle à nos jours*, Roanne, Howarth, 1989, p. 314.

89 ADR, 4 M 290, Antoine Chanoz, editor of *L'excommunié, Catéchisme de la Libre pensée*, n.p., 1873, confiscated by the police. Paul Antoin Chanoz (b. 1816) was a worker in the Lyons gas factory.

90 See Roger Magraw, *Workers and the Bourgeois Republic*, 2 vols, Blackwell, 1992, vol. 2, pp. 53–78.

91 ADR, 4 M 288, letter from Bishop Augustin David of Saint Brieuc.

92 Mario Praz, *La Chair, la mort et le diable dans la littérature du XIXe siècle, le romantisme noir*, Gallimard [1966], 1998.

93 Archives Municipales de Montpellier, D52 V, *Affiche du 24 mai 1871 annonçant l'ouverture de l'école laïque*.

94 *Le Salut Public*, 3 October 1870.

95 Active atheism did exist, however, and there were many secularists who wished to see atheism become the order of the day. Henri Verlet, *Le Peuple et la Révolution, l'athéisme et l'être suprême, la renaissance 1869–1870*, n.p., 1869?, p. 7, ADR, 4 M 289.

96 *Le Salut Public*, 30 November 1870.

97 *Le Salut Public*, 10 October 1870.

98 ADR, 4 M 293, Condamine in the name of the secular administration of the schools, 8 December 1870.

99 AAP, 542 Foss 73, 9 October 1870.

100 AVdP, VD6/791/6, I arrondissement, *Adresse du Maire au conseil*, October 1870.

101 *Procès verbaux du conesil municipal de Lyon*, session of 17 September 1870.

102 *Le Salut Public*, 11 November 1870. For instance, the arrest of Mgr Dubar, bishop of Carrathe (China).

103 Louis Garel, *La Révolution lyonnaise depuis le 4 septembre*, Lyons, Association typographique, 1871, p. 78. This view of the public salvation committee was renewed in the session of 20 September 1870 of the elected council of Lyons. AML, 4 M1 10003, *Procès verbaux du conseil municipal de Lyon*, 20 September 1870.

104 AVdP, VD6 0968, letter sent on 26 October 1870.

105 AML, 4 M1 13, *Procès verbaux du conseil municipal de Lyon*, 2 November 1870, p. 315.

106 Arnaud, Dumay, Clovis, Dupont and Pindy, 'Écoles laïques', in *Les Révolutions du XIXe siècle*, 10 vols, Paris, EDHIS, vol. 10, *Affiches, feuilles volantes, documents divers*, 1988, ff. 105.

107 Paul Fontoulieu, *Les Églises de Paris sous la Commune*, Dentu, 1873; Olivier Marion and Luc Perrin, 'La Commune et l'Église', Mémoire de Maîtrise, Université Paris X–XII, 1981.

108 Abbé G. Delmas, *Un Prêtre et la Commune de Paris en 1871*, pp. 40–5.

109 Abbé G. Delmas, *Un Prêtre et la Commune de Paris en 1871*, pp. 121–43.

110 Régère was later deported and took his son with him to New Caledonia. See Bernard Noël, *Dictionnaire de la Commune*, Fernand Hozon, 1971, vol. 2, pp. 202–3. Also Ernest Vizetelly, *My Adventures in the Commune*, London, Chatto and Windus, 1914, pp. 244–5.

111 This controversy on the 'Prussian' nature of Protestantism was mostly revived by Catholic bigots attempting to undermine their religious opponents who were, in their eyes at least, the great beneficiaries of the fall of the Second Empire. Anti-clerical writers and republicans also used similar terms to denounce the 'popes of Berlin'; see, for instance, M. Bédarrides, *Morale de l'invasion prussienne*, Paris, n.p., 1871, p. 11.

112 H.R. Blandeau, *Patriotisme du clergé catholique et des ordres religieux pendant la guerre de 1870–1*, Lecoffre, 1873; Comte Gazon de la Peyrière, *L'Église de France devant l'invasion prussienne*, Régis Ruffet, 1872.

113 F. Bournand, *Les Soeurs martyres, les soeurs Augustines, les soeurs des hôpitaux pendant la guerre (1870–1871); dévouements; témoignages des contemporains; les soeurs récompensées*, Tours, A. Cattier, 1894.

114 *Le Salut Public*, 22 November 1870.

115 AEP, 5b2 10, weekly letter from Abbot Rincazaux to the Archbishop of Paris from the fort of Saint Denis, 2 October 1870. AEP, 4 B244, André Belin, 'Les Aumôniers de 1870: essai de reconstitution de l'ordre de bataille des aumôniers de l'armée et de la marine française pendant la guerre de 1870–1871', typescript, 1972.

116 Abbé Jules Bonhomme, *Souvenirs du Fort de l'Est, près Saint-Denis*, Paris, Jacques Lecoffre, 1872, pp. 75–6.

117 Abbé Sterlin, *Souvenirs de la campagne 1870–1871*, Plainville, 1871, pp. 62–71.

118 ADR, V 21, Jacques-Marie-Achille Ginoulhiac, *Mandement à l'occasion de la fête de l'immaculée conception de la Sainte Vierge*, 21 November 1870.

119 Louis Veuillot, *Paris pendant les deux sièges*, 2 vols, Victor Palmé, 1871, vol. 1, pp. 25–6.

120 Bernard Ménager, '1848–1871, autorité ou liberté', in Jean-François Sirinelli, *Histoire des droites en France*, 3 vols, Gallimard, 1992, vol. 1, *Politiques*, pp. 104–7, 122–3.

121 Louis Veuillot, *Paris pendant les deux sièges*, vol. 2, pp. 166, 182–3.

122 On Veuillot, see B. Le Roux, *Louis Veuillot, un homme, un combat*, published by the author, 1984.

123 Louis Veuillot, *Paris pendant les deux sièges*, vol. 1, pp. 279–82.

124 J.A. Foulden, *Histoire de la vie et oeuvre de Mgr Darboy*, 1889.

125 On Trochu's reputation, see Roger L. Williams, *Manners and Murders in the World of Louis Napoleon*, University of Washington Press, 1975, pp. 152–91.

126 Rev. P. de Damas, *Souvenirs de guerre*, pp. 274–5.

127 All Saints' Day in the devastated cemetery of Montrouge, *Les Deux sièges de Paris, album pittoresque*, Au bureau du journal *L'Éclipse*, 1871.

128 See the very politically involved and Breton nationalist, Camille Le Mercier d'Erm, *Une 'Armée de Chouans': le drame politique de l'armée de Bretagne (1870–1871)*, Librairie académique Perrin, Armor Diffusion, 1975, pp. 92–5; *L'Étrange aventure de l'armée de Bretagne, 1870–1871*, Librairie académique Perrin, Armor Diffusion, 1975, who clearly placated Kératry Breton nationalist and secessionist views he did not share. Émile de Kératry, *Le 4 septembre et le gouvernement de la Défense Nationale, dépositions devant la commission d'enquête de l'assemblée nationale, mission diplomatique à Madrid*, Librairie Internationale A. Lacroix, Verboeckhoven et Cie, 1872.

129 Raymond A. Jonas, 'Anxiety, identity, and the displacement of violence during the "année terrible": the Sacred Heart and the Diocese of Nantes, 1870–1871', *French Historical Studies*, 21 (1998) 1, pp. 55–76.

130 Lt-Colonel d'Albiousse, *Le Drapeau du Sacré-Coeur, campagne de France, zouaves pontificaux*, Rennes, Hauvespre, 1871; Abbé Julien S. Allard, *Les Zouaves pontificaux, ou journal de Mgr Daniel, aumônier des zouaves*, Hugny, 1880.

131 Louis Veuillot, *Oeuvres complètes*, 23 vols, seconde série, correspondance, Lethielleux, 1932, vol. x, p. 321.

132 For an unsympathetic survey of popular credulity, see Judith Delvin, *The Superstitious Mind: French Peasants and the Supernatural in the Nineteenth Century*, Yale University Press, 1987, pp. 150–64.

133 Thomas A. Kselman, *Miracles and Prophecies in Nineteenth-Century France*, Rutgers University Press, 1983, pp. 115–30.

134 Anon, *Apparitions prophétiques d'une âme du purgatoire à une religieuse d'un monastère en Belgique en 1870, par l'auteur des 'voix prophétiques'*, Brussels, n.p., 1871.

135 *Le Corrézien*, 18 October 1870, 22 October 1870.

136 Letter of the *soeur supérieure* of the monastery, Ste Ursule de Blois, *La Marseillaise*, 15 October 1870. The nun of Blois was also described in *Le Réveil de la Province, L'Union*,

Le Constitutionel, Abbot Vincent, *Éphéméride de Frazé et mes impressions pendant la guerre franco-prussienne et la Commune de Paris*, ed. Abbot Roland Lefèvre, Bibliothèque diocésaine de Chartres, 1980, pp. 10, 26, 36, 62.

137 *Le Courier du Centre* (Limoges), 7 November 1870.

138 *Le Réveil de la Province* (Tulle), 6 December 1870, 9 December 1870, 12 January 1871.

139 Georges d'Heylli (ed.), *Télégrammes militaires de M. Léon Gambetta du 9 octobre 1870 au 6 février 1871*, Paris, L. Beauvais, 1871, 31 January 1871, evening.

140 All of this is glossed over in the hagiographic literature. François Bournand, *Le Clergé pendant la Commune, 1871*, Tolra, 1891, 2nd edn, 1892.

141 Avner Ben Amos, 'Molding the national memory: the state funerals of the Third Republic', unpublished thesis, Berkeley, 1988, p. 150. The funeral took place on 7 June 1871.

142 Mgr Dupanloup, *Lettre au clergé et aux fidèles de son diocèse sur les derniers malheurs de Paris pour demander de solennelles expiations*, Semaine Religieuse, 1871.

143 J.-C. Wastelle, 'Lyon 1873. Joseph Ducros, préfet de l'ordre moral', *L'Histoire*, 12 (1979), pp. 6–13.

144 Philippe Levillain, *Albert de Mun, Catholicisme Français et Catholicisme Romain, du Syllabus au Ralliement*, École Française de Rome, 1983.

145 Bernard, *La Justice française en Algérie, discours de la cour d'appel d'Angers, 1881*, quoted in Jean-Pierre Royer, Renée Martinage and Pierre Lecocq, *Juges et notables au XIXe siècle*, Presses Universitaires de France, 1982, p. 239.

146 Pierre Birnbaum, '*La France aux français*', pp. 86–99.

6 The enemy within: traitors and spies, gender and age

1 Jules Vallès, *L'Insurgé*, Maxipoche, 1998, p. 103.

2 Michel de Certeau, *Heterologies: Discourse on the Other*, Manchester University Press, 1986.

3 A multitude of almanacks, guidebooks and dictionaries of French communes provided this sort of information.

4 See, for instance, the fully illustrated descriptions of its range and use in the first days of the war in the periodical *La Guerre illustrée*.

5 Sophie Wahnich, *L'Impossible citoyen, l'étranger dans le discours de la révolution française*, Albin Michel, 1997, pp. 82–98.

6 ADHV, 4 M 210, *Expulsion des sujets allemands*, 19 August 1870.

7 Sutter-Laumann, *Histoire d'un trente sous (1870–1871)*, Paris, Albert Savine, 1891, pp. 51, 72–3.

8 This is, of course, recurrent in the First World War; see Panikos Panayi, *The Enemy in our Midst: Germans in Britain during the First World War*, Oxford, Berg, 1991, pp. 153–82.

9 ADR, 4 M 288, arrest on 12 December 1870 at Saincaize station.

10 Sophie Wahnich, *L'Impossible citoyen*, pp. 306–10, 361–2.

11 Francis Schiller, *Paul Broca, explorateur du cerveau*, Berkeley, University of California Press, 1979; French translation, Éditions Odile Jacob, 1990.

12 On fears, see François Ploux, 'L'Imaginaire social et politique de la rumeur dans la France du XIXe siècle (1815–1870)', *Revue Historique*, 614 (April/June 2000), pp. 395–434, pp. 412, 426. Rumours of the sudden death of Napoleon III and of clerical plots against the emperor had been numerous between 1851 and 1870.

13 ADR, 4 M 288, arrest of the so-called Favier, apparently a Prussian spy.

14 *Le Corrézien*, 20 September 1870.

15 AMM, 11, 11 November 1870.

16 Peter McPhee, *The Politics of Rural Life: Political Mobilization in the French Countryside, 1846–1852*, Clarendon Press, 1992.

17 On the proscrirtion of 1851 see John M. Merriman, *The Agony of the Republic: The Repression of the Left in Revolutionary France, 1848–1851*, Yale University Press, 1978.

18 Édouard Fleury, *Éphémérides de la guerre de 1870–71*, Imprimerie du journal de l'Aisne, Laon, 1871, pp. 44–5.

19 ADHV, 4 M 66, 16 October 1870; 22 September 1870; 12 September 1870.

20 *Le Courier du Centre* (Limoges), 4 November 1870.

21 Georges d'Heylli (ed.), *Télégrammes militaires de M Léon Gambetta du 9 octobre 1870 au 6 février 1871*, Paris, L. Beauvais, 1871, 1 November 1870.

22 *La République, journal du département de la Corrèze*, 5 February 1871.

23 *Compte rendu des travaux de la commission de désarmement de la Ville de Marseille, avec pièces à l'appui du 6 avril au 30 juin 1871*, Marseilles, Marius Olive, 1871, 26 March 1871.

24 ADHV, 4 R77, letter of 16 October 1870 backed by the signature of officers and NCOs of the National Guard. Neither signatories could spell the simple word 'signed'.

25 ADHV, 4 R77. Seven soldiers thus addressed the prefect: 'Dear Sir, we believed that when in a Republic everybody was equal, but we understand now that we are badly mistaken: favours will always exist.'

26 John Rothney, *Bonapartism after Sedan*, Ithaca, Cornell University Press, 1969, pp. 95–9; Jules Amigues, *Les Aveux d'un conspirateur bonapartiste. Histoires pour servir à l'Histoire de demain*, Lachaud et Burdin, 1874; Juliette Adam, *Mes angoisses et nos luttes*, Alphonse Lemerre, 1907, p. 85.

27 *La Nation française*, 11 April 1871.

28 Bazaine remained the eponymous traitor well into the twentieth century: Philip Guedalla, *The Two Marshals: Bazaine, Pétain*, Hodder and Stoughton, 1943; only foreigners had a less passionate view on the issue. Henry Brackenbury, *Les Maréchaux de France, étude de leur conduite dans la guerre de 1870*, Lachaud, 1872.

29 Anon, *Extrait des causes célèbres de tous les peuples, le maréchal Bazaine, relation complète*, Lebrun, 1874, p. 76

30 *Le Salut Public* (Lyons), 2 October 1870, 3 October 1870.

31 Le Marquis de la Rochethulon, *Du Rôle de la garde nationale et de l'armée de Paris dans les préparatifs de l'insurrection du 18 mars, rapport spécial fait à la commission d'enquête*, Léon Techener, 1872, p. 38.

32 See B. Taithe, *Defeated Flesh*, chs 8 and 9.

33 Paradoxically, the First World War was seen as having the opposite effect on French feminism and suffragettes. Christine Bard, *Les Filles de Marianne, histoire des féminismes, 1914–1940*, Fayard, 1995, pp. 46–87.

34 See, for instance, the medical positivism denounced in Deborah Dwork, *War is Good for Babies and Other Young Children*, Tavistock, 1987.

35 See the controversy over Mona Ozouf, *Les Mots des femmes, essai sur la singularité française*, Gallimard, 1999, pp. 399–421.

36 See James F. McMillan, *France and Women 1789–1914: Gender, Society and Politics*, Routledge, 2000, pp. 132–5.

37 Madelyn Gutwirth, '*Citoyens, Citoyennes*: cultural regression and the subversion of female citizenship in the French Revolution', in Renée Waldinger, Philip Dawson and Isser Woloch (eds), *The French Revolution and the Meaning of Citizenship*, Westport (Conn.), Greenwood Press, 1993, pp. 17–29; J.W. Scott, *Only Paradoxes to Offer: French Feminists and the Rights of Man*, Cambridge (Mass.), Harvard University Press, 1996; Olwen H. Hufton, *Women and the Limits of Citizenship in the French Revolution*, University of Toronto Press, 1992.

38 S. Michaud (ed.), *Flora Tristan, George Sand, Pauline Roland: Les femmes et l'invention d'une nouvelle morale, 1830–1848*, Créaphis, 1994.

39 Bard, *Les Filles de Marianne*, pp. 19–25.

40 Felicia Gordon, *The Integral Feminist: Madelein Pelletier, 1874–1939*, Cambridge, Polity Press, 1990, pp. 24–34; Steven C. Hause, *Hubertine Auclert: The French Suffragette*, New Haven, Yale University Press, 1987, pp. 21–9.

41 ADHV, 4 M 15.

42 H.A. Wauthoz, *Les Ambulances et les ambulanciers à travers les siècles*, Brussels, Lebègue, 1872, p. ix; Ilda de Crombrugghe, *Journal d'une infirmière pendant la guerre 1870–1871*, H. Plon, 1872, p. 10; J. Jurgensen, *Le Soir du combat, récit d'une infirmière, poème*, Geneva, Durafort, 1871; P. and H. de Trailles, *Les Femmes en France pendant la guerre et les deux sièges de Paris*, F. Polo Libraire, 1872.

43 A reform which had been simmering for a long while; Mme William Monod, *Les Héroïnes de la charité, soeur Marthe de Besançon et Miss Florence Nightingale*, Bellaire, 1873.

44 Sarah Bernhardt, *Ma Double vie*, 2 vols, Des Femmes, 1980, vol. 1, p. 245.

45 Pierre Durand, *Louise Michel : la passion*, Messidor, 1987.

46 It is important not to over-stress the validity of the imagery. The 'problem' of single motherhood tarnished the representation of femininity in the urban environment. See Rachel S. Fuchs, *Poor and Pregnant in Paris: Strategies for Survival in the Nineteenth Century*, Rutgers University Press, 1992, pp. 51–5.

47 Yves Chinon, *Enquêtes sur les apparitions de la vierge*, Perrin Marme, 1995; Philippe Boutry, 'Marie la grande consolatrice de la France au XIXe siècle', *L'Histoire*, 50 (1982), pp. 25–32.

48 Ruth Harris, *Lourdes: Body and Spirit in the Secular Age*, Harmondsworth, Allen Lane, 1999; Thomas A. Kselman, *Miracles and Prophecies in Nineteenth-Century France*, Rutgers University Press, 1983, pp. 116–17.

49 Ralph Gibson, 'Hellfire and damnation in nineteenth-century France', *Catholic Historical Review*, 74 (1988) 3, pp. 383–402.

50 David Barry, 'Hermance Leguillon (1812–1882): the diversity of French feminism in the nineteenth century', *French History*, 13 (1999), pp. 381–416, p. 387.

51 Mme William Monod, *La Mission des femmes en temps de guerre*, Bellaire, 1870.

52 AAP, 542 Foss 2, *Minutes des séances du Conseil Général des Hospices*, 29 October 1870, letter from Intendant Général Wolff to Brillon; GMP, 25 (1870), 531.

53 D.A. Shafer, '*Plus que des ambulancières*: women in articulation and defence of their ideals during the Paris Commune (1871)', *French History* (1993), pp. 85–101.

54 P. Durand, *Louise Michel: la passion*, Messidor, 1987, p. 16; J. Rougerie, *Procès des Communards*, Archives Julliard, 1976, p. 112. This type of mobilisation worked along-side more directly military organisations such as the *Légion des fédérées*; M.P. Johnson, 'Citizenship and gender: the *Légion des Fédérés* in the Paris Commune of 1871', *French History*, 8 (1994) 3, pp. 276–95; Eugene Schulkind, 'Socialist women in the 1871 Paris Commune', *Past and Present*, 106 (1985), pp. 124–63; Louise Michel, *La Commune, Histoire et Souvenirs*, 2 vols, Maspéro, 1970, vol. 2, pp. 7–15; Gay Gullickson, *Unruly Women of Paris: Images of the Commune*, Ithaca, Cornell University Press, 1996; Claire Goldberg Moses, *French Feminism in the Nineteenth Century*, Albany, State University of New York, 1984, pp. 190–4.

55 *Comité central de l'Union des femmes pour la défense de Paris et les soins aux blessés, Manifeste*, reproduced in *Les Révolutions du XIXe siècle*, 10 vols, Paris, EDHIS, vol. 10, *Affiches, feuilles volantes, documents divers*, 1988, p. 114.

56 SAT LY 16, *Déposition de Georges Clemenceau sur Louise Michel*.

57 Édouard Fleury, *Éphémérides de la guerre de 1870–71*, Imprimerie du journal de l'Aisne, Laon, 1871, p. 46.

58 Charles-Aimé Dauban, *Le Fond de la société sous la Commune* [1873], Slatkine-Megariotis Reprints, 1977, p. 21.

59 Gay Gullickson, *Unruly Women of Paris: Images of the Commune*, Ithaca, Cornell University Press, 1996.

60 The rules of the clubs often included the means of excluding drunken members. *Club Républicain, Démocratique et Socialiste du XIIIe Arrondissement*, reproduced in *Les Révolutions du XIXe siècle*, 10 vols, Paris, EDHIS, 1988, vol. 6, ff. 12, p. 3. W. Scott Haine, *The World of the Paris Café: Sociability among the French Working Class*, Johns Hopkins University Press, 1996, p. 19.

61 JORC, 4–15 April 1871.

62 L. Faze, *Histoire de la Guerre Civile de 1871*, Charpentier, 1879, p. 301.

63 P. Cattelain, *Souvenirs inédits du chef de la sûreté sous la Commune*, Juven, 1900, p. 69.

64 AML, 4 M1 10003, *Procès verbaux du conseil municipal de Lyon*, 15 October 1870.

65 Un avocat, *Le Drame de Lyon, 20 Decembre 1870 – assassinat du commandant Arnaud*, Lyons, P.N. Josserand, March 1871, pp. 19–20.

66 *Proclamation de la Commune à Narbonne. Compte Rendu Sténographique du procès d'Émile Digeon et de ses 31 coaccusés*, n.d., n.p., reprinted in *Les Révolutions du XIXe siècle*, 10 vols, Paris, EDHIS, 1988, vol. 8, ff. 15, p. 4.

67 Durand-Auzias, 'La journée du 4 septembre à Lyon', *Revue Hebdomadaire*, 3 September 1910, p. 23. This is a relatively unreliable witness who nevertheless offers the advantage of having reconstructed the history of the day from a strictly Bonapartist standpoint.

68 ADR, 4 M 223, *Rapport sur le club de la salle de bal parisienne*, 23 April 1871.

69 Firmin Maillard, *Les Publications de la rue pendant le siège et la Commune*, Auguste Aubry, 1874.

70 Ann-Louise Shapiro, *Breaking the Codes: Female Criminality in Fin-de-siècle Paris*, Stanford, Stanford University Press, 1996, pp. 156–7.

71 Jean Berleux, *La Caricature politique en France pendant la guerre, le siège de Paris et la Commune 1870–1871*, Labitte and E. Paul, 1890; Gonzalo J. Sanchez, 'The challenge of right-wing caricature journals: from the Commune amnesty campaign to the end of censorship, 1878–1881', *French History*, 10 (1996) 4, pp. 451–89.

72 Édith Thomas, *Les Pétroleuses*, Gallimard, 1963.

73 J.M.G. Roberts, *The Paris Commune from the right*, *English Historical Review*, Supplement 6, Longman, 1973.

74 Prosper Olivier Lissagaray, *The Paris Commune of 1871*, New Park Publications, 1976, p. 168.

75 Charles Sowerwine, *Sisters or Citizens? Women and Socialism since 1876*, Cambridge University Press, 1982, pp. 7–36.

76 Jean-Baptiste Millière, *Le 31 octobre. Compte rendu au 208e bataillon de la Garde Nationale par le Commandant Millière*, Paris, Association générale typographique, November 1870, reproduced in *Les Révolutions du XIXe siècle*, 10 vols, Paris, EDHIS, 1988, vol. 6, ff. 9, p. 16.

77 Dorinda Outram, *The Body and the French Revolution*, New Haven (Conn.), Yale University Press, 1989.

78 Late collections include: Lucien Nass, *Le Siège de Paris et la Commune, essais de pathologie historique*, Plon-Nourrit, 1914; Lucien Nass and M. Cabanès, *La Névrose révolutionnaire*, Société Française d'Imprimerie, 1906, reprinted A. Michel, 1924.

79 Sutter-Laumann, *Histoire d'un trente sous (1870–1871)*, Paris, Albert Savine, 1891, p. 304.

80 The veterans in French history have been too little studied; on the revolutionary veterans see the work of Isser Woloch, *The French Veteran from the Revolution to the Restoration*, University of North Carolina Press, 1979.

81 ADHV, 4 R 78, letter from Martin Nadaud, 10 November 1870.

82 AVdP, VD6 1775, *Corps civique de sécurité du neuvième arrondissement*, 16 October 1870.

83 AVdP, VD6/1333/1, *Rapports journaliers au maire de Paris, mairie du Ve, lettre au citoyen Treillard, chef du bataillon des vétérans du quartier du jardin des plantes et du quartier St Victor*, 19 November 1870.

84 AVdP, VD6 1775, 18 October 1871.

85 Catherine J. Kudlick, *Cholera in Post-Revolutionary Paris, a Cultural History*, Berkeley, University of California Press, 1996.

86 AVdP, VD6 2345, XVII arrondissement, 19 October 1870.

87 Major H. de Sarrepont, *Le Bombardement de Paris par les prussiens en janvier 1871*, Firmin Didot frères, 1872.

88 Émile Maury, *Mes souvenirs sur les èvènements des années 1870–1871*, ed. Alain Dalotel, La Boutique de l'Histoire, 1999, p. 50.

89 Sutter-Laumann, *Histoire d'un trente sous*, p. 78.

90 Maurice Dommanget, *Auguste Blanqui au début de la Troisième République, 1871–1880, dernière prison et ultimes combats*, Moraton, 1973.

91 Patricia O'Brien, *The Promise of Punishment: Prisons in Nineteenth Century France*, Princeton University Press, 1982, pp. 109–22. The term *vicieux*, found in the files of relatively few Communard children prisoners, was used much earlier, p. 144.

92 Marc Renneville, *La Médecine du crime: essai sur l'émergence d'un regard médical dur la criminalité en France (1785–1885)*, 2 vols, Villeneuve d'Asq, Presses Universitaires du Septentrion, 1996, 1998, vol. 2, pp. 546–55, 608–20.

93 Georges Jeanneret, *Paris pendant la Commune révolutionnaire de 71*, Neuchâtel, imp. Guillaume, 1871, p. 238.

94 Émile Maury, *Mes souvenirs sur les èvènements des années 1870–1871*, ed. Alain Dalotel, La Boutique de l'Histoire, 1999, p. 76.

95 SAT LY 127.

96 SAT LY 127, *Lettre au préfet maritime*, 7 October 1871.

97 SAT LY 127, *Situation au 1 juin 1872, conseil de guerre*; 3,315 wounded were arrested in May 1871, 552 of whom were under 20.

98 SAT LY 127, *Tilsitt*, 7 November 1871.

99 SAT LY 127, prison of Versailles, October 1871; another 94 were held in Rouen. We have more information on Versailles, Rouen and Cherbourg than on *Tilsitt*.

100 On the living conditions of waged apprentices and industrial workers and on reform programmes to ban under-age working, see Colin Heywood, *Childhood in Nineteenth-Century France: Work, Health and Education among the 'Classes Populaires'*, Cambridge University Press, 1988, pp. 97–213; family ties were stronger in the more industrial centres such as Saint-Étienne, see Michael P. Hanagan, *Nascent Proletarians: Class Formation in Post-Revolutionary France*, Basil Blackwell, 1989, pp. 135–44.

101 On the social analysis of the judicial elites, see Jean-Pierre Royer, Renée Martinage and Pierre Lecocq, *Juges et notables au XIXe siècle*, Presses Universitaires de France, 1982, pp. 11–25, 79–85.

102 Maxime du Camp, *La Charité privée à Paris, l'orphelinat d'Auteuil et l'abbé Roussel*, Ch. Des Granges, 1881, 2nd edn, Hachette, 1885, pp. 24–41, 81, 156, 164, 213, 251.

103 Charles J. Lecour, *La Prostitution à Paris et à Londres, 1789–1877*, Asselin, 1877, pp. 296–300.

104 Jules Simon, *L'Ouvrière*, [1861], St Pierre de Salerne, G. Montfort, 1977.

105 James F. McMillan, *Housewife or Harlot: The Place of Women in French Society 1870–1940*, Brighton, Harvester, 1981, pp. 29–45; Elinor A. Accampo, Rachel G. Fuchs and Mary Lynn Stewart, *Gender and the Politics of Social Reform in France, 1870–1914*, Johns Hopkins University Press, 1995, pp. 7–17.

106 David Barry, 'Community, tradition and memory among rebel working-class women of Paris, 1830, 1848, 1871', *European Review of History/Revue Européenne d'histoire*, 7 (2000) 2, pp. 261–76.

107 Georges Jeanneret, *Paris pendant la Commune révolutionnaire de 71*, Neuchâtel, imp. Guillaume, 1871, p. 116.

108 Jo Burr Margadant, *Madame le Professeur: Women Educators in the Third Republic*, Princeton University Press, 1990.

7 The brutalisation of French politics

1 B. Malon, *La Troisième défaite du prolétariat français*, Neuchâtel, Guillaume, 1871, p. 523.
2 R. Robertson, 'Civilization and the civilizing process: Elias, globalization and analytic synthesis', *Theory, Culture and Society*, 9 (1992) 1, pp. 211–27; George L. Mosse, *Fallen Soldiers: Reshaping the Memory of the World Wars*, Oxford University Press, 1990.
3 Juliette Adam, *Mes angoisses et nos luttes*, Alphonse Lemerre, 1907, p. 90.
4 On criminality and representation in the regional context see, for instance, Claude Chatelard, *Crime et criminalité dans l'arrondissement de St-Étienne au XIXème siècle*, Centre d'études Foréziennes, 1981, pp. 212–13
5 Mary Lynn McDougall, *After the Insurrections: The Workers' Movement in Lyon, 1834–1852*, Columbia University Press, 1973; Fernand Rude, *L'Insurrection Lyonnaise de novembre 1832. Le mouvement ouvrier à Lyon de 1827–1832*, Anthropos, Paris, 1969.
6 For a later period, see Odile Raynette-Gloud, 'L'Armée dans la bataille sociale: maintien de l'ordre et grèves ouvrières dans le nord de la France (1871–1906)', *Le Mouvement Social*, 179 (1997), pp. 93–104.
7 See George Holyoakes, *Sixty Years of an Agitator's Life*, 2 vols, Fisher Unwin, 1892, vol. 2, pp. 20–5; There were earlier precedents: Maxime du Camp, *Les Ancêtres de la Commune, l'attentat Fieschi*, Charpentier, 1877.
8 Robert Nye, *Masculinity and Male Codes of Honour in Modern France*, New York, Oxford University Press, 1993; also see Peter Gay, *The Cultivation of Hatred: The Bourgeois Experience, Victoria to Freud*, New York, HarperCollins, 1994.
9 Pierre Pelissier, *Émile de Girardin, prince de la presse*, Denoël, 1985.
10 *La Lanterne* denounced the murderer of Victor Noir, and the funeral of Noir led to a demonstration which offered the potential for an insurrection.
11 Roger Williams, *Manners and Murders in the World of Louis Napoleon*, University of Washington Press, 1975, pp. 112–27.
12 *The Parricide* was published in the local press of Lyons, Limoges and Tulle simultaneously during the war.
13 *Le Courier du Centre* (Limoges), 2 December 1870.
14 H.A. Frégier, *Des Classes dangereuses de la Population dans les Grandes Villes*, J.B. Baillière, 1840; Louis Chevalier, *Classes laborieuses et classes dangereuses*, Plon, 1958.
15 Jérôme Grévy, *La République des opportunistes*, Perrin, 1998, pp. 64–6.
16 Alan R.H. Baker, *Fraternity among the French Peasantry: Sociability and Voluntary Associations in the Loire Valley, 1815–1914*, Cambridge University Press, 1999, pp. 8–9.
17 John M. Merriman, *The Agony of the Republic: The Repression of the Left in Revolutionary France, 1848–1851*, Yale University Press, 1978.
18 *Troisième procès de l'association internationale des travailleurs à Paris*, Armand le Chevalier, 1870, pp. 66–96; un bourgeois républicain, *L'Histoire de l'internationale*, Brussels, n.p., 1873.
19 Ernest Cresson, *Cent jours à la Préfecture de Police, 2 novembre 1870–11 février 1871*, Nourrit, H. Plon, 1901.
20 Jean-Pierre Machelon, *La République contre les libertés? Les restrictions aux libertés publiques de 1879 à 1914*, Presses de la Fondation Nationale des Sciences Politiques, 1976; Benjamin F. Martin, *The Shame of Marianne: Crime and Criminal Justice under the Third Republic*, Baton Rouge, Louisiana State University Press, 1990.
21 Alain Corbin, *The Village of Cannibals: Rage and Murder in France, 1870*, Cambridge (Mass.), Harvard University Press, 1992.
22 His mother died soon after. *Le Courier du Centre*, 6 November 1870.
23 A. Corbin, *The Village of Cannibals: Rage and Murder in France, 1870*, Cambridge (Mass.), Harvard University Press, 1992, pp. 70–1.
24 *Le Réveil de la Province*, 7 March 1871.

NOTES

25 *Le Corrézien*, 20 December 1870.
26 *Le Réveil de la Province*, 21 August 1870.
27 The existence of *faits divers* in times of war is in itself a little paradoxical. Violent crimes and stories almost too horrible to narrate nevertheless abounded and provided some perverse relief in an age of violence and turmoil. Vanessa R. Schwartz, *Spectacular Realities: Early Mass Culture in Fin-de-siècle Paris*, University of California Press, 1998, pp. 26–40; David H. Walker, *Outrage and Insight: Modern French Writers and the 'Fait Divers'*, Oxford, Berg, 1995, pp. 2–6.
28 A. Corbin, *The Village of Cannibals*, p. 79.
29 *Le Réveil de la Province*, 21 August 1870.
30 A. Corbin, *The Village of Cannibals*, p. 86.
31 *Le Salut Public*, 10 February 1870.
32 Longer frameworks do not provide much enlightenment on the incident. Bruno Benoit, 'Relecture des violences collectives lyonnaises du dix-neuvième siècle', *Revue Historique*, 606 (1998), pp. 255–86; 'Les Malheurs des guerres civiles lyonnaises (1793–1794 et 1870–1871)', in A. Corvisier and Jean Jacquart (eds), *De la guerre réglée à la guerre totale*, vol. 2, 119 congrès des sociétés savantes, CTHS, 1997.
33 On the whole, there was a relative decline of clubbism between 1848 and 1870, even though each town of some importance had at least one.
34 ADR, 1 M 118.
35 Éric Bonhomme, 'Bordeaux et la Défense Nationale', *Annales du Midi*, 223 (1998), pp. 319–42, p. 330.
36 Yves Lequin, *Les Ouvriers de la région lyonnaise (1848–1914); les intérêts de classe et la république*, 2 vols, Presses Universitaires de Lyon, 1977, vol. 2, pp. 138–99.
37 Danielle Tartakowsky, *Le Pouvoir est dans la rue: crises politiques et manifestations en France*, Aubier, 1998; *Les Manifestations de rue en France, 1918–1968*, Publications de la Sorbonne, 1997, p. 797.
38 This notion of 'crowd *mentalité*' is also to be found in the work of Georges Lefebvre and Eric Hobsbawm.
39 Paul Lidsky, *Les Écrivains contre la Commune*, François Maspéro, 1970, pp. 60–3; Susanna Barrows, *Distorting Mirrors: Visions of the Crowd in Late Nineteenth-Century France*, New Haven, Yale University Press, 1981; Robert Nye, *Crime, Madness and Politics in Modern France: The Medical Concept of National Decline*, Princeton University Press, 1984; Louis Chevalier, *Classes laborieuses et classes dangereuses*, Plon, 1958.
40 Frédéric Bluche, *Septembre 1792, logiques d'un massacre*, Robert Laffont, 1986, pp. 125–7.
41 *Le Courier du Centre* (Limoges), 17 November 1870. The Mongré incident had a considerable echo in the regional press of unoccupied France.
42 *Le Salut Public* (Lyons), 14 November 1870. This report became the official version of events, and through the common cut-and-paste practices of the local press in rural France it was reproduced in many newspapers.
43 ADR, 4 M 290.
44 The conservative suspicion does seem grounded in fact, especially when one considers the fact that Denis Brack did not intervene in any negative or positive manner during the Arnaud affair but was simply seen agitating the day before. ADR, 4 M 289
45 ADR, 4 M 290.
46 ADR, 2RP 82, *Second conseil de guerre de la 8ème division militaire*.
47 *Le Salut Public*, 9 March 1871.
48 *Le Salut Public*, 8 March 1871.
49 Un avocat, *Le Drame de Lyon, 20 Decembre 1870 – assassinat du commandant Arnaud*, Lyons, P.N. Josserand, March 1871, p. 19.

50 Ann-Louise Shapiro, *Breaking the Codes: Female Criminality in Fin-de-siècle Paris*, Stanford, Stanford University Press, 1996, pp. 136–56.

51 Yves-Marie Bercé, *Révoltes et révolutions dans l'Europe moderne xvie–xviiie siècles*, PUF, 1980, p. 132.

52 Un avocat, *Le Drame de Lyon, 20 Decembre 1870 – assassinat du commandant Arnaud*, Lyons, P.N. Josserand, March 1871, p. 21.

53 *Le Salut Public*, 8 March 1871.

54 ADR, 4 M 289. The reporter of the assemblée nationale commission, devoted to the acts of Lyons during the war, attempted to have Andrieux indicted. He drew a profile of Andrieux which accused him of destroying all evidence relating to the AIT, of persecuting religious orders, of protecting Brack, Chol and Cluseret, of collusion with corrupt *francs-tireurs* leaders and of maintaining the red flag.

55 ADR 4 M 288.

56 Louis Andrieux, *À travers la République*, Payot, 1926, p. 74.

57 *Le Courier du Centre* (Limoges), 23 December 1870 and 28 December 1870.

58 Éric Bonhomme, 'Bordeaux et la Défense Nationale', *Annales du Midi* (1998) 223, pp. 319–42, p. 330. Bonhomme blames Crémieux for blowing the Arnaud case. This analysis probably underestimates the real impact of the murder on moderate republicans themselves.

59 On state funerals, a great republican tradition, see Avner Ben Amos, 'Molding the national memory: the state funerals of the Third Republic', unpublished thesis, Berkeley, 1988, p. 83.

60 ADR, 4 M 288.

61 On the red flag in Lyons, see Mary Lynn Stewart-McDougall, *The Artisan Republic: Revolution, Reaction and Resistance in Lyon, 1848–1851*, McGill Queen's/Alan Sutton, 1984, pp. 32–48.

62 This links the use of the black flag with earlier uses as the sign of mourning liberty in 1831. Benoit, 'Relecture des violences collectives', p. 267; F. Rude, *C'est nous les Canuts*, François Maspéro, 1977, p. 65.

63 *Le Salut Public*, 4 March 1871.

64 AML, 4 M1 10003, *Procès verbaux du conseil municipal de Lyon*, Lyon, séance du 20 December 1870, pp. 495–6.

65 *Le Salut Public*, 21 March 1871.

66 *La Revanche de la France et de la Commune, par un représentant du peuple de Paris*, Geneva, imprimerie coopérative, 1871, p. 6. Thomas was also accused of having shot at the people in June 1848 and, more recently, in January 1871.

67 Philip G. Nord, 'The Party of Conciliation and the Paris Commune', *French Historical Studies*, 15 (1987) 1, pp.1–35.

68 AML, 4 M1 10006, *Procès verbaux du conseil municipal de Lyon*, 10 April 1870.

69 *Ligue d'Union Républicaine des droits de Paris, à l'Assemblée Nationale et à la Commune de Paris*, reprinted in *Les Révolutions du XIXe siècle*, 10 vols, Paris, EDHIS, vol. 10, *Affiches, feuilles volantes, documents divers*, 1988, ff. 106.

70 AML, 4 M1 10006, *Procès verbaux du conseil municipal de Lyon*, 24 April 1871.

71 'Commission de conciliation du commerce, de l'industrie et du travail, Déclaration', in *Les Révolutions du XIXe siècle*, 10 vols, Paris, EDHIS, vol. 10, *Affiches, feuilles volantes, documents divers*, ff. 112.

72 *Le Courier du Centre* (Limoges), 3 April 1871; Marc César, *La Commune de Narbonne (mars 1871)*, Perpignan, Presses Universitaires de Perpignan, 1996.

73 B. Malon, *La Troisième défaite du prolétariat français*, Neuchâtel, Guillaume, 1871, 363–4; Ronald Aminzade, *Ballots and Barricades: Class Formation and Republican Politics in France, 1830–1871*, Princeton University Press, 1993, pp. 223–32. The trial in St-Étienne also ended with acquittals.

74 *La Nation Française* (Limoges), 10 June 1871.

75 *Ligue d'Union Républicaine des droits de Paris, Armistice de Neuilly, rapport des délégués, Les Révolutions du XIXe siècle*, 10 vols, Paris, EDHIS, vol. 7, ff. 6, 7, 8, 9, 10.

76 Marcel Cerf, *Édouard Moreau, l'âme du comité central de la république*, Éditions Denoël, 1971, pp. 171–203. Beaufort was the brother-in-law of Moreau.

77 The Beaufort case gave rise to a full enquiry by the Versailles forces. SAT LY 135.

78 Prosper Olivier Lissagaray, *The Paris Commune of 1871*, New Park Publications, 1976, p. 346.

79 SAT LY 135.

80 Lissagaray, *The Paris Commune of 1871*, p. 279.

81 *Le Salut Public*, 17 January 1871.

82 *Le Salut Public*, 26 March 1871.

83 See Robert Tombs' recent analysis in 'Les Communeux dans la ville: des analyses récentes à l'étranger', *Le Mouvement Social*, 179 (April–July 1997) 93–104, pp. 95–6, 105.

84 A recent catalogue of an exhibition at the Museum of Orsay in Paris (14 March to 10 June 2000) covers much of the photographic material produced in 1871. *La Commune Photographiée*, Réunion des Musée Nationaux, 2000, pp. 8–9.

85 Donald English, *The Political Uses of Photography in the Third Republic*, Ann Arbor, UMI Research Press, 1984.

86 *Le Figaro*, 26 November 1998.

87 ADCr, 4 M 107. The lists of suspects published in May 1871 contained 364 names; it was reduced to 163 in August.

88 Louise Michel, *La Commune, Histoire et Souvenirs*, 2 vols, Maspéro, 1970, vol. 2, p. 66; also see Georges Jeanneret, *Paris pendant la Commune révolutionnaire de 71*, Neuchâtel, imp. Guillaume, 1871, p. 193.

89 ADCr, 4 M107.

90 C.F. Laveau, 'Les Communards dans les prisons charentaises', *L'Actualité de l'Histoire*, 14 (1956), pp. 30–47, pp. 36–9.

91 This mass repression had a diversity of consequences and led to the rethinking of the prison provisions in France. Robert Badinter, *La Prison républicaine (1871–1914)*, Fayard, 1992, pp. 18–60.

92 On a revision of the debate, see Frédéric Bluche, *Septembre 1792, logiques d'un massacre*, Robert Laffont, 1986, pp. 17–18, 200–5.

93 AVdP, VD6 730 256.

94 Louis Fiaux, *L'Hygiène militaire, esquisses historiques et médicales à propos d'un bataillon de la garde mobile de l'armée de Paris*, Victor Rozier, 1871.

95 Louis Fiaux, *Jules Ferry, un malfaiteur public*, Librairie Internationale, 1886.

96 Louis Fiaux, *Histoire de la guerre civile de 1871, le gouvernement et l'assemblée de Versailles, la Commune de Paris*, Charpentier, 1879, p. 562.

8   The French state in question

1 E. Renan, *Qu'est-ce qu'une nation?*, Imprimerie Nationale, 1996, p. 241.

2 Pierre Nora (ed.), *Realms of Memory*, 3 vols, Columbia University Press, 1996–8.

3 See Bertrand Taithe, '*Monuments aux Morts?* Reading Nora's *Realms of Memory* and Samuel's *Theatres of Memory*', *History of the Human Sciences*, 12 (1999) 2, pp. 123–39.

4 Eugen Weber, *Peasants into Frenchmen: The Modernization of Rural France, 1870–1914*, Stanford University Press, 1976.

5 Another term used to signify the same thing is 'integration'; G. Férréol, *Intégration, lien social et citoyenneté*, Presses Universitaires du Septentrion, 1998.

6 A similar issue applies to immigration; see Gérard Noiriel, *Le Creuset français: histoire de l'immigration, XIXe–XXe siècle*, Éditions du Seuil, 1988, pp. 40–67.

7 National identity was not an invention of the nineteenth century although the nation state was, in many parts of Europe. French nationalism has been tracked back a long way. See enlightening studies of revolutionary *Cahiers généraux*: Beatrice Fry Hyslop, *French Nationalism in 1789 According to the General Cahiers*, New York, Octagon Books, 1968. Hyslop interestingly associated *etatism* to the more traditionally accepted components of French nationalism, pp. 24–6.

8 T.W. Margadant, 'Tradition and modernity in rural France during the nineteenth century', *Journal of Modern History*, 56 (1984), pp. 667–97; P. McPhee, 'A reconsideration of the "peasantry" of nineteenth-century France', *Journal of Peasant Studies*, 9 (1979), pp. 5–25; Charles Tilly, 'Did the cake of custom break?' in John Merriman (ed.), *Consciousness and Class Experience in Nineteenth-Century Europe*, New York, Holmes and Meier, 1979, pp. 17–44.

9 William Brustein, *The Social Origins of Political Regionalism, France 1849–1981*, University of California Press, 1988, pp. 124–8.

10 A surprisingly recent instance of this approach can be found in Sudhir Hazareesingh, 'The Société d'Instruction Républicaine and the propagation of civic republicanism in provincial and rural France, 1870–1877', *Journal of Modern History*, 71 (1999) 2, pp. 271–307.

11 See Jean-François Chanet, *L'École républicaine et les petites patries*, Aubier, 1996, pp. 204–23, 228–33.

12 A fascinating collection of articles on the subject can be found in no. 152 of the *Cahiers Trimestriels Jean-Jaurès*, 'Les "petites patries" dans la France Républicaine', 152 (April–June 1999).

13 Caroline Ford, *Creating the Nation in Provincial France: Religion and Political Identity in Brittany*, Princeton, 1993.

14 Peter McPhee, *The Politics of Rural Life: Political Mobilization in the French Countryside, 1846–1852*, Oxford, Clarendon, 1992.

15 Discourses on German education flourished in the aftermath of the conflict, although the real impact of German education in France is somewhat harder to assess. See Edmond Paul Dreyfus-Brisac, *L'Université de Bonn et l'enseignement en Allemagne*, Hachette, 1879; *L'Enseignement en France et à l'étranger considéré du point de vue politique et social*, A. Colin, 1880; Allan Mitchell, *The Divided Path: The German Influence on Social Reform in France after 1870*, Chapel Hill, University of North Carolina Press, 1991; George Weisz, *The Emergence of Modern Universities in France, 1863–1914*, Princeton University Press, 1983.

16 Mona Ozouf, *L'École, l'église et la république (1871–1914)*, Cana/Jean Offredo, 1982.

17 R.D. Anderson, *Education in France, 1848–1870*, Oxford, Clarendon, 1975; Robert Guildea, *Education in Provincial France, 1800–1914: A Study of Three Departments*, Clarendon, 1983, pp. 209–55.

18 ADC, R178, prefectoral report on conscription. There were, however, considerable variations from other forms of census showing that in the Bugeat sector two-thirds of men could read and write while in Jullac near Brive only one-third could.

19 Sarah Curtis, 'Supply and demand: religious schooling in nineteenth-century France', *History of Education Quarterly*, 39 (1999) 1, pp. 51–72; Raymond Grew and Patrick J. Harrigan, *School, State and Society: The Growth of Elementary Schooling in 19th Century France, a Quantitative Analysis*, Ann Arbor, University of Michigan Press, 1991.

20 The conference, edited by Léo Hamon, shows well how tenuous this link was. *Les Opportunistes: Les débuts de la République aux républicains*, Maison des Sciences de l'Homme, 1991; and *Les Républicains sous le Second Empire*, Maison des Sciences de l'Homme, 1993.

21 Frédéric Saluran, 'La Gauche avancée en 1849 et en 1870: le pourquoi de la chute', in Léo Hamon (ed.), *Les Républicains sous le Second Empire*, Maison des Sciences de l'Homme, 1993, pp. 93–111.

22 On this tension, see the interesting collection by Alan Forrest and Peter Jones, *Reshaping France: Town, Country and Region during the French Revolution*, Manchester University Press, 1991.

23 Benedict Anderson, *Imagined Communities*, Verso, 1991, pp. 37–65.

24 M. Gastu, *Le Peuple Algérien*, Challamel Ainé, 1884, pp. 101–8.

25 Many commentators were reluctant, and the conflict between colonists and metropolitan power is a constant feature of the French administration of Algeria. On legal reforms, see Ch. Roussel, 'La Justice en Algérie, les tribunaux indigènes', *Revue des Deux Mondes*, 1 August 1876, reprinted in Bruno Étienne (ed.), *Algérie 1830–1962*, Maisonneuve and Larose Valmonde, 1999, pp. 290–309.

26 AVdP, VD6/1567/1.

27 Roger V. Gould, *Insurgent Identities: Class, Community and Protest in Paris from 1848 to the Commune*, Chicago University Press, 1996; AVdP, VD6/1567/3.

28 Even the most anti-republican accounts make this point. Charles Besson, *Histoire d'un bataillon de mobiles, siège de Paris*, E. Lachaud, 1872, pp. 45–7, 135–6.

29 Thirteen thousand mayors attended the 14 July banquet in the year 2000. Interestingly, it was the President of the Senate who invited the mayors at the end of the twentieth century.

30 Louis Garel, *La Révolution lyonnaise depuis le 4 septembre*, Lyons, Association typographique, 1871, pp. 50–1.

31 Alain Corbin, *Les Cloches de la terre, paysage sonore et culture sensible dans les campagnes au XIXe siècle*, Albin Michel, 1994; Ted W. Margadant, *Urban Rivalries in the French Revolution*, Princeton University Press, 1992.

32 AML, 4 M1 10003, *Procès verbaux du conseil municipal de Lyon*, 19 November 1870.

33 Jean Aléxis Jacques Alguié, *Précis de doctrine médicale de l'école de Montpellier*, 3rd edn, Montpellier, 1843; *Nécessité de la doctrine médicale de Montpellier*, Montpellier, 1852.

34 W.G. MacCallum, 'The school of Montpellier', *The Johns Hopkins Hospital Bulletin*, 19 (1908), pp. 296–301; Louis Dulieu, *La Médecine à Montpellier*, 4 vols, Avignon, 1986.

35 George Weisz, *The Emergence of Modern Universities in France, 1863–1914*, Princeton University Press, 1983; *The Medical Mandarins: The French Academy of Medicine in the Nineteenth and Early Twentieth Centuries*, Oxford, 1995.

36 Mary Poovey, *Making a Social Body: British Cultural Formation, 1830–1864*, University of Chicago Press, 1995, pp. 115–16; Elizabeth Williams, *The Physical and the Moral: Anthropology, Physiology and Philosophical Medicine in France, 1750–1850*, Cambridge, 1994.

37 Lion Murard and Patrick Zylberman, *L'Hygiène dans la République: la santé publique en France ou l'utopie contrariée, 1870–1918*, Paris, 1997.

38 Ezra N. Suleiman, *Private Power and Centralization in France: The Notaires and the State*, Princeton University Press, 1987.

39 Christophe Charle, *Les Élites de la République, 1880–1900*, Fayard, 1987.

40 French notables were stubbornly resilient and adaptable, as is well shown in Thomas D. Beck and Martha W. Beck, *French Notables: Reflections of Industrialization and Regionalism*, New York, Peter Lang, 1987.

41 This is a leitmotif of republican government in France in 1870. See, for instance, the speeches of Jules Ferry. AAP, 542 Foss 3, 15 October 1870.

42 The government's decision of 28 October 1870 to limit the *Légion d'Honneur* to military service provoked uproar in the medical press. See *Recueil officiel des actes du Gouvernement*, p. 472; *Union médicale* (29 October 1870). Immediately after the armistice, Baron Larrey wrote 272 letters supporting medical applications.

43 Peter Gatrell, *A Whole Empire Walking, Refugees in Russia during World War I*, Bloomington, Indiana University Press, 1999, pp. 141–70.

44 *Six Semaines avec les Prussiens*, Tours, Mame, 1871, pp. 58–64.

45 ADHV, 4 R 177, report of 14 April 1871.

46 With Lafargue, Jules Guesde later played an important role in the making of the Parti Ouvrier Français. His main addition to the debates of 1871 was his *Livre Rouge de la justice rurale, documents pour servir à l'histoire d'une république sans républicains*, Geneva, 1871, which contains most of the worst Versailles' press reports on the Commune.

47 Martin Philip Johnson, 'Enlightening the "misguided brothers of the countryside": republican fraternalism and the Paris Commune of 1871', *French History*, 11 (1997) 4, pp. 411–37.

48 Martin Philip Johnson, *The Paradise of Association: Political Culture and Popular Organization in the Paris Commune of 1871*, University of Michigan Press, 1996, p. 66. Johnson relies on secondary evidence to overstate the success of Communards in the provinces,

49 Gaston Caulet du Tayrac, born in 1840. ADR, 4 M 290.

50 ADR, 4 M 289, Durand File, letter signed by G. Caulet du Tayrac; the letter was seized on visitor Audouard.

51 ADR, 4 M 290, copy of the debate at the municipal council, Gaston Caulet de Tayrac's file.

52 ADR, 4 M 290.

53 M.F. Crestin, *Souvenirs d'un lyonnais*, imprimerie Decléris et fils, 1897, p. 300. Crestin, like Andrieux, ended up suspecting Blanc of having been a Bonapartist or even Legitimist conspirator. This seems most unlikely, and Blanc's later political leaning towards Bonapartism should not be projected retrospectively on to his mishandled but probably genuine revolutionary activities of 1871.

54 Georges Jeanneret, *Paris pendant la Commune révolutionnaire de 71*, Neuchâtel, imp. Guillaume, 1871, pp. 71–2.

55 *Le Corrézien*, 27 May 1871.

56 Jacques Girault, *La Commune et Bordeaux (1870–1871), contribution à l'étude du mouvement ouvrier et de l'idéologie républicaine en province au moment de la Commune de Paris*, Éditions Sociales, 1971, pp. 130, 149–55.

57 ADCr, 4 M 107, directive of 2 May 1871. 'Check it and take the necessary measures to prevent the reunions that would aim to nominate delegates and raise funds. Be proactive and do not wait for new instructions to act … do not hesitate to arrest even the municipal councillors.'

58 Raymond Huard, *La Naissance des partis politiques en France*, Presses de Sciences Po, 1996, pp. 136–9.

59 AMM, H3 186 and *Délibérations du conseil municipal*, 57 D1, 9 May 1871.

60 Un Lyonnais, *Le candidat Barodet, sa vie, ses actes politiques et administratifs*, Paris, n.p., 1873, p. 79.

61 AMM, H3 186 and *Délibérations du conseil municipal*, 57 D1, 10 May 1871.

62 J.B. Ferrouillat, *Rapport présenté au conseil municipal de Lyon par le citoyen Ferrouillat au nom de la délégation envoyée à Versailles et à Paris*, 25 April 1871.

63 F.M. Atkinson (ed.), *Memoirs of Thiers, 1870–1873*, George Allen and Unwin, 1915, p. 136.

64 *La Nation Française*, 11 April 1871, leader.

65 Jacques Gouault, *Comment la France est devenue Républicaine: Les élections générales et partielles à l'assemblée Nationale de 1870–1871*, Cahiers de la Fondation Nationale des Sciences Politiques, 62, Armand Colin, 1954, pp. 72–5.

66 Besides a controversial decree by Gambetta, repealed only a few days before the elections had made ex-Bonapartist candidates ineligible, there were virtually no Bonapartist candidates in February 1871. Annie Moulin, *Peasantry and Society in France since 1789*, Cambridge University Press, 1988, pp. 87–9.

67 G. Marie de Ficquelmat, 'Les Élections législatives en Creuse de 1869 à 1885', *Mémoires de la Société des Sciences Naturelles et Archéologiques de la Creuse*, 39 (1975–7), pp. 852–73, p. 868.

68 Michel Lidove, 'Le Département de la Corrèze et la fondation de la Troisième République', *Bulletin de la Société des Lettres, Sciences et Arts de la Corrèze*, 68 (1964) 6–14, p. 9.
69 *La Nation Française*, 8 May 1871.
70 ADHV, 3 M 334, *Couleur politique des élus aux élections municipales de 1871*.
71 Gouault, *Comment la France est devenue Républicaine*, p. 116.
72 *Le Réveil de la Province*, 11 May 1871.
73 ADHV, R 188, Lubersac, 28 March 1871.
74 Maurice Agulhon, Gabriel Désert and Robert Specklin, *Histoire de la France rurale*, Le Seuil, 1976, vol. 3, pp. 372–6.
75 Daniel Dayen, *Martin Nadaud, ouvrier maçon et député, 1815–1898*, Limoges, Lucien Souny, 1998, p. 136.
76 Robert Tombs, *The War Against Paris, 1871*, Cambridge University Press, 1981, pp. 91–108.
77 ADCr, 1 M 198, *Dépêches*, 29 March 1871.
78 ADC, R188, Meymac, 29 March 1871; Ussel, 30 March 1871; Lubersac, 28 March 1871.
79 *L'Écho de la Dordogne*, 12 April 1871.
80 *La Gironde*, 13 April 1871.
81 Philip G. Nord, 'The Party of Conciliation and the Paris Commune', *French Historical Studies*, 15 (1987) 1, pp. 1–36.
82 Robert Tombs, *The War Against Paris, 1871*, Cambridge University Press, 1981.
83 Claude Digeon, *La Crise Allemande de la pensée française*, Presses Universitaires de France, 1959. A. Mitchell, *Victors and Vanquished: The German Influence on Army and Church in France*, Chapel Hill, University of North Carolina Press, 1984.
84 Judith F. Stone, *The Search for Social Peace: Reform Legislation in France, 1890–1914*, State University of New York Press, Albany, 1985, pp. 10, 102–3.
85 Pierre Arnaud (ed.), *Les Athlètes de la république, gymnastique, sport et idéologie républicaine 1870–1914*, Toulouse, Privat, 1987; Pierre Arnaud, *Le Militaire, l'écolier, le gymnaste: naissance de l'éducation physique en France, 1869–89*, Lyons, Presses Universitaires de Lyon, 1991.
86 Allan Mitchell, *Victors and Vanquished: The German Influence on Army and Church in France after 1870*, Chapel Hill, University of North Carolina Press, 1984, pp. 49–64.
87 Peter Sahlins, *Boundaries: The Making of France and Spain in the Pyrenees*, Berkeley, University of California Press, 1989. T. Baycroft, 'Changing identities in the Franco-Belgian borderland in the nineteenth and twentieth centuries', *French History*, 13 (1999) pp. 417–38.
88 This is a widespread anxiety amongst the French themselves, especially in the face of a perceived Anglo-Saxon domination. See Herman Lebovics, *True France: The Wars over Cultural Identity, 1900–1945*, Ithaca, Cornell University Press, 1992.
89 Jules Claretie, *Paris Assiégé*, reprinted Armand Colin, 1992, pp. 190–3. On Catholics in Brittany see C. Ford, *Creating the Nation in Provincial France*, Princeton University Press, 1993.
90 Charles d'Ariste, *Histoire d'un bataillon de la garde mobile 1870–1871*, Paris, Leautey, 1892, p. 13.
91 This is to a certain extent the point made by Brian Jenkins, *Nationalism in France: Class and Nation since 1789*, Routledge, 1990, pp. 11–12.
92 Michel de Certeau, D. Julia and J. Revel, *Une Politique de la langue, la Révolution française et les patois*, Gallimard, 1975.
93 On the importance of borders, see Timothy Baycroft, 'Changing identities in the Franco-Belgian borderland in the nineteenth and the twentieth centuries', *French History*, 13 (1999), pp. 417–38.
94 Christophe Charle, *Les Élites de la République, 1880–1900*, Fayard, 1987, pp. 27–72. Charle demonstrates how the republican state promoted further the meritocratic

ideals of the French Revolution and how the old elites responded to this challenge by investing further in education.

9 Union and unity: the Third Republic

1 Arthur Arnould, *Histoire populaire et parlementaire de la Commune de Paris*, Lyons, Jacques Marie Laffont, [1876] 1981, p. 275.
2 Brigitte Basdevant-Gaudemet, *La Commission de décentralisation de 1870: contribution à l'étude de la décentralisation en France au XIXe siècle*, Presses Universitaires de France, 1973, pp. 93–102.
3 Jean-Pierre Marichy, *La deuxième chambre dans la vie politique Française depuis 1875*, LGDJ, 1969.
4 Recent historiography casts this patronage culture in relation with established networking activities. D.L.L. Parry, 'Friends in high places: the favour sought by the Freemasons of Orléans', *French History*, 12 (1998) 2, pp. 195–212; Maurice Larkin, *Religion, Politics and Preferment in France since 1890*, Cambridge University Press, 1995.
5 Jean-Yves Mollier, *Le Scandale de Panama*, Fayard, 1991.
6 Jean Garrigues, *La République des hommes d'affaires (1870–1900)*, Aubier, 1997, pp. 14–18.
7 See Denis Baranger, *Parlementarisme des origines*, Presses Universitaires de France, 1999, pp. 359–71.
8 Jean-Pierre Machelon, *La République contre les libertés? Les restrictions aux libertés publiques de 1879 à 1914*, Presses de la Fondation Nationale des Sciences Politiques, 1976, p. 4.
9 Alain, *Éléments d'une doctrine radicale*, Gallimard, 1925.
10 André Siegfried, *France: A Study in Nationality*, New Haven, Yale University Press, 1930, pp. 103–4.
11 Lion Murard and Patrick Zylberman, *L'Hygiène dans la République: la santé publique en France ou l'utopie contrariée, 1870–1918*, Paris, 1997.
12 R.K. Gooch, *The French Parliamentary Committee System*, n.p., Archon Books [1935], 1969, p. 13.
13 Philip Nord, *The Republican Moment: Struggles for Democracy in Nineteenth Century France*, Cambridge (Mass.), Harvard University Press, 1995, p. 27. Freemasons, for instance, worked hard on a reconciliation programme.
14 Roger V. Gould, *Insurgent Identities: Class, Community and Protest in Paris from 1848 to the Commune*, Chicago University Press, 1995, p. 189.
15 Jacques Rougerie, *Paris Libre*, Le Seuil, 1971, p. 9.
16 It changed radically in exile. B. Malon, *La Troisième défaite du prolétariat français*, Neuchâtel, Guillaume, 1871, pp. 537–8.
17 Louis Andrieux, *À Travers la République*, Payot, 1926, pp. 262–4.
18 On the Pelletan dynasty, see Judith F. Stone, *Sons of the Revolution: Radical Democrats in France 1862–1914*, Louisiana State University Press, 1996.
19 Louise Michel, *La Commune, Histoire et Souvenirs*, 2 vols, Maspéro, 1970, vol. 1, p. 72.
20 Bernard Noël, *Dictionnaire de la Commune*, 2 vols, Flammarion, 1978, vol. 1, p. 258.
21 Daniel Mollenhauer, 'À la recherche de la vraie république: quelques jalons pour une histoire du radicalisme des débuts de la Troisième République', *Revue Historique*, 607 (1998), pp. 579–615.
22 Raymond Huard, *La Naissance des partis politiques en France*, Presses de Sciences Po, 1996, pp. 168–86.
23 Charles Chinchalle, *Les Survivants de la Commune*, Le Boulanger, 1885.
24 Michel Denis, Michel Lagrée and Jean-Yves Veillard, *L'Affaire Dreyfus et l'opinion publique*, Presses Universitaires de Rennes, 1995; Pierre Birnbaum (ed.), *La France de l'Affaire Dreyfus*, Gallimard, 1994, particularly the articles by Jean Estèbe, Christophe

Charle and Raymond Huard, pp. 19–119; Robert Elliot Kaplan, *Forgotten Crisis: The Fin-de-Siècle Crisis of Democracy in France*, Berg, 1995.

25 Edmond About, *Alsace, 1871–1872*, Paris, Librairie Hachette, 1906, p. 25; Dan P. Silverman, *Reluctant Union: Alsace Lorraine and Imperial Germany, 1871–1918*, Pennsylvania State University Press, 1972, pp. 23–69. Half a million Alsatians left the province between 1871 and 1914, leading to the gradual Germanisation of major cities such as Metz (41 per cent German in 1910).

26 Aimé Dupuy, *Sedan et l'enseignement de la revanche*, Institut National de Recherche et de Documentation Pédagogique, 1975.

27 Bertrand Joly, 'La France et la Revanche, 1871–1914', *Revue d'Histoire Moderne et Contemporaine*, 46 (1999) 2, pp. 325–47.

28 Edmond Béraud, *La République c'est la guerre*, n.p., 1885.

29 Quoted in Jean-François Martin and Marie-Françoise Rosset, *L'École Primaire dans le Rhône (1815–1940)*, Conseil général du Rhône/Archives départementales, 1997, p. 101.

30 Juliette Adam, *Mes angoisses et nos luttes*, Alphonse Lemerre, 1907.

31 Adrien Dansette, *Le Boulangisme*, Artheme Fayard, 1946. William D. Irvine, *The Boulanger Affair Reconsidered: Royalism, Boulangism and the Origins of the Radical Right in France*, Oxford University Press, 1989, pp. 80–6.

32 William D. Irvine, *The Boulanger Affair Reconsidered: Royalism, Boulangism and the Origins of the Radical Right in France*, Oxford University Press, 1989, pp. 80–6.

33 See, for instance, J.-J. Laguerre, *Les Allemands à Bar-le-duc et dans la Meuse 1870–1873*, Bar-le-Duc, Comte-Jacquet, 1874, pp. 221–308.

34 S.E. Cooper, 'Pacifism in France, 1889–1914: international peace as a human right', *French Historical Studies*, 17 (1991) 2, pp. 359–86.

35 Bertrand Joly, *Déroulède: l'inventeur du nationalisme français*, Perrin, 1998, pp. 75–166.

36 *Le Traitre* and *Dreyfus in Prison* were published on 13 and 20 January 1895; illustrated supplement of *Le Petit Journal*.

37 Émile Bader, *Mars-la-Tour et son monument national*, Mars-la-Tour, Ritter-Roscop, 1893.

38 See, for instance, the monument to the dead of the Haute-Vienne department in Limoges. Unlike in 1918, communes were not the centres of commemorations.

39 Clément de Lacroix, *Les Morts pour la patrie, tombes militaires et monuments élevés à la mémoire des soldats tués pendant la guerre, chronologie historique des événements de 1870–1871*, Chez l'auteur, 1891.

40 On the other hand, the phenomenon is well known for later conflicts. J. Winter, *Sites of Memory, Sites of Mourning: The Great War in European Cultural History*, Cambridge University Press, 1995.

41 For more information see B. Taithe, *Defeated Flesh: Welfare, Warfare and the Making of Modern France*, Manchester University Press, 1999, chapter 7. ADC, R244, *État nominatif des amputés*.

42 ADCr, 1 M 286, *Dossier des médailles militaires*. Also *Bulletin Officiel du Ministère de l'Intérieur*, 1911, p. 509 and 1912, pp. 111, 585.

43 ADR, 1 M 200, *Monuments commémoratifs*.

44 Serge Berstein, *Édouard Herriot, ou la république en personne*, Presses de la fondation nationale des sciences politiques, 1985.

45 ADR, 1 M 200, *Monument à la mémoire de Barodet, 28 Novembre 1910*.

46 Un Lyonnais, *Le candidat Barodet, sa vie, ses actes politiques et administratifs*, Paris, n.p., 1873, p. 69. '*Barodet c'est du raide! Barodet ça vous emporte la gueule à quinze pas … comme dirait votre ami le Père Duchesne.*'

47 Barodet himself had not been adverse to a little revisionism in his own lifetime; Désiré Barodet, *Éclaircissements historiques, lettre à monsieur le docteur Crestin*, Lyons, Delaroche, 1897.

48 D. Harvey, *Consciousness and the Urban Experience*, 2 vols, Oxford, Basil Blackwell, 1992, vol. 1, pp. 221–50; R.A. Jones, 'Monuments as ex-voto, monuments as historiography: the Basilica of Sacré Coeur', *French Historical Studies*, 18 (1993) 2, pp. 482–502.

49 Françoise Bayard and Pierre Cayez (eds), *Histoire de Lyon du XVIe siècle à nos jours*, Roanne, Howarth, 1989, p. 357.

50 Yves Lequin, *Les Ouvriers de la région Lyonnaise (1848–1914): les intérêts de classe et la République*, Presses Universitaires de Lyon, 1977, vol, 1, p. 142.

51 This debate has gone full circle. From being a pariah state in Europe, France became the peer of Germany regarding health and welfare provisions before 1914. Another revision to the debate is now taking place. Henri Hatzfeld, *Du Paupérisme à la sécurité sociale, 1850–1940*, Armand Colin, 1971; Timothy B. Smith, 'The plight of the able-bodied poor and the unemployed in urban France, 1880–1914', *European History Quarterly*, 30 (2000) 2, pp. 147–84.

52 Judith F. Stone, *The Search for Social Peace: Reform Legislation in France, 1890–1914*, Albany, State University of New York Press, 1985; Michelle Perrot, *Les Ouvriers en grève, France 1871–1890*, Mouton, 1974; Paul Farmer, *France Reviews its Revolutionary Origins: Social Politics and Historical Opinions in the Third Republic*, New York, Octagon Books [1944], 1973.

53 Allan Mitchell, 'Crucible of French anti-clericalism: the Conseil Municipal of Paris, 1871–1885', *Francia*, 8 (1980), pp. 395–405.

54 Henri Rollet, *L'Action sociale des catholiques en France 1871–1914*, Desclée de Brouwer, 1958; Timothy B. Smith, 'Republicans, Catholics and social reform: Lyon, 1870–1920', *French History*, 12 (1998) 3, pp. 246–75; M. Le Mansois Duprey, *L'Oeuvre sociale de la municipalité parisienne 1871–1891*, Imprimerie municipale, 1892.

55 Quoted in Raymond Huard, 'De la Commune à la fondation de la république, une démarche républicaine; Edgar Quinet à l'Assemblée de Versailles (1871–1875)', in Simone Bernard-Griffiths and Paul Viallaneix (eds), *Edgar Quinet, ce juif errant*, Presses Universitaires de Clermont Ferrand, 1978, pp. 119–22, p. 118.

56 Pierre Birnbaum, *'La France aux français', histoire des haines nationalistes*, Editions du Seuil, 1993, p. 11.

57 Michel Winock, *Édouard Drumont et Cie, antisémitisme et fascisme en France*, Le Seuil, 1982, pp. 35–66.

58 John Rothney, *Bonapartism after Sedan*, Ithaca, Cornell University Press, 1969.

59 *Le Corrézien*, 6 June 1871.

60 See Jean-Paul Bled, *Les Lys en exil, ou la seconde mort de l'Ancien Régime*, Fayard, 1992, pp. 214–79.

61 Jacques Gadille, *La Pensée et l'action politiques des évêques français au début de la Troisième République*, 2 vols, Hachette, 1967.

62 Steven D. Kale, 'The monarchy according to the king: the ideological content of the *Drapeau Blanc*, 1871–3', *French History*, 2 (1988) 4, pp. 399–426.

63 The entire concept of nobility in an age of classes turned its back on society. David Higgs, *Nobles in Nineteenth-Century France: The Practice of Inegalitarianism*, Johns Hopkins University Press, 1987.

64 Philippe Levillain, *Albert de Mun, Catholicisme Français et Catholicisme Romain, du Syllabus au Ralliement*, École Française de Rome, 1983, pp. 211–78; Robert Talmy, *Le Syndicalisme chrétien en France (1871–1930), Difficultés et controverses*, Bloud et Gay, 1966, pp. 14–22.

65 Robert R. Locke, *French Legitimists and the Politics of Moral Order in the Early Third Republic*, Princeton University Press, 1974, pp. 10–53. Locke shows that legitimism was socially diverse.

66 A. Jeanne Caron, *Le Sillon et la Démocratie Chrétienne 1894–1910*, Plon, 1967, pp. 17–76; Alexander Sedgwick, *The Ralliement in French Politics, 1890–1898*, Harvard University Press, 1965, pp. 7–55.

67 The Senate was later reformed in 1884 and then remained stable. Joseph-Barthélémy, *Le gouvernement de la France, tableau des institutions politiques, administratives et judiciaires de la France*, Payot, 1939, pp. 67–8, 73–4.

68 Léo Hamon (ed.), *Les Républicains sous le Second Empire*, Éditions de la Maison des Sciences de l'Homme, 1993, p. 208.

69 François Furet, *La Révolution 1770–1880*, 2 vols, Hachette, 1988.

70 See, for instance, the writings of Daniel Halévy, *Visites aux paysans du centre*, Librairie Grasset, 1921, pp. 28–32; a modern echo can be found in the work of Alain Corbin, *Le Monde retrouvé de Louis-François Pinagot, sur les traces d'un inconnu*, Flammarion, 1998, pp. 247–87. Pinagot realised the republican dream through his son, elected to the municipal council in 1871. On Halévy see Alain Silvera, *Daniel Halévy and his Times: A Gentleman-Commoner in the Third Republic*, Cornell University Press, 1966.

71 Maurice Agulhon, *Marianne au pouvoir, l'imagerie et la symbolique républicaines de 1880 à 1914*, Flammarion, 1989, pp. 30–1.

72 The royalists were unable to revise the suffrage and could only tinker with its application. Pierre Rosanvallon, *Le Sacre du citoyen, histoire du suffrage universel en France*, Gallimard, 1992, pp. 324–38.

73 Alan R.H. Baker, *Fraternity among the French Peasantry: Sociability and Voluntary Associations in the Loire Valley, 1815–1914*, Cambridge University Press, 1999, pp. 170–88, 313–16.

74 Robert R. Locke, *French Legitimists and the Politics of Moral Order in the Early Third Republic*, Princeton University Press, 1974, pp. 164–5.

Appendix 1   Chronological landmarks

1 Gustave Fischbach, *Guerre de 1870. Le siège et le bombardement de Strasbourg*, Cherbuliez, 1871 and Strasbourg, Libraires, 1870; Jacques Flach, *Strasbourg après le bombardement, 2 octobre 1870–30 septembre 1872, rapports sur les travaux du comité de secours strasbourgeois pour les victimes du bombardement*, Strasburg, Imp. de Fischbach, 1873.

2 Léon Belin, *Le Siège de Belfort, siège et bombardement*, Paris and Nancy, Berger Levrault, 1871.

Appendix 2   Detailed breakdown of the French war effort by departments

1 *Rapport présenté par le chef de la division administrative générale et départementale à M. Jules Cazot, secrétaire délégué du ministère de l'intérieur*, Organisation des gardes nationales mobilisés, Bordeaux, Émile Crugy, 1871, pp. 19–26.

2 Numbers taken from the analytical listing established by A. Martinier, *Corps auxiliaires créés pendant la guerre 1870–1871*, vol. 1, *Garde Nationale Mobile*, vol. 2, *Garde Nationale Mobilisée*, Edmond Dubois, 1896–7.

3 Based on the estimates of 53.7 per cent for the 20–59 age group at the 1851 census. The statistics are thus based on 40 per cent of all men aged 20–40. F. Braudel and E. Labrousse, *Histoire économique et sociale de la France*, 4 vols, Presses Universitaires de France, 1993, vol. 3, p. 236.

4 All figures from the 1861 census, *Almanach de Paris, 1866, annuaire général de diplomatie, de politique, d'histoire et de statistique*, Amyot, 1866, p. 51.

BIBLIOGRAPHY

Archival, newspaper and manuscript sources

I have used many archives to write this book, and newspapers and journals have added to the wealth of material. The major archival deposits of Paris have been used, and in particular the following *cotes*: Archives nationales: Dossiers des Commissaires de Police, les émigrés Polonais et l'Internationale, AN F7 12708; Ministère de l'Intérieur Janvier–Juin 1871, AN FIC1 131; Communards Amnistiés et Libérés, AN F7 12713 bis. Archives de l'Assistance Publique, where all the archives relating to the war and the Commune have been classified in 1991 under the register 542 Foss which goes from 542 Foss 1 to 125; Archives du Service de Santé des Armées de Terre et de Mer, where again all the archives have been collated in a series of 'boxes' 62, 63, 64, 65, 65bis, 66. The archives at the Vincennes Service Historique des Armées de Terre are also well organised and mostly under the label La 1–78, Lb 1–78, Lc 1–5, Ld 1–34, Le 1–59, Lf 1–14, Lg 1–7, Lh 1–13, Li 1–129, Lj 1–8, Lk 1–3, Ll 1–4, Lm1–48, Ln 1–17, Lo 1–79, Lhs 1–28, Lq 1–17, Lr 1–11, Lt 1–29, Lu 1–151, Lv 1–28, Lw 1–35, Lx 1–103. Another more detailed inventory exists for the Commune, previously Ly 1–26. The Archives de la Préfecture de Police de Paris suffered in the fires of May 1871 but still contain important quantities of material, mostly listed in the series Ba, Db and Da. The archives of Paris also suffered greatly in the fires, but enormous files are still accessible at the Archives de la Ville de Paris in the series of material deposited by arrondissement town halls ranging from VD6 715 to VD6 2696, deposited from 1860 onwards. The Archives Episcopales of the archbishopric of Paris are not so well organised but contain the files of Mgr Darboy and the elements relating to his death; other interesting files are the reports to the bishop from many army chaplains. The Archives of the Grand Orient de France are now mostly available at the Bibliothèque Nationale; an inventory exists.

I have also used some regional archives, notably the Archives départementales du Rhône, Lyons, de la Creuse, Guéret, de la Haute-Vienne, Limoges, de la Corrèze, Tulle, de l'Hérault, Montpellier. In all these regional archives the files studied belonged mainly to the M and R series. I also used the Montpellier Archives Municipales and the Lyons Archives Municipales.

The archives relating to overseas territories and colonies are kept in the wonderful archives of Aix-en-Provence, Archives d'Outre Mer, which contain numerous gems classified by territory and following the conventions of the Archives nationales.

Bibliography

This is a relatively short bibliography which should be used together with the one I have provided in *Defeated Flesh*, published in 1999. Readers should not be surprised if some rather obvious titles are not listed here; it is often because they were not central to my argument that I have chosen not to list them.

All French and English titles are published in Paris and London respectively unless otherwise specified. Obviously redundant publication details such as Oxford, Oxford University Press, have been simplified thus: 'Oxford University Press'.

Books and texts written before 1918

About, Edmond, *Alsace, 1871–1872*, Paris, Librairie Hachette, 1906.

Adam, Juliette, *Mes angoisses et nos luttes*, Alphonse Lemerre, 1907.

Aiguy, M. d', *Quel Gouvernement la France se donnera-t-elle?*, Lyons and Paris, Félix Girard, 1871.

Alain, *Elements d'une doctrine radicale*, Gallimard, 1925.

Albigny, Paul d', *Le Livre d'or du département de l'Ardèche, contenant la liste des enfants de ce département morts en 1870–1871*, privat, Roure, 1879.

Albiousse, Lt-Colonel d', *Le Drapeau du Sacré-Coeur, campagne de France, zouaves pontificaux*, Rennes, Hauvespre, 1871.

Alguié, Jean Aléxis Jacques, *Précis de doctrine médicale de l'école de Montpellier*, 3rd edn, Montpellier, 1843.

——*Nécessité de la doctrine médicale de Montpellier*, Montpellier, 1852.

Allard, Abbé Julien S., *Les Zouaves pontificaux, ou journal de Mgr Daniel, aumônier des zouaves*, Hugny, 1880.

Amigues, Jules, *La France à refaire : la Commune*, Lachaud, 1871.

——*Louis Nathaniel Rossel, papiers postumes recueillis et annotés par Jules Amigues*, Lachaud, 6th edn, 1871.

—— *Les Aveux d'un conspirateur bonapartiste. Histoires pour servir à l'Histoire de demain*, Lachaud et Burdin, 1874.

Anon, *L'Empereur Napoléon III et l'Italie*, Paris, Dentu, 1859.

—— *Apparitions prophétiques d'une âme du purgatoire à une religieuse d'un monastère en Belgique en 1870, par l'auteur des 'voix prophétiques'*, Brussels, n.p., 1871.

——*Six Semaines avec les Prussiens*, Tours, Mame, 1871.

——*Extrait des causes célèbres de tous les peuples, le maréchal Bazaine, relation complète*, Lebrun, 1874.

Appia, Louis and Moynier, Gustave, *La Guerre et la charité, traité théorique et pratique de philanthropie appliquée aux armées en campagne*, Geneva, Cherbuliez, 1867.

Arago, Étienne, *L'Hôtel de Ville de Paris au 4 Septembre et pendant le siège, réponse à monsieur le comte Daru*, Paris, Hetzel, 1871.

Ariste, Charles d', *Histoire d'un bataillon de la garde mobile 1870–1871*, Paris, Leautey, 1892.

Armagnac, L.,*15 jours de campagne, août–septembre 1870, étapes d'un franc-tireur parisien de Paris à Sedan*, 6th edn, Hachette, 1889.

Arnould, Arthur, *Histoire populaire et parlementaire de la Commune de Paris*, Lyons, Jacques Marie Laffont [1876], 1981.

Atkinson, F.M. (ed.), *Memoirs of Thiers, 1870–1873*, George Allen and Unwin, 1915.

Bader, Émile, *Mars-la-Tour et son monument national*, Mars-la-Tour, Ritter-Roscop, 1893.

Bakunin, M., *La révolution sociale ou la dictature militaire*, Geneva, 1871.

Bakunin, M., Léo, A. and Lefrançais, G., *Simples questions sociales*, Saint-Imier, Propagande socialiste, 1872.

Baldwin, Simon E., *The Relations of Education to Citizenship*, New Haven, Yale University Press, 1912.

Barodet, Désiré, *Éclaircissements historiques, lettre à monsieur le docteur Crestin*, Lyons, Delaroche, 1897.

Bastelica, André, *Appel aux français, lettre d'un proscrit*, Geneva, 1876.

Bauquier, Ch., *Les Dernières campagnes dans l'Est*, Lemerre, 1873.

Bédarrides, M., *Morale de l'invasion prussienne*, Paris, n.p., 1871.

Belin, Léon, *Le Siège de Belfort, siège et bombardement*, Paris and Nancy, Berger Levrault, 1871.

Bellina, A. de, *Les Polonais et la Commune de Paris*, n.p., 1871.

Benedetti, Comte Vincent, *Ma Mission en Prusse*, H. Plon, 1871.

Béquet, *Rapport au conseil de gouvernement, organisation du culte israélite en Algérie*, Imp. du gouvernement, 1858.

Béraud, Edmond, *Gambetta dictateur*, Poitiers, H. Oudin, 1881.

——*La République c'est la guerre*, n.p., 1885.

Berleux, Jean, *La Caricature politique en France pendant la guerre, le siège de Paris et la Commune 1870–1871*, Labitte and E. Paul, 1890.

Bernhardt, Sarah, *Ma Double vie*, 2 vols, Des Femmes, 1980.

Berquier, Jules Le, *Administration de la Commune de Paris et du département de la Seine*, Imprimerie et librairie administrative Paul Dupont, 1861.

Besson, C., *Histoire d'un bataillon de mobiles, siège de Paris*, E. Lachaud, 1872.

Blandeau, H.R., *La Dictature de Gambetta*, Amyot, 1871.

——*Patriotisme du clergé catholique et des ordres religieux pendant la guerre de 1870–1*, Lecoffre, 1873.

Bonhomme, Abbé Jules, *Souvenirs du Fort de l'Est, près Saint-Denis*, Paris, Jacques Lecoffre, 1872.

Bougeard, A., Brière, Dassis, Dourle, E. Dupas, Hamet, Leclerc, Leverdays, Lupin, Longuet, Maillard, Marchand, Martel, Vaillant, *Des Districts!!!*, 6 September, 1870, reproduced in *Les Révolutions du XIXe siècle*, 10 vols, Paris, EDHIS, 1988, vol. 6, ff. 1, p. 3.

Boulanger, Léon, *Compte rendu des travaux du Comité de Secours de la Sarthe*, Le Mans, 1871.

Bournand, François, *Le Clergé pendant la Commune, 1871*, Tolra, 1891, 2nd edn 1892.

——*Les Soeurs martyres, les soeurs Augustines, les soeurs des hôpitaux pendant la guerre (1870–1871) ; dévouements; témoignages des contemporains; les soeurs récompensées*, Tours, A. Cattier, 1894.

Brackenbury, Henry, *Les Maréchaux de France, étude de leur conduite dans la guerre de 1870*, Lachaud, 1872.

Broglie, Albert de, *Mémoires du duc de Broglie*, Calmann-Lévy, 1938.

Camp, Maxime du, *Les Ancêtres de la Commune, l'attentat Fieschi*, Charpentier, 1877.

——*La Charité privée à Paris, l'orphelinat d'Auteuil et l'abbé Roussel*, Ch. des Granges, 1881, 2nd edn, Hachette, 1885.

Casimir, P., *Les Pages douloureuses de la guerre*, Niort, L. Favre, 1872.

Cattelain, P., *Souvenirs inédits du chef de la sûreté sous la Commune*, Juven, 1900.

Chanzy, Général Antoine Eugène, *La Campagne de 1870–1871, la deuxième armée de la Loire*, H. Plon, 1871, reprinted Gautier, 1895.

Chenu, J.C., *De la mortalité dans l'armée et des moyens d'économiser la vie humaine*, Hachette, 1870.

Chinchalle, Charles, *Les Survivants de la Commune*, Le Boulanger, 1885.

Christot, F., *Le Massacre de l'ambulance de Saône-et-Loire, 21 Janvier 1871*, Lyons, Vingtrinier, 1871.

Claretie, Arsène Arnaud dit Jules, *Paris assiégé. Journal 1870–1871*, reprinted Armand Colin, 1992.

Claris, A., *Les Ennemis de l'internationale démasqués au congrès de la Haye*, Brussels, L. Verrycken, 1872.

——*La Proscription française en Suisse, 1871–72*, Geneva, 1872.

Clinquet, Arthur, *Le Général Chanzy*, Léon Chailley, 1883.

Court, Félicien, *Louis Ormières, 1851–1914, et l'ambulance du Grand Orient de France en 1870–1871*, Imprimerie Nouvelle, 1914.

——'Louis Ormières', *Bulletin du Grand Orient de France*, 26 (1870), pp. 380–92.

Cresson, Ernest, *Cent jours à la Préfecture de Police, 2 novembre 1870 – 11 février 1871*, Nourrit, H. Plon, 1901.

Crestin, M.F. *Souvenirs d'un lyonnais*, Imprimerie Decléris et fils, 1897.

Crombrugghe, I. de, *Journal d'une infirmière pendant la guerre 1870–1871*, H. Plon, 1872.

Damas, Rev. P. de, *Souvenirs de guerre et de captivité (France et Prusse)*, G. Téqui, 1883.

Dauban, Charles-Aimé, *Le Fond de la société sous la Commune* [1873], Slatkine-Megariotis Reprints, 1977.

Daudet, A., *Les Contes du Lundi* [1873], reprinted Maxipoche Classiques Français, 1995.

Delmas, Abbé G., *Un Prêtre et la Commune de Paris en 1871, récits historiques*, Josse, 1873.

Deluns-Montaud, Pierre, Aulard, A., Bourgeois, Émile and Reinach, Joseph, *Les Origines diplomatiques de la guerre de 1870–1871, recueil de documents publiés par le ministère des affaires étrangères*, 10 vols, Gustave Ficker, 1910–15.

Denormandie, M.E., *Le VIII arrondissement et son administration pendant le siège de Paris*, Garnier Frères, 1875.

Dreyfus-Brisac, Edmond Paul, *L'Université de Bonn et l'enseignement en Allemagne*, Hachette, 1879.

——*L'Enseignement en France et à l'étranger considéré du point de vue politique et social*, A. Colin, 1880.

Dunsany, E., *Gaul or Teuton? Considerations as to Our Allies of the Future*, London, Longman, Green, 1873.

Dupanloup, Mgr F., *Lettre à M le vicomte de la Guéronnière*, Charles Douniol, 1861.

——*Lettre au clergé et aux fidèles de son diocèse sur les derniers malheurs de Paris pour demander de solennelles expiations*, Semaine Religieuse, 1871.

Dupont, Léonce, *Tours et Bordeaux, souvenirs de la république à outrance*, Dentu, 1877.

Duportal, Armand, *La Commune à Toulouse, simple exposé des faits*, Imprimerie Générale Paul Savy, 1871.

Durand-Auzias, 'Le 4 Septembre à Lyon', *Revue Hebdomadaire*, 3 September 1910, pp. 20–38.

Durangel, H., *Rapport présenté par le chef de la division administrative générale et départementale à M Jules Cazot, secrétaire délégué du ministère de l'intérieur*, Organisation des gardes nationales mobilisés, Bordeaux, Émile Crugy, 1871.

Esboeufs, V. d' (Vergès), *La Vérité sur le gouvernement de la défense nationale, la Commune et les versaillais*, Geneva, 1871.

——*Le Coin du voile, trahison et défection au sein de la Commune*, Geneva, 1871.

Fauche, Amédée, *Montereau-Faut-Yonne, Journal de l'occupation prussienne*, Montereau, L. Zanote, 1871.

Favre, Jules, *Gouvernement de la Défense Nationale du 30 juin au 31 octobre 1870*, H. Plon, 1871.

Faze, Louis, *Histoire de la Guerre Civile de 1871*, Charpentier, 1879.

Ferrouillat, J.B., *Rapport présenté au conseil municipal de Lyon par le citoyen Ferrouillat au nom de la délégation envoyée à Versailles et à Paris*, 25 April 1871.

Fiaux, Louis, *L'Hygiène militaire, esquisses historiques et médicales à propos d'un bataillon de la garde mobile de l'armée de Paris*, Victor Rozier, 1871.

——*Histoire de la guerre civile de 1871, le gouvernement et l'assemblée de Versailles, la Commune de Paris*, Charpentier, 1879.

——*Jules Ferry, un malfaiteur public*, Librairie Internationale Achille Le Rey, 1886.

Fischbach, Gustave, *Guerre de 1870. Le siège et le bombardement de Strasbourg*, Cherbuliez, 1871, and Strasbourg, Libraires, 1870.

Flach, Jacques, *Strasbourg après le bombardement, 2 octobre 1870–30 septembre 1872, rapports sur les travaux du comité de secours strasbourgeois pour les victimes du bombardement*, Strasbourg, Imp. de Fischbach, 1873.

Fleury, A., *De l'assistance publique à Paris*, Rousseau, 1901.

Fleury, Édouard, *Éphémérides de la guerre de 1870–71*, Laon, Imprimerie du journal de l'Aisne, 1871.

Flourens, Gustave, *Paris Livré*, Verboeckhoven, A. Lacroix, 1871.

Fontoulieu, Paul, *Les Églises de Paris sous la Commune*, Dentu, 1873.

Foulden, J.A., *Histoire de la vie et oeuvre de Mgr Darboy*, n.p., 1889.

Frégier, H.A., *Des Classes dangereuses de la population dans les grandes villes*, J.B. Baillière, 1840.

Freycinet, Charles de, *Souvenirs, 1848–1878*, Delagrave, 1912.

Fuzier-Herman, Edmond, *La Province au siège de Paris – Garde Mobile du Tarn*, Paris, Librairie Militaire de J. Dumaine, 1871.

Garel, Louis, *La Révolution lyonnaise depuis le 4 septembre*, Lyons, Association typographique, 1871.

Garibaldi, Riciotti, *Souvenirs de la campagne de France 1870–71*, Nice, La Semaine Niçoise, 1899.

Gastu, François Joseph, *Le Peuple Algérien*, Challamel Ainé, 1884.

Gaulot, Paul, *La Vérité sur l'expédition du Mexique d'après les documents et souvenirs de Ernest Louet, payeur en chef du corps expéditionnaire*, 3 vols, P. Ollendorff, 1889–90.

Gavoy, Émile Alexandre, *Étude de faits de guerre: le service de santé militaire en 1870, hier, aujour-d'hui, demain*, Paris and Limoges, Henri Charles Lavauzelle, 1894.

Gazon de la Peyrière, Comte, *L'Église de France devant l'invasion prussienne*, Régis Ruffet, 1872.

Ginoulhiac, Mgr Jacques-Marie-Achille, *Mandement à l'occasion de la fête de l'immaculée conception de la Sainte Vierge*, 21 November 1870.

Goncourt, Edmond de, *Paris under Siege from the Goncourt Journal*, Ithaca, Cornell University Press, 1969.

Guéronnière, Alfred de la, *M. Thiers et sa mission*, Dentu, 1871.

Guesde, Jules, *Livre Rouge de la justice rurale, documents pour servir à l'histoire d'une république sans républicains*, Geneva, 1871.

Guldin, A., *Les Monuments des soldats de l'armée de Bourbaki décédés en Suisse en 1871*, St Gall, Imprimerie Merkur, 1898.

Hale, Colonel Lonsdale, *The 'People's War' in France, 1870–1871*, Hugh Rees, 1904.

Halévy, L., *Notes et souvenirs 1871–1872*, Calmann-Lévy, 1889.

Heylli, Georges d' (ed.), *Télégrammes militaires de M. Léon Gambetta du 9 octobre 1870 au 6 février 1871*, Paris, L. Beauvais, 1871.

Hodieu, A., *Du Principe électif à appliquer à la ville de Lyon pour la nomination de son conseil municipal*, Lyons, 1864.

Holyoakes, G., *Sixty Years of an Agitator's Life*, 2 vols, Fisher Unwin, 1892.

Husson, A., *Les Consommations de Paris*, Guillaumin, 1856.

Jacqmin, François Prosper, *Les Chemins de fer pendant la guerre de 1870–1871*, Hachette, 1872.

Jeanneret, Georges, *Paris pendant la Commune révolutionnaire de 71*, Neuchâtel, Imp. Guillaume, 1871.

Joubert, Charles and Vresse, Arnauld de, *De la Défense de Paris pendant le siège au point de vue de l'alimentation*, Arnauld de Vresse, 1871.

Jurgensen, J., *Le Soir du combat, récit d'une infirmière, poème*, Geneva, Durafort, 1871.

Kératry, Émile de, *Le 4 septembre et le gouvernement de la Défense Nationale, dépositions devant la commission d'enquête de l'assemblée nationale, mission diplomatique à Madrid*, Librairie Internationale A. Lacroix, Verboeckhoven, 1872.

Lacroix, Clément de, *Les Morts pour la patrie, tombes militaires et monuments élevés à la mémoire des soldats tués pendant la guerre, chronologie historique des événements de 1870–1871*, chez l'auteur, 1891.

Laguerre, J.-J., *Les allemands à Bar-le-duc et dans la Meuse 1870–1873*, Bar-le-Duc, Comte-Jacquet, 1874.

Lay, P. (ed.), *Lettres d'un homme [Victor Desplats] à la femme qu'il aime pendant le siège de Paris et la Commune*, Jean-Claude Lattès, 1980.

Le Bonapartisme condamné par l'Armée: protestations des officiers français internés en Allemagne contre la restauration impériale, Librairie Internationale, A. Lacroix, Verboeckhoven, 1871.

Lecour, Charles J., *La Prostitution à Paris et à Londres, 1789–1877*, Asselin, 1877.

Lefrançais, G., *Étude sur le mouvement communaliste à Paris en 1871*, Neuchâtel, 1871.

Le Mansois Duprey, M., *L'Oeuvre sociale de la municipalité parisienne 1871–1891*, Imprimerie municipale, 1892.

Lemonnyer, J., *Essai bibliographique sur les publications de la proscription française ou catalogue raisonné d'une bibliothèque socialiste, communaliste et de libre pensée*, Versailles, Au Palais de l'Assemblée Nationale, 1873.

Léo, André (Léodile Champseix), *La guerre sociale, discours prononcé au congrès de la Paix à Lausanne*, Neuchâtel, 1871.

Les Deux sièges de Paris, album pittoresque, Au bureau du journal *L'éclipse*, 1871.

L'Humaniste, Amédée, *Les cent jours de l'Algérie*, Algiers, Typographie de l'Association Ouvrière, 1871.

Lissagaray, Prosper Olivier, *The Paris Commune of 1871*, New Park Publications, 1976.

Long, Xavier, *Rapport au sujet de la répartition des secours faite par la société anglaise des Amis, Quakers aux victimes innocentes de la guerre en France, 1870–1871*, n.p., 1872.

Lordat, Jacques, *Réponse à des objections faites contre la doctrine anthropologique enseignée à Montpellier dans laquelle le dynamisme humain est considéré comme composé de deux principes actifs*, Montpellier, 1852, 2nd edn 1854.

Louis-Lande, L., *Récits d'un soldat, les fusiliers marins au siège de Paris, un invalide, le Sergent Hoff, la Hacienda de Camaron [sic]*, H. Lecène et H. Oudin, 1886.

MacCallum, W.G., 'The school of Montpellier', *The Johns Hopkins Hospital Bulletin*, 19 (1908).

MacCormac, William, *Notes and Recollections of an Ambulance Surgeon*, J.A. Churchill, 1871.

Maillard, Firmin, *Les Publications de la rue pendant le siège et la Commune*, Auguste Aubry, 1874.

Maitron, J. (ed.), *Henri Messager, lettres de déportation, 1871–1876*, Le Sycomore, 1979.

Malon, B., *La Troisième Défaite du prolétariat français*, Neuchâtel, Guillaume, 1871.

Marchal, Charles Jacob (de Calvi), *La Guerre de 1870, formule du Communalisme*, Pau, Imprimerie Véronèse, March 1871.

Martinier, A., *Corps auxiliaires créés pendant la guerre 1870–1871*, vol. 1, *Garde Nationale Mobile*, vol. 2, *Garde Nationale Mobilisée*, Edmond Dubois, 1896–7.

Maurin, Dr A., *L'Humaniste, les cent jours de l'Algérie*, Algiers, Typographie de l'Association Ouvrière, 1871.

Maury, Émile, *Mes souvenirs sur les évènements des années 1870–1871*, ed. Alain Dalotel, La Boutique de l'Histoire, 1999.

Meffray, Col. Comte de, *Les Fautes de la Défense de Paris*, Verboeckhoven, A. Lacroix, 1871.

Messager, Henri, *Henri Messager, lettres de déportaion, 1871–1876*, Jean Maitron (ed.), Le Sycomore, 1979.

Michel, Louise, *La Commune, Histoire et Souvenirs*, 2 vols, Maspéro, 1970.

Michiels, Alfred, *Histoire de la guerre franco-prussienne et de ses origines*, Alphonse Picard, 1871.

Middleton, Robert, *Garibaldi, ses opérations à l'armée des Vosges*, Garnier Frères, 1872, and Brussels, C. and A. Vanderauwera, 1871.

Millière, Jean-Baptiste, *Le 31 octobre. Compte rendu au 208e bataillon de la Garde Nationale par le Commandant Millière*, Paris, Association générale typographique, November 1870.

Moilin, Tony (ed.), *Rapport du Comité Républicain du VIe arrondissement* [club de l'école de médecine, 5 December 1870] reprinted in *Les Révolutions du XIXe siècle*, 10 vols, Paris, EDHIS, 1988, vol. 6, ff. 15, pp. 3–4.

Molinari, G. de, *Les Clubs Rouges pendant le siège de Paris*, Garnier Frères, 1871.

Monod, Henri, *Rapport du comité évangélique auxiliaire de secours pour les soldats blessés ou malades, 1870–1871*, Sandoz and Fichbacher, 1875.

Monod, Mme William, *La Mission des femmes en temps de guerre*, Bellaire, 1870.

——*Les Héroines de la charité, soeur Marthe de Besançon et Miss Florence Nightingale*, Bellaire, 1873.

Moynier, Gustave, 'Notes sur la création d'une institution judiciaire internationale, propre à prévenir et à réprimer les infractions à la convention de Genève', *Bulletin International*, III (1872), pp. 122–34.

——*Notes sur la création d'une institution judiciaire internationale, propre à prévenir et à réprimer les infractions à la Convention de Genève*, Geneva, Comité International, 1872.

——'La Convention de Genève pendant la guerre Franco-Allemande de 1870', *Bulletin International*, IV (1873), pp. 51–104.

——*La Convention de Genève, ou la guerre Franco-Allemande*, Soullier et Wirth, 1873.

——*Les Dix Premières Années de la Croix Rouge, comité international de secours aux blessés militaires*, Geneva, Fick, 1873.

——*La Croix Rouge, son passé, son avenir*, Sandoz et Thuillier, 1882.

——*Essais sur les caractères généraux des lois de la guerre*, Geneva, Eggimann, 1895.

Nass, Lucien, *Le Siège de Paris et la Commune, essais de pathologie historique*, Plon-Nourrit, 1914.

Nass, Lucien and Cabanès, M., *La Névrose révolutionnaire*, Société Française d'Imprimerie, 1906, reprinted A. Michel, 1924.

Nouveau Manuel de la Garde Nationale, règlement du 16 mars 1869, revu et mis en ordre par un officier d'État-Major, adapté pour les Gardes Nationales Mobilisés, Hachette, 1870.

Ollivier, Émile, *The Franco-Prussian War and its Hidden Causes*, Isaac Pitman and Sons, 1913.

Organisation de la Garde Nationale, Librairie Administrative Dupont, 1870.

Pain, A., *Des Divers modes de l'assistance publique*, Baillière, 1865.

Poincaré, Raymond, *Ce que demande la cité*, Hachette, 1912.

Poujoulat, M., *Réponse à la brochure de M. de la Guéronnière*, Charles Douniol, 1861.

Proclamation de la Commune à Narbonne. Compte Rendu Sténographique du procès d'Émile Digeon et de ses 31 coaccusés, n.d., n.p., reprinted in *Les Révolutions du XIXe siècle*, 10 vols, Paris, EDHIS, 1988, vol. 8, ff. 15, pp. 105–11.

Prolès, Charles, *Les Hommes de la révolution de 1871, Raoul Rigault, la préfecture de Police sous la Commune, les otages*, Chamuel, 1898.

Rapport présenté par le chef de la division administrative générale et départementale à M. Jules Cazot, secrétaire délégué du ministère de l'intérieur, Organisation des gardes nationales mobilisés, Bordeaux, Émile Crugy, 1871.

Razoua, E., *Petit manuel du Garde Nationale républicain*, Chevalier, 1870 (September).

Richard, Albert, *Aux Français : simples appréciations d'un révolutionnaire*, Lyons, December 1870, reproduced in *Les Révolutions du XIXe siècle*, 10 vols, Paris, EDHIS, vol. 10, *Affiches feuilles volantes, documents divers*, 1988.

Rinn, L., *Histoire de l'insurrection de 1871 en Algérie*, n.p., Algiers, 1891, AOM, 3XI Rinn papers.

Robin, Colonel, *L'Insurrection de la Grande Kabylie en 1871*, Henri Charles Lavauzelle, 1900.

Roche, Charles, *La Rue Grolée*, Lyons, Lepagnez, s.d., 1890.

Rochethulon, Le Marquis de la, *Du Rôle de la garde nationale et de l'armée de Paris dans les préparatifs de l'insurrection du 18 mars, rapport spécial fait à la commission d'enquête*, Léon Techener, 1872.

Rossel, Louis Nathaniel, *Mémoires et correspondance de Louis Rossel*, preface by Victor Margueritte with a biography by Isabella Rossel, P.V. Stock, 1908.

Rothan, Gustave, *Souvenirs diplomatiques, l'affaire du Luxembourg, le prélude de la guerre de 1870*, Calmann-Lévy, 1882.

Roussel, Ch., 'La Justice en Algérie, les tribunaux indigènes', *Revue des Deux Mondes*, 1 August 1876, reprinted Bruno Étienne (ed.), *Algérie 1830–1962*, Maisonneuve and Larose Valmonde, 1999, 290–309.

Saint-Edme, Ernest, *La Science pendant le siège de Paris*, Dentu, 1871.

Sarrepont, Major H. de, *Le Bombardement de Paris par les prussiens en janvier 1871*, Firmin Didot Frères, 1872.

Ségur, Louis Philippe Antoine Charles de, *Les Marchés de la guerre à Lyon et à l'armée de Garibaldi*, H. Plon, 1873.

Simon, Jules, *L'Ouvrière*, [1861] St Pierre de Salerne, G. Montfort, 1977.

——*Souvenirs du 4 Septembre, origine et chute du Second Empire*, Calmann-Lévy, 1876.

——*Dieu, Patrie, Liberté*, Calmann-Lévy, 1883.

Sorel, Albert, *Histoire diplomatique de la guerre franco-allemande*, 2 vols, H. Plon, 1875.

Sterlin, Abbé, *Souvenirs de la campagne 1870–1871*, Plainville, 1871.

Stoffel, Baron Eugène, *Rapports militaires écrits de Berlin*, Garnier Frères, 1871.

Stusi, *L'Invasion, le siège et la Commune*, n.p., 1901.

Sutter-Laumann, *Histoire d'un trente sous (1870–1871)*, Paris, Albert Savine, 1891.

Testut, Oscar, *L'Internationale*, E. Lachaud, 1871.

Thiebault, Edmond, *Riciotti Garibaldi et la 4ème brigade, récit de la campagne de 1870–1*, Godet Jeune, 1872.

Thiers, Adolphe, *De la propriété*, Paulin, L'Heureux, 1848.

——*Discours de M.A. Thiers, le 24 mai 1873*, Paris, Degorce-Cadot, 1873.

——*Occupation et Libération du territoire, 1871–1873, correspondances*, 2 vols, Calmann-Lévy, 1903.

Tissier, Albert, *De l'Application du décret du 24 octobre 1870 sur les israélites indigènes de l'Algérie*, Algiers, Adolphe Jourdan, 1891.

Trailles, P. and H. de, *Les Femmes en France pendant la guerre et les deux sièges de Paris*, F. Polo Libraire, 1872.

Trochu, L.J., *L'Armée française en 1867*, Amyot, 1867.

Troisième procès de l'Association Internationale des travailleurs à Paris, Les grands procès politiques, Paris, Armand le Chevalier, 1870.

Un avocat, *Le Drame de Lyon, 20 Decembre 1870 – assassinat du commandant Arnaud*, Lyons, P.N. Josserand, March 1871.

Un bourgeois républicain, *Histoire de l'internationale (1862–1872)*, Londres–Paris–Bruxelles, Combe et Vande Weghe, 1873.

Un Lyonnais, *Le candidat Barodet, sa vie, ses actes politiques et administratifs*, Paris, n.p., 1873.

Vallès, Jules, *L'Insurgé*, Maxipoche, 1998.

——*Oeuvres complètes: Souvenirs d'un étudiant pauvre, le candidat des pauvres, lettre à Jules Mirès*, Éditeurs Français Réunis, 1972.

Verlet, Henri, *Le Peuple et la Révolution, l'Athéisme et l'être suprême, la renaissance 1869–1870*, n.p., 1869.

Vésinier, P., *Histoire de la Commune de Paris*, London, 1871.

Veuillot, Louis, *Paris pendant les deux sièges*, Victor Palmé, 1871, 2 vols, 1872.

—— *Oeuvres complètes*, 23 vols, second série, correspondance, Lethielleux, 1932.

Vincent, Abbot, *Éphéméride de Frazé et mes impressions pendant la guerre franco-prussienne et la Commune de Paris*, ed. Abbot Roland Lefèvre, Bibliothèque diocésaine de Chartres, 1980.

Vizetelly, Ernest, *My Adventures in the Commune*, London, Chatto and Windus, 1914.

Vuillaume, Maxime, Bellenger, H. and de Marancour, L., *Hommes et choses du temps de la Commune*, Geneva, 1871.

Wauthoz, H.A., *Les Ambulances et les ambulanciers à travers les siècles*, Brussels, Lebègue, 1872.

Zola, Émile, *La Débâcle*, La Pleïade, reprinted 1990.

Books and articles written since 1918

Accampo, Elinor A., Fuchs, Rachel G. and Stewart, Mary Lynn, *Gender and the Politics of Social Reform in France, 1870–1914*, Johns Hopkins University Press, 1995.

Adriance, T.J., *The Last Gaiter Button: A Study of the Mobilisation and Concentration of the French Army in the War of 1870*, Westport, Greenwood Press, 1987.

Agulhon, Maurice, Désert, Gabriel and Specklin, Robert, *Histoire de la France rurale*, vol. 3, Le Seuil, 1976.

——*Marianne au pouvoir, l'imagerie et la symbolique républicaines de 1880 à 1914*, Flammarion, 1989.

Aisenberg, Andrew R., *Contagion: Disease, Government and the 'Social Question' in Nineteenth-Century France*, Stanford University Press, 1999.

Aldrich, Robert, *Greater France: A History of French Overseas Expansion*, Macmillan, 1996.

Aminzade, R., *Ballots and Barricades: Class Formation and Republican Politics in France, 1830–1871*, Princeton University Press, 1993.

Anceau, Éric, *Dictionnaire des députés du Second Empire*, Presses Universitaires de Rennes, 1999.

Anderson, Benedict, *Imagined Communities*, Verso, 2nd edn, 1991.

Anderson, R.D., *Education in France, 1848–1870*, Oxford, Clarendon Press, 1975.

Andrieux, Louis, *À Travers la République*, Payot, 1926.

Ansky, Michel, *Les Juifs d'Algérie du décret Crémieux à la libération*, Éditions du Centre, 1950.

Arnaud, Pierre (ed.), *Les Athlètes de la république, gymnastique, sport et idéologie républicaine 1870–1914*, Toulouse, privat, 1987.

——*Le Militaire, l'écolier, le gymnaste: naissance de l'éducation physique en France, 1869–89*, Lyons, Presses Universitaires de Lyon, 1991.

Aron, Raymond, *Penser la guerre, Clausewitz*, 2 vols, Gallimard, 1976.

Assouline, David and Lallaoui, Mehdi, *Un Siècle d'immigrations en France*, 3 vols, vol. 1, *Première période 1851–1918, de la mine au champ de bataille*, Syros, 1996.

Attal, Robert, *Regard sur les juifs d'Algérie*, L'Harmattan, 1996.

Aubert, Jacques (ed.), *L'État et sa police en France (1789–1914)*, Geneva, Librairie Droz, 1979.

Audoin-Rouzeau, Stéphane, *1870, la France dans la guerre*, Armand Colin, 1989.

Auspitz, Katherine, *The Radical Bourgeoisie: The 'Ligue de l'Enseignement' and the Origins of the Third Republic, 1866–1885*, Cambridge University Press, 1982.

Ayoun, R., 'Le Décret Crémieux et l'insurrection de 1871 en Algérie', *Revue d'Histoire Moderne et Contemporaine*, XXXV (January–March 1988), pp. 61–87.

Badinter, Robert, *La Prison républicaine (1871–1914)*, Fayard, 1992.

Baker, Alan R.H., *Fraternity among the French Peasantry: Sociability and Voluntary Associations in the Loire Valley, 1815–1914*, Cambridge University Press, 1999.

Balibar, Étienne, *Droit de Cité*, Éditions de l'Aube, 1998.

Baranger, Denis, *Parlementarisme des origines*, Presses Universitaires de France, 1999.

Bard, Christine, *Les Filles de Marianne, histoire des féminismes, 1914–1940*, Fayard, 1995.

Barker, Nancy Nichols, 'Napoleon III and the Hohenzollern candidacy for the Spanish throne', *The Historian*, 29 (1967), pp. 421–50.

——*The French Experience in Mexico, 1821–1861: A History of Constant Misunderstanding*, Chapel Hill (NC), University of North Carolina Press, 1979.

Barrows, Susanna, *Distorting Mirrors: Visions of the Crowd in Late Nineteenth-Century France*, New Haven, Yale University Press, 1981.

Barry, David, 'Hermance Leguillon (1812–1882): the diversity of French feminism in the nineteenth century', *French History*, 13 (1999), pp. 381–416.

——'Community, tradition and memory among rebel working-class women of Paris, 1830, 1848, 1871', *European Review of History/Revue Européenne d'histoire*, 7 (2000) 2, pp. 261–76.

Barthélémy, Joseph, *Le Gouvernement de la France, tableau des institutions politiques, administratives et judiciaires de la France*, Payot, 1939.

Basdevant-Gaudemet, Brigitte, *La Commission de décentralisation de 1870: contribution à l'étude de la décentralisation en France au XIXe siècle*, Presses Universitaires de France, 1973.

Bassford, Christopher, *Clausewitz in English: The Reception of Clausewitz in Britain and America, 1815–1845*, Oxford University Press, 1994.

Bayard, Françoise and Cayez, Pierre (eds), *Histoire de Lyon du XVIe siècle à nos jours*, Roanne, Howarth, 1987.

Baycroft, Timothy, 'Changing identities in the Franco-Belgian borderland in the nineteenth and the twentieth centuries', *French History*, 13 (1999), pp. 417–38.

Beck, Thomas D. and Beck, Martha W., *French Notables: Reflections of Industrialization and Regionalism*, New York, Peter Lang, 1987.

Becker, Jean-Jacques, *The Great War and the French People*, Leamington Spa, Berg, 1985.

Bellet, Roger, *Jules Vallès*, Fayard, 1995.

Ben Amos, Avner, 'Molding the national memory: the state funerals of the Third Republic', unpublished thesis, Berkeley, 1988.

Benoit, Bruno, 'Relecture des violences collectives lyonnaises du dix-neuvième siècle', *Revue Historique*, 606 (1998), pp. 255–86.

Bercé, Yves-Marie, *Révoltes et révolutions dans l'Europe moderne xvie–xviiie siècles*, PUF, 1980.

Bernard-Griffiths, M. and Viallaneix, Paul (eds), *Edgar Quinet, ce juif errant*, Clermont Ferrand University Press, 1978.

Berstein, Serge, *Édouard Herriot, ou la république en personne*, Presses de la fondation nationale des sciences politiques, 1985.

Birnbaum, Pierre, *'La France aux français', histoire des haines nationalistes*, Editions du Seuil, 1993.

——(ed.), *La France de l'Affaire Dreyfus*, Gallimard, 1994.

—— *Le Moment antisémite, un tour de France en 1898*, Fayard, 1998.

Bled, Jean-Paul, *Les Lys en exil, ou la seconde mort de l'Ancien Régime*, Fayard, 1992.

Bluche, Frédéric (ed.), *Le Prince, le peuple et le droit, autour des plébisicites de 1851 et 1852*, Presses Universitaires de France, Paris, 2000.

——*Septembre 1792, logiques d'un massacre*, Robert Laffont, 1986.

Bonhomme, Éric, 'Bordeaux et la Défense Nationale', *Annales du Midi*, 223 (1998), pp. 319–42.

Boutry, Philippe, 'Marie la grande consolatrice de la France au XIXe siècle', *L'Histoire*, 50 (1982).

Bowlan, J., 'Polygamists need not apply: becoming a French citizen in colonial Algeria, 1918–1938', *Proceedings of the Annual Meeting of the Western Society for French History*, 24 (1997), pp. 110–19.

Braudel, F. and Labrousse, E., *Histoire économique et sociale de la France*, Presses Universitaires de France, 4 vols, Quadrige, 2nd edn, 1993.

Brustein, William, *The Social Origins of Political Regionalism, France 1849–1981*, University of California Press, 1988.

Bulmer, Martin and Rees, Anthony (eds), *Citizenship Today: The Contemporary Relevance of T.H. Marshall*, UCL Press, 1996.

Bur, Michel (ed.), *Histoire de Laon et du Laonnois*, Toulouse, privat, 1987.

Burdeau, François, *Liberté, Libertés locales chéries!*, Paris, Editions Cujas, 1983.

Bury, John Patrick T., *Gambetta and the National Defence: A Republican Dictatorship in France*, Longman, 1936.

——*Gambetta and the Making of the Third Republic*, Longman, 1973.

Bury, John Patrick T. and Tombs, Robert P., *Thiers 1797–1877*, Allen and Unwin, 1986.

Cahm, É., *Société Internationale d'histoire de l'affaire Dreyfus*, 6 (1998–9), pp. 47–9.

Caron, Jeanne, *Le Sillon et la Démocratie Chrétienne 1894–1910*, H. Plon, 1967.

Carrot, Georges, 'La Garde Nationale 1789–1871, une institution de la nation', thèse de doctorat de 3ième cycle, Université de Nice, 1979.

Case, Lynn M., *Franco-Italian Relations, 1860–1865: The Roman Question and the Convention of September*, Philadelphia, University of Pennsylvania Press, 1932.

Casevitz, Jean, *Une Loi manquée : la loi Niel 1866–1868, l'armée française à la veille de la guerre de 1870*, Presses Universitaires de France, 1959.

Cerf, Marcel, *Édouard Moreau, l'âme du comité central de la république*, Éditions Denoël, 1971.

Certeau, Michel de, *L'Écriture de l'histoire*, Gallimard, 1975.

——*Heterologies: Discourse on the Other*, Manchester University Press, 1986.

Certeau, Michel de, Julia, D. and Revel, J., *Une Politique de la langue, la Révolution française et les patois*, Gallimard, 1975.

Certeau, Michel de, Giard, Luce and Mayol, Pierre, *L'Invention du quotidien*, 2 vols, Gallimard, 1994.

César, Marc, *La Commune de Narbonne (mars 1871)*, Perpignan, Presses Universitaires de Perpignan, 1996.

Challener, Richard D., *The French Theory of the Nation in Arms, 1866–1939*, New York, Columbia University Press, 1965.

Chanet, Jean-François, *L'École républicaine et les petites patries*, Aubier, 1996.

Charle, Christophe, *Les Élites de la République, 1880–1900*, Fayard, 1987.

Chatelard, Claude, *Crime et criminalité dans l'arrondissement de St-Étienne au XIXème siècle*, Centre d'études Foréziennes, 1981.

Chevalier, Louis, *Classes laborieuses et classes dangereuses*, Plon, 1958.

Chinon, Yves, *Enquêtes sur les apparitions de la vierge*, Perrin Marme, 1995.

Clancy-Smith, J.A., *Rebel and Saint: Muslim Notables, Populist Protest, Colonial Encounters (Algeria and Tunisia 1800–1914)*, Berkeley, University of California Press, 1984.

Claretie, J., *Paris Assiégé*, reprinted Armand Colin, 1992.

Cole, Alistair and Campbell, Peter, *French Electoral Systems and Elections since 1789*, Aldershot, Gower, 1989.

Conklin, Alice L., 'Colonialism and human rights, a contradiction in terms? The case of France and West Africa, 1895–1914', *American Historical Review*, 103 (1998) 2, pp. 419–43.

Cooper, S.E., 'Pacifism in France, 1889–1914: international peace as a human right', *French Historical Studies*, 17 (1991) 2, pp. 359–86.

Corbin, A., *Archaisme et modernité en Limousin au XIXe siècle, 1845–1880*, 2 vols, Limoges, PULIM [1975], 1998.

——*The Village of Cannibals: Rage and Murder in France, 1870*, Cambridge (Mass.), Harvard University Press, 1992.

——*Les Cloches de la terre, paysage sonore et culture sensible dans les campagnes au XIXe siècle*, Albin Michel, 1994.

——*Time, Desire and Horror: Towards a History of the Senses*, Cambridge, Polity Press, 1997.

—— *Le Monde retrouvé de Louis François Pinagot, sur les traces d'un inconnu, 1798–1876*, Flammarion, 1998.

Corvisier, André (ed.), *Histoire militaire de la France*, 4 vols, vol. 2, Presses Universitaires de France, 1992.

Corvisier, A. and Jacquart, Jean (eds), *De la Guerre réglée à la guerre totale*, vol. 2, 119 congrès des sociétés savantes, CTHS, 1997.

Crossley, Ceri, *French Historians and Romanticism: Thierry, Guizot, the Saint-Simonians, Quinet, Michelet*, Routledge, 1993.

Cubitt, Geoffrey, 'Memory and fidelity in French Legitimism: Crétineau Joly and the Vendée', *Nineteenth Century Contexts, an Interdisciplinary Journal*, 21 (2000) 4, pp. 593–610.

Culpitt, Ian, *Welfare and Citizenship: Beyond the Crisis of the Welfare State?*, Sage, 1992.

Curtis, Sarah, 'Supply and demand: religious schooling in nineteenth century France', *History of Education Quarterly*, 39 (1999) 1, pp. 51–72.

Dalotel, Alain, Faure, Alain and Freiermuth, Jean-Claude, *Aux origines de la Commune : le mouvement des réunions publiques à Paris, 1868–1870*, François Maspéro, 1980.

Dansette, Adrien, *Le Boulangisme*, Artheme Fayard, 1946.

Danziger, Raphael, *Abd al-Qadir and the Algerian Resistance to the French and Internal Consolidation*, New York, Holmes and Meier, 1977.

Dayen, D., *Martin Nadaud, ouvrier maçon et député, 1815–1898*, Limoges, Lucien Souny, 1998.

Déloye, Yves, *École et citoyenneté. L'individualisme républicain de Ferry à Vichy : controverses*, Presses de Sciences Po, 1994.

Delvin, Judith, *The Superstitious Mind: French Peasants and the Supernatural in the Nineteenth Century*, Yale University Press, 1987.

Denis, Michel, Lagrée, Michel and Veillard, Jean-Yves, *L'Affaire Dreyfus et l'opinion publique*, Presses Universitaires de Rennes, 1995.

Digeon, Claude, *La Crise Allemande de la pensée française*, Presses Universitaires de France, 1959.

Disjkra, Bram, *Idols of Perversity: Fantasies of Feminine Evil in Fin-de-Siècle Culture*, Oxford University Press, 1986.

Dommanget, Maurice Auguste, *Blanqui au début de la Troisième République, 1871–1880, dernière prison et ultimes combats*, Moraton, 1973.

Duchesne, Sophie, *Citoyenneté à la française*, Presses de Sciences Po, 1997.

Dugdale, E.T.S (ed.), *German Diplomatic Documents, 1871–1914*, 4 vols, Methuen, 1928.

Dulieu, Louis, *La Médecine à Montpellier*, 4 vols, Avignon, 1986.

Dunwoodie, Peter, *Writing French Algeria*, Clarendon Press, Oxford, 1998.

Dupuy, Aimé, *Sedan et l'enseignement de la revanche*, Institut National de Recherche et de Documentation Pédagogique, 1975.

Durand, Pierre, *Louise Michel : la passion*, Messidor, 1987.

Dwork, Deborah, *War is Good for Babies and Other Young Children*, Tavistock, 1987.

Echard, W.E., *Napoleon III and the Concert of Europe*, Baton Rouge, Louisiana State University Press, 1983.

——*Foreign Policy of the Second Empire: A Bibliography*, New York, Greenwood Press, 1988.

Echenberg, Myron, *Colonial Conscripts: The Tirailleurs Sénégalais in French West Africa, 1857–1960*, Portsmouth (NH), Heinemann, London, James Currey, 1991.

Egrat, Madeleine, 'La Boulangerie Parisienne sous le Second Empire', *L'Actualité de l'Histoire*, 14 (1956), pp. 12–29.

Eksteins, Modris, *Rites of Spring: The Great War and the Birth of the Modern Age*, Bantam Press, 1989.

Elias, N., *La Société des individus*, Fayard, 1987, pp. 52–3, 216.

English, Donald, *The Political Uses of Photography in the Third Republic*, Ann Arbor, UMI Research Press, 1984.

Farmer, Paul, *France Reviews its Revolutionary Origins: Social Politics and Historical Opinions in the Third Republic*, New York, Octagon Books [1944], 1973.

Ferguson, Priscilla Parkhurst, *Paris as Revolution: Writing the Nineteenth Century City*, University of California Press, 1994.

Férréol, G., *Intégration, lien social et citoyenneté*, Presses Universitaires du Septentrion, 1998.

Ficquelmat, G. Marie de, 'Les Élections législatives en Creuse de 1869 à 1885', *Mémoires de la Société des Sciences Naturelles et Archéologiques de la Creuse*, 39 (1975–7), pp. 852–73.

Fischer, Fabienne, 'Les Alsaciens et les Lorrains en Algérie avant 1871', *Revue Française d'Histoire d'Outre Mer*, 84 (1997) 317, pp. 57–69.

Ford, Caroline, *Creating the Nation in Provincial France: Religion and Political Identity in Brittany*, Princeton, 1993.

Forrest, Alan and Jones, Peter, *Reshaping France: Town, Country and Region during the French Revolution*, Manchester University Press, 1991.

Förster, Stig and Nagler, Jörg (eds), *On the Road to Total War: The American Civil War and the German Wars of Unification, 1861–1871*, German Historical Institute (Washington D.C.) series, Cambridge University Press, 1997.

Fuchs, Rachel S., *Poor and Pregnant in Paris: Strategies for Survival in the Nineteenth Century*, Rutgers University Press, 1992.

Furet, François, *La Révolution 1770–1880*, 2 vols, Hachette, 1988.

Furlough, Ellen, *Consumer Cooperation in France: The Politics of Consumption, 1834–1930*, Ithaca, Cornell University Press, 1991.

Gadille, Jacques, *La Pensée et l'action politiques des évêques français au début de la Troisième République*, 2 vols, Hachette, 1967.

Gaillard, Jeanne, *Commune de province, Commune de Paris 1870–1871*, Flammarion, Question d'Histoire, 1971.

——*Paris, la ville*, Lille, Université de Lille III, H. Champion, 1976.

Garrigues, Jean, *La République des hommes d'affaires (1870–1900)*, Aubier, 1997.

Gatrell, Peter, *A Whole Empire Walking : Refugees in Russia during World War I*, Bloomington, Indiana University Press, 1999.

Gay, Peter, *The Cultivation of Hatred: The Bourgeois Experience, Victoria to Freud*, New York, HarperCollins, 1994.

Gérard, A., 'Le Thème de la Révolution/religion dans l'historiographie républicaine de Michelet à Mathiez', *Recherches Institutionelles*, 5 (1982), pp. 12–25.

——'Action humanitaire et pouvoir politique : l'engagement des médecins Lillois au XIXe siècle', *Revue du Nord*, 332 (October–December 1999), pp. 817–36.

Gibson, Ralph, 'Hellfire and damnation in nineteenth century France', *Catholic Historical Review*, 74 (1988) 3, pp. 383–402.

Giesberg, Robert I., *The Treaty of Frankfurt: A Study in Diplomatic History, September 1870–September 1873*, Philadelphia, University of Pennsylvania Press, 1966.

Girard, Louis, *Problèmes politiques et constitutionnels du Second Empire*, 2 vols, Paris, CDU, 1964–5.

Girard, Louis, Prost, A. and Gossez, R., *Les Conseils Généraux en 1870 : étude statistique d'un personnel politique*, Presses Universitaires de France, 1967.

Girault, Jacques, *La Commune et Bordeaux (1870–1871), contribution à l'étude du mouvement ouvrier et de l'idéologie républicaine en province au moment de la Commune de Paris*, Éditions Sociales, 1971.

Goguel, François, *Géographie des élections françaises sous la troisième et la quatrieme République*, Cahiers de la Fondation Nationale des Sciences Politiques, 159, Armand Colin, 1970.

Gooch, R.K., *The French Parliamentary Committee System*, n.p., Archon Books [1935], 1969.

Gordon, Felicia, *The Integral Feminist: Madelein Pelletier, 1874–1939*, Polity Press, 1990.

Gouault, Jacques, *Comment la France est devenue Républicaine : Les élections générales et partielles à l'assemblée Nationale de 1870–1871*, Cahiers de la Fondation Nationale des Sciences Politiques, 62, Armand Colin, 1954.

Gould, Roger V., *Insurgent Identities: Class, Community and Protest in Paris from 1848 to the Commune*, Chicago University Press, 1995.

Greenberg, Louis, *Sisters of Liberty: Marseille, Lyon, Paris and the Reaction to the Centralized State*, Cambridge (Mass.), Harvard University Press, 1971.

Grévy, Jérôme, *La République des opportunistes*, Perrin, 1998.

Grew, Raymond and Harrigan, Patrick J., *School, State and Society: The Growth of Elementary Schooling in Nineteenth-Century France – A Quantitative Analysis*, Ann Arbor, University of Michigan Press, 1991.

Grubb, Alan, *The Politics of Pessimism: Albert de Broglie and Conservative Politics in the Early Third Republic*, Newark, University of Delaware Press, 1996.

Guedalla, Philip, *The Two Marshals: Bazaine, Pétain*, Hodder and Stoughton, 1943.

Guildea, Robert, *Education in Provincial France, 1800–1914, A Study of Three Departments*, Clarendon Press, 1983.

Gullickson, Gay, *Unruly Women of Paris: Images of the Commune*, Ithaca, Cornell University Press, 1996.

Guthrie, Christopher E., 'The battle for the Third Republic in the arrondissement of Narbonne', *French History*, 2 (1988) 1, pp. 45–73.

——'Émile Digeon and socialism in the Narbonnais', *French History*, 12 (1998) 1, pp. 43–67.

Haine, W. Scott, *The World of the Paris Café: Sociability among the French Working Class*, Johns Hopkins University Press, 1996.

Halay, T., *Le Mont-de-Piété des origines à nos jours*, L'Harmattan, 1994.

Halévy, Daniel, *Visites aux paysans du centre*, Librairie Grasset, 1921.

Hamon, Léo (ed.), *Les Opportunistes : Les débuts de la République aux républicains*, Maison des Sciences de l'Homme, 1991.

——(ed.), *Les Républicains sous le Second Empire*, Maison des Sciences de l'Homme, 1993.

Hanagan, Michael P., *Nascent Proletarians: Class Formation in Post-Revolutionary France*, Basil Blackwell, 1989.

Hansen, Philip, *Hannah Arendt: Politics, History and Citizenship*, Cambridge, Polity, 1993.

Harbaoui, Chaâbane, 'Le Statut rhétorique du "Peuple" et de la "Révolution" dans le discours de Michelet', in Christian Croisille and Jean Ehrard (eds), *La Légende de la Révolution*, Clermont Ferrand University Press, 1988, pp. 379–92.

Harris, Ruth, ' "The child of the barbarian": rape, race and nationalism in France during the First World War', *Past and Present*, 141 (1993), pp. 170–206.

—— *Lourdes: Body and Spirit in the Secular Age*, Harmondsworth, Allen Lane, 1999.

Harrison, Carol E., *The Bourgeois Citizen in Nineteenth-Century France: Gender, Sociability, and the Uses of Emulation*, Oxford University Press, 1999.

Hartley, Dean, *Welfare, Law and Citizenship*, Harvester Wheatsheaf, 1996.

Harvey, David, *Consciousness and the Urban Experience: Studies in the History and Theory of Capitalist Urbanization*, Oxford, Blackwell, 1985.

Hatzfeld, Henri, *Du Paupérisme à la sécurité sociale, 1850–1940*, Armand Colin, 1971.

Hause, Steven C., *Hubertine Auclert: The French Suffragette*, Yale University Press, 1987.

Hazareesingh, Sudhir, *From Subject to Citizen: The Second Empire and the Emergence of French Democracy*, Princeton, 1998.

——'The Société d'Instruction Républicaine and the propagation of civic republicanism in provincial and rural France, 1870–1877', *Journal of Modern History*, 71 (1999) 2, pp. 271–307.

Hebey, Pierre, *Alger 1898: la grande vague antijuive*, Paris, Nil Eden, 1996.

Heywood, Colin, *Childhood in Nineteenth-Century France: Work, Health and Education among the 'Classes Populaires'*, Cambridge University Press, 1988.

Higgs, David, *Nobles in Nineteenth-Century France: The Practice of Inegalitarianism*, Johns Hopkins University Press, 1987.

Holmes, Richard, *Road to Sedan: The French Army 1866–1870*, Royal Historical Society, 1984.

Horne, John and Kramer, Alan, 'German "atrocities" and Franco-German opinion, 1914: the evidence of German soldiers' diaries', *The Journal of Modern History*, 66 (1994) 1, pp. 1–33.

Howard, Michael, *The Franco-Prussian War: the German Invasion of France, 1870–1871*, New York, Dorset Press, 1961, rep. 1990.

Huard, Raymond, *La Préhistoire des partis, le mouvement républicain en bas languedoc*, Presses de Sciences Po, 1982.

——*La Naissance des partis politiques en France*, Presses de Sciences Po, 1996.

Hufton, O.H., *Women and the Limits of Citizenship in the French Revolution*, University of Toronto Press, 1992.

Hutchinson, John F., 'Rethinking the origins of the Red Cross', *Bulletin of the History of Medicine*, 63 (1989), pp. 557–78.

——*Champions of Charity: War and the Rise of the Red Cross*, Oxford, Westview Press, 1996.

Hutton, Patrick H., *The Cult of the Revolutionary Tradition: The Blanquists in French Politics, 1864–1893*, Berkeley, University of California Press, 1981.

Hyslop, Beatrice Fry, *French Nationalism in 1789 according to the General Cahiers*, New York, Octagon Books, 1968.

Ichilov, Orit, *Citizenship and Citizenship Education in a Changing World*, Woburn, 1998.

Igersheim, François, *Politique et Administration dans le Bas-Rhin (1848–1870)*, Presses Universitaires de Strasbourg, 1993.

Irvine, William D., *The Boulanger Affair Reconsidered: Royalism, Boulangism and the Origins of the Radical Right in France*, Oxford University Press, 1989.

Jauffret, Jean-Charles, *Parlement, gouvernement, commandement: l'armée de métier sous la IIIème, 1871–1914*, 2 vols, SAT, 1987.

Jenkins, Brian, *Nationalism in France: Class and Nation since 1789*, Routledge, 1990.

Johnson, Martin Philip, 'Citizenship and gender: the *Légion des Fédérés* in the Paris Commune of 1871', *French History*, 8 (1994) 3, pp. 276–95.

——*The Paradise of Association: Political Culture and Popular Organization in the Paris Commune of 1871*, University of Michigan Press, 1996.

——'Enlightening the "misguided brothers of the countryside": republican fraternalism and the Paris Commune of 1871', *French History*, 11 (1997) 4, pp. 411–37.

Joly, Bertrand, *Déroulède : l'inventeur du nationalisme français*, Perrin, 1998.

——'La France et la Revanche, 1871–1914', *Revue d'Histoire Moderne et Contemporaine*, 46 (1999) 2, pp. 325–47.

Jonas, Raymond A., 'Anxiety, identity, and the displacement of violence during the *année terrible*: the Sacred Heart and the diocese of Nantes, 1870–1871', *French Historical Studies*, 21 (1998) 1, pp. 55–76.

Jones, P.M., *Politics and Rural Society: The Southern Massif Central c. 1750–1880*, Cambridge University Press, 1985.

Jones, R.A., 'Monuments as ex-voto, monuments as historiography: the Basilica of Sacré Coeur', *French Historical Studies*, 18 (1993) 2, pp. 482–502.

Jordan, David P., *Transforming Paris: The Life and Labour of Baron Haussmann*, University of Chicago Press, 1995.

Joyce, P., *Visions of the People*, Cambridge University Press, 1991.

Kale, Steven D., 'The monarchy according to the king: the ideological content of the *drapeau blanc*, 1871–3', *French History*, 2 (1988) 4, pp. 399–426.

Kamenka, Eugene, *Paradigm for Revolution? The Paris Commune, 1871–1971*, Canberra, Australian National University Press, 1972.

Kaplan, Robert Elliot, *Forgotten Crisis: The Fin-de-Siècle Crisis of Democracy in France*, Berg, 1995.

Karsten, P., *Law, Soldiers and Combat*, Westport, Greenwood Press, 1978.

Katz, Philip M., *From Appomattox to Montmartre: Americans and the Paris Commune*, Cambridge (Mass.), Harvard University Press, 1998.

Kselman, Thomas A., *Miracles and Prophecies in Nineteenth-Century France*, Rutgers University Press, 1983.

Kudlick, Catherine J., *Cholera in Post-Revolutionary Paris, A Cultural History*, Berkeley, University of California Press, 1996.

Lackey, Scott, 'The Habsburg army and the Franco-Prussian war: the failure to intervene and its consequences', *War in History*, 2 (1995) 2, pp. 151–79.

Langford, Rachael, *Jules Vallès and the Narration of History: Contesting the French Third Republic in the Jacques Vingtras Trilogy*, Bern, Peter Lang, 1999.

Larkin, Maurice, *Religion, Politics and Preferment in France since 1890*, Cambridge University Press, 1995.

Laveau, C.F., 'Les Communards dans les prisons charentaises', *L'Actualité de l'Histoire*, 14 (1956), pp. 30–47.

Lebovics, Herman, *True France: The Wars over Cultural Identity, 1900–1945*, Ithaca, Cornell University Press, 1992.

Lecaillon, Jean-François, *Napoléon III et le Mexique : Les illusions d'un grand dessein*, L'Harmattan, 1994.

Leclère, Bernard and Wright, Vincent, *Les Préfets du Second Empire*, Fondation Nationale des Sciences Politiques, 1973.

Léon, Pierre, *Géographie de la fortune et structures sociales à Lyon au XIXe siècle (1815–1914)*, Centre d'Histoire économique et sociale de la région lyonnaise, 1974.

Lequin, Yves, *Les Ouvriers de la région Lyonnaise (1848–1914) : les intérêts de classe et la République*, Presses Universitaires de Lyon, 1977.

Lerou, Paule and Dartevelle, Raymond, *Pratiques religieuses, mentalités et spiritualités dans l'Europe Révolutionnaire (1770–1820)*, Brepols, 1988.

Lévêque, Pierre, *Histoire des forces politiques en France 1789–1880*, Armand Colin, 1992.

Levillain, Philippe, *Albert de Mun, Catholicisme Français et Catholicisme Romain, du Syllabus au Ralliement*, École Française de Rome, 1983.

Levillain, Philippe and Vigezzi, Brunello (eds), *Opinion Publique et politique extérieure, 1870–1915*, Università di Milano/Collection de l'école française de Rome, 54, 1981.

Levillain, Philippe and Riemenschneider, Reiner (eds), *La Guerre de 1870–1871 et ses conséquences*, Bonn, Bouvier Verlag, 1990.

Lidove, Michel, 'Le Département de la Corrèze et la fondation de la troisième république', *Bulletin de la Société des Lettres, Sciences et Arts de la Corrèze*, 68 (1964), pp. 6–14.

Lidsky, Paul, *Les écrivains contre la Commune*, François Maspéro, 1970.

Locke, Robert R., *French Legitimists and the Politics of Moral Order in the Early Third Republic*, Princeton University Press, 1974.

Lorcin, Patricia M.E., *Imperial Identities: Stereotyping, Prejudice and Race in Colonial Algeria*, I.B. Tauris, 1995.

Lüsebrink, Hans-Jürgen, *Les Troupes coloniales dans la guerre : présences, imaginaires et représentations*, Images et Colonies, BDIC-ACHAC, 1993.

McDougall, Mary Lynn, *After the Insurrections: The Workers Movement in Lyon, 1834–1852*, Columbia University Press, 1973.

Machelon, Jean-Pierre, *La République contre les libertés? Les restrictions aux libertés publiques de 1879 à 1914*, Presses de la Fondation Nationale des Sciences Politiques, 1976.

MacKenzie, John M., *Orientalism, History, Theory and the Arts*, Manchester University Press, 1995.

MacMaster, Neil, *Colonial Migrants and Racism: Algerian in France, 1900–62*, Macmillan, 1997.

McMillan, James F., *Housewife or Harlot: The Place of Women in French Society 1870–1940*, Brighton, Harvester, 1981.

——*France and Women 1789–1914: Gender, Society and Politics*, Routledge, 2000.

McPhee, Peter, 'A reconsideration of the "peasantry" of nineteenth-century France', *Journal of Peasant Studies*, 9 (1979), pp. 5–25.

——*The Politics of Rural Life: Political Mobilization in the French Countryside, 1846–1852*, Oxford, Clarendon Press, 1992.

Magraw, Roger, *Workers and the Bourgeois Republic*, 2 vols, Blackwell, 1992.

Mailhe, G., *Deportations en Nouvelle Calédonie des Communards et des révoltés de la Grande Kabylie (1872–1876)*, L'Harmattan, 1994.

Marais, Jean-Luc, *Histoire du Don en France de 1800 à 1939, dons et legs charitables, pieux et philanthropiques*, Presses Universitaires de Rennes, 1999.

Margadant, Jo Burr, *Madame le Professeur: Women Educators in the Third Republic*, Princeton University Press, 1990.

Margadant, Ted W., 'Tradition and modernity in rural France during the nineteenth century', *Journal of Modern History*, 56 (1984), pp. 667–97.

——*Urban Rivalries in the French Revolution*, Princeton University Press, 1992.

Marichy, Jean-Pierre, *La Deuxième Chambre dans la vie politique Française, depuis 1875*, LGDJ, 1969.

Marion, Olivier and Perrin, Luc, 'La Commune et l'Église', Mémoire de Maîtrise, Université Paris X–XII, 1981.

Martin, Benjamin F., *The Shame of Marianne: Crime and Criminal Justice under the Third Republic*, Baton Rouge, Louisiana State University Press, 1990.

Martin, Jean-François and Rosset, Marie-Françoise, *L'École Primaire dans le Rhône (1815–1940)*, Conseil général du Rhône/Archives départementales, 1997.

Martin, Marie-Madeleine, *Histoire de l'Unité française : l'idée de patrie en France, des origines à nos jours*, Paris, Presses Universitaires de France, 2nd edn, 1982.

Masson, André, 'L'Opinion française et les problèmes coloniaux à la fin du Second Empire', *Revue Française d'histoire d'outre-Mer*, 69 (1962), pp. 366–437.

Maurain, Jean, *La Politique écclesiastique du Second Empire de 1852 à 1869*, Paris, Félix Alcan, 1930.

Mayeur, J.M. (ed.), *Libre Pensée et religion laïque en France, de la fin du Second Empire à la fin de la Troisième République*, Strasbourg, Cerdic Publications, 1980.

Ménager, Bernard, *La Vie politique dans le département du Nord de 1851 à 1877*, 3 vols, Atelier National, reproduction des thèses, Lille III, 1983.

—— *Les Napoléons du Peuple*, Paris, Aubier, 1988.

Mercier d'Erm, Camille Le, *L'Étrange aventure de l'armée de Bretagne, 1870–1871*, Librairie académique Perrin, Armor Diffusion, 1975.

——*Une 'Armée de Chouans' : le drame politique de l'armée de Bretagne (1870–1871)*, Librairie académique Perrin, Armor Diffusion, 1975.

Merriman, John M., *The Agony of the Republic: The Repression of the Left in Revolutionary France, 1848–1851*, Yale University Press, 1978.

——*The Red City: Limoges and the French Nineteenth Century*, Oxford University Press, 1985.

Michaud, S. (ed.), *Flora Tristan, George Sand, Pauline Roland: les femmes et l'invention d'une nouvelle morale, 1830–1848*, 1994.

Miller, Susan Gilson (ed.), *Disorienting Encounters: Travels of a Moroccan Scholar in France in 1845–1846. The Voyage of Muhammad As-Saffar*, University of California Press, 1992.

Mitchell, Allan, 'Crucible of French anti-clericalism: the Conseil Municipal of Paris, 1871–1885', *Francia*, 8 (1980), pp. 395–405.

——*Victors and Vanquished: The German Influence on Army and Church in France after 1870*, Chapel Hill, University of North Carolina Press, 1984.

—— *The Divided Path: The German Influence on Social Reform in France after 1870*, Chapel Hill, University of North Carolina Press, 1991.

Moissonnier, Maurice, *La Première Internationale et la Commune à Lyon*, Éditions sociales, 1972.

Mollenhauer, Daniel, 'À la recherche de la vraie république : quelques jalons pour une histoire du radicalisme des débuts de la Troisième République', *Revue Historique*, 607 (1998), pp. 579–615.

Mollier, Jean-Yves, *Le Scandale de Panama*, Fayard, 1991.

Monsieur Thiers: d'Une république à l'autre, Published, 1998.

Montroy, Jacques Dumont de, *Napoléon III et la réorganisation de l'armée de 1866 à 1870, la loi Niel mutilée du 1 février 1868*, l'auteur, 1996.

Morris, Lydia, *Dangerous Classes: The Underclass and Social Citizenship*, Routledge, 1994.

Moses, Claire Goldberg, *French Feminism in the Nineteenth Century*, Albany, State University of New York, 1984.

Mosher, R., Kenny, R.A., Jr, and Garrod, A., *Preparing for Citizenship: Teaching Youth to Live Democratically*, Westport, Praeger, 1995.

Mosse, George L., *Fallen Soldiers: Reshaping the Memory of the World Wars*, Oxford University Press, 1990.

Moulin, Annie, *Peasantry and Society in France since 1789*, Cambridge University Press, 1988.

Murard, Lion and Zylberman, Patrick, *L'Hygiène dans la République : la santé publique en France ou l'utopie contrariée, 1870–1918*, Paris, 1997.

Nicolet, Claude, *L'Idée républicaine en France, essai d'histoire critique*, Gallimard, 1982.

Noël, Bernard, *Dictionnaire de la Commune*, Fernand Hozon, 1971.

Noiriel, Gérard, *Le Creuset français : histoire de l'immigration, XIXe–XXe siècle*, Éditions du Seuil, 1988.

Nora, Pierre (ed.), *Realms of Memory*, 3 vols, Columbia University Press, 1996–8.

Nord, Philip G., 'The Party of Conciliation and the Paris Commune', *French Historical Studies*, 15 (1987) 1, pp. 1–35.

——*The Republican Moment: Struggles for Democracy in Nineteenth Century France*, Cambridge (Mass.), Harvard University Press, 1995.

Nye, Robert, *Crime, Madness and Politics in Modern France: The Medical Concept of National Decline*, Princeton University Press, 1984.

——*Masculinity and Male Codes of Honour in Modern France*, New York, Oxford University Press, 1993.

O'Brien, Patricia, *The Promise of Punishment: Prisons in Nineteenth-Century France*, Princeton University Press, 1982.

Oldfield, Adrian, *Citizenship and Community: Civic Republicanism and the Modern World*, Routledge, 1990.

Olivesi, A., *La Commune de 1871 à Marseille et ses origines*, Rivière, 1950.

Outram, Dorinda, *The Body and the French Revolution*, New Haven (Conn.), Yale University Press, 1989.

Ozouf, Mona, *L'École, l'église et la république (1871–1914)*, Cana/Jean Offredo, 1982.

——*Les Mots des femmes, essai sur la singularité française*, Gallimard, 1999.

Panayi, Panikos, *The Enemy in our Midst: Germans in Britain during the First World War*, Oxford, Berg, 1991.

Paret, Peter, *Clausewitz and the State, the Man, His Theories and His Times*, Princeton University Press [1976], 1985.

Parry, D.L.L., 'Friends in high places: the favour sought by the Freemasons of Orléans', *French History*, 12 (1998) 2, pp. 195–212.

Pédroncini, Guy (ed.), *La Défense sous la troisième république*, vol 1, *Vaincre la défaite, 1872–1881*, SAT, 1989.

Pelissier, Pierre, *Émile Girardin, prince de la presse*, Denoël, 1985.

Perkins, Kenneth J., *Qadis, Captains and Colons: French Military Administration in the Colonial Maghrib, 1844–1934*, New York, Africana Publishing, 1981.

Pérouas, Louis, *Histoire de Limoges*, Toulouse, privat, 1989.

Pérouas, Louis and D'Hollander, Paul, *La Révolution Française, une rupture dans le christianisme? Le cas du Limousin (1775–1822)*, Naves, Les Monédières, 1988.

Perrot, Michelle, *Les Ouvriers en grève, France 1871–1890*, Mouton, 1974.

Pick, Daniel, *War Machine: The Rationalisation of Slaughter in the Modern Age*, New Haven, Yale University Press, 1993.

Pinkney, David H., *Napoleon III and the Rebuilding of Paris*, Princeton University Press, 1958.

Ploux, François, 'L'Imaginaire social et politique de la rumeur dans la France du XIXe siècle (1815–1870)', *Revue Historique*, 614 (April/June 2000), pp. 395–434.

Plumridge, J.H., *Hospital Ships and Ambulance Trains*, Seeley, Service, 1975.

Poovey, Mary, *Making a Social Body: British Cultural Formation, 1830–1864*, University of Chicago Press, 1995.

Porter, Roy (ed.), *Rewriting the Self: Histories from the Renaissance to the Present*, Routledge, 1997.

Praz, Mario, *La Chair, la mort et le diable dans la littérature du XIXe siècle, le romantisme noir*, Gallimard [1966], 1998.

Rancière, Jacques, *Les Noms de l'Histoire*, Le Seuil, 1992.

Raynette-Gloud, Odile, 'L'Armée dans la bataille sociale : maintien de l'ordre et grèves ouvrières dans le nord de la France (1871–1906)', *Le Mouvement Social*, 179 (1997), pp. 93–104.

Recham, Balkacem, *Les Musulmans Algériens dans l'armée française (1919–1945)*, L'Harmattan, 1996.

Rémond, René, *Les Droite en France*, Aubier, 1982.

Renan, E., *Qu'est-ce qu'une nation?*, Imprimerie Nationale, 1996, p. 186.

Renneville, Marc, *La Médecine du crime : essai sur l'émergence d'un regard médical sur la criminalité en France (1785–1885)*, Villeneuve d'Asq, Presses Universitaires du Septentrion, 1998, 2 vols, 1996.

Robert, Frédéric, *La Marseillaise*, Les nouvelles éditions du pavillon, Imprimerie Nationale, 1989.

Roberts, J.M.G., *The Paris Commune from the Right*, *English Historical Review*, Supplement 6, Longman, 1973.

Robertson, R., 'Civilization and the civilizing process: Elias, globalization and analytic synthesis', in *Theory, Culture and Society*, 9 (1992) 1, pp. 211–27.

Roche, Maurice, *Rethinking Citizenship: Welfare, Ideology and Change in Modern Society*, Cambridge, Polity Press, 1992.

Rollet, Henri, *L'Action sociale des catholiques en France 1871–1914*, Desclée de Brouwer, 1958.

Rosanvallon, Pierre, *L'État en France de 1789 à nos jours*, Le Seuil, 1990.

——*Le Sacre du citoyen, histoire du suffrage universel en France*, Gallimard, 1992.

Roth, François, *La Guerre de 1870*, Fayard, 1990.

Rothney, J., *Bonapartism after Sedan*, Ithaca, Cornell University Press, 1969.

Rougerie, Jacques, *Paris Libre*, Le Seuil, 1971.

——*Procès des communards*, Archives Julliard, 1976.

Roux, B. Le, *Louis Veuillot, un homme, un combat*, published by the author, 1984.

Royer, Jean-Pierre, Martinage, Renée and Lecocq, Pierre, *Juges et notables au XIXe siècle*, Presses Universitaires de France, 1982.

Rude, Fernand, *L'insurrection Lyonnaise de novembre 1832. Le mouvement ouvrier à Lyon de 1827–1832*, Anthropos, Paris, 1969.

——*C'est nous les Canuts*, François Maspéro, 1977.

——'Bakounine en 1870–1871', *Cahiers d'histoire*, 24 (1979) 4, pp. 75–83.

Rudelle, Odile, *La République absolue, aux origines de l'instabilité constitutionelle de la France républicaine 1870–1889*, Publications de la Sorbonne, 1982.

—— (ed.) *Jules Ferry : La république des citoyens*, 2 vols, Imprimerie Nationale, 1996.

Sahlins, Peter, *Boundaries: The Making of France and Spain in the Pyrenees*, Berkeley, University of California Press, 1989.

Sainte Marie, A., 'La Province d'Alger vers 1870, l'établissement du Douar Commun et la fixation de la nature de la propriété dans le cadre du Senatus Consulte du 22 avril 1863', *Revue de l'Occident Musulman et de la méditerranée*, 9 (1971), pp. 37–61.

Sanchez, Gonzalo J., 'The challenge of right-wing caricature journals: from the Commune amnesty campaign to the end of censorship, 1878–1881', *French History*, 10 (1996) 4, pp. 451–89.

Schiller, Francis, *Paul Broca, explorateur du cerveau*, Berkeley, University of California Press, 1979, French trans. Éditions Odile Jacob, 1990.

Schroeder, H.J. (ed.), *Disciplinary Decrees of the General Councils*, Herder, 1937.

Schulkind, Eugene, *The Paris Commune of 1871: The View from the Left*, New York, Grove Press, 1974.

——'Socialist women in the 1871 Paris Commune', *Past and Present*, 106 (1985), pp. 124–63.

Schwartz, Vanessa R., *Spectacular Realities: Early Mass Culture in Fin-de-siècle Paris*, University of California Press, 1998.

Schwarzfuchs, Simon, *Les Juifs d'Algérie et la France (1830–1855)*, Centre de recherches sur les Juifs d'Afrique du Nord, Jerusalem, Ben Zvi, 1981.

Scott, John, *Poverty and Wealth: Citizenship, Deprivation and Privilege*, Longman, 1994.

Scott, J.W., *Only Paradoxes to Offer: French Feminists and the Rights of Man*, Cambridge (Mass.), Harvard University Press, 1996.

Sedgwick, Alexander, *The Ralliement in French Politics, 1890–1898*, Harvard University Press, 1965, pp. 7–55.

Semmel, Stuart, 'Reading the tangible past: British tourism, collecting and memory after Waterloo', *Representations*, 69 (2000), pp. 9–37.

Shafer, D.A., '*Plus que des ambulancières* : women in articulation and defence of their ideals during the Paris Commune (1871)', *French History* (1993), pp. 85–101.

Shafir, Gershon (ed.), *The Citizenship Debates, a Reader*, University of Minnesota Press, 1998.

Shapiro, Ann-Louise, *Breaking the Codes: Female Criminality in Fin-de-siècle Paris*, Stanford, Stanford University Press, 1996.

Siegfried, André, *France: A Study in Nationality*, New Haven, Yale University Press, 1930.

Silvera, Alain, *Daniel Halévy and His Times: A Gentleman-Commoner in the Third Republic*, Cornell University Press, 1966.

Silverman, Dan P., *Reluctant Union: Alsace Lorraine and Imperial Germany, 1871–1918*, Pennsylvania State University Press, 1972.

Sirinelli, Jean François (ed.), *Histoire des droites en France*, 3 vols, Gallimard, 1992.

Smith, Timothy B., 'Republicans, Catholics and Social Reform: Lyon, 1870–1920', *French History*, 12 (1998) 3, pp. 246–75.

——'The plight of the able-bodied poor and the unemployed in urban France, 1880–1914', *European History Quarterly*, 30 (2000) 2, pp. 147–84.

Smith, W.A., 'Napoléon III and the Spanish Revolution of 1868', *Journal of Modern History* (1953), pp. 214–24.

Sowerwine, Charles, *Sisters or Citizens? Women and Socialism since 1876*, Cambridge University Press, 1982.

Stedman-Jones, Gareth, *Languages of Class: Studies in English Working-Class History, 1832–1982*, Cambridge University Press, 1983.

Stewart-McDougall, Mary Lynn, *The Artisan Republic: Revolution, Reaction and Resistance in Lyon, 1848–1851*, McGill Queen's, Alan Sutton, 1984.

Stone, Judith F., *The Search for Social Peace: Reform Legislation in France, 1890–1914*, State University of New York Press, Albany, 1985.

——*Sons of the Revolution: Radical Democrats in France 1862–1914*, Louisiana State University Press, 1996.

Suleiman, Ezra N., *Private Power and Centralization in France: The Notaires and the State*, Princeton University Press, 1987.

Taithe, Bertrand, 'The Red Cross flag in the Franco-Prussian war: civilians, humanitarians and war in the "modern" age', in R. Cooter, S. Sturdy and M. Harrison (eds), *Medicine, War and Modernity*, Sutton, 1998, pp. 22–47.

——*Defeated Flesh: Welfare, Warfare and the Making of Modern France*, Manchester University Press, 1999, Rowman and Littlefield, 2000.

——'De la supériorité de l'Angleterre sur la France? Regards sur la France dans la crise de 1870 et naissance de l'humanitaire', in K. de Queiros Mattoso (ed.), *L'Angleterre et le Monde, XVIIIe–XXe siècle, l'histoire entre l'économique et l'imaginaire, hommage à François Crouzet*, Paris, L'Harmattan, 1999, pp. 311–39.

Taithe, B. and Thornton, T. (eds), *Propaganda: Political Rhetoric and Identity, 1300–2000*, Sutton, 1999.

Talmy, Robert, *Le Syndicalisme chrétien en France (1871–1930), Difficultés et controverses*, Bloud et Gay, 1966.

Tartakowsky, Danielle, *Les Manifestations de rue en France, 1918–1968*, Publications de la Sorbonne, 1997.

——*Le Pouvoir est dans la rue: crises politiques et manifestations en France*, Aubier, 1998.

Tate, Trudi, *Modernism, History and the First World War*, Manchester University Press, 1998.

Taylor, Lucy, 'Textbook citizens: education for democracy and political culture in El Salvador', *Democratization*, 6 (1999) 3, pp. 62–83.

Temmime, Émile, 'La Politique française à l'égard de la migration Algérienne: le poid de la colonisation', *Le Mouvement Social*, 188 (July 1999), pp. 77–89.

Thériault, Jean-Yvan, 'La Citoyenneté entre narrativité et factualité', *Sociologie et Sociétés*, XXXI (1999) 2, pp. 5–14.

Thody, Philip, *French Caesarism from Napoleon I to Charles de Gaulle*, Macmillan, 1989.

Thomas, Édith, *Les Pétroleuses*, Gallimard, 1963.

—— *Rossel 1844–1871*, Gallimard, 1967.

Thuillier, Guy, *La Bureaucratie en France aux XIXe et XXe siècles*, Economica, 1989.

Tilly, Charles, 'Did the cake of custom break?, in John Merriman (ed.), *Consciousness and Class Experience in Nineteenth Century Europe*, New York, Holmes and Meier, 1979, pp. 17–44.

——(ed.) 'Citizenship, identity and social history', *International Review of Social History*, Supplement 3, 1995.

Tombs, Robert, *The War Against Paris, 1871*, Cambridge University Press, 1981.

——'Prudent rebels: the Second Arrondissement during the Paris Commune of 1871', *French History*, 5 (1991) 4, pp. 393–413.

——(ed.), *Nationhood and Nationalism in France*, HarperCollins, 1991.

——'Les Communeux dans la ville : des analyses récentes à l'étranger', *Le Mouvement Social*, 179 (April–July 1997), pp. 93–104.

Troyansky, David G., 'Monumental politics: national history and local memory in French *Monuments aux Morts* in the Department of Aisne since 1870', *French Historical Studies*, 15 (1987) 1, pp. 121–41.

Vernon, James, *Re-Reading the Constitution*, Cambridge University Press, 1996.

Vernon, Richard, *Citizenship and Order: Studies in French Political Thought*, University of Toronto Press, 1986.

Viallaneix, Paul and Ehrard, Jean (eds), *La Bataille, l'Armée, la Gloire, 1745–1871*, 2 vols, Clermont Ferrand, 1985.

Virolli, M., *For Love of Country: An Essay on Patriotism and Nationalism*, Oxford, Clarendon, 1995.

Vivier, Nadine, *Propriété collective et identité communale, les biens communaux en France, 1750–1914*, Publications de la Sorbonne, 1998.

Vovelle, Michelle, *Religion et Révolution, la déchristianisation de l'an II*, Hachette, 1976.

Wahnich, Sophie, *L'Impossible Citoyen, l'étranger dans le discours de la Révolution française*, Albin Michel, 1997.

Waldinger, Renée, Dawson, Philip and Woloch, Isser (eds), *The French Revolution and the Meaning of Citizenship*, Westport (Conn.), Greenwood Press, 1993.

Walker, David H., *Outrage and Insight: Modern French Writers and the 'Fait Divers'*, Oxford, Berg, 1995.

Wastelle, J.-C., 'Lyon 1873. Joseph Ducros, préfet de l'ordre moral', *L'Histoire*, 12 (1979), pp. 6–13.

Weber, Eugen, *Peasants into Frenchmen: The Modernization of Rural France, 1870–1914*, Stanford University Press, 1976.

Weisz, George, *The Emergence of Modern Universities in France, 1863–1914*, Princeton University Press, 1983.

——*The Medical Mandarins: The French Academy of Medicine in the Nineteenth and Early Twentieth Centuries*, Oxford University Press, 1995.

Wells, Charlotte C., *Law and Citizenship in Early Modern France*, Johns Hopkins University Press, 1995.

White, Patricia, *Civic Virtue and Public Schooling: Educating Citizens for a Democratic Society*, Teachers' College Press, 1996.

Williams, Elizabeth, *The Physical and the Moral: Anthropology, Physiology and Philosophical Medicine in France, 1750–1850*, Cambridge, 1994.

Williams, Roger L., *The French Revolution of 1870–1871*, London, Weidenfeld and Nicolson, 1969.

——*Manners and Murders in the World of Louis Napoleon*, University of Washington Press, 1975.

Winock, M., *Édouard Drumont et Cie, antisémitisme et fascisme en France*, Le Seuil, 1982.

Winter, J., *Sites of Memory, Sites of Mourning: The Great War in European Cultural History*, Cambridge University Press, 1995.

Woloch, Isser, *The French Veteran from the Revolution to the Restoration*, University of North Carolina Press, 1979.

Wright, V., 'Les Préfets de police pendant le second empire : personnalités et problèmes', in Jacques Aubert (ed.), *L'État et sa police en France (1789–1914)*, Geneva, Librairie Droz, 1979, pp. 83–102.

Yates, Lynn (ed.), *Citizenship and Education*, Bundoora Victoria, La Trobe University Press, 1995.

Zeldin, Theodore, *Émile Ollivier and the Liberal Empire of Napoleon III*, Oxford, Clarendon Press, 1963.

INDEX